"I've long admired Missy and her ability to create beautiful, thoughtful, and simply delicious technique-driven dishes with ease. This book is an immersion in the love of craft, storytelling, and dedication to all of that."

—*Kristen Kish*, chef, TV personality, and author of *Kristen Kish Cooking*

"In Italy, pasta is more than a food. It is a religion. I was raised with a mother and grandmother in the kitchen rolling out egg pasta dough every day. Flipping through this book, I was reminded of their gestures and loving hands as they worked the dough into multiple shapes and forms. Missy and Talia have explored the far corners of the Italian pasta rituals through storytelling, recipes, and delicate imagery to illustrate how joyful and rewarding pasta making can be. They have captured the essence of the craft and added fine details to foster anyone's desire to master the skill. Bravissime!"

—*Massimo Bottura*, chef/owner, Osteria Francescana, Modena, Italy

pasta

Missy Robbins
AND TALIA BAIOCCHI

Food Photography by Kelly Puleio
Location Photography by Stephan Alessi
Illustrations by Nick Hensley

TEN SPEED PRESS
California | New York

The Spirit and Craft of Italy's
Greatest Food, with Recipes

pasta

Quanto Basta xi

Introduction 1

How to Make Pasta 7

About Flour 10

Equipment 12

Fresh Pasta 17
Egg Dough 18
Semolina Dough 19
Green Dough 22
Ricotta Gnocchi Dough 24
Gnudi Dough 25
Whole-Wheat Dough 26
Chestnut Dough 27
Espresso Dough 28
Chickpea Dough 29
Buckwheat Dough 30
Cocoa Dough 31

Rolling and Sheeting Your Dough 32

Extruded Pasta 36
Extruded Dough 41

The Shapes 45

Hand Cut 48
Fettuccine 49
Maccheroncini di Campofilone 50
Mandilli di Seta 51
Pappardelle 54
Pizzoccheri 55
Strangozzi 56
Tagliatelle 57
Tagliolini 60
Tajarin 61

Hand Shaped 62
Fileja 63
Busiate 64
Gnudi 65
Malloreddus 67
Orecchiette 68
Trofie 70
Pici 71
Ricotta Gnocchi 74
Stricchetti 75

Filled 76
Balanzoni 77
Agnolotti 80
Agnolotti dal Plin 84
Cannelloni 86
Cappelletti 87
Caramelle 88
Casunziei 89
Cjalsons 92
Culurgiones 94
Mezzelune 95
Occhi 98
Pansotti 100
Ravioli 104
Tortelli 106
Tortellini 110

Outliers 112
Corzetti 113
Canederli 114
Bigoli 115
Spaghetti alla Chitarra 119

Extruded 120
Bucatini 121
Casarecce 121
Linguine 122
Mafaldine 122
Rigatoni 123
Spaghetti 123
Penne 124
Ziti 124

How to Cook Pasta 127

Cook Pasta Like a Cook 128

Rules to Cook By 132

Building a Pasta Tool Kit 135

FAQ 138

Italian American Classics 143

Simple Red Sauce 147

30-Clove Sauce 148

Diavola Sauce 149

Fettuccine Alfredo 150

Ravioli Red Sauce 153

Baked Ziti with Aged Provolone and Caciocavallo 154

Penne alla Vodka 155

Spaghetti Meatballs 156

Lobster Fra Diavolo with Linguine 159

Cannelloni 161

Pasta e Fagioli 162

Spaghetti Vongole 165

Lasagna 168

North 175

Trofie al Pesto Genovese
Pasta with Pine Nut Pesto 178

Pansotti con Salsa di Noci
*Herb-Filled Pasta with
Walnut Sauce* 180

Tajarin al Tartufo
Pasta with White Truffles 182

Pizzoccheri alla Valtellinese
*Buckwheat Pasta with Potatoes,
Cabbage, and Brown Butter* 183

Tortelli di Zucca
*Squash-Filled Pasta with Sage
Brown Butter* 184

Canederli
Speck and Rye Bread Dumplings 188

Passatelli in Brodo
*Bread and Parmigiano Dumplings
in Brodo* 189

Bigoli in Salsa
Pasta in Anchovy Sauce 191

Casunziei all'Ampezzana
*Beet-Filled Pasta with Brown Butter,
Poppy Seeds, and Smoked Ricotta* 194

Cjalsons
*Sweet and Savory Pasta with Brown
Butter and Cinnamon* 197

Tortellini in Brodo
Pork-Filled Pasta in Brodo 198

Tagliatelle alla Bolognese
Pasta with Bolognese Ragù 202

Balanzoni Burro e Salvia
*Mortadella and Ricotta–Filled Pasta
with Brown Butter and Sage* 205

Agnolotti dal Plin
*Brisket and Caramelized Onion–
Filled Pasta* 209

Corzetti alle Erbe
Pasta with Herbs and Pine Nuts 213

Central 215

Spaghetti alla Carbonara
*Pasta with Eggs, Guanciale, and
Pecorino* 218

Timballo alla Teramana
*Abruzzese Lasagna with Cheese,
Spinach, and Beef* 220

**Spaghetti alla Chitarra con
Pallottine**
*Pasta with Abruzzese Meatballs and
Lamb Sugo* 224

Pappardelle al Ragù di Coniglio
Pasta with Braised Rabbit Ragù 226

Pici al Ragù d'Anatra
Pasta with Duck Ragù 228

Strangozzi alla Norcina
*Pasta with Black Truffles and
Anchovy* 232

Cacio e Pepe
*Pasta with Pecorino and
Black Pepper* 233

Bucatini all'Amatriciana
*Pasta with Tomato, Guanciale,
and Pecorino* 234

Gnudi alla Fiorentina
*Spinach and Ricotta Dumplings with
Brown Butter and Sage* 238

**Maccheroncini di Campofilone
al Sugo Tradizionale**
*Pasta with Short Ribs and
Tomato Sugo* 240

South 243

Culurgiones alla Nuorese
*Cheese and Potato–Filled Pasta in
Tomato Sauce* 246

Busiate alla Pesto Trapanese
*Pasta with Tomato and Almond
Pesto* 248

Bucatini con le Sarde
*Pasta with Sardines, Currants,
Pine Nuts, and Fennel* 249

Spaghetti ai Ricci di Mare
Pasta with Sea Urchin 252

Orecchiette con Cime di Rapa
*Pasta with Broccoli Rabe, Anchovies,
Garlic, and Chile Flakes* 253

Spaghetti alla Puttanesca
*Pasta with Tomatoes, Olives, Capers,
and Anchovies* 256

Malloreddus alla Campidanese
*Sardinian Gnocchi with Sausage,
Saffron, and Tomato Ragù* 258

**Casarecce con Pesce Spada,
Pistacchi e Capperi**
*Pasta with Swordfish, Pistachios,
and Capers* 263

Couscous alla Trapanese
Couscous with Fish Brodo 264

Fileja alla 'Nduja
*Pasta with 'Nduja and
Tomato Sauce* 267

Modern Classics

Spaghetti with Garlic Four Ways 273

Spaghetti with Lemon, Pine Nuts, and Parmigiano 274

Sheep's Milk Cheese–Filled Agnolotti with Saffron, Dried Tomato, and Honey 276

Linguine with Anchovies, Corbara Tomatoes, and Lemon 280

Potato-Filled Cappelletti with Speck, Horseradish, and Caraway 281

Ricotta Gnocchi with Broccoli Pesto, Basil, and Pistachios 282

Fettuccine with Spicy Lamb Sausage and Tomato Passata 286

Rigatoni Diavola 289

Potato and Crème Fraîche–Filled Ravioli with Garlic and Rosemary 290

Ricotta and Tuscan Kale–Filled Cappelletti with Fennel Pollen 294

Parmigiano Fonduta–Filled Tortellini in Brodo 298

Spaghetti alla Chitarra with Ramps, Lemon, and Ricotta Salata 300

Ravioli with Taleggio Fonduta, Peas, and Speck 302

Eggplant-Filled Mezzelune with Simple Sauce and Ricotta Salata 306

Pappardelle with Porcini and Veal Bolognese 309

Prosciutto and Goat Cheese–Filled Cappelletti with Pistachios 312

Caramelle with Caramelized Onion, Brown Butter, and Balsamic 316

Mafaldine with Pink Peppercorns and Parmigiano-Reggiano 319

Tagliatelle with Ossobuco and Soffritto 320

Spinach and Ricotta–Filled Tortelli with Brown Butter and Ricotta Salata 322

Sunchoke-Filled Agnolotti with Walnuts, Lemon, and Thyme 326

Spaghetti with Pancetta, Black Pepper, and Spring Onions 329

Strangozzi with Pork Sugo, Nutmeg, and Parmigiano 330

Cocoa Pici with Braised Cinghiale 333

Corn-Filled Cappelletti with Black Pepper and Pecorino 335

Chickpea Pappardelle with Chickpeas, Rosemary, and Garlic 338

Sheep's Milk Ricotta–Filled Occhi with Lemon and Bottarga 340

Espresso Tagliolini with Smoked Ricotta and Chiles 342

Corzetti with Sungold Tomatoes, Pecorino, and Herbs 343

Spaghetti alla Chitarra with Lobster and Fresh Chiles 346

Spaghetti with Colatura, Garlic, and Bread Crumbs 348

Corzetti with Chanterelles and Aged Goat Cheese 350

Mandilli di Seta with Dried Cherry Tomatoes and Herbed Bread Crumbs 351

Stricchetti with Smashed Peas and Prosciutto 354

Tagliatelle with Matsutake Mushrooms, Lemon, and Mint 357

Contorni

Charred Treviso with Walnuts and Saba 364

Bitter Lettuces and Herbs with House Vinaigrette 366

Escarole with Anchovy Vinaigrette, Ricotta Salata, and Crispy Garlic 367

Snap Peas with Black Pepper, Lemon, and Lardo 369

Broccoli Rabe with Parmigiano and Calabrian Chile Oil 370

Olive Oil–Poached Zucchini with Grilled Bread and Oregano 371

Roasted Eggplant with Olives and Sun-Dried Tomato Vinaigrette 374

Fennel with Celery, Walnuts, and Parmigiano 375

Porcini with Rosemary and Garlic 377

Asparagus with Mint Pesto and Almonds 378

Pinzimonio 379

Grilled and Marinated Baby Artichokes with Bay Leaf and Orange 380

Grilled Summer Beans and Garlic Vinaigrette 383

Braised Savoy Cabbage with Onions and Nutmeg 384

Roasted Kabocha Squash with Hot Honey and Bread Crumbs 385

Acknowledgments 390

Index 392

Quanto Basta

Pasta making is, at its most basic, an act of humility. It's repetitive, precise manual labor—a simple gift to the gods of gluten offered up in flour-dusted basements and prep kitchens around the world. It is ceremonious only in its utter lack of ceremony. What has always appealed to me is how the frank marriage of two ingredients—whether flour and water or flour and eggs—splinters into hundreds of variations of stuffed, rolled, extruded, dried, stamped, and hand-cut shapes; how each has its own origin story, rhythmic set of motions, and tools; and how mastery can sometimes come down to an elusive sleight of hand: the flick of a wrist, the perfect twist of the index finger away from the thumb. Movements learned only through practice.

In the two years between leaving A Voce in Manhattan and opening my first restaurant, Lilia, in Brooklyn, I spent most of my days at home learning, for the first time since I was a kid, what it meant to cook not for accolades or recognition but for comfort. There was no Michelin. No *New York Times.* No owners. No need to prove that a Jewish kid from Connecticut with no Italian heritage had any business cooking Italian food. No longer were my thoughts, Is this nice enough? or Is this cool enough? but rather, What kind of food do I want to eat? or What food do I want to cook? and most importantly, Why?

I was cooking pasta that paid homage to Italy's iconic regional dishes, sure, but the virtue of craveability was paramount. It's why my food at Lilia and my second restaurant, Misi, is so rooted in home cooking, and it's perhaps the only way to explain how a dish as simple as rigatoni with red sauce ended up on Lilia's opening menu, and then once again at Misi. I wanted to serve the food that I like to eat—the food I'd always been cooking, just stripped down to the studs and rebuilt with a simple mantra in mind: quanto basta.

In Italian cookbooks, quanto basta is typically represented as "q.b." It translates to "as much as is necessary," and it appears when an ingredient is listed without an exact quantity. It's essentially the Italian version of "salt to taste," but it has come to symbolize a shift in focus for me—one that places simplicity and comfort first and always makes me ask, Is this really necessary?

It took me decades to get here. This book is meant as a ride-along, from red sauce to regional classics to the pastas I've made my own. At its core is a journey back to the home regions of some of my favorite pastas in an effort to understand them with new clarity—to gain a deeper knowledge of not only how they are faring in a country undergoing constant culinary evolution but also of their sense of place.

Perhaps more than anything, though, this book is my love letter to pasta. What has made pasta the cornerstone of Italian culinary culture for centuries, an indelible part of so many Americans' early food memories, and a food so eminently alluring that even the gluten averse cannot resist its siren song is that it asks, first and foremost, something elemental of us: that we enjoy it.

Introduction

My earliest pasta memory was a dish called "milk spaghetti," a gooey, unnatural brick-orange tangle of pasta, Campbell's tomato soup, Cracker Barrel Cheddar cheese, butter, and milk baked in the oven, cut into squares, and scooped out of a casserole dish with a spatula. It was passed down to my mother from my grandmother Mildred, a woman with a fairly limited stash of culinary provocations.

Needless to say, as a Jewish kid from Connecticut raised in a kosher home, I wasn't exactly reared on carbonara. It was milk spaghetti and, when we went out to our local Italian spots, fettuccine Alfredo, stuffed shells, and the stray cheese-filled ravioli. But my heart belonged to baked ziti. On the weekends, we were regulars at Leon's, a real Saturday night kind of place with white tablecloths and those ubiquitous garnet-colored Venetian candles that give so many red-sauce joints their Dick Tracy luster. The ziti, topped with about a pound of mozzarella baked to golden perfection, would come careening through the dining room on giant platters. On weeknights, we'd do the same thing at Bimonte's, a pizzeria with psych-ward lighting, red-leather booths, and scuffed linoleum floors. I'd wash down my ziti with a Foxon Park white birch soda, the local soft drink of choice, while my father tackled a meatball sub and a Pepsi. We'd order a pizza on the side.

By the time I was flirting with adolescence, we'd taken to buying fresh pasta at a place called Connie's Macaroni, one of many Italian American pastifici in the New Haven area. A jewel box of a shop, it teemed with Italians: mamas picking up red sauce on the way home from Mass; a constant gaggle of older men there only to loiter. We'd load up on linguine and fettuccine.

Eventually, we got around to making our own pasta. By then I'd cultivated a fascination, hitching along on my mother's trips to the market just to park myself in the dried goods aisle, obsessively scanning the boxes of pasta to try and commit the shapes and their names to memory. She ended up buying me a pasta extruder when I was eleven—a white Simac PastaMatic that was nearly impossible to clean. We'd make fettuccine mostly, which we'd promptly smother in Alfredo sauce.

This is all to say that there was always pasta. Yet while I'd love to be able to draw a straight line from my two beloved childhood red-sauce joints to what I do today, I cannot. Nor can I really suggest that my obsession with pasta shapes or my early forays into extrusion were profound bits of foreshadowing. Instead, my path to pasta has been more about chance than fate.

Go F*ck Yourself, Lisa. I'm Busy.

During my senior year of college, I started cooking professionally at 1789, a New American restaurant in Georgetown. I was making smoked salmon platters, goat cheese–crusted racks of lamb, Caesar salad—the kind of square-plate food that reigned in 1993. It was hardly enough to inspire a young cook today, but it was a hell of a lot more appealing than a master's degree in psychology. After graduation, I went north and spent a summer filled with French men and terrines as a cook at a fancy restaurant in the Berkshires. By fall, I'd enrolled in culinary school in New York. After six months, I was interning with Wayne Nish at March before moving on to the kitchen at Anne Rosenzweig's Arcadia. By 1997, after nearly two years back at March, I returned to work with Anne as sous chef at her second restaurant, Lobster Club.

At the time, Lobster Club was one of the hottest restaurants in New York—a converted brownstone on East Eightieth Street that seemed to capture every bit of energy the Upper East Side had to offer. I was in my midtwenties and the daytime sous, which basically meant I'd be out most nights just shy of 4:00 a.m. and would show up less than three hours later to prep—invariably hungover but still brimming with ambition. I'd have every one of the burners going by 8:00 a.m.; by 4:00 p.m., I'd be in the basement rolling out the menu's only pasta. It became my favorite time of day, and I guarded that private time almost maniacally. I have a vivid memory of an afternoon right before service when one of the cooks rushed downstairs to the basement while I was stuffing ravioli to tell me that the building next door was on fire, that the fire was coming into the restaurant, and that I needed to evacuate—immediately. To which I replied, "Go fuck yourself, Lisa. I'm busy."

After two years working six days per week at Lobster Club, I was beat-up and nursing an urge to cook outside of New York. I'd visited Italy with my parents in college, and while I had very little recollection of the details of the trip, I remembered how Italy made me feel. I chose it because it was the only country I had a visceral connection to, even if I wasn't sure I wanted to cook Italian food or, frankly, what Italian food actually was. But Anne agreed to help me secure an internship, and she came back with three waiting. There was just one problem: I had no money. When I told Anne I wasn't sure how I'd get there, she looked me straight in the eye and said flatly, "Well, go find the money."

You Understand What You Want to Understand!

Five weeks later, I piled into a taxi with my Discman, two Berlitz Italian CDs, an English-Italian dictionary, a handful of novels, and a few changes of clothes. I was headed to Ristorante Righi in San Marino, a weird autonomous country of its own within Emilia-Romagna known mostly for being a weird autonomous country of its own within Emilia-Romagna. I didn't speak a word of Italian, and I'd made only two pastas in my life: my teenage fettuccine and Lobster Club's lone ravioli.

The first thing I learned was how to drink espresso. I lived with the sous chef and his wife and two line cooks. Every morning we'd meet downstairs and walk to the restaurant. It was a literal minute away, but we'd still stop for a cappuccino on our way to the cappuccino we'd have when we arrived at the restaurant. The two cappuccini would then be followed by a midmorning espresso, followed by lunch, followed by an espresso, followed by lunch service, followed by another espresso, a nap, a predinner espresso, dinner, and a final postdinner espresso.

The second thing I learned was how to make gnocchi. The restaurant had a pasta room run by a woman in her forties who was almost certainly born with a cigarette in her mouth. She'd sit in the room all day, a Merit resting on her bottom lip while she rolled out pasta dough. One day it'd be ravioli, the next it'd be strozzapreti, the following tagliatelle—but gnocchi day was always my favorite. It was a three-person job: the first would break down the potatoes, the second would add the flour, and the third would roll out the dough. The trick was that you had to do it all while the potatoes were still hot. I still make potato gnocchi this way.

I spent two months at Righi, followed by a brief stint at a restaurant on the Emilian coast before moving on to Il Convivio in Sansepolcro, in eastern Tuscany. Il Convivio was a husband-and-wife operation housed in Palazzo Bourbon del Monte, which was built by Lorenzo de' Medici's architect during the Renaissance. Paolo was the town's mayor by day, and by night he'd hold court in the restaurant as host while his wife, Fernanda, ran the small kitchen with a staff of four. Every day during the midday break between lunch and dinner she'd make the pasta—all from hand-rolled northern-style dough of egg and 00 flour. Her buddies would stop by to help, and they'd turn out these beautiful sheets of pasta that she'd drape over the counter to dry. From them, we'd cut wide ribbons of pappardelle that would be smothered in a ragù made from a grab bag of wild game, tiny tortellini packed with mortadella and served in brodo (broth), and ravioli stuffed with ricotta, bitter greens, and nutmeg. I never went home for break once in my month at the restaurant. At night, I'd bring my copy of the *International Herald Tribune* to the local wine bar and practice my Italian with the bartender over a bowl of pappardelle with chickpeas and rosemary, a dish that, in numerous iterations, would follow me throughout my career.

My last stop was Agli Amici, a white-tablecloth thirty-seat restaurant in a village outside of Udine, in Friuli. I landed there shortly after it had received a Michelin star, and was packed into a dorm above the restaurant with a few other interns. I spent about a month cleaning bathrooms and being yelled at on the line in Friulian dialect. "You understand what you want to understand!" was a common refrain, which I only understood later, after imploring a fellow line cook to translate for me. It's here that I really learned how to cook pasta—how to finish pasta by "marrying" it with the sauce, allowing the pasta to absorb its flavor without beating it into soggy submission. Four years later, when Tony Mantuano, the founding chef at Spiaggia in Chicago, would talk about the importance of the "marriage ceremony," I knew precisely what he meant.

"Hey, It's Alfred . . . Have You Heard of Spiaggia?"

After five months in Italy, I was back in New York and in need of a job. I called Alfred, a headhunter who was eager to place me in an Italian restaurant. I applied to Felidia and the now long-gone Va Tutto, but nothing felt right. Within a month, I ran into John DeLucie at a Barnes & Noble. I'd met him about a year earlier at Colina, a short-lived Jonathan Waxman restaurant in what is now ABC Kitchen, where he'd worked as chef de cuisine. He had landed at the Soho Grand, reluctantly, after the restaurant was panned by the *New York Times* and then shuttered a few months later. On the spot, he asked if I wanted to be his sous chef. "No, thank you," I said. "I am not working in a hotel."

But John is what I like to call "positively manipulative." I spent the next three and a half years at the Soho Grand cooking a slightly more "eclectic" version of the food I was making my senior year in college: short-rib sliders, pierogi, the occasional upscale mac and cheese. There were twenty-five-dollar "grand margaritas" and a DJ. I hated every minute of it. By late 2002, I was back in touch with Alfred. He had a lead.

"Hey, it's Alfred. When you came back from Italy you said you'd go to Chicago or San Francisco. Have you heard of Spiaggia? They're looking for a CdC [chef de cuisine]."

I took a call with Tony Mantuano, by then a fixture in Chicago, revered for bringing high-end Italian food to the city. We spent nearly an hour on the phone. Years later, he told me that as soon as he hung up he turned to his wife and said, "Damn, I hope she can cook, because I think she's the one."

I moved to Chicago five weeks later.

Tony was, and still is, a traditionalist—albeit one who sought to filter Italy's iconic dishes through a Michelin lens. But when he made tortelli di zucca, he made them exactly the way he'd learned to make them at Dal Pescatore, in Lombardy. The ingredients were always pristine, the plating was refined, but there were no tricks. It was, in some ways, a continuation of what I'd learned in Italy, and in others a learning curve that felt precipitous. I didn't yet have the knowledge of regional Italian cuisine or my own point of view, and I didn't yet understand his. But I spent the next five years studying—devouring cookbooks and whatever Tony was willing to teach me, convinced that his fine-dining approach to regional Italian cooking would be the foundation of the food I'd eventually cook on my own.

In many ways it was. I still make pasta by hand the same way I did at Spiaggia, and Tony's voice loosely quoting Marcella Hazan—"The most important ingredient is the one you leave out"—still plays in my head. I'd take a similar approach to Italian food with me to A Voce in 2008, but it was never entirely natural for me. I developed a deep understanding of Italian regional cuisine, and I learned how to translate that for Michelin-seeking owners and a high-end clientele. But it was more intellectual than emotional, and it always felt divorced from the humility and soulfulness that drew me to Italian food in the first place—that idea of quanto basta.

It was also a different time for Italian food in New York. Del Posto would soon be the first Italian restaurant since 1974 to receive four stars from the *New York Times;* Michael White's brand of rich, complex Italian food was on the rise. Scott Conant was cooking a similar version of refined, technique-driven food at Scarpetta that was gaining him accolades. A new model had been established for Italian food that held its most acclaimed practitioners to French fine-dining standards, even as the concept of fine dining was in decline.

I was craving something different. What, I wondered, would happen if I just stripped away all of the bullshit? What would happen if I just cooked what I wanted to eat? In 2013, I left A Voce and the brand of more baroque Italian cooking I'd established there with no plan except to go and find the inspiration I was missing. I went to Vietnam, back to Italy, to Hong Kong, to Thailand. Eventually I landed squarely in my home kitchen, cooking for my friends, for my partner, and for myself. It was simple food driven by craving and inspired by ingredient—no third or fourth garnish, no three-pan pickups. It was rigatoni with red sauce, spaghetti with garlic and parsley, and braised broccoli rabe. And it was the happiest I'd felt in the kitchen since I was a kid.

This, I thought, is the food I want to eat. This is the food I want to cook.

How to Make Pasta

I'll say this up front in case you've landed here with the hope of finding science or even a replicable, mathematical pattern that can squash the mystique of pasta making. I'm not that kind of chef. I cannot tell you about the anatomy of different flour types—the precise ratio of glutenin and gliadin that yields the right chew—or even why one flour works and another doesn't. The people who taught me how to make pasta couldn't explain this either, and I had different questions anyway.

What I do know is how—not why—my methods work and how to replicate them at home. But these lessons are not foolproof. The most important "q.b." is you, and my approach is not to eliminate that variable, but to accentuate it by carefully explaining my technique and reminding you to trust yourself. Don't get caught up in registering the precise graduation of the settings on your hand-cranked pasta machine, or "sheeter." Pay attention instead to the way the pasta feels in your hand, how the dough drapes around the pads of your fingers when it reaches its ideal thinness, how it grips the board when it needs an extra dusting of flour, and, likewise, how the friction on its surface tells you when you've added too much. Don't count down the seconds of cooking time as you marry a pan of butter sauce and mafaldine. Listen instead for the gentle slapping sound it makes, like water gently lapping the shoreline, when the sauce and the pasta become one. Record it to memory so it becomes your equivalent of an expired timer. You have to *feel* it.

What follows is all of the information I have gathered in fifteen years of cooking, traveling, and reading about pasta. This is my way of showing you how I make pasta so you can find out how you do it. The recipes are here to say "this way" and to guide you for as long as you need until you know your way.

About Flour

The simplicity of my approach to flour is either refreshing or maddening, depending on whom you ask. First, and up front, I do not mill my own flour. This is not because I do not believe in the practice. It's undeniable that freshly milled flour is more vibrant and flavorful. But I have a general philosophy that in order to be a great craftsperson, you cannot be a jack of all crafts. My approach to cooking has always been to learn my part of the craft and find great product from people who are great at theirs—and to support them.

For my egg dough I use Molino Spadoni Gran Mugnaio tipo 00, which was the first brand I encountered in Italy—its blue-and-white-striped bag as iconic for me as a bottle of Campari. But I work with a variety of flour brands at home—from King Arthur to Rustichella d'Abruzzo to Molino Grassi Organic—and there are now an increasing number of local farms all over the country milling great flour. So play around, and if you want to go deep and mill your own, even more power to you. Here's a crash course in flour types.

The Big Two: Grano Tenero and Grano Duro

There are two types of wheat you'll encounter in pasta making: grano tenero and grano duro, which are basically your classic soft wheat and durum wheat, respectively. The former is graded based on the amount of crusca (bran) left in the flour after milling—from tipo 00 (the finest ground, which contains no bran) to integrale (aka whole wheat). Tipo 00 is most commonly used in central and northern Italy to make handmade pastas, whereas durum wheat, or semolina, is common across the south. These are the three types of wheat flour I use for pasta:

Farina di Grano Tenero Tipo 00

This is a soft-wheat flour that is essentially pasta's all-purpose flour. Its extremely fine, powdery texture yields a smooth and consistent dough, making it ideal for egg dough.

Farina di Grano Tenero Integrale

I use whole-wheat flour in a variety of pastas but never on its own. As with chestnut flour and chickpea flour (see the opposite page), I think whole-wheat flour is at its best when cut with tipo 00, as it helps avoid the chalkiness and lack of elasticity you get from some low-gluten and gluten-free flours.

Semola Rimacinata di Grano Duro

This is twice-milled semolina flour that is finer than classic semolina but will still result in more texture and bite than tipo 00. I use it for my extruded pastas and semolina dough.

Heirloom and Specialty Wheat Flours

Hundreds of varieties of wheat are currently in production in Italy. Some are disappearing, some are being revived, and others are cultivated in such small quantities that they are consumed only at the farm or winery at which they are grown. There are also other types of wheat flour that have production processes that make them utterly unique in both appearance and flavor from other flours. Two of note are grano arso and Senatore Cappelli.

Grano Arso

Grano arso, aka burnt grain, is essentially just that: wheat that has been scorched before milling. The flour lends both a dark color and a smoky, charred flavor to pastas. It originated in Puglia, and like so many southern products, it came about as a way to make use of something that would have otherwise been tossed out. But in recent years, grano arso has had a trendy resurgence in baking and pasta making. Note that its flavor profile is bold, so cut it either 70:30 or 60:40 tipo 00 to grano arso, depending on your preference.

Senatore Cappelli

While a number of heritage wheat strains are now cultivated across Italy—think Carosella, Frassineto, and Biancolilla—Senatore Cappelli has been consistently used to make artisanal pastas, particularly in central Italy. Selected and cultivated beginning in the early 1900s, it is prized for its higher levels of protein and antioxidants compared with modern durum wheat.

Alternative Flours

Throughout Italy, you'll find pasta made from a variety of different flours, from buckwheat in the Alps to chestnut along the Riviera and down through Tuscany. Note that while making pasta entirely from these flours is customary in many places, I consistently cut them with tipo 00, as you'll see in my dough recipes for each.

Chestnut Flour

The most common alternative pasta flour in Italy is chestnut, which finds its way into trofie and testaroli in Liguria and gnocchi in Lombardy, among many others. It tastes exactly how you'd expect it to: nutty, slightly sweet, and perfect for fall.

Chickpea Flour

Chickpea flour is more commonly used in breads, fritters, and savory cakes, such as farinata in Liguria and panelle in Sicily. I love it for its ability to lend subtle earthiness and richness to pasta dough.

Buckwheat Flour

Buckwheat tangles with pasta in pretty much every alpine region. In Lombardy, it's pizzoccheri; in the Carnic Alps in Friuli, blecs; and in Trentino–Alto Adige, spaetzle, among others. Buckwheat not only gives the dough a nutty, bran-like flavor but also contributes a rough-and-tumble, toothsome texture.

Rye Flour

Rye flour is typically used in Trentino–Alto Adige, but it can also be found in parts of the south, particularly Calabria, where it was once combined with other scrap flours from the mills and used to make rustic pastas.

Equipment

Pasta making does not want for merch. There are boards for gnocchi, malloreddus, cavatelli; dozens of rolling pins and cutters; stamps; drying racks; sheeters and extruders; and irons for fusilli, passatelli, and busiate. You get the idea. The list of essentials below is truly an exercise in restraint. If you're anything like me and a single gnocchi board just won't do, there are a number of online specialty stores that specialize in pasta esoterica. My favorites are Fante's Kitchen Shop and Artisanal Pasta Tools.

Bench scraper: I use this tool primarily to keep my station clean, scraping up dough and flour when it sticks to the board. It can also be used as an aid in folding and mixing dough.

Box grater: While most cooks use a Microplane grater, I have always preferred a box grater for both fine and coarse grating. Even the extra-coarse Microplane can't quite achieve the same thickness and texture the box grater can.

Brass ferretto (maccheroni iron): This long, thin rod, or ferretto, is used to make coiled shapes like fusilli and busiate. Look for a square-sided rod, rather than the one that resembles a knitting needle, as it is much easier to work with.

Cavarola board: This rectangular wooden board, which distinguishes itself from the gnocchi board with its herringbone-like pattern, can be used to shape gnocchi, cavatelli, and, in my case, mandilli di seta.

Chitarra: No pasta maker's arsenal is complete without a chitarra, the metal-stringed tool used to make spaghetti alla chitarra. I've found that the most durable, high-quality model is available from Fante's.

Corzetti stamps: A bunch of places throughout Italy sell these stamps, and several remaining artisans, such as Franco Casoni (francocasoni.it) and Pietro Picetti, still make custom stamps to order in Liguria. In the United States, you can find beautiful stamps from Artisanal Pasta Tools. You can also order from Romagnoli Pasta Tools, a maker in Florence, Italy, via Etsy.

Digital scale: All of my pasta recipes are in grams for accuracy, so you'll need a slim kitchen scale. I prefer Escali or Oxo brand.

Dough divider: This pastry cutter with an accordion design allows you to cut pasta sheets into uniform strips more efficiently, which is especially handy when making shapes such as pansotti and tortelli. I opt for the five-blade divider with a lock from JB Prince, in festooned (aka fluted) and smooth.

Food mill: A couple recipes call for milling tomatoes and potatoes. You can certainly mash by hand, but milling is going to produce a superior texture. For potatoes, a ricer will also do.

Gnocchi board: The classic gnocchi board is about the size of two decks of cards side by side and has tight ridges that give the exterior of the dough its grip. I like a version from Eppicotispai, which comes with a garganelli rod—two in one. I also often use a cavarola board for gnocchi, which gives them a crosshatched pattern.

KitchenAid stand mixer with dough hook: While you can use the well method for mixing your dough (see page 18), the KitchenAid is a trusty all-in-one tool if you plan to make pasta regularly. I use it to mix my dough, but it also comes with attachments for sheeting and cutting.

Ladle: Your standard stainless-steel kitchen ladle comes in a number of sizes. Opt for a 2 oz size, which is used during the pasta marriage process for adding pasta cooking water to the pan as you toss to combine.

Large wooden work surface: A 24 by 18-inch Boos board is what I use for rolling out my dough—and for all general prep—at home. If you're lucky enough not to be rolling out pasta in a New York City apartment, the bigger the board, the better.

Malloreddus board: This board, shaped like a Ping-Pong paddle, is similar to a gnocchi board (it's used to make Sardinian gnocchi, after all) but smaller and with ridges that are arranged farther apart to produce the shape's deeper, wider grooves.

Meat grinder: If you have a KitchenAid, getting the meat grinder attachment is your best bet. If not, just be sure to get a grinder that is all metal. Note that this isn't just for meat. You'll see that I also use it for vegetables, particularly to make soffritto (finely cut vegetable base).

Microplane graters: While I rely on a box grater for most cheeses, I use a Microplane zester grater for ricotta salata. I also use a zester grater for spices, such as nutmeg.

Passatelli iron: A traditional two-handled passatelli iron isn't exactly available everywhere, but you can purchase one from Artisanal Pasta Tools, or you can substitute a potato ricer.

Pasta basket: This may seem like a cheffy indulgence, but I assure you having two 5-inch baskets (I like Desco), for two servings each, is essential (don't try and fit all four servings into one). They will ensure that you get all of your pasta out at the same time, with none lost to the murk of the pot, and that you don't break the pasta by using tongs to remove it.

Pasta drying tray: A mesh-topped pasta (or fruit) drying tray with short legs that lift it above the work surface, allowing for air circulation, is ideal for drying extruded pasta. It is a design that means less turning and babysitting.

Pasta extruder: There are a number of relatively compact extruders on the market, ranging in price from a couple of hundred dollars to thousands of dollars for the restaurant-grade extruders that use bronze dies. See page 38 for what's available.

Pasta sheeter: While pasta sheeters for home use can range in price from under a hundred dollars to about fifteen hundred dollars, I recommend starting with a small Imperia Model 150, which is manual rather than motorized. A motor will give you greater control and speed, but the manual sheeter is great for learning purposes.

Pastry bags: To reduce single-use plastic, you can use reusable pastry bags for piping your pasta fillings, but they can be hard to clean. Be sure to remove all the residue from your previous batch so you don't add unwelcome flavor to your next one.

Pepper mill: This might seem like an unnecessary addition, but I am putting it here to remind you that all recipes that call for pepper call for freshly ground pepper. No shortcuts.

Rolling pin: I like to use a skinnier pin—with a circumference of about 3 inches—for more control. The pin is used to get your dough to a point where you can pass it through the sheeter.

Round pastry cutter: You'll want these for cutting ravioli, occhi, mezzelune, and more. While less expensive metal versions are available, they tend to bend over time. I prefer the Exoglass cutters from JB Prince for that reason. Grab a fluted set for flair and a smooth set for general use.

Ruler: Many recipes for long cut and filled pastas call for a specific width. But a ruler is also a helpful guide to ensure straight lines when cutting pasta by hand.

Single pastry cutters: These will be your go-to cutters for long pasta. I pick these up when I am traveling the same way I do stamps for corzetti. But for everyday use, I love La Gondola's heavy-duty brass cutters with wooden handles. Get a set of two: one fluted and one with a plain edge.

Spray bottle: When making filled shapes, keep a spray bottle on hand to mist your dough when it feels as though it's drying out.

Table fan: When making extruded pasta the day you plan to cook it, knowing your pasta hasn't dried by the time your guests arrive is not the best feeling. Setting up a small fan next to your drying trays will speed up the drying process and help mitigate the higher humidity levels that might be keeping it from drying.

Tamis: While testing recipes for this book, our tester, Laurie Ellen Pellicano, took to making fun of my attachment to the tamis ("Here comes the tamis again!"). This fine-mesh sieve is indeed a staple and the key to making a fluffy, creamy cheese filling. Get to know, and love, your tamis.

Torchio bigolaro: Think of a bigolaro as a hand-crank bronze extruder for thick spaghetti. It costs a few hundred dollars, clips onto a tabletop, and requires plenty of elbow grease, but you can get more mileage out of it than you might think. Bottene's torchio #6 is the best choice for home use.

Fresh Pasta

What defines fresh pasta? The obvious answer is that it is pasta made fresh and meant to be cooked the day it was made (or within 24 hours). In Emilia-Romagna, the undisputed capital of fresh pasta making, it is predominantly made from tipo 00 flour and egg yolks. That formula yields a pasta that is at once rich and light on its feet and was the delight of kings, popes, and aristocracy before it became an everyday delicacy. Yet it is but one type. Fresh pasta can be made from a variety of flours—wheat to chestnut to buckwheat to rye—with whole eggs or just yolks; with or without oil; with salt or without salt; with the addition of potato, ricotta, spinach, saffron; or simply with semolina flour and water. There are hundreds of ways to make great pasta. In fact, I'd even wager that if you were to ask a dozen pasta chefs to send you their dough recipes, no two would be the same. But none of them would argue where great fresh pasta begins.

Great Pasta Starts with Great Dough

To say that great fresh pasta starts with great dough is a cliché. But it is a cliché for a reason. If you do not begin with a great base, no amount of determination or technique will allow you to correct course. Luckily, making dough is the step in the pasta-making process in which you can exert the most control (hence, why all ingredients are measured by weight, which allows for the most accuracy), but it still requires touch and instinct, especially when it comes to adjusting to your environment. Mino Rosato, whose family owns the pasta shop L'Oriecchietta, in Puglia, insists that pasta making at the shop varies in difficulty depending on which wind is blowing (the humid sirocco versus the dry, cool tramontana). Regardless of where you're working, seasons and temperatures will impact the pasta-making process. The formulas and advice that follow are the result of testing in multiple environments and seasons to offer my most foolproof dough recipes.

There are two ways to make dough: via the traditional well method or using a trusty KitchenAid stand mixer. Although using a KitchenAid with a dough hook attachment is easier (see page 24), I recommend mastering the well method first. For the bakers out there, it's like making pie dough by hand, which allows you to feel how the butter changes as it's kneaded and comes to temp, and how that impacts the overall texture of your dough. Pasta is similarly all about touch, and the well allows you to get acquainted with the dough as you mix and knead it and to commit the texture of the final product to memory.

The recipes begin with egg dough, specifically one made with nearly equal weights of egg yolk and tipo 00 flour and nothing else. I want all of my hydration to come from fat-rich yolks and all of the salt to come from my pasta water. Many pasta cooks will tell you that the addition of the protein-rich egg white is crucial for filled pastas, as it yields a more durable dough. But after experimenting with countless doughs over the years, I beg to differ. Egg white adds a chew that I find less refined than a yolk-only egg dough, which gives finished pasta a tenderness that has become the stylistic hallmark to which I always aspire. True, a yolk-only egg dough is delicate and can be more challenging to work with, but every recipe that calls for it is written to account for that.

In addition to egg dough, I've included a recipe for semolina-and-water dough, which is called for in trofie, orecchiette, and a few other hand-formed pastas that require the kind of elasticity and spring that it provides, and a handful of alternative flour doughs: chickpea, chestnut, espresso, cocoa, and spinach. While they may seem like novelties, all, perhaps with the exception of espresso dough, are rooted in Italian tradition. A number of recipes specifically call for these outlier doughs, but they can also be swapped in for egg dough whenever the inspiration strikes.

Egg Dough

To begin, place the flour on your wooden work surface and create a barricade with a center sanctuary for your yolks that is 5 to 6 inches in diameter but not more. If you create too much space, your barricade won't be strong enough to hold the yolks as you begin to incorporate the flour. To avoid any additional risk to your barricade, mix, but do not beat, your yolks before adding them to the well. Kick off by adding half of the yolks to the well and use a fork to incorporate the inner layer of flour, stirring in a continuous motion around the circumference to combine. Continue adding the rest of the yolks, incorporating the flour as you go. If you bust through your barricade, not to worry. Use your bench scraper to catch the egg mixture and fold it back into the flour, doing this at every edge until you have a mixture that is thick enough to contain itself. Set your tools aside, roll up your sleeves, and get to work kneading. The dough will be sticky at first, so as you work it, continue to remove the dough that clings to your hands and return it to the mass.

The dough will begin to firm up as the gluten is activated by kneading, but if it feels a touch too dry and is not integrating (this can happen when the environment is drier, such as during the winter or when you're working in an arid climate), gradually add about 1 tablespoon room-temperature water to loosen it. The kneading motion is simple, but it does take some time to get the rhythm right. You essentially want to fold the dough in on itself, pressing down and away from your body with the heel of your dominant hand, relying on the weight of your body to do so. (You can hold the edge of the dough closest to you with your other hand to keep it in place as you stretch it away from you.) Rotate it 180 degrees, fold, and press again. Repeat this rotating, folding, and pressing motion until the dough is smooth and relatively firm to the touch, 8 to 10 minutes. Use your bench scraper to clean off any pieces of dough that clump and stick as you're kneading. Lightly dust the board with flour if needed; be careful not to add too much, as it will dry out the dough.

When properly kneaded, the dough should resemble the texture of Play-Doh and should spring back just slightly when poked. Cover the dough with plastic wrap and set it aside for at least 30 minutes. This allows the dough to become more pliable. If you're not forming pasta until the evening or the next day, place the dough in the refrigerator and remove it 20 minutes before you plan to roll it out so it returns to room temperature. Use the dough within 24 hours.

500g tipo 00 flour, plus more for kneading q.b.
454g (24 to 26) egg yolks

Semolina Dough

In a bowl, combine the 00 flour and semolina flour and stir until fully integrated. Turn out the flour mixture onto your wooden work surface and create a barricade with a center sanctuary for the water that is 5 to 6 inches in diameter but not more. If you create too much space, your barricade won't be strong enough to contain the water as you begin to incorporate the flour. Because water does not have the viscosity and thus self-containment that egg yolks do, add the water to the well slowly, using a fork to incorporate the inner layer of flour and stirring in a continuous motion around the circumference to combine. Continue adding water, incorporating the flour as you go, until you have used up all of the water. If you bust through your barricade, not to worry. Use your bench scraper to catch the water and incorporate it into the flour, doing this at every edge until you have a mixture that is thick enough to contain itself. Set your tools aside, roll up your sleeves, and get to work kneading. The dough will be sticky at first, so as you work it, continue to remove the bits that cling to your hands and return them to the mass.

The dough will begin to firm up as the gluten is activated by kneading, but if it feels a touch too dry and is not integrating (this can happen when the environment is drier, such as during the winter or if you're working in an arid climate), gradually add about 1 tablespoon room-temperature water to hydrate it. The kneading motion is simple, but it does take some time to get the rhythm right. You essentially want to fold the dough in on itself, pressing down and away from your body with the heel of your dominant hand, relying on the weight of your body to do so. (You can hold the edge of the dough closest to you with your other hand to keep the dough in place as you stretch it away from you.) Rotate it 180 degrees, fold, and press again. Repeat this rotating, folding, and pressing motion until the dough is smooth and relatively firm to the touch, 10 to 15 minutes. (Note that this dough will be firmer and harder to knead than the egg-based doughs, so ready your forearms.) Use your bench scraper to clean off any pieces of dough that clump and stick as you're kneading. Lightly dust the board with flour if needed; be careful not to add too much, as it will dry out the dough.

Unlike egg dough, which will resemble the texture of Play-Doh when properly kneaded, flour-and-water dough will be a bit less tender and more elastic. Cover the dough with plastic wrap and set it aside for at least 30 minutes. This allows the dough to become more pliable. If you're not forming pasta until the evening or the next day, place the dough in the refrigerator and remove it 20 minutes before you plan to roll it out so it returns to room temperature. Use the dough within 24 hours.

325g tipo 00 flour
175g semolina flour
250g lukewarm water

Green Dough

Bring a large pot of water to a boil. Prepare an ice-water bath and set a colander in it. Drop the spinach into the boiling water and blanch until tender but still bright green, 30 seconds to 1 minute. Transfer the spinach to the ice-water bath to stop the cooking. Drain the spinach and place in a clean kitchen towel. Enclose the spinach in the towel, folding in each of the sides to cover the spinach, then wring out all the excess water. Transfer the spinach to a high-speed blender and blend to a smooth, liquefied puree (if you're having a hard time getting it moving, add a bit of water to the blender, 1 Tbsp at a time, until loosened enough to blend). Measure out 250g puree and set aside. Transfer any overage to an airtight container and freeze for another use.

Place the flour on your wooden work surface and create a barricade with a center sanctuary for the water that is 5 to 6 inches in diameter but not more. If you create too much space, your barricade won't be strong enough to contain the yolks as you begin to incorporate the flour. To avoid any additional risk of breaking through your barricade, mix, but do not beat, your yolks before adding them to the well. Stir the spinach puree into the yolks until well blended. Add half of the egg mixture to the well and use a fork to incorporate the inner layer of flour, stirring in a continuous motion around the circumference to combine. Continue adding the rest of the mixture, incorporating the flour as you go. If you bust through your barricade, not to worry. Use your bench scraper to catch the egg mixture and fold it back into the flour, doing this at every edge until you have a mixture that is thick enough to contain itself. Set your tools aside, roll up your sleeves, and get to work kneading. The dough will be sticky at first, so as you work it, continue to remove the dough that clings to your hands and return it to the mass.

The dough will begin to firm up as the gluten is activated by kneading, but if it feels a touch too dry and is not integrating (this can happen when the environment is drier, such as during the winter or if you're working in an arid climate), gradually add about 1 tablespoon room-temperature water to hydrate it. The kneading motion is simple, but it does take some time to get the rhythm right. You essentially want to fold the dough in on itself, pressing down and away from your body with the heel of your dominant hand, relying on the weight of your body to do so. (You can hold the edge of the dough closest to you with your other hand to keep the dough in place as you stretch it away from you.) Rotate it 180 degrees, fold, and press again. Repeat this rotating, folding, and pressing motion until the dough is smooth and relatively firm to the touch, 8 to 10 minutes. Use your bench scraper to clean off any pieces of dough that clump and stick as you're kneading. Lightly dust the board with flour if needed; be careful not to add too much, as it will dry out the dough.

When properly kneaded, the dough should resemble the texture of Play-Doh, will be an even bright green color, and should spring back just slightly when poked. Cover the dough with plastic wrap and set it aside for at least 30 minutes. This allows the dough to become more pliable. If you're not forming pasta until the evening or the next day, place the dough in the refrigerator and remove it 20 minutes before you plan to roll it out so it returns to room temperature. Use the dough within 24 hours.

454g spinach leaves
630g tipo 00 flour, plus more for kneading q.b.
118g (6 to 7) egg yolks

Nota bene

If you're making the spaghetti alla chitarra with ramps on page 300 or you simply want to make ramp dough, use half spinach leaves and half leafy green ramp tops.

Ricotta Gnocchi Dough

In a large bowl, combine the ricotta and parmigiano and stir until well mixed. Add the eggs, a little at a time, mixing well after each addition until thoroughly combined.

In a medium bowl, combine the semolina and 00 flour and stir until fully integrated. Gradually add the flour mixture to the ricotta mixture with a rubber spatula, using broad strokes to smear and fold the mixtures together. Keep folding until the mixture is integrated, but be careful not to overwork the dough. It should not appear entirely smooth and uniform like a traditional pasta dough. Cover and refrigerate for at least 1 hour or up to 24 hours. This makes it easier to roll the gnocchi.

408g ricotta
120g finely grated
    parmigiano-reggiano
150g (about 3) eggs
78g semolina flour
108g tipo 00 flour

What About Using the KitchenAid?

Once you've used the well method to commit the texture and tenderness of the ideal dough to memory, the KitchenAid will save you the elbow grease. Set the KitchenAid with the dough hook attachment to "stir." Add the flour and then begin adding the yolks or water slowly, about one-quarter of the volume at a time. As the yolks or water and flour begin to integrate, they will create a well in the mixer bowl. Stop the machine periodically and use a spatula to push the flour down from the sides of the bowl and into the mass. Turn the machine up to "2" and mix until integrated, about 2 minutes. Stop the machine again, strip the dough from the hook, and return it to the bowl. Turn the machine to "stir" for 2 more minutes. Stop the machine and transfer the dough to a lightly floured wooden board. I like to finish my dough by kneading it by hand until smooth, 3 to 5 minutes.

Gnudi Dough

Bring a large pot of water to a boil over high heat. Generously salt the water. Prepare an ice-water bath and set a colander in it.

Drop the spinach into the boiling water and cook until tender but still bright green, 30 seconds to 1 minute. Transfer the spinach to the ice-water bath to stop the cooking. Drain the spinach, transfer to a kitchen towel, and squeeze out the excess water.

Finely chop the spinach and return it to the towel, wringing it out once more to make sure you've removed as much water as possible.

Put the ricotta into a food processor and pulse just until it is as smooth as cake frosting and has a sheen.

In a large bowl, combine the whipped ricotta, spinach, egg yolks, pecorino, lemon peel, salt, and grated nutmeg q.b. Mix until the ingredients are well integrated.

Sprinkle the surface of the ricotta mixture with the flour and fold just until combined.

Using a stand mixer on medium-high speed, whip the egg whites until they form stiff peaks, 3 to 5 minutes. Gently fold the whipped whites into the spinach mixture one-third at a time.

Cover and let rest in the refrigerator until thoroughly chilled, at least 1 hour or up to overnight.

454g / 1 lb baby spinach
522g / 2¼ cups ricotta (see "whipped" ricotta, page 139)
36g / 2 egg yolks
150g / 1⅔ cups finely grated pecorino romano
Peel of 1 lemon, pith removed and peel finely chopped
½ teaspoon salt, plus more q.b.
Whole nutmeg, q.b.
95g / ¾ cup tipo 00 flour, plus more for dusting
162g / 5 to 6 egg whites

Whole-Wheat Dough

In a bowl, combine the 00 flour and whole-wheat flour and stir until fully integrated. Turn out the flour mixture onto your wooden work surface and create a barricade with a center sanctuary for the egg yolks that is 5 to 6 inches in diameter but not more. If you create too much space, your barricade won't be strong enough to contain the yolks as you begin to incorporate the flour. To avoid any additional risk of breaking through your barricade, mix, but do not beat, your yolks before adding them to the well. Add half of the egg mixture to the well and use a fork to incorporate the inner layer of flour, stirring in a continuous motion around the circumference to combine. Continue adding the rest of the egg mixture, incorporating the flour as you go. If you bust through your barricade, not to worry. Use your bench scraper to catch the egg mixture and fold it back into the flour, doing this at every edge until you have a mixture that is thick enough to contain itself. Set your tools aside, roll up your sleeves, and get to work kneading. The dough will be sticky at first, so as you work it, continue to remove the dough that clings to your hands and return it to the mass.

The dough will begin to firm up as the gluten is activated by kneading, but if it feels a touch too dry and is not integrating (this can happen when the environment is drier, such as during the winter or if you're working in an arid climate), gradually add about 1 tablespoon room-temperature water to hydrate it. The kneading motion is simple, but it does take some time to get the rhythm right. You essentially want to fold the dough in on itself, pressing down and away from your body with the heel of your dominant hand, relying on the weight of your body to do so. (You can hold the edge of the dough closest to you with your other hand to keep the dough in place as you stretch it away from you.) Rotate it 180 degrees, fold, and press again. Repeat this rotating, folding, and pressing motion until the dough is smooth and relatively firm to the touch, 8 to 10 minutes. Use your bench scraper to clean off any pieces of dough that clump and stick as you're kneading. Lightly dust the board with flour if needed; be careful not to add too much, as it will dry out the dough.

When properly kneaded, the dough should resemble the texture of Play-Doh and should spring back just slightly when poked. Cover the dough with plastic wrap and set it aside for at least 30 minutes. This allows the dough to become more pliable. If you're not forming pasta until the evening or the next day, place the dough in the refrigerator and remove it 20 minutes before you plan to roll it out so it returns to room temperature. Use the dough within 24 hours.

300g tipo 00 flour, plus more for kneading q.b.
200g whole-wheat flour
454g (24 to 26) egg yolks

Chestnut Dough

In a bowl, combine the chestnut flour and 00 flour and stir until fully integrated. Turn out the flour mixture onto your wooden work surface and create a barricade with a center sanctuary for the egg yolks that is 5 to 6 inches in diameter but not more. If you create too much space, your barricade won't be strong enough to contain the yolks as you begin to incorporate the flour. To avoid any additional risk of breaking through your barricade, mix, but do not beat, your yolks before adding them to the well. Add half of the egg mixture to the well and use a fork to incorporate the inner layer of flour, stirring in a continuous motion around the circumference to combine. Continue adding the rest of the egg mixture, incorporating the flour as you go. If you bust through your barricade, not to worry. Use your bench scraper to catch the egg mixture and fold it back into the flour, doing this at every edge until you have a mixture that is thick enough to contain itself. Set your tools aside, roll up your sleeves, and get to work kneading. The dough will be sticky at first, so as you work it, continue to remove the dough that clings to your hands and return it to the mass.

The dough will begin to firm up as the gluten is activated by kneading, but if it feels a touch too dry and is not integrating (this can happen when the environment is drier, such as during the winter or if you're working in an arid climate), gradually add about 1 tablespoon room-temperature water to hydrate it. The kneading motion is simple, but it does take some time to get the rhythm right. You essentially want to fold the dough in on itself, pressing down and away from your body with the heel of your dominant hand, relying on the weight of your body to do so. (You can hold the edge of the dough closest to you with your other hand to keep the dough in place as you stretch it away from you.) Rotate it 180 degrees, fold, and press again. Repeat this rotating, folding, and pressing motion until the dough is smooth and relatively firm to the touch, 8 to 10 minutes. Use your bench scraper to clean off any pieces of dough that clump and stick as you're kneading. Lightly dust the board with flour if needed; be careful not to add too much, as it will dry out the dough.

When properly kneaded, the dough should resemble the texture of Play-Doh and should spring back just slightly when poked. Chestnut flour often yields a dough that, even when properly kneaded, is still a bit stickier than your classic egg dough. This generally means that you may need to add a bit more flour to your work surface when you roll out the dough. For now, cover the dough with plastic wrap and set it aside for at least 30 minutes. This allows the dough to become more pliable. If you're not forming pasta until the evening or the next day, place the dough in the refrigerator and remove it 20 minutes before you plan to roll it out so it returns to room temperature. Use the dough within 24 hours.

125g chestnut flour
375g tipo 00 flour, plus
more for kneading q.b.
454g (24 to 26) egg yolks

Espresso Dough

In a bowl, combine the 00 flour, whole-wheat flour, and coffee and stir until fully integrated. Turn out the flour mixture onto your wooden work surface and create a barricade with a center sanctuary for the egg yolks that is 5 to 6 inches in diameter but not more. If you create too much space, your barricade won't be strong enough to contain the yolks as you begin to incorporate the flour. To avoid any additional opportunity to break through your barricade, mix, but do not beat, your yolks before adding them to the well. Add half of the egg mixture to the well and use a fork to incorporate the inner layer of flour, stirring in a continuous motion around the circumference to combine. Continue adding the rest of the egg mixture, incorporating the flour as you go. If you bust through your barricade, not to worry. Use your bench scraper to catch the egg mixture and fold it back into the flour, doing this at every edge until you have a mixture that is thick enough to contain itself. Set your tools aside, roll up your sleeves, and get to work kneading. The dough will be sticky at first, so as you work it, continue to remove the dough that clings to your hands and return it to the mass.

The dough will begin to firm up as the gluten is activated by kneading, but if it feels a touch too dry and is not integrating (this can happen when the environment is drier, such as during the winter or if you're working in an arid climate), gradually add about 1 tablespoon room-temperature water to hydrate it. The kneading motion is simple, but it does take some time to get the rhythm right. You essentially want to fold the dough in on itself, pressing down and away from your body with the heel of your dominant hand, relying on the weight of your body to do so. (You can hold the edge of the dough closest to you with your other hand to keep the dough in place as you stretch it away from you.) Rotate it 180 degrees, fold, and press again. Repeat this rotating, folding, and pressing motion until the dough is smooth and relatively firm to the touch, 8 to 10 minutes. Use your bench scraper to clean off any pieces of dough that clump and stick as you're kneading. Lightly dust the board with flour if needed; be careful not to add too much, as it will dry out the dough.

When properly kneaded, the dough should resemble the texture of Play-Doh and should spring back slightly when poked. Cover the dough with plastic wrap and set it aside for at least 30 minutes. This allows the dough to become more pliable. If you're not forming pasta until the evening or the next day, place the dough in the refrigerator and remove it 20 minutes before you plan to roll it out so it returns to room temperature. Use the dough within 24 hours.

300g tipo 00 flour, plus more for kneading q.b.
200g whole-wheat flour
7g / 1 Tbsp finely ground espresso-roast coffee
454g (24 to 26) egg yolks

Chickpea Dough

In a bowl, combine the 00 flour and chickpea flour and stir until fully integrated. Turn out the flour mixture onto your wooden work surface and create a barricade with a center sanctuary for the egg yolks that is 5 to 6 inches in diameter but not more. If you create too much space, your barricade won't be strong enough to contain the yolks as you begin to incorporate the flour. To avoid any additional risk of breaking through your barricade, mix, but do not beat, your yolks before adding them to the well. Add half of the egg mixture to the well and use a fork to incorporate the inner layer of flour, stirring in a continuous motion around the circumference to combine. Continue adding the rest of the egg mixture, incorporating the flour as you go. If you bust through your barricade, not to worry. Use your bench scraper to catch the egg mixture and fold it back into the flour, doing this at every edge until you have a mixture that is thick enough to contain itself. Set your tools aside, roll up your sleeves, and get to work kneading. The dough will be sticky at first, so as you work it, continue to remove the dough that clings to your hands and return it to the mass.

The dough will begin to firm up as the gluten is activated by kneading, but if it feels a touch too dry and is not integrating (this can happen when the environment is drier, such as during the winter or if you're working in an arid climate), gradually add about 1 tablespoon room-temperature water to hydrate it. The kneading motion is simple, but it does take some time to get the rhythm right. You essentially want to fold the dough in on itself, pressing down and away from your body with the heel of your dominant hand, relying on the weight of your body to do so. (You can hold the edge of the dough closest to you with your other hand to keep the dough in place as you stretch it away from you.) Rotate it 180 degrees, fold, and press again. Repeat this rotating, folding, and pressing motion until the dough is smooth and relatively firm to the touch, 8 to 10 minutes. Use your bench scraper to clean off any pieces of dough that clump and stick as you're kneading. Lightly dust the board with flour if needed; be careful not to add too much, as it will dry out the dough.

When properly kneaded, the dough should resemble the texture of Play-Doh and should spring back slightly when poked. Cover the dough with plastic wrap and set it aside for at least 30 minutes. This allows the dough to become more pliable. If you're not forming pasta until the evening or the next day, place the dough in the refrigerator and remove it 20 minutes before you plan to roll it out so it returns to room temperature. Use the dough within 24 hours.

350g tipo 00 flour, plus more for kneading q.b.
150g chickpea flour
454g (24 to 26) egg yolks

Buckwheat Dough

In a bowl, combine the 00 flour and buckwheat flour and stir until fully integrated. Turn out the flour mixture onto your wooden work surface and create a barricade with a center sanctuary for the egg yolks that is 5 to 6 inches in diameter but not more. If you create too much space, your barricade won't be strong enough to contain the yolks as you begin to incorporate the flour. To avoid any additional risk of breaking through your barricade, mix, but do not beat, your yolks before adding them to the well. Add half of the egg mixture to the well and use a fork to incorporate the inner layer of flour, stirring in a continuous motion around the circumference to combine. Continue adding the rest of the egg mixture, integrating the flour as you go. If you bust through your barricade, not to worry. Use your bench scraper to catch the egg mixture and fold it back into the flour, doing this at every edge until you have a mixture that is thick enough to contain itself. Set your tools aside, roll up your sleeves, and get to work kneading. The dough will be sticky at first, so as you work it, continue to remove the dough that clings to your hands and return it to the mass.

The dough will begin to firm up as the gluten is activated by kneading, but if it feels a touch too dry and is not integrating (this can happen when the environment is drier, such as during the winter or if you're working in an arid climate), gradually add about 1 tablespoon room-temperature water to hydrate it. The kneading motion is simple, but it does take some time to get the rhythm right. You essentially want to fold the dough in on itself, pressing down and away from your body with the heel of your dominant hand, relying on the weight of your body to do so. (You can hold the edge of the dough closest to you with your other hand to keep the dough in place as you stretch it away from you.) Rotate it 180 degrees, fold, and press again. Repeat this rotating, folding, and pressing motion until the dough is smooth and relatively firm to the touch, 8 to 10 minutes. Use your bench scraper to clean off any pieces of dough that clump and stick as you're kneading. Lightly dust the board with flour if needed; be careful not to add too much, as it will dry out the dough.

When properly kneaded, the dough should resemble the texture of Play-Doh and should spring back slightly when poked. Cover the dough with plastic wrap and set it aside for at least 30 minutes. This allows the dough to become more pliable. If you're not forming pasta until the evening or the next day, place the dough in the refrigerator and remove it 20 minutes before you plan to roll it out so it returns to room temperature. Use the dough within 24 hours.

300g tipo 00 flour, plus more for kneading q.b.
75g buckwheat flour
340g (18 to 20) egg yolks

Cocoa Dough

In a bowl, combine the 00 flour and cocoa powder and stir until fully integrated. Turn out the flour mixture onto your wooden work surface and create a barricade with a center sanctuary for the egg yolks that is 5 to 6 inches in diameter but not more. If you create too much space, your barricade won't be strong enough to contain the yolks as you begin to incorporate the flour. To avoid any additional opportunity to break through your barricade, mix, but do not beat, your yolks before adding them to the well. Add half of the egg mixture to the well and use a fork to incorporate the inner layer of flour, stirring in a continuous motion around the circumference to combine. Continue adding the rest of the egg mixture, incorporating the flour as you go. If you bust through your barricade, not to worry. Use your bench scraper to catch the egg mixture and fold it back into the flour, doing this at every edge until you have a mixture that is thick enough to contain itself. Set your tools aside, roll up your sleeves, and get to work. The dough will be sticky at first, so as you work it, continue to remove the dough that clings to your hands and return it to the mass.

The dough will begin to firm up as the gluten is activated by kneading, but if it feels a touch too dry and is not integrating (this can happen when the environment is drier, such as during the winter or if you're working in an arid climate), gradually add about 1 tablespoon room-temperature water to hydrate it. The kneading motion is simple, but it does take some time to get the rhythm right. You essentially want to fold the dough in on itself, pressing down and away from your body with the heel of your dominant hand, relying on the weight of your body to do so. (You can hold the edge of the dough closest to you with your other hand to keep the dough in place as you stretch it away from you.) Rotate it 180 degrees, fold, and press again. Repeat this rotating, folding, and pressing motion until the dough is smooth and relatively firm to the touch, 8 to 10 minutes. Use your bench scraper to clean off any pieces of dough that clump and stick as you're kneading. Lightly dust the board with flour if needed; be careful not to add too much, as it will dry out the dough.

When properly kneaded, the dough should resemble the texture of Play-Doh and should spring back just slightly when poked. Cover the dough with plastic wrap and set it aside for at least 30 minutes. This allows the dough to become more pliable. If you're not forming pasta until the evening or the next day, place the dough in the refrigerator and remove it 20 minutes before you plan to roll it out so it returns to room temperature. Use the dough within 24 hours.

470g tipo 00 flour, plus more for kneading q.b.
30g natural cocoa powder, sifted
454g (24 to 26) egg yolks

Rolling and Sheeting Your Dough

There is a tactile satisfaction to cutting a piece of that perfect, covetable dough, rolling it out with a rolling pin, and then slowly, patiently guiding it through the pasta machine until it's just thin enough to make out the contours of your palm through it. A sheet of pasta requires that you treat it with a white-glove reverence, and I always delight in indulging myself, and it, by taking it slow. Pasta has a way of rewarding the patient.

The instructions that follow assume that you're using a manual sheeter. If you're working with the KitchenAid attachment or another motorized sheeter, more power to you. It will undoubtedly make your life easier, and the instructions that follow will be more detailed than necessary, though they will still apply. I do recommend, however, starting with a manual sheeter, as it will help you learn to make decisions based on feel rather than prescription. For instance, cranking by hand assists you in determining, by the tension in the handle, whether your dough sheet needs to go through the same setting again (and again) or if it's ready to go down (or up) one.

To start, cut your dough into quarters so you're working with smaller, more manageable pieces. Begin with one piece and cover the remaining pieces with the plastic wrap. Dust your board and rolling pin with a bit of 00 flour. Roll the dough out to an oval ¼ to ½ inch thick and about 8 inches long. You want it to be thin enough to fit through the widest setting on the sheeter, but not so wide that it doesn't have room to expand widthwise as it's fed through. Feed the dough through once, cranking with your dominant hand while you very gently lead the dough through with your nondominant hand. Then fold the dough into thirds by bringing one end to the middle and then the other end over the top as if folding a business letter. Lightly press on top to seal and then feed one narrow end of the dough through the sheeter again. What you're doing at this point is essentially rekneading the dough and making sure there is no extra air in it. Repeat the fold and feed at least three times, until the dough is smooth and uniform. Decrease the setting on your sheeter (to "5" on the Imperia or "2" on the KitchenAid) and feed the dough through again. At this point, the sheet will be long enough to be a bit unwieldy to work with. You can return it to your floured board, cut it in half and work with only one length at a time, covering the length(s) not in use with a kitchen towel or plastic wrap.

The shape you intend to make will determine how thin you sheet the dough from this point. Some shapes, such as strangozzi (page 56), are cut at this point in the process, while others are fed through three more gradually narrowing settings, yielding a sheet through which you can easily see the outline of your hand—even the lines of your palm. As the sheet becomes longer and thinner, you will need to handle it with more care. Don't be afraid to pause and adjust or to cut your sheet in half if it becomes a bit unwieldy to work with. (Just cover the half you've set aside with a kitchen towel or plastic wrap.) The dance between cranking the machine and feeding the dough through on one end while catching it on the other is not second nature—indeed, it's a job better suited to three hands than two. It will be awkward at first, and you will certainly turn out more than a couple of unseemly sheets. You can always fold the sheet in half and feed it through again to even it out. Continue this process until you've achieved the desired thickness for the shape you intend to make (see pages 34–35). As you work, your sheet may become tacky and require a light dusting of 00 flour; be careful not to add too much or you'll end up with a sheet that's too dry. Lightly dust with 00 flour and transfer to a parchment-lined sheet tray, layering parchment between each sheet to ensure they do not stick together. Cover with plastic wrap or a kitchen towel and repeat the process until you have sheeted your full batch of dough. Follow the directions for trimming the sheet(s) in the recipe for your desired shape.

On pages 34 and 35 you'll find a chart showing the shapes and settings you should sheet up to on an Imperia Model 150 or down to on a KitchenAid attachment when making each one, as well as how many times to pass the sheet through the final setting.

For long pastas and for flat pastas like corzetti (page 113), the thickness to which you roll your dough can come down to preference without compromising the integrity of the dish. For instance, at Misi I roll my fettuccine (page 49) as thin as many roll their mandilli di seta (page 51), while my strangozzi (page 56) is a true outlier at nearly ⅛ inch thick. Precision in sheeting is most important with filled pastas, which can break easily, either in the pan or in the pot, if the dough is too thin. If the dough is rolled too thick, filled pastas can lose their delicacy and overpower the filling you've worked so hard to make.

While this may all seem daunting at first, after you roll and sheet dough for a handful of shapes and taste how their thickness impacts how they're shaped and cooked, you will slowly begin to move away from having to use this section as you go. After all, that is the goal: to internalize this advice so you can ultimately break free of following recipes and instructions.

The Sfoglino Method

I remember the first time I saw someone roll a sfoglia, or sheet of pasta, by hand. I was working at a restaurant in Sansepolcro, a Tuscan town a stone's throw from the Emilia-Romagna border and two hours from Bologna, where the country's best sfogline have, for centuries, turned the process of rolling out dough into an art form. The family I worked for may have been cooking in Tuscany, but they came from a line of Romagnese who'd been rolling sfoglie a particular way for as long as anyone alive could recall. Every morning, I'd watch the matriarch, Fernanda, as she wielded a mattarello more than half her size to roll out dough sheets about the size of a circular dining table for six. She'd then drape the sheets over a table to rest for a few minutes, and I'd move through them, cutting each sfoglia down to uniform squares that she'd fashion into what seemed like hundreds of tortellini per day. She did all of this with only three tools: a rolling pin, a wooden table, and her hands. This is how I learned to make pasta, and how many sfogline like Fernanda still make pasta today. It's not a method I've ever incorporated into my kitchens, which is why you won't find instructions for rolling out your dough by hand here. But, as always, follow your curiosity and experiment beyond these pages.

Guide to Pasta-Rolling Settings and Pass-Throughs

Shapes		With KitchenAid (setting / times passed through)	With Imperia (setting / times passed through)
	Fettuccine	6 / 1x	2 / 2x
	Maccherroncini di Campofilone	5 / 2x	2 / 1x
	Mandilli di Seta	6 / 1x (without board)	2 / 2x (without board)
	Pappardelle	6 / 1x	2 / 2x
	Pizzoccheri	3 / 2x	4 / 2x
	Strangozzi	2 / 2x	5 / 2x
	Tagliatelle	6 / 1x	2 / 2x
	Tagliolini	4 / 2x	3 / 2x
	Tajarin	4 / 2x	3 / 2x
	Fileja	N/A	N/A
	Busiate	N/A	N/A

Shapes		With KitchenAid (setting / times passed through)	With Imperia (setting / times passed through)
	Gnudi	N/A	N/A
	Malloreddus	N/A	N/A
	Orecchiette	N/A	N/A
	Trofie	N/A	N/A
	Pici	N/A	N/A
	Ricotta Gnocchi	N/A	N/A
	Stricchetti	6 / 3x	2 / 3x
	Balanzoni	6 / 3x	2 / 3x
	Agnolotti	6 / 3x	2 / 3x
	Agnolotti dal Plin	6 / 3x	2 / 3x
	Cannelloni	5 / 2x	2 / 1x

Shapes		With **KitchenAid** (setting / times passed through)	With **Imperia** (setting / times passed through)
	Cappelletti	6 / 3x	2 / 3x
	Caramelle	6 / 3x	2 / 3x
	Casunziei	6 / 3x	2 / 3x
	Cjalsons	6 / 3x	2 / 3x
	Culurgiones	4 / 2x	3 / 2x
	Mezzelune	6 / 3x	2 / 3x
	Occhi	6 / 3x	2 / 3x
	Pansotti	6 / 3x	2 / 3x
	Ravioli	6 / 3x	2 / 3x
	Tortelli	6 / 3x	2 / 3x
	Tortellini	6 / 3x	2 / 3x
	Corzetti	4 / 2x	3 / 2x

Shapes		With **KitchenAid** (setting / times passed through)	With **Imperia** (setting / times passed through)
	Canederli	N/A	N/A
	Bigoli	N/A	N/A
	Spaghetti alla Chitarra	2 / 2x	4 / 1x
	Bucatini	N/A	N/A
	Casarecce	N/A	N/A
	Linguine	N/A	N/A
	Mafaldine	N/A	N/A
	Rigatoni	N/A	N/A
	Spaghetti	N/A	N/A
	Penne	N/A	N/A
	Ziti	N/A	N/A

Extruded Pasta

It's true that watching ziti being spit out of a machine isn't quite as sexy as rolling, filling, and sealing a perfect raviolo. This is perhaps why the craftsmanship involved in making great extruded pasta, as well as its importance not just in central and southern Italy's pasta culture but also in the history of pasta itself, is often overlooked. However, if it weren't for the tradition of drying pasta, none of us would be eating it, I'd never have become a chef, and all of us would probably be at least 60 percent less happy. Not to mention the fact that high-quality extruded dried pasta—whether you make it yourself or you buy it in a store—is just as texturally complex and delicious as fresh pasta. Without both traditions, Italy would never have taken a border-crossing Mediterranean staple of the Middle Ages and turned it into a culturally significant, complex cuisine.

To understand why fresh and dried pastas are equally important, I like to think of them as completely different art forms that serve different purposes. They are, after all, not made the same way. Today, extruded pasta is pasta made by a machine that mixes flour and water into dough, kneads it, and then forces it through a die, or mold, that extrudes the selected shape. That shape is then dried and packaged for sale—or, in my case, cooked in the restaurants that night, but I'll get to that next. Sounds easy enough, at least until you learn, as I did the first time I visited Faella in the Campanian town of Gragnano (effectively Mecca for dried pasta), that there are at least a dozen decisions a producer makes during each step that will determine whether the end result is a bland industrial pasta or a flavorful artisanal pasta. If you want to understand just how widely quality can vary, go and buy spaghetti from three high-quality brands (see page 39) and three mass-market brands and taste them side by side. You will tell the difference.

Before I get to how I make extruded pasta at home, which I assure you is far less complex than what follows, it's helpful to understand how it's done at the commercial level, especially by artisanal producers. If nothing else, it will give you an appreciation for what actually goes into a really good box of pasta. First, great extruded pasta begins with great grain and grain handling. The level of protein in the wheat strain, where it comes from, how it is milled, and how fast that milled flour is used can impact everything from how the pasta dries to how it tastes. (In fact, it's in the name of quality and taste that many of Italy's best producers of extruded pastas have taken to resurrecting high-protein, heirloom strains of durum wheat like Saragolla, the variety that made Neapolitan pasta famous for its quality in the eighteenth and nineteenth centuries.)

The second consideration is water. Part of what makes pasta di Gragnano unique is not just its geographic position and its early mastery of the natural drying process but also its water source. It's no accident that the world's greatest pizza and dried pasta comes from the same place; what unifies them is water. The third consideration is the choice of material from which the dies are made. It's indisputable that bronze dies produce the highest-quality extruded pastas, as they yield shapes that are more porous, textured, and less dense; each of those qualities allows the pasta to absorb flavor all the way through the shape and to bind well to sauces. Larger, more commercial pasta makers often use Teflon, which results in a smooth, denser product. It's all visible to the naked eye. Get up close to a strand of Ronzoni spaghetti next to a strand of, say, Rustichella d'Abruzzo spaghetti and you will notice two things: the Ronzoni, which is made by Teflon die, has a polished texture and a darker color. That slick surface does not cling to sauces like a bronze die–cut pasta will, and what you want from a great extruded pasta is that cling. And about that darker color? It's often the result of drying at higher temperatures, which is great for producing more pasta but not so great for the pasta itself.

Since the documented dawn of drying pasta for trade and transport began more than eight centuries ago, it's been the most important, and most challenging, part of the process. Before the introduction of machines that could artificially, and uniformly, dry pasta, it was done outside in the sun. (There is mention of specific methods for drying this way as far back as the fourteenth century.) By the turn of the twentieth century, machines for drying were used at pasta factories all over Italy, from Sicily to the north, where drying in the sun was previously difficult or even impossible given the cooler climate. Today, the highest-quality pastas are typically dried at 95° to 110°F over the course of 24 hours to a few days, depending on the shape and temperature. By contrast, many industrial producers dry pastas at temperatures as high as 220°F for just a few hours, which essentially precooks the pasta, altering both texture and flavor, rendering the pasta less flavorful, or worse, bitter. The goal is to dry the pasta slowly enough that it doesn't alter the flavor and nutritional value of the flour, but not so slowly that it begins to grow mold (or who knows what else). This usually involves drying in two or three stages at different temperatures and/or humidity levels.

In short, this is a Process with a capital P. But the good news is that doing this at home for your own table does not require a temperature-controlled dedicated pasta sweat lodge or a few days of drying time. You just need one very heavy—and not exactly cheap—piece of equipment, a desk fan, semolina flour, and water.

Making Extruded Pasta at Home

I spent years making pasta before I even attempted to extrude my own. Part of this is because I came up making pasta in the northern tradition, and extruded pasta was, to my point above, a completely different craft. Besides, I'd had enough bad extruded pasta made in-house—too many cooked rigatoni that collapsed onto themselves, too many gummy strands of linguine—to know that it was not something to undertake in a cavalier way. When we began cooking regional menus at A Voce, we did not go out and buy an extruder to take for a test drive once we made our way to Lazio and on south. Instead, we relied on great artisanal dried pastas from folks who had been making them since well before I was born.

But as I was planning to open Lilia, I knew that many of the pasta dishes I wanted to serve relied on extruded shapes, and that I could only feel good about making them a permanent part of my menus if I figured out how to make them myself. After months of trial and error—of testing different machines, different ratios of flour to water, flour brands, and, most importantly, methods of drying and drying times—I landed on a style of extruded pasta that is neither fully dried nor fresh but finds a third path that has broadened my understanding of pasta.

Choosing an Extruder

We can't talk about making spaghetti or rigatoni at home without first talking about the machine you're going to need to buy. Extruders are like espresso machines in that neither can reasonably be considered an "essential" item for a kitchen (I beg to differ in my case, though I realize I am, at best, an outlier). The difference between a serviceable machine and a good machine is four digits, both are typically hell to clean, and there is generally no good place to put one, particularly if you reside in a New York apartment. This is a luxury purchase, plain and simple, and while I am not doing a particularly good job of selling it, if you know how to use one, it's worth every penny. To my point above about a "third path," the best argument for owning an extruder is not so you can mimic the dried pasta traditions of Gragnano at home (if you want to do that, you're better off buying great pasta) but so you can explore the possibilities for texture and flavor that exist between fresh and dried.

There are extruders that start at $200 and go as high as $10,000, but it's not an even graduation in price. There are a number of options under $500, and from there you jump to about $2,000 and up. The lower-end options are unified by their use of plastic dies, sometimes cast in aluminum and sometimes not. Will they make pasta? Yes, sure, they technically work, but there is a major discrepancy in quality between these machines and a proper extruder. They are useful only as a low-risk starting point—an opportunity to get a feel for the process and see if you want to go deeper. If you really want to make great extruded pasta, though, you will need to invest.

Arcobaleno's AEX5 "Vita"

At both restaurants I use Emiliomiti extruders, but for home use I like Arcobaleno's AEX5 "Vita," which can do almost everything I do at the restaurant on a smaller scale. It's about as compact, light, and affordable ($1,800) as a proper extruder can be. The main distinction is that the machine uses brass dies instead of bronze (the company also offers a limited selection of copper dies for this model), but the difference in texture is almost imperceptible. A notable bonus is that a wide range of dies are available, from bucatini to campanelle, with each running about $85.

Emiliomiti Lillo Due

If you want to take the next step up, Emiliomiti's Lillo Due, the company's smallest model, is an excellent machine at $2,300 and is certainly more oriented toward professionals. To that end, be forewarned: you'll need at least three people to lift it. The bronze dies for the Lillo Due run about $135 for standard shapes.

My Favorite Dried Pasta Brands

While the extrusion press became a fixture of pasta making in the sixteenth century, thus paving the way for its more widespread commercialization, it wasn't until the Industrial Revolution that dried pasta became big business, spreading from the Alps on down to the southern shore of Sicily, where the seeds of trade had been sown hundreds of years before. The evidence of the boom is still everywhere, as many of the most renowned names in pasta, both industrial and artisanal, were established in the 1800s, particularly in and around Gragnano and Torre Annunziata outside Naples, the two towns that still form the cradle of dried pasta production in Italy. Some of my favorite brands hail from these two towns, but with the introduction of machine drying at the turn of the last century, great pasta making became possible everywhere, regardless of climate, as evidenced by the geographical spread that the following brands represent.

Rustichella d'Abruzzo (from Penne, Abruzzo)

Born in the aptly named town of Penne in 1924 as Pastificio Gaetano Sergiacomo, Rustichella d'Abruzzo is now one of the more widely distributed medium-size artisanal pasta brands in Italy. The company makes dozens of shapes across several lines, but I am particularly fond of the Triticum line, which features pasta made from 100 percent organic heirloom durum wheat strains, such as Saragolla and Senatore Cappelli.

Faella (from Gragnano, Campania)

Alongside Di Martino and Gentile, Faella (established 1907) is one of the most recognizable brands from Gragnano. What struck me most when I visited Faella was the age of its machinery. Much of it dates to the 1950s and 1960s, and it is kept in use as a way of preserving the continuity of the product, even though it also means a much slower process with less output. That effort shows in the pasta, however, which I love for its sturdiness and bite.

Monograno Felicetti (from Predazzo, Trentino–Alto Adige)

Located at the foot of the Dolomites, in Trentino–Alto Adige, Monograno Felicetti pasta factory turns out pastas made from 100 percent organic durum wheat and water sourced from mountain springs. Sounds like great marketing, but the quality is there, particularly in the long pastas made from Senatore Cappelli "Il Cappelli" and those from other wheat varieties, such as Kamut.

De Cecco (from Fara San Martino, Abruzzo)

"Small batch" doesn't always mean high quality, and "high volume" doesn't always mean low quality, and to me no other Italian brand illustrates the latter quite like De Cecco. Yes, those blue-and-yellow boxes are ubiquitous in American supermarkets, but the brand, which was established in 1886 in Abruzzo and is still run by the De Cecco family, manages to make great pasta at scale, using bronze dies and a low-temperature, longer-drying process to preserve the integrity of the wheat. Of all of the large pasta brands in Italy, this is far and away my top choice. In fact, in a blind tasting we conducted to test my brand allegiances, it not only beat out all of the producers of comparable size but also some of the most respected names in artisanal dried pasta.

Extruded Dough

Like all pasta dough, extruded pasta dough begins with a ratio. Mine is 25 to 30 percent water to semolina by weight. Most home pasta extruders have a capacity of 500g at a time, which will yield about four regular portions of pasta or six smaller portions, once you account for losing about one-quarter to one-third of the batch at the beginning of the process (more on that later), hence the flour and water measurements for this dough. Feel free to use smaller amounts, so long as you keep the ratio intact. From here, pretty much the entire process diverges from the making of fresh pasta.

To begin, attach your preferred die to the machine and open the hopper. Add the full volume of semolina, and then turn the machine to "mix." While the machine is in motion, gradually add the water about 1 Tbsp or so at a time. Before you add the full amount of water, pause the machine and check the hydration. (I do this once I've added three-quarters of the water.) Open the hopper and grab some of the "dough" in your hand. In the mixing chamber, it should appear loose and crumbly, like the top of a coffee cake. When you make a fist with the "dough," it should bind together and hold the impression of your hand but still easily break up into a crumb-like texture. If it does not bind at all, add a very small amount of water—about 1 Tbsp—keeping in mind that the word *dough* is deceiving. The mixture should be fairly dry in the mix phase, as it does not actually become a dough until it goes through the die.

Return the machine to mix for 5 minutes. Pause it again and open the hopper to check the texture of the "dough," scraping down any that is clinging to the sides of the machine. Let the "dough" rest in the machine for 5 minutes. Line a sheet pan with parchment paper and generously dust with semolina. Set it next to the machine.

Switch the machine to "extrude." As the pasta begins to emerge from the machine, it will appear both rigid and a bit gnarled and untrue to form, no matter what die you're using. Texture is what you're looking for on the surface of the pasta, but not so much that the pasta appears as though someone chewed it up and spit it out. This ragged debut is what happens as the machine heats up but hasn't quite reached the optimal temperature for extrusion, and the dough is not yet binding uniformly. You will inevitably have to discard some of your batch (generally 50 to 100g), particularly on your first run. As the machine warms it up, the pasta will begin extruding with greater ease and the surface texture will reveal a delicate ridged pattern—looking almost like a strand of hair under a microscope. Use a bench scraper to cut the pasta, and set it aside on the sheet pan. (If you're making a long pasta, be sure to pull it out of the machine gently, untangling any strands as they emerge.) When the entirety of the "dough" has been extruded, shut off the machine, sprinkle the pasta on the sheet pan with another layer of semolina, and set aside to dry uncovered at room temperature.

500g semolina flour, plus more for dusting q.b. (preferably Rustichella d'Abruzzo semola rimacinata)
175g water, at room temperature

Drying Your Pasta

Whenever I find something wrong with the extruded pasta at one of the restaurants, it's often because it is either over- or underdried. If it is underdried, it will have a tacky texture when cooked, verging on the slithery quality of tapioca rather than the sturdy chew you're looking for. If it's overdried, it tends to break when handling or in the pan when marrying and will certainly take much longer to cook.

Drying is not an exact science, especially if you're drying at home without the luxury of temperature control and with a variable level of heat and humidity. Even between the two restaurants, which are one mile from each other, the drying times are totally different. If you live in a place with four seasons, your pasta will dry faster in fall and winter than it does in spring and summer. If you live in a place with a relatively consistent climate, lucky you. Not only do you likely enjoy a better quality of life, but you will be able to nail down a mostly consistent process. For the rest of us, drying pasta successfully is more about identifying doneness than it is about prescriptive drying times, though you should plan for somewhere between 3 and 6 hours, depending on shape (tubular pastas generally take a bit longer), climate, and whether you're using a fan.

For my style of extruded pasta, "done" means that the shape does not feel wet or malleable but is not so dry that when you take, say, a piece of rigatoni between your thumb and index finger and squeeze gently, it doesn't crack into pieces. (You will likely see little fissures when you squeeze it, but it won't break.) Further, if you go to separate it into two pieces, it should offer some resistance, not quite as if it's peeling apart but not a clean break either. There should also be an evenness to the texture, which is achieved by either flipping over the "nests" of long pasta shapes or shaking the pan holding tubular pasta. Do this every hour or so until the pasta is done drying. To avoid having to babysit the pasta quite so much while it's drying, purchase a pasta drying tray on legs for maximum airflow (see page 14).

Planning Ahead

One of the questions I am most frequently asked is, How far in advance should I be making my pasta? And, maddeningly, the answer is, it depends. One thing you don't want to do is start this process too late on the day you're entertaining, which is why I always recommend making it in the morning. If you can't, make the pasta the day before, let it dry for 4 to 6 hours, until "done," and then cover it tightly with plastic wrap and refrigerate it until you're ready to use it (it will keep for up to 3 days).

Using a desk fan to aid the drying process will undoubtedly speed it up and is particularly useful in the summer months, when humidity levels are higher in many places. The constant circulation of air also offers a more even drying process, but be sure to place the fan at least 3 feet away and set the control to low so the pasta doesn't dry too fast.

The Shapes

There are hundreds of traceable pasta shapes. Some we're lucky enough to know by name, by contour, and by flavor. Others we might find in a book but will likely never put a fork to in modern Italy. And still hundreds, perhaps thousands more have been lost to time, their names or shapes never committed to writing—the domain of a single family or town that has long forgotten them. Of what we do know and have documented, the sheer number is as awe-inspiring as it is bewildering; to acknowledge this diversity is to acknowledge that mastery is an impossibility when it comes to making pasta. Let no one tell you otherwise.

As such, what you'll find here is not comprehensive by any stretch; it's personal. These are the forty-five shapes that I have spent the most time learning, tuning, relearning, and cooking since I started down this path. There are a handful of others that I don't regularly cook but are either so classic or so idiosyncratic in their reflection of place and history that they simply can't be omitted. They may not be on my menus, but they've been a part of my development, stoking my curiosity and always reminding me of just how much more there is to know about this craft.

I've organized the shapes into categories, beginning with hand-cut shapes—that is, fettuccine, pappardelle, and the like. These are the pastas that I recommend starting with, as they will give you a feel for rolling out dough and for how thickness impacts cooking. From there, we head into hand-shaped pastas, those that are formed by your two hands and often with the aid of a simple tool like a gnocchi board or maccheroni iron. While they may look simple, these are often the most difficult pastas to master, as they are truly about repetition in pursuit of muscle memory. In other words, looks are deceiving. (My pasta-making path is paved with mangled orecchiette.) Next, of course, are the filled pastas, from the classic ravioli to tortellini and culurgiones, which vary in degree of difficulty depending on the enclosure and size of the pasta. Then there are the outliers: the pastas that don't fit neatly into any category, like spaghetti alla chitarra or corzetti. These are some of my favorite shapes, and while a few of them have an advanced level of difficulty, many in this section will prove to be a great starting point, too. You'll also find a reference for the extruded shapes. Because your machine does most of the work for these, it's really a guide to cutting by shape. Lastly, each shape entry identifies where the shape can be found in Italy and provides additional ideas for how to serve it.

Now, before you dive in, a few how-to-use-this-section housekeeping items:

Experimentation is encouraged. While each of these shapes corresponds to a specific dish or dishes, I've included a "How I serve it" section that is meant to encourage you to think beyond the recipes in this book.

Read up on rolling and sheeting first. The recipes that follow pick up where those instructions end (see pages 32–33). Also review the handy chart that acts as a visual cheat sheet on how thick or thin to roll out your dough by shape (see pages 34–35).

Overage isn't a sign of error. My dough recipes are scaled to account for the natural waste that occurs when cutting and shaping pasta—whether it's human error or routine stamping and trimming. One batch of dough may still yield more pasta than the finished recipe calls for. If you're left with extra dough or sheets, try a different shape and store it in the refrigerator for the next night. With the exception of the filled shapes, everything will keep well in the refrigerator for 24 hours. Or store your dough and get back to work the next day.

When in doubt, lean on the illustrations. I've included illustrations of key steps in the process when the placement of your hands is essential to producing the final product.

Don't get discouraged. Some shapes you will nail on your first try; others will require you to be acquainted, and comfortable, with failure. Don't get down on yourself if you don't get it on your first, second, or third try. It happens to me all the time, even with shapes I think I've committed to memory. Pasta making requires constant practice.

All-Purpose Lasagna Sheets

While the lasagna sheet is absolutely its own shape, I also treat it as an all-purpose sheet. Cut it into squares to make quadrati, or into mismatched shapes to make maltagliati, or, yes, use it layer your lasagna (page 168).

Simply choose your preferred egg-based dough (pages 18, 22, and 26–31) and follow the directions for rolling and sheeting (pages 32–33), referring to the chart on pages 34–35 for the prescribed thickness of the shape you're cutting. Lightly dust a wooden work surface with 00 flour. Line a sheet pan with parchment paper and lightly dust with semolina. Lay your sheet(s) of pasta on the work surface. Use a knife to cut 4 by 12-inch sheets, removing the scraps from the unclean edges (save them for soup). Transfer each sheet to the prepared sheet pan, and layer a piece of parchment and a light dusting of semolina between each sheet to prevent them from sticking. Cover with a kitchen towel. Repeat with the remaining sheets.

For quadrati, simply cut each sheet into 1½ by 1½-inch squares and arrange in an even layer on the prepared sheet pan. Dust lightly with semolina and cover with a kitchen towel.

Let dry for 20 to 30 minutes at room temperature. If not using right away, cover the sheet pan with plastic wrap and refrigerate for up to 24 hours.

Hand Cut

Fettuccine

It's tough to say whether fettuccine would have quite the mental hold on this country without Alfredo. The shape, which is found primarily in central Italy, is really Lazio's answer to Emilia-Romagna's tagliatelle (page 57). By definition it tends to be a little narrower and thicker than its neighbor to the northeast, but in practice they are sometimes the same. (In fact, some even argue that, to the contrary, fettuccine should be wider. Not in my house.)

In the same way that tagliatelle is a fixture of Bolognese food, fettuccine is a pillar of Roman and central Italian cuisine—and is served in a variety of preparations based on who, where, and what time of year it is. I think of it as a more all-purpose version of the former, as it's generally not quite as thin or breakable. But for the sake of ease, in this book fettuccine and tagliatelle are rolled to the same thinness—halfway between where each would fall—and I differentiate them by their widths and how they are cut.

Where it's found

Central Italy, particularly in Lazio.

How I serve it

With whatever is in the refrigerator, the pantry, or my market haul and, of course, with butter, parmigiano, and black pepper (no cream!).

1   Prepare your selected egg-based dough (pages 18, 22, and 26–31) and follow the instructions for rolling and sheeting (pages 32–33).

2   Lightly dust a wooden work surface with 00 flour. Line a sheet pan with parchment paper and lightly dust with semolina.

3   Lay your sheet(s) of pasta on the work surface. Use a knife to cut 18-inch-long sheets, removing the scraps from the unclean edges (save them for soup). Cover the sheets with plastic wrap or a kitchen towel.

4   Place the fettuccine cutter on your hand-cranked pasta machine or KitchenAid. (If you do not have a cutter attachment or you prefer to hand-cut your fettuccine, fold one pasta sheet in half and then in thirds until you end up with a small packet about 4½ by 6 inches. Position the packet horizontally with the longer side parallel to you. Trim any uneven edges and discard. Beginning at the left or right edge of your packet, move inward and cut ¼-inch-wide strips. Follow steps 6 through 9.)

5   To cut the pasta using the machine, holding one end of the pasta sheet with your nondominant hand, gently feed the opposite end into the cutter and begin cranking with your dominant hand. Keep the sheet nearly perpendicular to the machine as you crank. As the pasta moves through the machine, move your nondominant hand under the cutter to catch it. (If you are using a KitchenAid, feed with one hand and catch with the other.)

6   Generously dust your strands of fettuccine with 00 flour and gently shake them to separate. Curl the batch into a nest and place it on the prepared sheet pan.

7   Repeat with the remaining sheets.

8   Let dry for 20 to 30 minutes at room temperature.

9   If not using right away, cover the sheet pan with plastic wrap and refrigerate for up to 24 hours.

Maccheroncini di Campofilone

I like to think of maccheroncini di Campofilone as thin tagliolini (page 60), which themselves are especially thin tagliatelle (page 57). But in the case of Campofilone's famous egg-dough pasta, when I say thin, I mean *thin* (often less than 1 millimeter wide) and cut by hand.

The shape, which comes from the Fermo Province of the Marche (otherwise famous for its production of shoes), dates to at least the sixteenth century. And while it remained a hyper-regional specialty until the latter part of the twentieth century, it has since become regarded as one of Italy's great egg pastas. It's now dried and sold packaged primarily through its two most famous producers, Spinosi and La Campofilone, but if you find yourself anywhere near the town of Ascoli Piceno, do yourself a favor and detour to taste it fresh.

The trick is to cook it very quickly and marry it without it turning to mush. When you nail both, it's impossibly silky and delicate—so thin it almost disappears into the sauce. It's a selfless shape that lets whatever you pair it with take the lead.

Where it's found

The Marche, in the province of Fermo, in and around the towns of Ascoli Piceno and Campofilone.

How I serve it

It's traditionally served with a beef-spiked red sauce or fish ragù. I like to serve it with the former.

1   Prepare your selected egg-based dough (pages 18, 22, and 26–31) and follow the instructions for rolling and sheeting (pages 32–33).

2   Lightly dust a wooden work surface with 00 flour. Line a sheet pan with parchment paper and lightly dust with semolina.

3   Lay your sheet(s) of pasta on the work surface. Use a knife to cut 18-inch-long sheets, removing the scraps from the unclean edges (save them for soup). Cover the sheets with plastic wrap or a kitchen towel.

4   Place one sheet on your work surface. Fold the sheet in half and then in thirds until you end up with a small packet about 4½ by 6 inches. Position the packet horizontally with the longer side parallel to you. Trim any uneven edges and discard. Beginning at the left or right edge of your packet, move inward and cut ⅒-inch-wide strands.

5   Generously dust your strands of tajarin with 00 flour and gently shake them to separate. Curl the batch into a nest and place it on the prepared sheet pan.

6   Repeat with the remaining sheets.

7   Let dry for 20 to 30 minutes at room temperature.

8   If not using right away, cover the sheet pan with plastic wrap and refrigerate for up to 24 hours.

Mandilli di Seta

The name *mandilli di seta* aptly translates to "silk handkerchiefs." Think of these as extra-thin lasagna sheets that are cut into rectangles, boiled, and, in their home region of Liguria, are often smothered in pesto or meat sauce. As with tagliatelle, how thin the pasta was rolled was not only a symbol of the cook's prowess but also of culinary sophistication.

Today, mandilli have been eclipsed by their more ubiquitous Riviera brethren, trofie (page 70) and pansotti (page 100). But I've always taken to the shape, which might appear to be a simple affair but is actually one of the more difficult shapes to cook and marry. When done properly, though, it is a pasta to behold, its smooth texture and folds resembling a pile of rippling silk.

Like other delicate shapes, you must cook them quickly in the water but also to coat them properly during the marriage—again, quickly—in the pan to ensure that the delicate layers don't fuse themselves into accidental lasagna.

Where it's found

Liguria, particularly around Genoa.

How I serve it

With pesto al Genovese, primarily, or with fresh tomatoes or other light vegetables like zucchini.

1   Prepare your selected egg-based dough (pages 18, 22, and 26–31) and follow the instructions for rolling and sheeting (pages 32–33).

2   Lightly dust a wooden work surface with OO flour. Line a sheet pan with parchment paper and lightly dust with semolina.

3   Lay your sheet(s) of pasta on the work surface. Use a knife to cut 4 by 4½-inch sheets, removing the scraps from the unclean edges (save them for soup). Cover the sheets with plastic wrap or a kitchen towel.

4   This step, which calls for a cavarola board (see page 12), adds texture and further thins out and lengthens the pasta. If you don't have a cavarola board, feed your sheets through the sheeter one more time at the same setting and move ahead to step 5. Lightly dust your cavarola board with OO flour and lay an individual sheet on it with the longer side vertical. Applying moderate pressure, roll your rolling pin over the sheet two or three times until the pattern from the board has indented the pasta.

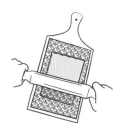

5   Generously dust each sheet with OO flour and group them in stacks of 8 to 10 on the prepared sheet pan.

6   Repeat steps 3 through 5 with the remaining sheets.

7   Let dry for 20 to 30 minutes at room temperature.

8   If not using right away, cover the sheet pan with plastic wrap and refrigerate for up to 24 hours.

Pappardelle

Pappardelle are said to have originated in Tuscany, and while the shape has migrated to surrounding regions (and beyond), I still associate it with its home base, and more specifically with pappardelle al ragù di coniglio (page 226).

The pairing of rabbit ragù and pappardelle is so classic that in *The Singular Doctrine*, published in 1560, food writer Domenico Romoli, who wrote extensively about Roman and Tuscan cuisine, name-checks pappardelle ("fine, delicate, and tender lasagne") five times—notably as pappardelle alla romana, pappardelle alla fiorentina, and pappardelle con lepre (hare). No recipes appear for alla fiorentina or alla romana, but clearly pappardelle were already in heavy rotation on the sixteenth-century banquet circuit. In fact, they appear in the writings of dozens of prominent culinary writers, from Romoli to Pellegrino Artusi, in various preparations but primarily as a canvas for game ragù.

When it comes to the shape itself, Romoli's description isn't far off. While it was historically made with flour and water, today it's almost exclusively made with egg dough that is rolled out into thin sheets, and then cut into ribbons about 1¼ inches wide.

I make two versions: my classic egg dough pappardelle and one made from my chickpea dough.

Where it's found

Throughout Italy, with its densest concentration in Tuscany.

How I serve it

With any ragù that suits, or with chickpeas and rosemary (page 338), a combination that has been burned in my memory since I tried it in Sansepolcro twenty years ago.

1   Prepare your selected egg-based dough (pages 18, 22, and 26–31) and follow the instructions for rolling and sheeting (pages 32–33).

2   Lightly dust a wooden work surface with OO flour. Line a sheet pan with parchment paper and lightly dust with semolina.

3   Lay your sheet(s) of pasta on the work surface. Use a knife to cut 9-inch-long sheets, removing the scraps from the unclean edges (save them for soup).

4   Lightly dust each sheet with OO flour and neatly stack them two or three high. Using your fluted pastry cutter, cut around the edges of the stacked sheets so all of the edges are ruffled.

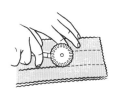

5   Beginning at the long edge of the sheet stack, move inward and cut 1¼-inch-wide strips. (You can use a ruler or other straightedge to keep your lines even while you get acquainted with the fluted cutter.)

6   Separate the strips, lightly dust each one with OO flour, and then return the strips to neat stacks, each ten to twelve pieces high, and place the stacks on the prepared sheet pan. Repeat with the remaining stacks.

7   Repeat with the remaining sheets.

8   Let dry for 20 to 30 minutes at room temperature.

9   If not using right away, cover the sheet pan with plastic wrap and refrigerate for up to 24 hours.

Pizzoccheri

Until a few decades ago—and, frankly, still for the most part—pizzoccheri were a classic regional oddity, a rustic, hand-cut pasta made from an unloved grain (er, seed) and consumed with a gut-busting combo of cheese, potatoes, butter, and cabbage. They were eaten either by tourists with snow chains and a lift ticket or folks born in Lombardy's alpine Valtellina, where pizzoccheri originated some four hundred years ago.

Today, pizzoccheri, which are essentially toothsome tagliatelle made from cold-resistant buckwheat, are such a point of local pride that they have their own consortium dedicated to the protection of their shape and traditional preparation. While that consortium's recipe describes a combination of one part 00 flour and four parts buckwheat flour, I flip the flour ratio and add egg yolk instead of water to make a dough that is slightly less gritty and more pliable.

Where it's found

In the Valtellina in Lombardy.

How I serve it

To me, this shape is inseparable from pizzoccheri alla valtellinese (page 183), but it also works great in similarly hearty, vegetable-forward pastas that are built for fall eating.

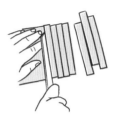

---

1   Prepare your buckwheat dough (page 30) and follow the instructions for rolling and sheeting (pages 32–33).

2   Lightly dust a wooden work surface with 00 flour. Line a sheet pan with parchment paper and lightly dust with semolina.

3   Lay your sheet(s) of pasta on the work surface. Use a knife to cut 18 by 4½-inch sheets, removing the scraps from the unclean edges (save them for soup). Cover the sheets with plastic wrap or a kitchen towel.

4   Place one sheet on your work surface. Position the sheet horizontally with the longer side nearest you. Beginning at the left or right edge of your sheet, move inward and cut ½-inch-wide strands.

5   Generously dust your strands of pizzoccheri with 00 flour, gently shake them to separate, and arrange them in a single layer on the prepared sheet pan.

6   Repeat with the remaining sheets.

7   Let dry for 20 to 30 minutes at room temperature.

8   If not using right away, cover the sheet pan with plastic wrap and refrigerate for up to 24 hours.

Strangozzi

Umbria's most famous native pasta shape, strangozzi (aka stringozzi) are essentially thicker, more sturdy fettuccine. The name is said to have originated from stringhe da scarpa, or "shoelaces," or stringa, or "string." Turns out both descriptions fit the shape, which can vary from a slightly irregular version of spaghetti alla chitarra (string) to a wider fettuccine (shoelaces) and can be made from flour, water, and oil or egg dough.

While the strangozzi are typically rolled and hand cut, there are related shapes, some of which are presented as synonyms, that are rolled into long strands, in the same way that pici (page 71), umbricelli, or bringoli are made. They are close relatives but not exactly interchangeable with strangozzi.

My version of the shape follows the shoelace model and relies on egg dough. I've always considered it to be a shape that works best with rich, meat-based sauces or the umami bomb that is strangozzi alla norcina (page 232), mostly because it has a thicker, toothsome quality that is up for the challenge. Think of strangozzi as fettuccine that stand at attention.

Where it's found

Umbria, primarily around the town of Spoleto as strangozzi or stringozzi.

How I serve it

I believe this shape's highest calling is to be paired with black truffles, often in a sauce that also includes garlic, anchovy, and olive oil. But I also love pairing it with a simple tomato sauce kicked up with black pepper (à la strangozzi alla spoletina) or with various ragùs.

1   Prepare your selected egg-based dough (pages 18, 22, and 26–31) and follow the instructions for rolling and sheeting (pages 32–33).

2   Lightly dust a wooden work surface with 00 flour. Line a sheet pan with parchment paper and lightly dust with semolina.

3   Lay your sheet(s) of pasta on the work surface. Use a knife to cut 9-inch sheets, removing the scraps from the unclean edges (save them for soup). Cover the sheets with plastic wrap or a kitchen towel.

4   Place the fettuccine cutter on your hand-cranked pasta machine or KitchenAid.

5   To cut the pasta, hold one end of the pasta sheet with your nondominant hand, gently feed the opposite end into the cutter, and begin cranking with your dominant hand. Keep the sheet nearly perpendicular to the machine as you crank. As the pasta moves through the machine, move your nondominant hand under the cutter to catch it. (If you are using a KitchenAid, feed with one hand and catch with the other.)

6   Generously dust your strands of strangozzi with 00 flour and gently shake them to separate. Curl the batch into a horseshoe shape and place it on the prepared sheet pan.

7   Repeat with the remaining sheets.

8   Let dry for 30 to 40 minutes at room temperature.

9   If not using right away, cover the sheet pan with plastic wrap and refrigerate for up to 24 hours.

Tagliatelle

In tagliatelle's origin tale, Lucrezia Borgia stars as the main character. The story goes that the shape, a nod to Ms. Borgia's long, blond hair, was created by the Bolognese chef Zafirano to commemorate her marriage to Alfonso I d'Este in 1502. (Her pasta fame does not end there, however. In rival legends, both her belly button and that of Venus are credited with being the inspiration for tortellini.)

Tagliatelle are essentially synonymous with fettuccine but rolled out thinner (another legend holds that the pasta was so thin its inventor could see Bologna's Basilica di San Luca through it) and are claimed by Emilia-Romagna, even though they can now be found throughout the north.

Bologna's Accademia Italiana della Cucina describes them as precisely ⅓ inch wide, but they show up in varying widths all over the region. I have personally always differentiated them from my fettuccine, which are rolled to the same thinness in this book, by cutting them a touch wider, ½ inch, and although not exactly traditional, I further distinguish the shapes by using a fluted cutter for tagliatelle.

Where it's found

Emilia-Romagna and the surrounding regions, and in Lazio as fettuccine.

How I serve it

I use it with a hearty ragù or with simple, light sauces based on butter and cheese, incorporating everything from mushrooms to zucchini, depending on the season.

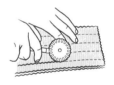

1　Prepare your selected egg-based dough (pages 18, 22, and 26–31) and follow the instructions for rolling and sheeting (pages 32–33).

2　Lightly dust a wooden work surface with OO flour. Line a sheet pan with parchment paper and lightly dust with semolina.

3　Lay your sheet(s) of pasta on the work surface. Use a knife to cut 12-inch-long sheets, removing the scraps from the unclean edges (save them for soup).

4　Lightly dust each sheet with OO flour and neatly stack them two or three high. Using your fluted pastry cutter, cut around the edges of the stacked sheets so all of the edges are ruffled.

5　Beginning at the long edge of the stack of sheets, move inward and cut ½-inch-wide strands. (You can use a ruler or other straightedge to keep your lines even while you get acquainted with the fluted cutter.)

6　Generously dust your strands of tagliatelle with OO flour and gently shake them to separate. Curl the batch into a horseshoe shape and place it on the prepared sheet pan.

7　Repeat with the remaining sheets.

8　Let dry for 20 to 30 minutes at room temperature.

9　If not using right away, cover the sheet pan with plastic wrap and refrigerate for up to 24 hours.

Pasta

Tagliolini

Tagliolini show up in almost every region under different names. They are served in a sauce of anchovies and pecorino; in a ragù, seafood sauce, or brodo; and even baked. In Piedmont, they go by the dialectal name *tajarin* (opposite page) and tangle with white truffles, ragù, and more. In the Marche, they go by maccheroncini di Campofilone and are accompanied by meat-spiked red sauce. In other words, they adapt to their region of consumption, finding a home nearly anywhere pasta is sold, morphing ever so slightly in the dough they call for and their precise thickness from place to place as they travel.

Unlike for tajarin or maccheroncini, I often use a pasta machine to cut tagliolini, and I roll the dough a bit thicker. The differences among these three shapes might seem annoyingly nuanced, but they do show in the finished dish, especially when working with sauces engineered to let the pasta shine. If you are prepared to tackle the trio, tagliolini is a great place to start.

Where it's found

All over Italy, from Molise to Trentino–Alto Adige, under various aliases.

How I serve it

When I think of tagliolini, I always think of crab. They are a fantastic companion to light seafood sauces but can also stand nearly alone in a clean lemon butter and parmigiano sauce (al limone) or similarly minimalist combinations.

1   Prepare your selected egg-based dough (pages 18, 22, and 26–31) and follow the instructions for rolling and sheeting (pages 32–33).

2   Lightly dust a wooden work surface with OO flour. Line a sheet pan with parchment paper and lightly dust with semolina.

3   Lay your sheet(s) of pasta on the work surface. Use a knife to cut 18-inch-long sheets, removing the scraps from the unclean edges (save them for soup). Cover the sheets with plastic wrap or a kitchen towel.

4   Place the tagliolini cutter on your hand-cranked pasta machine or KitchenAid. (If you do not have a cutter attachment or you prefer to hand-cut your tagliolini, fold one pasta sheet in half and then in thirds until you end up with a small packet about 4½ by 6 inches. Position the packet horizontally with the longer side parallel to you. Trim any uneven edges and discard. Beginning at the right or left edge of your packet, move inward and cut ⅛-inch-wide strands. Follow steps 6 through 9.)

5   To cut the pasta using the machine, hold one end of the pasta sheet with your nondominant hand, gently feed the opposite end into the cutter, and begin cranking with your dominant hand. Keep the sheet nearly perpendicular to the machine as you crank. As the pasta moves through the machine, move your nondominant hand under the cutter to catch it. (If you are using a KitchenAid, feed with one hand and catch with the other.)

6   Generously dust your strands of tagliolini with OO flour and gently shake them to separate. Curl the batch into a nest and place it on the prepared sheet pan.

7   Repeat with the remaining sheets.

8   Let dry for 20 to 30 minutes at room temperature.

9   If not using right away, cover the sheet pan with plastic wrap and refrigerate for up to 24 hours.

Tajarin

Maccheroncini, tagliolini, and tajarin are all regional variations on a very thin, rich egg pasta. Tajarin, however, have always been more of a northern flex, incorporating from twenty to forty egg yolks per kilo of 00 flour, depending on who is doing the flexing. The shape embedded itself in the Langhe hills outside Turin as far back as the fifteenth century and remained a fixture of Piedmontese nobility throughout the nineteenth century (it was a favorite of Victor Emmanuel II). Even today, it has retained its noble status, primarily through its most famous pairing: Alba white truffles and Barolo. I, like many others, have flown four thousand miles and driven another one hundred without regret just to eat it in season.

While the combination with truffles is iconic, tajarin are a year-round pasta that can be found paired with butter and sage, in a ragù, in a sauce of chicken livers, or with butter and the juice of roasted meat. Regardless of whether they come topped with seventy-five dollars' worth of truffles, tajarin always manage to retain an air of prestige.

What sets this pasta apart from its fine-stringed brethren is the use of egg yolk, almost to excess. Most chefs have a separate dough they use for it, but my egg dough is already yolk-only and far more decadent than the average egg dough.

Where it's found

Piedmont, particularly in the Langhe hills south of Turin—aka home of Barolo and Barbaresco.

How I serve it

No one, at least not me, will argue against white truffles and tajarin, but I see the shape more broadly as a shortcut to refinement without much adornment. You can serve it in a simple butter sauce finished with parmigiano and it will wow based on its texture and delicacy alone.

1   Prepare your selected egg-based dough (pages 18, 22, and 26–31) and follow the instructions for rolling and sheeting (pages 32–33).

2   Lightly dust a wooden work surface with 00 flour. Line a sheet pan with parchment paper and lightly dust with semolina.

3   Lay your sheet(s) of pasta on the work surface. Use a knife to cut 18-inch-long sheets, removing the scraps from the unclean edges (save them for soup). Cover the sheets with plastic wrap or a kitchen towel.

4   Place one sheet on your work surface. Fold the sheet in half and then in thirds until you end up with a small packet about 4½ by 6 inches. Position the packet horizontally with the longer side parallel to you. Trim any uneven edges and discard. Beginning at the left or right edge of your packet, move inward and cut ¹⁄₁₀-inch-wide strands.

5   Generously dust your strands of tajarin with 00 flour and gently shake them to separate. Curl the batch into a nest and place it on the prepared sheet pan.

6   Repeat with the remaining sheets.

7   Let dry for 20 to 30 minutes at room temperature.

8   If not using right away, cover the sheet pan with plastic wrap and refrigerate for up to 24 hours.

Hand Shaped

Fileja

In the south of Italy, dozens of pasta shapes are made using a maccheroni iron, or ferretto, a thin iron rod that resembles a knitting needle (which is often used in its place) and is either round or square; I prefer the latter.

Fileja is from Calabria, specifically near the town of Tropea, of onion fame, and is made by taking a thin rope of pasta dough, pressing the maccheroni iron into it, and then gently rolling the iron back and forth until the pasta forms a rustic tube shape. I learned this method not in Calabria but in Sardinia, where a shape called maccheroni al ferretto or macarrones de busa is made according to virtually the same method.

Where it's found

Calabria, specifically near Tropea.

How I serve it

It's classically served in a tomato-based sauce flavored with 'nduja, a type of spicy soft sausage native to Calabria (page 267). It's a toothsome shape, so it tends to pair best with heartier sauces.

1   Prepare your semolina dough (page 19). Lightly dust a wooden work surface with OO flour. Line a sheet pan with parchment paper and lightly dust with semolina.

2   Divide your dough into quarters. Place one piece of dough on your work surface and cover the other pieces with plastic wrap or a kitchen towel.

3   Use your hands to form the dough into a large rope. Place all four fingertips of both hands next to one another at the center of the rope and begin rolling the dough back and forth on the work surface, moving both hands outward, away from each other, toward the ends of the dough.

4   Repeat this motion, gently applying pressure as you go, to elongate the dough into a rope about ½ inch in diameter—about the thickness of a Sharpie. (If your rope gets too long to manage easily, cut it in half and roll out each half separately.)

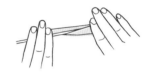

5   Using a knife or bench scraper, divide the rope(s) into 1-inch-long pieces. Cover any pieces you are not forming with plastic wrap or a kitchen towel.

6   Using one 1-inch piece of dough, repeat steps 3 and 4, rolling a smaller rope about 5 inches long and the thickness of a pencil.

7   Position the rope lengthwise parallel to you. Using your iron, shape your pasta by pressing the iron into the right edge of your rope, angling its left end beneath the rope. Place all four fingers of each hand at opposite ends of the iron and roll the iron upward and away from your body, pressing down lightly to flatten the rope as you go along. The rope will wrap around the iron in a wide coil.

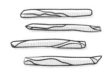

8   Once the rope has fully wrapped around the iron, position it lengthwise parallel to you and gently roll it back and forth on the board to ensure it is of even thickness. (Make sure to do this gently; if you push too hard, the shape will stick to the iron and will uncoil when you remove it.)

9   Gently pull the finished pasta off the iron and place it on the prepared sheet pan. Repeat with the remaining pieces from the batch.

10   Repeat steps 3 through 9 with the remaining dough.

11   Let the pasta dry for 1 to 2 hours, until it just begins to harden and hold its shape when handling.

12   If not using right away, cover the sheet pan with plastic wrap and refrigerate for up to 24 hours.

Busiate

Busiate belongs to the pasta al ferro family, a group of tubular pastas shaped around a maccheroni iron, or ferretto. The name, however, derives from busa, the large Mediterranean reed that was used to form the shape in lieu of a maccheroni iron. In Sicily, the shape barely finds its way outside the western side of the island, where it is best known for its starring role in busiate alla pesto trapanese, Sicily's retort to Liguria's pesto al Genovese.

I went all the way to Trapani to learn to make busiate, only to find out how difficult it is to achieve consistency in the tightness and thickness of the spiral. The key is to roll it in a single, steady motion and dry it properly before cooking, as it tends to lose its coil in the pot.

Where it's found

In Sicily, particularly the western side of the island, and in Sardinia as busa.

How I serve it

While I love the way the shape squirrels away pesto alla trapanese (page 248), it's also a great companion to classic red sauce or fresh tomato sauce and to a hearty ragù like pork sugo (page 330).

1   Prepare your semolina dough (page 19). Lightly dust a wooden work surface with OO flour. Line a sheet pan with parchment paper and lightly dust with semolina.

2   Divide your dough into quarters. Place one piece of dough on your work surface and cover the other pieces with plastic wrap or a kitchen towel.

3   Use your hands to form the dough into a large rope. Place all four fingertips of both hands next to one another at the center of the rope and begin rolling the dough back and forth on the work surface, moving both hands outward, away from each other, toward the ends of the dough.

4   Repeat this motion, gently applying pressure as you go, to elongate the dough into a rope about ¼ inch in diameter. (If your rope gets too long to manage easily, cut it in half and roll out each half separately.)

5   Using a knife or bench scraper, divide the rope(s) into 3-inch-long pieces. Cover any pieces you are not forming with plastic wrap or a kitchen towel.

6   Using one 3-inch piece of dough, repeat steps 3 and 4, rolling a smaller rope about ⅛ inch in diameter and 6 inches in length.

7   Position the rope lengthwise parallel to you. Using your maccheroni iron, shape the pasta by pressing the iron into the right end of the rope, angling its left end beneath the rope. Place all four fingers of each hand at opposite ends of the iron and roll the iron upward and away from your body, pressing down lightly to flatten the rope as you go along. The rope will wrap around the iron in a tight coil.

8   Once the rope has fully wrapped around the iron, position it lengthwise parallel to you and gently roll it back and forth on the board to ensure the shape is of even thickness. (Make sure to do this gently; if you push too hard, the shape will stick to the iron and uncoil when you remove it.)

9   Gently pull the finished pasta off the iron and place it on the prepared sheet pan. Repeat with the remaining pieces from the batch.

10   Repeat steps 3 through 9 with the remaining dough.

11   Let the pasta dry for 1 to 2 hours at room temperature, until it just begins to harden and hold its shape when handling.

12   If not using right away, cover the sheet pan with plastic wrap and refrigerate for up to 24 hours.

Gnudi

The direct translation of *gnudi* is, yes, "nudes," and the best way to think of them is ravioli cooked "nude," or without their pasta cloak. Ravioli gnudi, as they are also called, date to at least the thirteenth century, as evidenced in Salimbene di Adam's *Cronica*, begun in the early 1280s. In it, the celebrity friar and chronicler describes eating "raviolis sin crusta de pasta" (ravioli without their pasta wrapping). These ravioli gnudi went on to become a staple of the Renaissance table and today are typically found in the area around Arezzo, in Tuscany, and further north, in Lombardy, where they are often larger and referred to as malfatti, or "badly shaped," a name that also sometimes attends them in Tuscany.

They are made by combining eggs, flour, ricotta, greens (spinach, chard, or nettles, most commonly), parmigiano, and spices such as nutmeg. The greens are blanched, squeezed dry, finely chopped, and mixed with the other ingredients to form gnudi about the size of a chestnut. They're then boiled in salted water and are traditionally served in a variety of sauces, from the classic butter-and-sage alla fiorentina (see page 238) to red sauce.

Where it's found

Tuscany, particularly in the areas surrounding Arezzo, and in Lombardy near Brescia.

How I serve it

As ever, with butter and sage.

---

1 Lightly dust a wooden work surface with OO flour. Line a sheet pan with parchment paper and lightly dust with semolina.

2 Working in batches using a small spring scoop or tablespoon measure, portion your gnudi dough (page 25) into 15g pieces and transfer to your work surface.

3 Dust each of your hands with OO flour and form the pieces into 1½-inch–diameter spheres. Transfer in a single layer to your prepared sheet pan. Give the pan an extra dusting of semolina to prevent sticking.

4 Cover with plastic wrap and refrigerate for at least 1 hour and up to 24 hours.

Malloreddus

Even though they are often referred to as Sardinian gnocchi, or gnocchetti sardi, malloreddus have more in common with cavatelli—or even orecchiette—than with what most people think of when thinking of gnocchi. Indeed, they are part of a family of pastas sometimes referred to as strascinati, so named for the method of producing them, in which tiny pieces of dough are dragged across a board.

The name *malloreddus* is said to originate either from the Latin malleolus, or "small hammer," or from the dialectal Sardinian malloru, or "baby calf," in an obscure reference to being made (er, born) from the dough left over from making another shape. The pasta tends to resemble tiny shells with a ribbed or checkered exterior, the result of making the shape on the inside of a basket or on a textured piece of glass. It also comes in a variety of sizes, from the length of a peanut shell to as small as a fingernail, and is made from a semolina-and-water dough sometimes flavored with saffron.

This is one of the easiest, most versatile shapes to make. My version strays a bit from the traditional with the use of egg dough for a bit more lightness, but you can use just about any dough that strikes your fancy.

Where it's found

Sardinia, particularly in the south near Cagliari.

How I serve it

While I love the traditional malloreddus alla campidanese (page 258), I've got a soft spot for how this shape performs in a light seafood brodo (I have served it with clams, sea beans, and saffron at Misi) or a simple red sauce flavored with saffron.

1   Prepare your selected egg-based or semolina dough (pages 18, 22, and 26–31). Lightly dust a wooden work surface with OO flour. Line a sheet pan with parchment paper and lightly dust with semolina.

2   Divide your dough into quarters. Place one piece of dough on your work surface and cover the other pieces with plastic wrap or a kitchen towel.

3   Use your hands to form the dough into a large rope. Place all four fingertips of both hands next to one another at the center of the rope and begin rolling the dough back and forth on the work surface, moving both hands outward, away from each other, toward the ends of the dough.

4   Repeat this motion, gently applying pressure as you go, to elongate the dough into a rope about ½ inch in diameter—about the thickness of a Sharpie. (If your rope gets too long to manage easily, cut it in half and roll out each half separately.)

5   Using a knife or bench scraper, divide the rope(s) into ¾-inch pieces. Cover any pieces you are not forming with plastic wrap or a kitchen towel.

6   Using your gnocchi or malloreddus board (or the back of a fork, a cheese grater, or a bamboo mat), shape your pasta by pressing your thumb into the board and then dragging the pasta down the surface while turning your thumb out and away from your body. Your malloreddus should curl into shell-like shapes with the board giving them a finely ribbed exterior that will cling well to sauce. Repeat with the remaining pieces from the batch.

7   Place the finished pasta in a single layer on the prepared sheet pan.

8   Repeat steps 3 through 7 with the remaining dough.

9   If not using right away, cover the sheet pan with plastic wrap and refrigerate for up to 24 hours.

Orecchiette

If you have even the most casual interest in pasta, you've probably encountered Puglia's famous "little ear." The shape, which dates at least to the sixteenth century, is part of a family of pastas called strascinati, from the Italian verb for "to drag", a reference to how they are made. Strascinati are also a somewhat ill-defined shape that takes many forms, depending on how they are dragged and with how many fingers. Today, they most often appear in the shape of much larger, more cylindrical orecchiette, and are made in a similar way: by using a knife to drag a piece of dough across a board, leaving it smooth on one side and rough on the other. I bring up strascinati mostly because you will likely make a few accidental versions of them in pursuit of orecchiette.

Orecchiette differ from strascinati both in size (they're smaller) and in the second half of the method, which calls for pulling the dough from the tip of the knife onto your thumb and flipping it inside out like a rubber party popper. The shape can vary from about the size of a quarter to as small as a dime, especially in and around Bari, where orecchiette reach their apex. The dough is always a mixture of water and semolina, durum wheat flour, grano arso, or some mixture of two of the three flours.

Now, if you've had orecchiette, you might look at them and say, "That looks easy enough." But let me be the first person to tell you that this is one of the most difficult shapes to make, and getting it right is truly about making at least five hundred terrible versions of it (still edible though!) until you can get that transition from knife to thumb to work seamlessly. Do not be discouraged.

Where it's found

Puglia, primarily, but also in Calabria, Basilicata, Molise, and as far north as Abruzzo.

How I serve it

With red sauce and ricotta salata or with anchovy, garlic, and broccoli rabe (page 253).

---

1 Prepare your semolina dough (page 19). Lightly dust a wooden work surface with OO flour. Line a sheet pan with parchment paper and lightly dust with semolina.

2 Divide your dough into quarters. Place one piece of dough on your work surface and cover the other pieces with plastic wrap or a kitchen towel.

3 Use your hands to form the dough into a large rope. Place all four fingertips of both hands next to one another at the center of the rope and begin rolling the dough back and forth on the work surface, moving both hands outward, away from each other, toward the ends of the dough.

4 Repeat this motion, gently applying pressure as you go, to elongate the dough into a rope about ½ inch in diameter—the thickness of a Sharpie—and about 18 inches in length. (If your rope gets too long to manage easily, cut it in half and roll out each half separately.)

5 Using a knife or bench scraper, divide the rope(s) into ½-inch-long pieces. (When you're first starting out, you can cut them a bit bigger to make shaping them easier.) Cover any pieces you are not forming with plastic wrap or a kitchen towel.

6   Using the serrated edge of a butter knife, shape your pasta by positioning the top of your knife, serrated edge down, at a 30-degree angle to the edge of the piece of dough. Drag the dough along your work surface toward you. (Make sure you don't have too much flour on your work surface, or there will not be enough friction to complete this step.) Don't be afraid to apply a good amount of pressure; semolina dough can take it, and you want the center of the shape to be relatively thin. If you stopped here, you'd essentially have a cavatello. It's the next step that sets orecchiette apart.

7   Using your first two fingers, pull the dough off the knife and over your thumb, essentially turning that cavatello-like shape inside out while pressing upward with your thumb to form a dome. (If this sounds challenging, it's because it's about as easy to describe as it is to make. Repeat with the remaining pieces from the batch.)

8   Place the finished pasta in a single layer on the prepared sheet pan.

9   Repeat steps 3 through 8 with the remaining dough.

10   Let the pasta dry for 1 to 2 hours at room temperature, until it just begins to harden and hold its shape when handling.

11   If not using right away, cover the sheet pan with plastic wrap and refrigerate for up to 24 hours.

Trofie

Trofie, which get their name from the verb *strofinare*, or "to rub," are the result of more precision than meets the eye. Made by rubbing a small piece of dough across a board with the palm of your hand opposite the thumb, they require just the right upward-dog motion of the hand and pressure. This is perhaps why the art of making these by hand in Liguria is dying out.

Trofie are, like so many hand-formed shapes, a descendant of the gnocchi family, which is why they are sometimes referred to as Ligurian dumplings. While trofie are more commonly made from 00 flour and water, both chestnut flour and potato were once common in the region. The former is still used, and for my money, it's the combination of trofie made from chestnut dough with its primary companion, pesto al Genovese, that represents one of the great culinary treasures of Liguria, if not all of Italy.

Trofie resemble tiny spirals, about 1 to 2 inches long and tapered into a point at each end. Some makers take a slightly different tack, rubbing a jelly bean–size piece of dough between two palms; this is a great method when you're starting out. I prefer to use the board, as the friction of the wood surface produces a more textured shape that clings well to sauce.

---

1   Prepare your semolina dough (page 19). Line a sheet pan with parchment paper and lightly dust with semolina.

2   Place your dough on the work surface and cover with plastic wrap or a kitchen towel. (Keep the towel or plastic wrap loose so you can pick up pieces of dough as you work.)

3   Pick a piece of dough from the mass about the size of a shelled peanut and place it on the board in front of you. Trofie is made in a single motion, employing the outside of your palm and requires that the work surface has enough friction to form the shape, so start without flouring it as you would to make other shapes. If the dough is tacky and sticks to the board, add a very light dusting of flour.

4   Using the outside edge of your palm, roll the dough upward at a 45-degree angle (to the left if you are right-handed, and to the right if you are left-handed), applying moderate pressure in a gentle rocking motion, and then downward at a 90-degree angle parallel to the bottom of the board, applying heavier pressure as you drag the outer edge of your palm down the board.

5   As you drag the piece of dough downward, it should begin to curl into a small spiral that is tapered at both ends at the edge of your palm. Important: It is impossible to get the motion correct on the first few tries; it requires a lot of repetition to get the angle and pressure to align to form the spiraled shape. Don't lose hope.

6   Place the finished pasta in a single layer on the prepared sheet pan.

7   Repeat with the remaining dough.

8   Let the pasta dry for 1 to 2 hours at room temperature, until it just begins to harden and hold its shape when handling.

9   If not using right away, cover the sheet pan with plastic wrap and refrigerate for up to 24 hours.

Where it's found

Liguria, particularly along the eastern Riviera near Recco and Camogli.

How I serve it

It's hard to argue that anything can surpass the combination of trofie and pesto (page 178). That understood, this delicate shape also pairs well with tomato sauces.

Nota bene

My recipe for chestnut dough is egg based, which won't work for trofie. If you want to make chestnut trofie (and I hope you do), replace 100g of tipo 00 flour in my semolina dough recipe with the same amount of chestnut flour.

Pici

Despite the protestations of Arezzo residents to the contrary (they claim their similar shape, bringoli, was cribbed by the Sienese), pici are Siena's great contribution to the pasta canon. The shape, which is a thick, hand-rolled—and thus irregularly shaped—form of spaghetti, is a staple in and around the province of Siena. Today, it is so well traveled that it crosses into at least two border regions, where it assumes a variety of aliases.

While pici are typically made by rolling out a dough made from tipo 00 flour, water, oil, and salt, today you will often find a more classic northern egg dough used. The shape finds its way into myriad dishes, from peasant classics, such as pici con le briciole (with fried bread crumbs) to richer sauces, like pici al ragù di cinghiale (wild boar ragù). Work the dough slowly and avoid using too much flour on the board, as both will make it more difficult to keep the shape from breaking as you're forming it.

Where it's found

Tuscany, particularly in the areas surrounding Siena and Grosseto; around Arezzo as bringoli; in Umbria as umbrici, umbricelli, or umbrichelli; and in Lazio as umbrichelli or lombrichetti.

How I serve it

Pici are toothsome and flavorful enough, especially if you make them with egg dough, to be paired with minimalist sauces, but my preferred pairing is a hearty ragù (page 228).

1   Prepare your selected egg-based dough (pages 18, 22, and 26–31). Lightly dust a wooden work surface with 00 flour. Line a sheet pan with parchment paper and lightly dust with semolina.

2   Divide your dough into quarters. Place one piece of dough on your work surface and cover the other pieces with plastic wrap or a kitchen towel.

3   Lightly dust the dough with 00 flour. Using your rolling pin, roll the dough out to an oval about 5 inches long by ¼ inch thick.

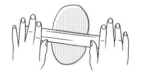

4   Position the oval of dough horizontally on your work surface with the longer side parallel to you. Beginning at the edge and working in, use your knife to cut strips of dough ¼ inch wide. (Note that not all the pieces will be 5 inches long. Not to worry. Part of the charm of pici, like that of all handmade pastas, is its imperfection.)

5   Position one strip of dough horizontally on your work surface with the longer side parallel to you. Place all four fingertips of both hands next to one another at the center of the strip and begin rolling the dough back and forth on the work surface, moving both hands outward, away from each other, toward the ends of the dough. As you go along, you may need to add a bit more 00 flour to your board to ensure the dough does not stick. Be careful not to add too much, however, or you'll end up with the opposite issue: not enough friction on the board to roll easily.

6   Repeat this motion, gently applying pressure as you go, to elongate the strip of dough to a strand of thick spaghetti 16 to 18 inches in length. (As you're learning this shape, it's not uncommon to apply a bit too much pressure and accidentally sever the strand in the center. Simply cut it in half and roll out two pieces instead of one. Again, this pasta is forgiving.)

7   Generously dust your strands of pici with 00 flour and gently shake to separate. Lay them on the prepared sheet pan. Repeat with each strip of dough from the batch.

8   Repeat steps 3 through 7 with the remaining dough. (Because pici take time to roll out, no additional drying time is needed before cooking.)

9   If not using right away, cover the sheet pan with plastic wrap and refrigerate for up to 24 hours.

Ricotta Gnocchi

I could write an entire book on the shapes that collect under the umbrella of gnocchi. To most Americans, the word is synonymous with potato gnocchi, a shape that is canon in both Italian American cuisine and regional Italian cooking; in fact, while they are found in greater density in northern Italy, potato gnocchi are virtually boot-wide.

But gnocchi are far from one thing. They can be made from bread; from ricotta; from a mixture of semolina, milk, butter, eggs, and cheese (gnocchi alla romana); and from a mixture of water and flour. They come in myriad shapes and sizes and are finished with as many sauces. Gnocchi, in short, are all around us.

I've made them every which way, but only one recipe has become part of my repertoire. I love the lightness of well-made ricotta gnocchi, how they have not only just enough structure to differentiate themselves from gnudi (page 65) but also a pillowy richness that is addictive and easy to eat in quantity. The trick to avoiding the gummy fate of so many that have come before is dependent upon how you work your dough. Take care not to overknead or apply too much force when forming the shape. For light gnocchi, you must have a light touch.

Where it's found

Although not region specific, it is most often found in central Italy, in Umbria and Lazio in particular.

How I serve it

While you'll find them sauced with broccoli pesto in this book (page 282), to me almost nothing beats ricotta gnocchi with simple red sauce (page 147).

1   Prepare your ricotta gnocchi dough (page 24).

2   Lightly dust a wooden work surface with OO flour. Line a sheet pan with parchment paper and lightly dust with semolina.

3   Take a small handful of dough, place it on your prepared work surface, and use your hands to gently roll it into a rope roughly ¾ inch in diameter. If the dough is sticky and difficult to roll, lightly dust your hands with OO flour, taking care not to use much. Repeat with the remaining dough.

4   Using your knife or bench scraper, cut the ropes into 1-inch pieces.

5   Lightly dust a wooden gnocchi board or the back of a fork with OO flour. Press a piece of the dough with your thumb into the board or back of the fork, dragging it down the surface while turning your thumb out and away from your body. The gnocchi should curl into shell-like shapes, with the board or fork giving it a finely ribbed exterior that will cling well to sauce.

6   Repeat with the remaining pieces. As the gnocchi are formed, place them, ribbed side up, on the prepared sheet pan.

7   Cover the sheet pan with plastic wrap and chill for at least 30 minutes or up to 24 hours before cooking.

Stricchetti

Stricchetti are perhaps better known as farfalle, or, if you're reading this from North America, bow-tie pasta. In Italy, they have at least a dozen more aliases—fiocchetti, sciancon, nocchette, canestri, and so on—but I refer to them by their name in Emilia-Romagna, stricchetti (or stricchettoni, stringhetti), which derives from the dialectal word for "pinch."

The shape's origin isn't clear, but by the second half of the twentieth century, it begins to spread across the country. In Emilia-Romagna it's made, like most pastas of the region, with egg dough and served in sauces that often contain vegetables flavored with meat, whether peas and prosciutto in spring or cavolo nero or cardoons with sausage in winter.

The shape can vary in size, from about an inch to quite a bit larger, depending on the maker and the place it's being made. Mine are about 2 inches long, fluted on all edges for flair, and pinched tightly in the center. It's important to dry this shape longer than you would any of the other egg pastas in the book—about 4 hours—as it tends to lose its shape very easily when cooked.

Where it's found

Emilia-Romagna, and across Italy under various aliases.

How I serve it

I love it served classically, as in Italy in spring, with peas and prosciutto (page 354), or with butter and parmigiano as pure, kid-approved comfort.

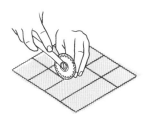

1   Prepare your selected egg-based dough (pages 18, 22, and 26–31) and follow the instructions for rolling and sheeting (pages 32–33).

2   Lightly dust a wooden work surface with OO flour. Line a sheet pan with parchment paper and lightly dust with semolina.

3   Lay your sheet(s) of pasta on the work surface. Using a fluted dough divider, cut your pasta sheet(s) into 1½ by 2-inch rectangles. (Alternatively, use a fluted pastry cutter and a ruler.) Cover the rectangles with plastic wrap or a kitchen towel.

4   With your index finger and thumb facing each other, pinch the top and bottom of one rectangle in the center to form a bow-tie shape, making sure the center is pinched tightly, as stricchetti tend to lose their shape when cooked.

5   Repeat with all of the rectangles. As the stricchetti are shaped, place them in a single layer on the prepared sheet pan.

6   Let dry for 3 to 4 hours at room temperature, until the center of each shape feels sturdy and secure. (To test whether the pasta is sufficiently dried, bring a small amount of water to a boil and cook a single stricchetto to ensure it holds its shape.)

7   If not using right away, cover the sheet pan with plastic wrap and refrigerate for up to 24 hours.

Filled

Balanzoni

I had balanzoni for the first time only a few years ago, at a restaurant called Vâgh iń ufézzi in Bologna, where they are served classically, in a sauce of butter, sage, and parmigiano. The shape, which is variably called tortellacci verdi, tortelloni verdi, tortelli verdi, and tortelli matti (or "crazy tortelli"), is essentially oversized tortellini made with spinach egg dough, stuffed with mortadella, cheese, and spices, and finished in a sauce of butter and sage.

Balanzoni are supposedly named for a Bolognese carnevale character known as Dottore Balanzone or, simply, Il Dottore. The reason is a matter of lore (some say the shape resembles his hat, others his mask), but the doctor has always sported a portly figure, and so too do balanzoni. Whatever the reason behind the homage, it's a shape to behold. My filling (page 205) sticks close to tradition, marrying parmigiano, ricotta, mortadella, and plenty of nutmeg.

Where it's found
Emilia-Romagna, particularly in the city of Bologna.

How I serve it
It can play different positions, but I find that it's always best paired with a simple butter-based sauce.

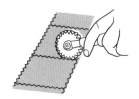

1   Prepare your green dough (page 22) and follow the instructions for rolling and sheeting (pages 32–33).

2   Lightly dust a wooden work surface with 00 flour. Line a sheet pan with parchment paper and lightly dust with semolina.

3   Lay one sheet of pasta on the work surface. Use a plain-edged or fluted dough divider to cut 2½-inch squares. (Alternatively, use a plain or fluted pastry cutter and a ruler or a knife and a ruler.) Cover the squares with plastic wrap or a kitchen towel.

4   Spoon your filling into a pastry bag. Cut a ½-inch hole in the tip of your pastry bag and pipe a circle of filling about the size of a quarter in the center of each square.

5   Evaluate your dough. If it feels moderately tacky, you can eliminate this next step. If it feels a bit dry, hold your spray bottle 8 to 10 inches above the work surface and spray the squares. This will help you securely seal the pasta.

6   Lift a square off the work surface and hold it in the palm of your nondominant hand. With your dominant hand, fold one corner over to the opposite corner to create a triangle, lining up the edges.

7   Using your thumb and index finger, pinch the edge closed around the filling, making sure to force out any air. Go back and forth a few times, pinching to make sure it is sealed well.

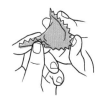

8   While holding the piece in your nondominant hand, make a dimple in the center of the filled side of the pasta with your index finger.

9   Then, holding the bottom points of the triangle with both thumbs and index fingers, bring the two points together at the underside of the filling, forming a large ring (there should be space between the filling and the closure). Pinch the ends together firmly to close and flatten to about the thickness of the rest of the shape, which will ensure more even cooking.

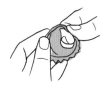

continued

Balanzoni

continued

10   Place the finished pasta on the prepared sheet pan. Repeat with all of the squares, arranging them in a single layer on the prepared pan. Give the pan an extra dusting of semolina to prevent sticking.

11   Repeat this process with the remaining portion of the sheet and then with all the remaining sheets.

12   Place in the refrigerator uncovered (if they are covered, they will sweat and become too wet) to dry for 45 minutes to 1 hour. If not using right away, remove from the refrigerator, loosely cover the sheet pan with plastic wrap, and return to the refrigerator for up to 8 hours.

Agnolotti

Like ravioli or tortelli, agnolotti take many shapes. They can be made by cutting squares and then folding the squares in half to form a rectangular version of mezzelune (page 95). They can be made in long rows and cut into the shape of a lumbar pillow or, in the case of their most famous iteration, agnolotti dal plin (page 84), made into tiny meat-filled pockets that resemble bloated envelopes. Outside of agnolotti dal plin, which are a clearly defined shape, the shape of agnolotti is a product of the imagination of the maker and the town that maker is from.

Agnolotti originated in Piedmont at least as far back as the late eighteenth century but can now be found everywhere from Lombardy to Puglia. They also boast as many filling variations as there are iterations on their contour, whether it be veal brains, fonduta (Piedmontese fondue), greens, or the more classic mixture of stewed meats left over from a Sunday feast.

My all-purpose agnolotti take the lumbar approach to the shape, forming long pockets that can hold more filling than both tortelli and ravioli. This is a main point of differentiation, and what I generally point to when someone asks me why I chose agnolotti for the Lilia dish (page 276) that has become the menu's first-in-command. I also love the way agnolotti look on the plate, and how they hold their shape when cooked. They are regal but still approachable—a dressed-down version of agnolotti dal plin that are easier to make.

Where it's found

Piedmont mostly but also Lombardy, Tuscany, and farther south.

How I serve it

I think of agnolotti as interchangeable with any other robust filled shape. But I particularly lean on them when I am working with a delicate whipped cheese filling that I want to be the star of a dish.

1   Prepare your selected egg-based dough (pages 18, 22, and 26–31) and follow the instructions for rolling and sheeting (pages 32–33).

2   Lightly dust a wooden work surface with 00 flour. Line a sheet pan with parchment paper and lightly dust with semolina.

3   Lay your sheet(s) of pasta on the work surface. Use a knife to cut 18-inch-long sheets, removing the scraps from the unclean edges (save them for soup). Cover the sheets with plastic wrap or a kitchen towel.

4   Place one sheet on the work surface lengthwise parallel to you. Spoon your filling into a pastry bag. Cut a ½-inch hole in the tip of your pastry bag and pipe a thick rope of filling—about the thickness of a Sharpie—½ inch from the bottom edge of your sheet.

5   Evaluate your dough. If it feels moderately tacky, you can eliminate this next step. If it feels a bit dry, hold your spray bottle 8 to 10 inches above the work surface and spray the pasta. This will help you securely seal the pasta.

6   Flip the bottom edge of the sheet up and around the filling so the pasta hugs the filling. Seal the dough to the bottom sheet, rolling the filled side over itself just slightly and taking care to force out any air so you have a continuous tube of tightly filled pasta.

7   Using your two index fingers spaced about 3 inches apart, press and seal the agnolotti, starting from the left edge and working your way right to yield 3-inch-wide pillows. Go back over the areas you pressed to make sure they are well sealed.

8 Along the seam where the pasta meets, use your fluted pastry cutter to cut away the unfilled pasta sheet, getting as close to the seam as you can. Detach and reserve the remainder of the sheet (you will use it to form another line of pasta just like this one).

9 Using the pastry cutter, separate the pillows by cutting between them, positioning the cutter exactly in the center of where you have made your finger depression to seal.

10 Separate the pieces and carefully transfer them in a single layer to your prepared sheet pan. Give the pan an extra dusting of semolina to prevent sticking.

11 Repeat this process with the remaining portion of the sheet and then with all of the remaining sheets.

12 Place in the refrigerator uncovered (if they are covered, they will sweat and become too wet) to dry for 45 minutes to 1 hour. If not using right away, remove from the refrigerator, loosely cover the sheet pan with plastic wrap, and return to the refrigerator for up to 8 hours.

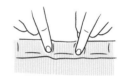

Agnolotti dal Plin

Agnolotti dal plin, or commonly agnolotti col plin, essentially translates to "agnolotti with the pinch." It's certainly not "in a pinch," as this tiny version of agnolotti is a labor-intensive and deliberate affair. A single serving amounts to twenty-five to thirty pockets of meat, each the size of a postage stamp.

The shape was said to have originated in the courts but quickly became a staple of the Piedmontese middle class as a means to use up leftover stewed meats and braises from a robust Sunday supper. As with cjalsons (page 92) and casunziei (page 89), the name of the pasta identifies its shape and is synonymous with its most famous preparation, which is finished in a pan sauce made from butter and the juices from roasted meat. In case you forgot about the French influence on Piedmontese cuisine, here's your reminder.

Both the size and the pinch are what differentiate this from its larger sibling. Generally, the shape is made by piping the filling into a pasta shape in a single line, rolling the pasta sheet over the filling, pinching the filling at 1-inch intervals, and then cutting through the pinch with a fluted pastry cutter. I do not pipe the filling in a continuous line, however, because a meat filling makes it hard to ensure you've secured the pasta well enough that it won't bust open when you cut through it (though if you're using my sunchoke filling, this method works just fine). Instead, I pipe the filling for each agnolotto individually and then follow the same process from there. This method makes for a clean cut and better closure overall.

Where it's found

Piedmont, particularly the Langhe and Monferrato.

How I serve it

The classic preparation of agnolotti dal plin (page 209) is one of my favorite recipes in this book, but I also use the shape for fillings that feature ingredients that do not need volume to impress, such as sunchoke or fonduta.

1   Prepare your selected egg-based dough (pages 18, 22, and 26–31) and follow the instructions for rolling and sheeting (pages 32–33).

2   Lightly dust a wooden work surface with OO flour. Line a sheet pan with parchment paper and lightly dust with semolina.

3   Lay your sheet(s) of pasta on the work surface. Use a knife to cut 18-inch-long sheets, removing the scraps from the unclean edges (save them for soup). Cover the sheets with plastic wrap or a kitchen towel.

4   Place one sheet on the work surface lengthwise. Spoon your filling into a pastry bag. Cut a ¼-inch hole in the tip of your pastry bag and pipe beads of filling—about the size of a hazelnut—½ inch from the bottom edge of your sheet and about 1 inch apart. If your filling is dense, such as a meat filling, pinch off each piece of filling and place it by hand.

5   Evaluate your dough. If it feels moderately tacky, you can eliminate this next step. If it feels a bit dry, hold your spray bottle 8 to 10 inches above the work surface and spray the pasta. This will help you securely seal the pasta.

6   Flip the bottom edge of the sheet up and around the filling so the pasta hugs the filling. Seal the top edge to the bottom sheet of pasta.

7   Using your thumb and index finger, pinch the dough on either side of each bead of filling to seal it. (You may want to go back over the areas you pinched to make sure they are well sealed.)

8   Along the seam where the top edge and bottom sheet meet, use your fluted pastry cutter to cut away the sheet, getting as close to the seam as you can. Detach and reserve the remainder of the sheet (you will use it to form another line of pasta just like this one).

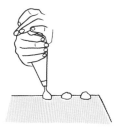

9   Using the pastry cutter, separate the pieces by cutting between them, positioning the cutter exactly in the center of where you pinched to seal the dough. As you cut, each piece should roll over onto itself to form an envelope.

10   Separate the pieces and carefully transfer them in a single layer to your prepared sheet pan. Give the pan an extra dusting of semolina to prevent sticking.

11   Repeat this process with the remaining portion of the sheet and then with all the remaining sheets.

12   Place in the refrigerator uncovered (if they are covered, they will sweat and become too wet) to dry for 45 minutes to 1 hour. If not using right away, remove from the refrigerator, loosely cover the sheet pan with plastic wrap, and return to the refrigerator for up to 8 hours.

Cannelloni

For Americans, cannelloni are perhaps better known as manicotti—or, if you find yourself rubbing elbows with an Italian American from New York's Tri-state area (or you've heard of a show called *The Sopranos*), simply "manicot."

Their region of origin is unknown, but cannelloni appear to be both relatively modern and pretty diffuse. They can be found as far north as the Aosta Valley and as far south as Sicily. Although most of us in America know and love the version filled with spinach and cheese and submerged in red sauce, cannelloni can be stuffed with meat, greens, fish, and ragù and smothered in béchamel and cheese, red sauce, and more. One thing is constant regardless of where you find cannelloni or what stuffing is used: this is a pasta al forno, meaning it is assembled in a pan and baked in the oven.

Cannelloni can be made ahead, stored, popped in the oven with very little oversight required, and then paraded to the table with fanfare. To that end, the virtue of this dish lies not in its refinement but in how easy it is to make—and love.

Where it's found

All over Italy but particularly in Emilia-Romagna, where it's filled with meat and smothered in béchamel, and in Abruzzo, Tuscany, and farther south, in Campania.

How I serve it

Italian American style, stuffed with cheese and spinach, then topped with red sauce and even more cheese (page 161).

1   Prepare your selected egg-based dough (pages 18, 22, and 26–31) and follow the instructions for rolling and sheeting (pages 32–33).

2   Lightly dust a wooden work surface with OO flour. Line a sheet pan with parchment paper and lightly dust with semolina.

3   Lay your sheet(s) of pasta on the work surface. Use a plain pastry cutter to cut 5 by 7-inch sheets, removing the scraps from the unclean edges (save them for soup). (Alternatively, use a knife and a ruler.)

4   Separate the pieces, dust each one lightly with OO flour, and stack in groups on the prepared sheet pan. Give the pan an extra dusting of semolina to prevent sticking.

5   Bring a large pot of water to a boil over high heat. Generously salt the water. Line another sheet pan with parchment paper and brush the paper with a tiny bit of olive oil.

6   Blanch the pasta sheets for about 1 minute, until tender but not soft. Using a spider, remove from the water and lay flat in a single layer on the prepared pan, using sheets of lightly oiled parchment to separate the layers.

7   Line another sheet pan with parchment paper and brush with a tiny bit of olive oil. Spoon your filling into a pastry bag. Cut a 1-inch hole in the tip of your pastry bag. Clean off your wooden work surface. Select one of your cooked sheets and position it lengthwise parallel to you. Pipe your filling in a line ½ inch from either side and 1 inch from the bottom of the sheet.

8   Gently flip the bottom edge of the pasta sheet over the filling, using your thumbs to ensure that it hugs the filling. Roll the pasta over itself again to create a cylinder.

9   Place the finished pasta, seam side down, on the second oiled sheet pan.

10   Fill and roll the remaining sheets, adding them to the oiled sheet pan.

11   If not using right away, cover the cannelloni with plastic wrap and refrigerate for up to 24 hours.

Cappelletti

Long overshadowed by its more prime-time relative, tortellini, cappelletti—named for their resemblance to a medieval hat, or capello—deviate in their cutting, folding, and size. Like nearly all filled pastas from northern Italy, cappelletti date back to the Middle Ages, when they were a fixture of the upper-class table. By the mid-1800s, however, they'd become a more widespread, middle-class affair. While in the past tortellini and cappelletti were often differentiated by their fillings (meat for the former, cheese for the latter) and origin within Emilia-Romagna, today the term *cappelletti* refers to the shape itself, which is formed from circles, not squares, and tightly fastened against the filling. Stylistically, the shape can vary, most commonly if the maker decides to form a collar by flipping the brim up to hug the filling.

Where it's found

Emilia-Romagna, particularly Reggio Emilia.

How I serve it

It's truly a choose-your-own-adventure (see pages 281, 294, 312, and 335), but I tend to pair a bold filling with a simple sauce, like butter and pepper or butter and pasta water with fennel pollen (page 294), which allows the shape to own the plate.

1   Prepare your selected egg-based dough (pages 18, 22, and 26–31) and follow the instructions for rolling and sheeting (pages 32–33).

2   Lightly dust a wooden work surface with 00 flour. Line a sheet pan with parchment paper and lightly dust with semolina.

3   Lay one sheet of pasta on the work surface. Using your #70 (2⅜-inch) plain or fluted round cutter, cut circles about ⅛ inch apart.

4   Spoon your filling into a pastry bag. Cut a ½-inch hole in the tip of the pastry bag and pipe a small circle of filling about the diameter of a quarter in the center of each circle.

5   Evaluate your dough. If it feels moderately tacky, you can eliminate this next step. If it feels a bit dry, hold your spray bottle 8 to 10 inches above the work surface and spray the circles. This will help you securely seal the pasta.

6   Lift a circle off the work surface and hold it in the palm of your nondominant hand. With your dominant hand, fold the top half of the circle over the bottom half to create a half-moon, lining up the edges.

7   Using your thumb and index finger, pinch the edge closed around the filling, making sure to force out any air. Go back and forth a few times, pinching to make sure it is sealed well.

8   While holding the piece in your nondominant hand, make a dimple in the center of the filled side of the pasta with your index finger.

9   Then, holding both ends of the half-moon with the dimple side closest to you, gently bring the edges of the pasta together on a slight downward angle so they meet. Cross the ends over each other and pinch them closed.

10   Place the finished pasta on the prepared sheet pan. Repeat with all of the circles, arranging them in a single layer on the prepared pan. Give the pan an extra dusting of semolina to prevent sticking.

11   Repeat with the remaining sheets.

12   Place in the refrigerator uncovered (if they are covered, they will sweat and become too wet) to dry for 45 minutes to 1 hour. If not using right away, remove from the refrigerator, loosely cover the sheet pan with plastic wrap, and return to the refrigerator for up to 8 hours.

Caramelle

While caramelle have become ubiquitous in the United States of late, no one seems to know exactly where they came from, and when. The most likely origin story is that caramelle are a modern mutation of Piacenza's feast-day tortelli piacentini (aka turtei cu la cua), a shape that recalls culurgiones (page 94), but with a tail on each end that's either fanned or pinched.

Caramelle, in contrast, do not have a braided enclosure and are made in either a cylindrical form (like a mini Tootsie Roll) or shorter and fatter (like a piece of saltwater taffy). Because they don't appear to have a traditional preparation, they are effectively used like ravioli—that is, stuffed with whatever you please and finished with the same freedom.

Where it's found
Emilia-Romagna and, well, the United States.

How I serve it
Regardless of the filling, I always pair caramelle with a sauce that won't obscure the shape, whether it be a drizzle of balsamic or a simple butter sauce (page 316).

1   Prepare your selected egg-based dough (pages 18, 22, and 26–31) and follow the instructions for rolling and sheeting (pages 32–33).

2   Lightly dust a wooden work surface with OO flour. Line a sheet pan with parchment paper and lightly dust with semolina.

3   Lay one sheet of pasta on the work surface. Using a straight-edged dough divider, cut your pasta sheet(s) into 2½ by 3-inch rectangles. (Alternatively, use a plain pastry cutter and a ruler or a knife and a ruler.) Cover the rectangles with plastic wrap or a kitchen towel.

4   Spoon your filling into a pastry bag. Cut a ½-inch hole in the tip of your pastry bag. Pipe a 1½-inch-long rope of filling about ½ inch from the 3-inch-wide bottom edge.

5   Gently roll the bottom edge of the rectangle over the filling to create a cylinder. Using your index fingers, press down on either side of the filling to seal the dough, making sure to force out any air.

6   Using your thumb and index finger, pinch the closure on either side of the filling to form a shape that looks like a wrapped piece of candy.

7   Place the finished pasta on the prepared sheet pan. Repeat with all of the rectangles, arranging them in a single layer on the prepared pan. Give the pan an extra dusting of semolina to prevent sticking.

8   Repeat with the remaining sheets.

9   Place in the refrigerator uncovered (if they are covered, they will sweat and become too wet) to dry for 45 minutes to 1 hour. If not using right away, remove from the refrigerator, loosely cover the sheet pan with plastic wrap, and return to the refrigerator for up to 8 hours.

Casunziei

I like to think of casunziei, cjalsons, and casoncelli as all part of a single family of alpine mezzelune that ride an intriguing line between sweet and savory—each a product of high-altitude bounty, or austerity, depending on how you look at it. Casoncelli are effectively casunziei from Lombardy (they are variably called casunziei here, too) that are filled with a mix of cured meat, bread crumbs, nutmeg, and often amaretti cookies, raisins, or cinnamon. In the Veneto that filling becomes, most classically, beets. And in the Friulian Alps, cjalsons are a grab-bag mixture of dried fruits, spices, cheese, and wild herbs.

When I think of casunziei, I do not think of the Lombardian version, but of casunziei from Cortina d'Ampezzo, a ski town perched amid a particularly picturesque slice of the Dolomite range. This, to me, is perhaps the Alps' greatest contribution to pasta, a full spectrum of sweet, savory, smoky, and rich that is as beautiful to look at as it is a pleasure to eat. Although you will find green or golden versions of casunziei that make use of alpine herbs, turnips, and potato, it's the beet-filled version (page 194) that has become as famous as the town itself.

Where it's found

Veneto, specifically in the alpine town of Cortina d'Ampezzo.

How I serve it

For me, classic is the only way to go: foamy butter, poppy seeds, and smoked ricotta (page 194).

1   Prepare your egg dough (page 18) and follow the instructions for rolling and sheeting (pages 32–33).

2   Lightly dust a wooden work surface with 00 flour. Line a sheet pan with parchment paper and lightly dust with semolina.

3   Lay one sheet of pasta on the work surface. Using your #70 (2¾-inch) fluted pastry cutter, cut circles ⅛ inch apart.

4   Spoon your filling into a pastry bag. Cut a ½-inch hole in the tip of your pastry bag and pipe a small circle about the diameter of a quarter in the center of each circle. (This filling is fairly loose, so take care when piping it.)

5   Evaluate your dough. If it feels moderately tacky, you can eliminate this next step. If it feels a bit dry, hold your spray bottle 8 to 10 inches above the work surface and spray the circles. This will help you securely seal the pasta.

6   Lift a circle off the work surface and hold it in the palm of your nondominant hand. With your other hand, fold the top half of the circle over the bottom half to create a half-moon, lining up the edges.

7   Using your thumb and index finger, pinch the edge closed around the filling, making sure to force out any air. Go back and forth a few times, pinching to make sure it is sealed well.

8   Place the finished pasta on the prepared sheet pan. Repeat with all of the circles, arranging them in a single layer on the prepared pan. Give the pan an extra dusting of semolina to prevent sticking.

9   Repeat with the remaining sheets.

10   Place in the refrigerator uncovered (if they are covered, they will sweat and become too wet) to dry for 45 minutes to 1 hour. If not using right away, remove from the refrigerator, loosely cover the sheet pan with plastic wrap, and return to the refrigerator for up to 8 hours.

Cjalsons

These sweet-savory Friulian half-moon ravioli, native to the Carnic Alps, are an omnipresent and beloved part of northern Friulian culture. In fact, the shape inspires such pride that literally dozens of variations exist—not only from town to town but from household to household.

Cjalsons are clearly a product of Arab influence in their use of sweetness and spices, many of which migrated north from Sicilian kitchens during the reign of the Holy Roman emperor Frederick II. However odd sweet pasta may seem to us now, it was actually customary to serve pastas in a sauce of butter, cheese, and spices until as recently as the eighteenth century. (The Renaissance, in particular, is replete with pastas that rely on sweetness and spice as a status symbol.) In this way, cjalsons feel like a relic from an earlier time—preserved but constantly changing.

If I could pinpoint a single pasta that helped me grasp just how diverse Italy was from region to region, I'd choose that first bite of cjalsons I had in 1999 at a restaurant I was interning at in Udine. Its version relied on potato dough stuffed with apple, cinnamon, cocoa, lemon, and smoked and fresh ricotta and served in brown butter with shaved smoked ricotta. My version is a mash-up of that bite and cjalsons di Piedim from Gianni Cosetti's bible of traditional Carnia-area recipes, *Vecchia e nuova cucina di Carnia*, that combines cocoa, dried fruit, ricotta, and citrus zest. I further diverge in that I angle my filling (page 197) more toward savory than sweet so the pasta can still slot in as a genuine primo without shock and awe.

Where it's found

Friuli, specifically in the Carnic Alps.

How I serve it

As you tend to find it in the Alps, with butter, shaved smoked ricotta, cocoa, and/or cinnamon (page 197).

---

1 Prepare your selected egg-based dough (pages 18, 22, and 26–31) and follow the instructions for rolling and sheeting (pages 32–33).

2 Lightly dust a wooden work surface with 00 flour. Line a sheet pan with parchment paper and lightly dust with semolina.

3 Lay one sheet of pasta on the work surface. Using your #70 (2¾-inch) fluted pastry cutter, cut circles ⅛ inch apart.

4 Spoon your filling into a pastry bag. Cut a ½-inch hole in the tip of your pastry bag and pipe a small circle of filling about the diameter of a quarter in the center of each circle.

5 Evaluate your dough. If it feels moderately tacky, you can eliminate this next step. If it feels a bit dry, hold your spray bottle 8 to 10 inches above the work surface and spray the circles. This will help you securely seal the pasta.

6 Lift a circle off the work surface and hold it in the palm of your nondominant hand. With your dominant hand, fold the top half of the circle over the bottom half to create a half-moon, lining up your edges.

7 Using your thumb and index finger, pinch the edge closed around the filling, making sure to force out any air. Go back and forth a few times, pinching to make sure it is sealed well.

8   Place the finished pasta on the prepared sheet pan. Repeat with all of the circles, arranging them in a single layer on the prepared pan. Give the pan an extra dusting of semolina to prevent sticking.

9   Repeat with the remaining sheets.

10   Place in the refrigerator uncovered (if they are covered, they will sweat and become too wet) to dry for 45 minutes to 1 hour. If not using right away, remove from the refrigerator, loosely cover the sheet pan with plastic wrap, and return to the refrigerator for up to 8 hours.

Culurgiones

Culurgiones have more names than an English royal: angiullotus, culurjones, gurigliones, culinjonis, spighitti, and, perhaps the only truly helpful entry, Sardinian ravioli. While the shape bears little resemblance to that of classic ravioli, it's now as ubiquitous and important to Sardinian cuisine as ravioli are to mainland Italy. Although other variations exist, culurgiones tend to take two main forms: the first, a tiny cheese-filled bota bag, and the second, a teardrop whose braided closure looks like a fishtail braid or a sheaf of wheat. The latter is most common in the shape's birthplace in Sardinia's mountainous east, near the town of Nuoro. That resemblance to wheat is symbolic; not only was the shape originally made to celebrate the wheat harvest, but by extension it was considered to be something of a talisman meant to celebrate bounty and prevent deprivation.

Fillings can certainly vary, but a combination of greens or fresh herbs, fresh and aged pecorino sardo, and potato is most common.

Where it's found
Sardinia.

How I serve it

In a simple tomato sauce and garnished with mint and fiore sardo (see page 246).

Nota bene

The sheets and the filling can become too soft to work with as they sit out. To remedy, place them in the refrigerator and remove in batches.

1   Prepare your semolina dough (page 19) and follow the instructions for rolling and sheeting (pages 32–33).

2   Lightly dust a wooden work surface with 00 flour. Line a sheet pan with parchment paper and lightly dust with semolina.

3   Lay one sheet of pasta on the work surface. Using your #90 (3½-inch) fluted pastry cutter, cut circles ⅛ inch apart.

4   Spoon about 16g of filling in the center of each circle.

5   Evaluate your dough. If it feels tacky, you can eliminate this next step. If your pasta feels a bit dry, hold your spray bottle 8 to 10 inches above the work surface and spray the circles. This will help you securely seal the pasta.

6   Lift a circle off the table and cup it in the palm of your nondominant hand. With your dominant hand, bring the sides of the pasta up to form a taco-like shape.

7   Starting at the left or right end of the circle, use your index finger to fold the end of the circle in onto the filling.

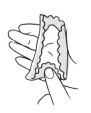

8   Using your middle finger and your thumb, pinch the sides of the dough together over the end that has been folded in, creating a triangular closure. Use your index finger to press the top of the closure into the filling. Repeat the process of pinching and folding to create a braided closure that resembles a fishtail braid. Pinch the end of the shape closed to create a small tail.

9   Place the finished pasta on the prepared sheet pan. Repeat with all of the circles, arranging them in a single layer on the prepared pan. Give the pan an extra dusting of semolina to prevent sticking.

10   Repeat with the remaining sheets.

11   Place in the refrigerator uncovered (if they are covered, they will sweat and become too wet) to dry for 45 minutes to 1 hour. If not using right away, remove from the refrigerator, loosely cover the sheet pan with plastic wrap, and return to the refrigerator for up to 8 hours.

Mezzelune

Mezzelune are effectively a subgenre of ravioli that are sealed in the shape of a half-moon, hence the name. Within this subgenre, mezzelune take dozens of names—from schlutzkrapfen in Alto Adige to casunziei in the Veneto—depending on where they're made and what they're filled with. The only stylistic variation, aside from the choice of filling, is the type of pastry cutter used. (I prefer to use a fluted pastry cutter, which gives the shape a bit more visual intrigue on the plate.)

Each of the shape's regional variations has its own origin story, and though mezzelune can be found all over the country, they are perhaps most ubiquitous in the north, particularly across the Alps and even across the Italian border in neighboring German-speaking countries. For me, the greatest argument for mezzelune is their ease. They are one of the simplest filled shapes to master.

Where it's found

Across Italy, with a particular concentration in the Alps.

How I serve it

Any which way (for example, see page 306). It's great if you're in a rush or have a shape that has a bold filling that does not quite need the interior real estate ravioli offer in order to pop on the plate.

1   Prepare your selected egg-based dough (pages 18, 22, and 26–31) and follow the instructions for rolling and sheeting (pages 32–33).

2   Lightly dust a wooden work surface with 00 flour. Line a sheet pan with parchment paper and lightly dust with semolina.

3   Lay one sheet of pasta on the work surface. Using your #70 (2¾-inch) fluted pastry cutter, cut circles ⅛ inch apart.

4   Spoon your filling into a pastry bag. Cut a ½-inch hole in the tip of your pastry bag and pipe a small circle of filling about the diameter of a quarter in the center of each circle.

5   Evaluate your dough. If it feels tacky, you can eliminate this next step. If your pasta feels a bit dry, hold your spray bottle 8 to 10 inches above the work surface and spray the circles. This will help you securely seal the pasta.

6   Lift a circle off the table and hold it in the palm of your nondominant hand. With your dominant hand, fold the top half of the circle over the bottom half to create a half-moon, lining up the edges.

7   Using your thumb and index finger, pinch the edge closed around the filling, making sure to force out any air. Go back and forth a few times, pinching to make sure it is sealed well.

8   Place the finished pasta on the prepared sheet pan. Repeat with all of the circles, arranging them in a single layer on the prepared pan. Give the pan an extra dusting of semolina to prevent sticking.

9   Repeat with the remaining sheets.

10   Place in the refrigerator uncovered (if they are covered, they will sweat and become too wet) to dry for 45 minutes to 1 hour. If not using right away, remove from the refrigerator, loosely cover the sheet pan with plastic wrap, and return to the refrigerator for up to 8 hours.

Occhi

I guess it was inevitable that I'd someday unwittingly name my own shape. I still swear that occhi, a diminutive take on round ravioli with each occhio resembling one very wide eye, were listed by name at Trattoria La Buca, a restaurant I ate at in the town of Zibello, in Emilia-Romagna, in 2013. The funny thing is, the restaurant, it turns out, has never heard of the shape. Did we have too much wine? Step into another dimension filled with abundant occhi?

New York magazine did a story on it, making an effort to track down the shape. It ends up reading like a parody of pasta nomenclature. (There is a shape called occhi di lupo, or "wolf's eyes," but it bears no resemblance to our occhi, which the restaurant claims were actually agnolini, despite agnolini looking nothing like occhi.) This is precisely why we've got twenty names for each shape.

I still hold strong to the belief that there are occhi out there in Zibello waiting to lay claim, but until then, we've got to claim them as ours. At Misi, I stuff occhi with sheep's milk ricotta and marry them with a simple sauce of butter, lemon zest, and bottarga.

Where it's found

Until the real occhi stand up, New York City.

How I serve it

As described in the recipe headnote, but consider them as versatile as ravioli. You can stuff them with whatever and serve them however you please.

1   Prepare your selected egg-based dough (pages 18, 22, and 26–31) and follow the instructions for rolling and sheeting (pages 32–33).

2   Lightly dust a wooden work surface with OO flour. Line a sheet pan with parchment paper and lightly dust with semolina.

3   Lay your sheet(s) of pasta on the work surface. Use a knife to cut 18-inch-long sheets, removing the scraps from the unclean edges (save them for soup). Cover the sheets with plastic wrap or a kitchen towel.

4   Lay one pasta sheet on your work surface. Spoon your filling into a pastry bag. Cut a 1-inch hole in the tip of your pastry bag and pipe small circles of filling about 1½ inches wide and ½ inch high evenly across your sheet, spacing them about 1½ inches apart.

5   Evaluate your dough. If it feels moderately tacky, you can eliminate this next step. If the pasta feels a bit dry, hold your spray bottle 8 to 10 inches above the work surface and spray the pasta. This will enable the second sheet to stick.

6   Lay a second sheet of pasta gently over the first, making sure the edges line up and there aren't any wrinkles.

7   Using your two index fingers, gently press around each circle of filling to eliminate any air pockets. For extra insurance, flip your #30 (1⅛-inch) plain round cutter to the dull side and press over each dollop again to express any excess air and make an even circle.

8   Using your #40 (1½-inch) plain round cutter, press down around the first occhio with the palm of your hand flat on top of the cutter. After you have pressed down, gently move the cutter clockwise while still pressing, to ensure a full cut. This pasta will have a very small border around the edge when sealed.

9   Gently remove the scraps surrounding the occhi by lifting the sheets from one end. Discard the excess dough or reserve for use in soup.

10 Place the finished pasta in a single layer on the prepared sheet pan. Give the pan an extra dusting of semolina to prevent sticking.

11 Repeat with the remaining sheets.

12 Place in the refrigerator uncovered (if they are covered, they will sweat and become too wet) to dry for 45 minutes to 1 hour. If not using right away, remove from the refrigerator, loosely cover the sheet pan with plastic wrap, and return to the refrigerator for up to 8 hours.

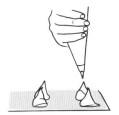

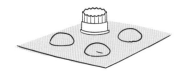

Pansotti

Pansotti are essentially the Italian Riviera's version of tortelli (page 106). The only real difference in the way they are made is how they are closed: folded not into a triangle and fastened, but instead in half with the sides pulled around the front until the filling creates a pasta paunch—hence the name, which derives from the word *panzia*, or "belly."

Pansotti are traditionally stuffed with local prescinsêua cheese (think of it as a more acidic, sour ricotta) or ricotta mixed with parmigiano and preboggion, a collection of seven wild herbs and plants that are combined and briefly boiled. Most can't agree on what comprises the seven herbs at any given time of year, but you'll generally find some combination of borage, anise, chard, wild chicory, poppy, parsley, and nettle. However, in what will be a surprise to no one, each subregion, maker, family, and restaurant has its own take—some of which exceed seven ingredients to total ten or more. Preboggion is used in a number of Ligurian dishes (torta salata, focaccia, omelets), but its highest calling is pansotti.

What you're really looking for from the greens in the filling is a combination of herbal, bitter, and aromatic—how you combine them is often a matter of personal taste and, in the spirit of foraging them in their birthplace, of what is available to you.

Where it's found
Liguria.

How I serve it
True to form, in salsa di noci (page 180), though you can absolutely serve them in a simple sauce of pasta water and butter. There's enough flavor in the filling to carry the dish.

1   Prepare your selected egg-based dough (pages 18, 22, and 26–31) and follow the instructions for rolling and sheeting (pages 32–33).

2   Lightly dust a wooden work surface with 00 flour. Line a sheet pan with parchment paper and lightly dust with semolina.

3   Lay one sheet of pasta on the work surface. Using a straight-edged dough divider, cut your pasta sheet into 4 by 3½-inch rectangles. (Alternatively, use a plain pastry cutter and a ruler or a knife and a ruler.) Cover the rectangles with plastic wrap or a kitchen towel.

4   Spoon your filling into a pastry bag. Cut a 1-inch hole in the tip of your pastry bag and pipe a generous circle of filling about the size of an unshelled walnut in the center of each circle.

5   Evaluate your dough. If it feels moderately tacky, you can eliminate this next step. If it feels a bit dry, hold your spray bottle 8 to 10 inches above the work surface and spray the pasta. This will help you securely seal the pasta.

6   Fold one long side over the filling to meet the other long side, lining up the edges.

7   Using your thumb and index finger, pinch the edge closed around the filling, making sure to force out any air. Go back and forth a few times, pinching to make sure it is sealed well.

8   While holding the piece in your nondominant hand, make a dimple in the center of the filled side of the pasta with your thumb.

9   Grasp the bottom tips of the rectangle with your thumbs and index fingers. Pull one side around to join it to the other side in front of the filling, forming a collar around the filling. Pinch the ends together firmly to close.

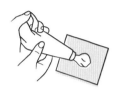

10 Place the finished pasta on the prepared sheet pan. Repeat with all of the rectangles, arranging them in a single layer on the prepared pan. Give the pan an extra dusting of semolina to prevent sticking.

11 Repeat with the remaining sheets.

12 Place in the refrigerator uncovered (if they are covered, they will sweat and become too wet) to dry for 45 minutes to 1 hour. If not using right away, remove from the refrigerator, loosely cover the sheet pan with plastic wrap, and return to the refrigerator for up to 8 hours.

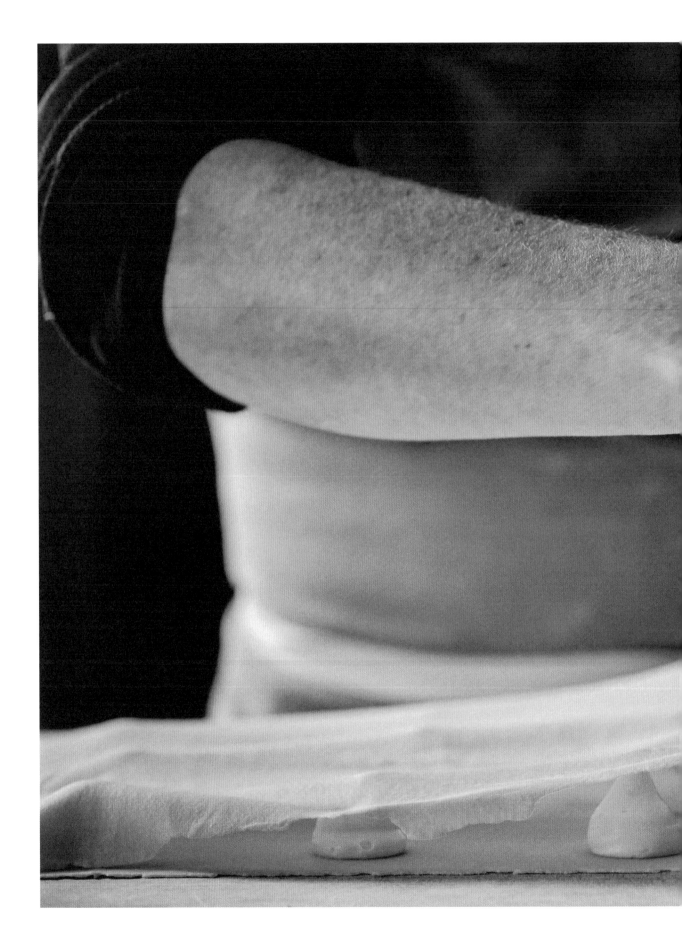

Ravioli

Ravioli are effectively the filled equivalent of spaghetti: a shape that is so ubiquitous throughout Italy that it has become a synonym for pasta itself. While descriptions of a shape similar to ravioli date to the twelfth century, it's later, during the Renaissance, that the shape, well, takes greater shape—and by name. Chef Martino of Como includes several versions in his *Libro de arte coquinaria (The Art of Cooking)*, published in the mid-fifteenth century. One, a thin dough stuffed with cheese, herbs, meat, and spices and cooked in brodo, matches what we understand to be ravioli today. Many other chefs of the era describe a similar filled pasta prepared in myriad ways in the regal courts of Lombardy.

Today, ravioli are found everywhere from their supposed birthplace in the north to as far south as Sicily, not to mention their role as an icon of the Italian American table. They are stuffed with whatever you can possibly dream up and sauced with the same sense of boundless possibility. In that spirit, ravioli, to me, have always been the ideal starting point for making filled pasta—a shape that resists dogma and invites experimentation. They can be made round or square, big or small. For the restaurants, my ravioli are round, typically about 2 inches in diameter, and with a ruffled edge. But I've given instructions for making them square as well, in a hat tip to red-sauce nostalgia.

Where it's found

North to south, and the world over.

How I serve it

There are few dishes I find more fulfilling than red sauce and ravioli (page 153). That said, ravioli are really best enjoyed as a test model for any filling you can dream up (for example, see pages 290 and 302). I can no longer count the many versions I've made over the years.

---

1   Prepare your selected egg-based dough (pages 18, 22, and 26–31) and follow the instructions for rolling and sheeting (pages 32–33).

2   Lightly dust a wooden work surface with 00 flour. Line a sheet pan with parchment paper and lightly dust with semolina.

3   Lay your sheet(s) of pasta on the work surface. Use a knife to cut 18-inch-long sheets, removing the scraps from the unclean edges (save them for soup). Cover the sheets with plastic wrap or a kitchen towel.

4   Place one pasta sheet on your work surface. Spoon your filling into a pastry bag. Cut a 1-inch hole in the tip of your pastry bag and pipe circles of filling about 1½ inches wide and ½ inch high evenly across your sheet, spacing them about 2 inches apart.

5   Evaluate your dough. If it feels moderately tacky, you can eliminate this next step. If the pasta feels a bit dry, hold your spray bottle 8 to 10 inches above the work surface and spray the pasta. This will enable the second sheet to stick.

6   Lay a second sheet of pasta gently over the first, making sure the edges line up and there aren't any wrinkles.

7   Using your two index fingers, gently press around each dollop of filling to express any air pockets. For extra insurance, flip your #30 (1⅛-inch) plain round cutter to the dull side and gently press over each dollop to express any excess air.

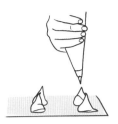

8   If you're making square ravioli, use a fluted pastry cutter or fluted dough divider to cut the ravioli into 2½-inch squares. You can also use a 2½-inch fluted square cutter to the same effect.

9   If you are making round ravioli, use your #60 (2⅜-inch) plain round cutter, pressing it down first with the palm of your hand flat on top of the cutter. After you have pressed down, gently move the cutter clockwise while still pressing to ensure a full cut.

10   Gently remove the scraps surrounding the ravioli by lifting the sheets from one end. Discard the excess dough or reserve for use in soup.

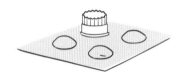

11   Place the finished pasta on the prepared sheet pan in a single layer. Give the pan an extra dusting of semolina to prevent sticking.

12   Repeat with the remaining sheets.

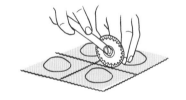

13   Place in the refrigerator uncovered (if they are covered, they will sweat and become too wet) to dry for 45 minutes to 1 hour. If not using right away, remove from the refrigerator, loosely cover the sheet pan with plastic wrap, and return to the refrigerator for up to 8 hours.

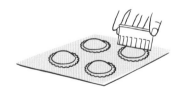

Tortelli

Tortelli are not one shape. Instead, the moniker encompasses a whole motley crew of iterations—squares, triangles, half-moons, circles—that have rendered them almost interchangeable with ravioli. In fact, the history of tortelli is perhaps best defined by its ability to shape-shift, often as a means of signaling what it's stuffed with.

My tortelli, which are inspired by a version I stumbled across in Milan many years ago, have always closely resembled tortelloni, which are a larger version of tortellini that are almost always stuffed with cheese or a mixture of cheese and greens or herbs. The difference is in both how I cut and how I close the shape. I use a fluted cutter and essentially make a triangular pasta. You could stop here and still call it tortelli, but I do not! I close it like I would tortellini, but instead of having the closure form a ring along the bottom, I overlap the edges to make a boatlike shape. You could call my tortelli a close cousin of cappellacci di zucca, a squash-filled shape from the town of Ferrara, in Emilia-Romagna.

The point is, tortelli are defined by their big-tent identity, and I've always loved them for being resistant to dogma and open to interpretation. My version is merely one of dozens.

Where it's found

All over Italy but particularly in Emilia-Romagna and Lombardy.

How I serve it

Stuffed with squash flavored with mostarda (page 186), or filled with cheese and greens and sauced with restraint (page 322). Tortelli like the spotlight.

1   Prepare your selected egg-based dough (pages 18, 22, and 26–31) and follow the instructions for rolling and sheeting (pages 32–33).

2   Line a sheet pan with parchment paper and lightly dust with semolina.

3   Lay one sheet of pasta on the work surface. Using a fluted dough divider, cut your pasta sheet into 2½-inch squares. (Alternatively, use a fluted pastry cutter and a ruler or a knife and a ruler.) Cover the squares with plastic wrap or a kitchen towel.

4   Spoon your filling into a pastry bag. Cut a ½-inch hole in the tip of your pastry bag and pipe a small circle of filling about the diameter of a quarter in the center of each square.

5   Evaluate your dough. If it feels moderately tacky, you can eliminate this next step. If it feels a bit dry, hold your spray bottle 8 to 10 inches above the work surface and spray the squares. This will help you securely seal the pasta.

6   Lift a square off the work surface and hold it in the palm of your nondominant hand. Using your dominant hand, fold one corner to meet the opposite corner just below the top edge so the ruffled edges appear tiered.

7   Using your thumb and index finger, pinch the edges closed around the filling, making sure to force out any air. Go back and forth a few times, pinching to make sure it is sealed well.

8   While holding the piece in your nondominant hand, make a dimple in the center of the filled side of the pasta with your index finger.

9 Then, holding both ends of the triangle with the dimple side closest to you, gently bring the edges of the pasta together and ever so slightly cross the ends over each other to form a canoe shape with the filling at the center. Pinch the ends closed well.

10 Place the finished pasta on the prepared sheet pan. Repeat with all of the squares, arranging them in a single layer on the prepared pan. Give the pan an extra dusting of semolina to prevent sticking.

11 Repeat with the remaining sheets.

12 Place in the refrigerator uncovered (if they are covered, they will sweat and become too wet) to dry for 45 minutes to 1 hour. If not using right away, remove from the refrigerator, loosely cover the sheet pan with plastic wrap, and return to the refrigerator for up to 8 hours.

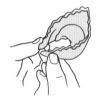

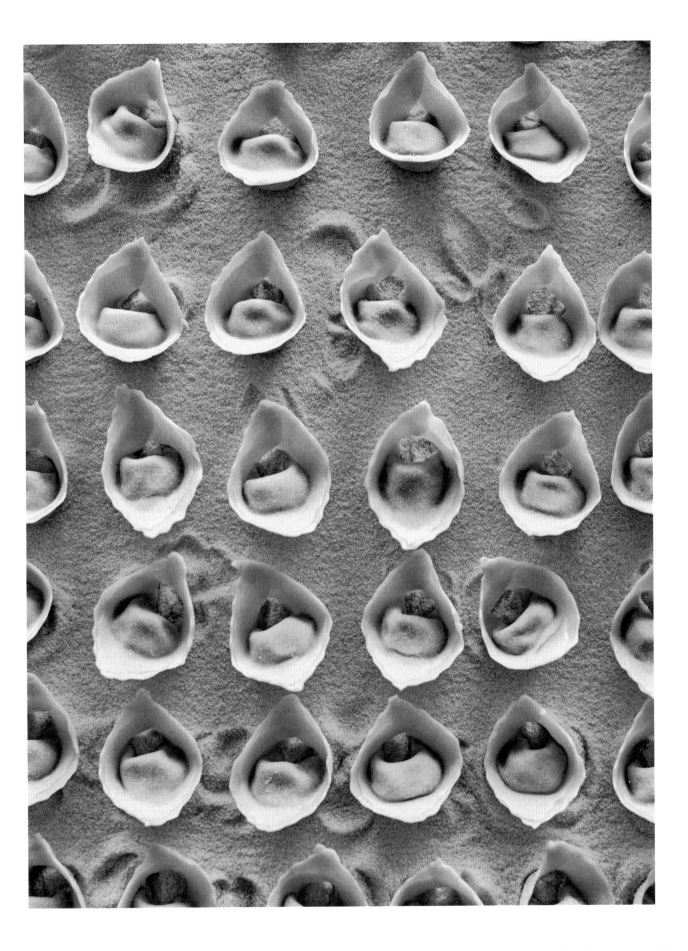

Tortellini

Like any shape of comparable acclaim, tortellini have their own origin legends. They are said to have been modeled after two different belly buttons—that of the goddess Venus, presumably on holiday in Bologna, and that of Lucrezia Borgia—depending on who's spinning the yarn. Although the shape does indeed resemble a belly button, its actual origin story likely follows that of many other famous stuffed pastas, which pop up with frequency in the Middle Ages and become codified as upper-class fare during the fifteenth and sixteenth centuries.

Now an everyday affair in their birthplace of Emilia-Romagna, tortellini nevertheless maintain a dignified air. They are still primarily served in their most traditional form—in brodo, unadorned, as if to declare that they need nothing else. And they don't.

Although the fillings can vary quite widely, they are almost always made from a combination of cured meats (plus either ground pork, veal, or chicken), parmigiano, and nutmeg. I stick relatively close to that combo for my classic filling but diverge at the restaurants, where I like to fill tortellini with a smooth parmigiano fonduta, which becomes liquefied and creamy when cooked.

Where it's found
Emilia-Romagna, primarily in Modena and Bologna.

How I serve it
In brodo (page 198), end of story.

1   Prepare your selected egg-based dough (pages 18, 22, and 26–31) and follow the instructions for rolling and sheeting (pages 32–33).

2   Lightly dust a wooden work surface with 00 flour. Line a sheet pan with parchment paper and lightly dust with semolina.

3   Lay one sheet of pasta on the work surface. Using a straight-edged dough divider, cut your pasta sheet into 1¾-inch squares. (Alternatively, use a plain pastry cutter and a ruler or a knife and a ruler.) Cover the squares with plastic wrap or a kitchen towel.

4   Spoon your filling into a pastry bag. Cut a ¼-inch hole in the tip of your pastry bag and pipe a small circle of filling about the size of a hazelnut in the center of each square. If your filling is dense, like a meat filling, pinch off each piece of filling and place it by hand.

5   Evaluate your dough. If it feels moderately tacky, you can eliminate this next step. If it feels a bit dry, hold your spray bottle 8 to 10 inches above the work surface and spray the squares. This will help you securely seal the pasta.

6   Lift a square off the work surface and hold it in the palm of your nondominant hand. With your dominate hand, fold one corner to the opposite corner to form a triangle, lining up the edges.

7   Using your thumb and index finger, pinch the edge closed around the filling, making sure to force out any air. Go back and forth a few times, pinching to make sure it is sealed well.

8   Grasp the bottom tips of the triangle with your thumb and index finger. Pull one side around your other index finger to join it to the other at the underside of the filling, forming a ring. Pinch the ends together firmly to close and flatten to about the thickness of the rest of the shape, which will ensure more even cooking.

9   Place the finished pasta on the prepared sheet pan. Repeat with all of the squares, arranging them in a single layer on the prepared pan. Give the pan an extra dusting of semolina to prevent sticking.

10   Repeat with the remaining sheets.

11   Place in the refrigerator uncovered (if they are covered, they will sweat and become too wet) to dry for 45 minutes to 1 hour. If not using right away, remove from the refrigerator, loosely cover the sheet pan with plastic wrap, and return to the refrigerator for up to 8 hours.

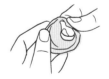

Outliers

Corzetti

There are technically two types of corzetti. One is made by pressing two fingers into small pieces of dough to create figure-eight-shape gnocchi known as croset, crosit, or crosetti. But I've always known corzetti—aka croxetti or corzetti stampati—as flat coin shapes made by pressing a carved stamp into them. The carved wooden stamps, which can be found in artisan pasta shops along the Italian Riviera and elsewhere, are as beautiful as the shape itself, imprinted with everything from abstract patterns to vegetal motifs to designs that mimic coins in circulation during the height of the Genovese republic.

The shape dates to the late thirteenth century, when it was often stamped with a family's coat of arms and served on special occasions. It has remained a staple of the Riviera, where it's something of a canvas for whatever the maker has on hand, though herb- and nut-based sauces or a simple fresh tomato sauce are most common. It's a shape that is all about delicacy—think of it almost as pasta carpaccio—and performs best in simple preparations. I tend to pair corzetti with a fresh sauce of just-busted Sungold tomatoes and herbs in the summer or sweet Italian broccoli, pine nuts, and pecorino in the winter.

Where it's found
Liguria.

How I serve it
In simple herb-based sauces (page 213), such as pesto, or with in-season vegetables. In the winter, I love to swap in chestnut dough and pair the shape with mushrooms and parmigiano.

Nota bene

Sometimes the edge of a well-loved corzetti stamp will dull over time and no longer cut. Use the ring in your set of round pastry cutters to cut out the circle and then use the stamp to imprint it.

1   Prepare your selected egg-based dough (pages 18, 22, and 26–31) and follow the instructions for rolling and sheeting (pages 32–33).

2   Lightly dust a wooden cutting board with OO flour. Line a sheet pan with parchment paper and lightly dust with semolina.

3   Lay a sheet of pasta on the work surface. Using the hollow side of your corzetti stamp, cut circles ⅛ inch apart.

4   Flip the stamp to the patterned side and press it into each circle, pressing hard enough to make it textured, but not so hard that it flattens the shape too much. You may need to use additional OO flour to dust one or both sides of your corzetti so they press and release more easily from your stamp. Repeat with all of the circles.

5   Place the finished pasta on the prepared sheet pan, arranging them in a single layer and separating the layers with parchment dusted with semolina.

6   Repeat with the remaining sheets.

7   Let dry for 15 to 20 minutes at room temperature. If not using right away, cover the sheet pan with plastic wrap and refrigerate for up to 24 hours.

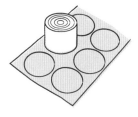

Canederli

Are canederli, aka Knödel in Austria or Germany, pasta? Cross the border from the Italian Alps, where these bread dumplings proliferate, and the answer would be "no." But plop them into the alpine towns that comprise South Tyrol, and there's no arguing that canederli are pasta. In fact, here they are often referred to as gnocchi di pane, or "bread gnocchi."

While canederli are of Austrian origin, the use of stale bread to make a dough pops up all over Italy (see passatelli, page 189, for one) as a means of both thrift and necessity in regions where growing food presents a challenge for many months out of the year. This is, plain and simple, sustenance cooking. Two versions tend to proliferate in the Alps: canederli di speck, combining smoked cured ham with bread, eggs, flour, and chives, and canederli di spinaci, made with cheese, spinach, and parsley.

My version is inspired by a dish I had at Walbichl, a small rifugio outside of Merano, in Alto Adige. I diverge in the use of rye bread instead of plain white, which gives another layer of flavor and aroma to the dish. It also has precedent, as some versions of traditional canederli incorporate rye flour.

---

1   Line a sheet pan with parchment paper.

2   Lightly wet your hands and work in batches to form the canederli dough (page 188) into 54g balls the size of golf balls. Transfer to the sheet pan.

3   Cover with plastic wrap and refrigerate for up to 24 hours.

Where it's found
Italian Alps, particularly in Trentino–Alto Adige.

How I serve it
The classic way, either in a sage-and-butter sauce or in brodo.

Nota bene

The canederli can be cooked ahead. Following the instructions for boiling the canederli on page 188, cook them in batches and transfer to a sheet pan to cool. Once they've cooled, cover the sheet pan with plastic wrap and refrigerate for up to 24 hours before serving.

Bigoli

Bigoli are a hyper-regional pasta most associated with Venice, though they are also found in surrounding areas of the Veneto, in Istria—where they are known as fusarioi—and in eastern Lombardy, specifically in the town of Mantua. They are similar to Tuscan pici save for a few key differences. First, they are often made with buckwheat or whole-wheat flour as well as milk, butter, and eggs. Second, they are extruded rather than hand-rolled, through their own namesake tool, the bigolaro—a tabletop hand press that spits out long, thick strands of pasta that are then cut by hand to about 12 inches long.

While some may opt to rely entirely on whole-wheat or buckwheat flour for their bigoli, as with all pastas that include alternative flours, I always combine these flours with 00 flour. I also choose to omit both butter and milk from the recipe. The addition of one or both can yield a more decadent pasta, but it's at the expense of bite. And bigoli are all about bite.

Where it's found

The Veneto, specifically Venice; Istria; and southeastern Lombardy, in and around the town of Mantua.

How I serve it

They are most famously paired with a sauce of anchovies and onions (page 191), which is fairly ubiquitous in Venice, or a sauce of sardines and onions, which is more common in Mantua (I prefer the former). I love the classic preparation but also pair them with rich, meat-based sauces.

1   Prepare your whole-wheat dough (page 26).

2   Lightly dust a wooden work surface with 00 flour. Line a sheet pan with parchment paper and lightly dust with semolina. Attach your bigolaro to the edge of your work surface.

3   Divide your dough into quarters. Place one piece on the work surface. Cover the other pieces with plastic wrap or a kitchen towel.

4   Form the dough into a cylinder about 2 inches in diameter. (It should be just small enough to fit into the chamber of the bigolaro.)

5   Place the dough cylinder into the bigolaro and turn the lever to extrude. Using a knife, cut 12-inch-long strands.

6   Generously dust your strands with 00 flour and gently shake them to separate. Curl each batch into a horseshoe shape and place it on the prepared sheet pan.

7   Repeat with the remaining dough quarters.

8   Let dry for 20 to 30 minutes at room temperature.

9   If not using right away, cover the sheet pan with plastic wrap and refrigerate for up to 24 hours.

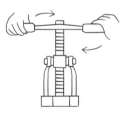

Pasta

Spaghetti alla Chitarra

Arguably Abruzzo's greatest contribution to the pasta canon, spaghetti alla chitarra are named for the tool that has been used to make the pasta since at least the early 1800s. While it's called a chitarra (guitar) for its resemblance to the instrument, it looks more like a tabletop harp. The square-shaped spaghetti, also known across the border in Lazio as tonnarelli, are made by rolling out thick sheets (⅛ inch versus the typical 1/16 inch thick) of egg dough and then placing them atop the fine metal wires of the chitarra. The pasta is then rolled out again until the wires have cut the sheet into square strands that collect in the box below. You can make only a single order at a time, and it's this bit of deliberate inefficiency that has always attracted me to the pasta and also probably why you see many Abruzzese make it by machine today.

The shape originated in the province of Chieti but is now found all over the region in a number of preparations. Its most common partner, however, is lamb—whether tiny meatballs in a rich tomato-based sauce (page 224) or lamb ragù. It's also frequently served with vegetables, especially zucchini, cooked with saffron.

I've experimented with the shape for a decade in a variety of different preparations, but it's generally during the spring that it shows up on my menus, often alongside ramps (which I often work into the dough), fava beans, and spring peas. What makes spaghetti alla chitarra so versatile and appealing is its texture, which is perhaps best described as, no pun intended, springy.

Where it's found

In Abruzzo as maccheroni alla chitarra, spaghetti alla chitarra, and pasta alla chitarra; in Lazio as tonnarelli.

How I serve it

Its versatility is a calling card, so think of it as a handmade substitute for spaghetti. Of my many experiments and experiences with it, I had my most memorable version at a restaurant in the backwaters of Abruzzo, where it was served with zucchini, saffron, and pancetta. It's this kind of simple, vegetable-focused preparation that I favor, though let us not forget its spiritual bond with lamb (page 224) and other ragùs of varying composition.

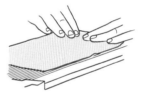

1   Prepare your selected egg-based dough (pages 18, 22, and 26–31) and follow the instructions for rolling and sheeting (pages 32–33).

2   Lightly dust a wooden cutting board with OO flour. Line a sheet pan with parchment paper and lightly dust with semolina.

3   Lay your sheet(s) of pasta on the work surface. Use a knife to cut your pasta into 8 by 9-inch sheets, removing the scraps from the unclean edges (save them for soup). Cover the sheets with plastic wrap or a kitchen towel.

4   Place one pasta sheet on your work surface. Lightly dust both sides of the sheet with OO flour. A typical chitarra has two sides with strings arranged at two widths. Lay your sheet over the chitarra strings on the narrower side. Press your rolling pin into the sheet, moving back and forth while applying enough pressure so the strings cut through the pasta. (This requires more force than you might expect.)

5   Gather the strands and generously dust them with OO flour. Gently shake to separate, curl the batch into a nest, and place it on the prepared sheet pan.

6   Repeat with the remaining sheets.

7   Let the pasta dry for 20 to 30 minutes at room temperature. If not using right away, cover the sheet pan with plastic wrap and refrigerate for up to 24 hours.

Extruded

Bucatini

Among certain pasta-loving circles, bucatini is the only true threat to spaghetti's dominance. Part of its appeal is directly related to its most famous dish, bucatini all'amatriciana (page 234), and part of it may simply be the charm of spaghetti with a hole through the center. While it's a fixture in Lazio, it can be found throughout the south, notably as a frequent companion to Sicily's pasta con le sarde (page 249).

1   Line a sheet pan with parchment paper and generously dust with semolina. Follow the recipe for extruded dough (page 41).

2   When the machine has warmed and the pasta is properly extruding, gently pull on the pasta to ensure that it comes out evenly in a straight line (you want to avoid the pasta curling as it emerges from the extruder) and lightly dust with semolina.

3   Use a bench scraper to cut the pasta into 18-inch lengths, then curl into a horseshoe shape and place in a single layer on the prepared sheet pan.

4   Let the pasta dry for 2 to 6 hours, until it has very little give and has semihardened. If not using right away, cover the sheet pan with plastic wrap and refrigerate for up to 36 hours.

Where it's found

Countrywide, but notably in Lazio, Campania, and Sicily.

How I serve it

With classic red sauce, traditionally in all'amatriciana (page 234) and pasta con le sarde (page 249), or with heartier ragùs.

Casarecce

I can't separate casarecce from a single dish served in a tiny restaurant called Trattoria I Rizzari on the Sicilian coast just south of Catania: a brothy, briny fresh tomato sauce with sweet shrimp no bigger than a quarter, and fresh mint. It was only after this dish burrowed into my memory that I began cooking with casarecce. While popular throughout the south, the shape—which roughly translates to "homemade"—is most frequently encountered in Sicily, where it's often paired with seafood.

1   Line a sheet pan with parchment paper and generously dust with semolina. Follow the recipe for extruded dough (page 41).

2   When the machine has warmed and the pasta is properly extruding, use a bench scraper to cut the pasta into 3-inch pieces and place in a single layer on the prepared sheet pan.

3   Let the pasta dry for 2 to 6 hours, until it has very little give and has semihardened. If not using right away, cover the sheet pan with plastic wrap and refrigerate for up to 36 hours.

Where it's found

Sicily, primarily.

How I serve it

In sauces that incorporate seafood, in simple red sauce, and with pesto, whether Genovese (page 178) or Trapanese (page 248).

Linguine

While linguine tends to get short shrift, it's more than just a stand-in for spaghetti. For me, the shape differentiates itself by offering a bit more bite and heft. Linguine originates in Liguria, where it's sometimes called trenette, and is a common stand-in for trofie in pesto al Genovese (page 178).

1   Line a sheet pan with parchment paper and generously dust with semolina. Follow the recipe for extruded dough (page 41).

2   When the machine has warmed and the pasta is properly extruding, gently pull on the pasta to ensure that it comes out evenly in a straight line (you want to avoid the pasta curling as it emerges from the extruder) and lightly dust with semolina.

3   Use a bench scraper to cut the pasta into 18-inch lengths, then portion into nests and place in a single layer on the prepared sheet pan.

4   Let the pasta dry for 2 to 6 hours, until it has very little give and has semihardened. If not using right away, cover the sheet pan with plastic wrap and refrigerate for up to 36 hours.

Where it's found
Countrywide.

How I serve it
I tend to call on linguine in dishes that employ seafood, whether it's clams (page 165) or a red sauce kicked up with plenty of anchovy (page 280).

Mafaldine

This dense, ribbon-shaped pasta with ruffled edges (think of it as a more toothsome pappardelle) is said to have been created in honor of Princess Mafalda of Savoy shortly after her birth, in 1902, but its exact origin is unknown.

1   Line a sheet pan with parchment paper and generously dust with semolina. Follow the recipe for extruded dough (page 41).

2   When the machine has warmed and the pasta is properly extruding, gently pull on the pasta to ensure that it comes out evenly in a straight line (you want to avoid the pasta curling as it emerges from the extruder) and lightly dust with semolina.

3   Use a bench scraper to cut the pasta into 18-inch lengths, then portion into nests and place in a single layer on the prepared sheet pan.

4   Let the pasta dry for 2 to 6 hours, until it has very little give and has semihardened. If not using right away, cover the sheet pan with plastic wrap and refrigerate for up to 36 hours.

Where it's found
While not exactly ubiquitous, it can be found bootwide.

How I serve it
I've gladly pigeonholed myself into serving mafaldine one way (page 319), but really any sauce you'd want to get caught in their grooves without obscuring them is a great fit.

Rigatoni

Big, bold, sauce-catching, rigatoni is the rough-and-tumble alternative to spaghetti's fine-stranded refinement. They both are synonymous with classic pomodoro sauce, but rigatoni brings a kind of jovial charisma to the dish. Like bucatini, rigatoni has a strong presence in Lazio but is a more widespread fixture in the south.

Where it's found
Countrywide, but especially prevalent in Sicily.

How I serve it
Exclusively with red sauce (page 289).

1   Line a sheet pan with parchment paper and generously dust with semolina. Follow the recipe for extruded dough (page 41).

2   When the machine has warmed and the pasta is properly extruding, use a bench scraper to cut the pasta into 2-inch pieces and place in a single layer on the prepared sheet pan.

3   Let the pasta dry for 2 to 6 hours, until it has very little give and has semihardened. If not using right away, cover the sheet pan with plastic wrap and refrigerate for up to 36 hours.

Spaghetti

Is there anything more emblematic of Italy's greatest food than spaghetti? Our childhood cravings and wanderlust for Italy are all captured in the twirl of a forkful. While string-like pasta made from semolina that is dried before cooking dates back to at least the ninth century, spaghetti (at least its name) is fairly young. Its moniker is commonly attributed to the poet Antonio Vivano, who aptly pointed out that spaghetti look like "little strings."

Where it's found
Countrywide.

How I serve it
As this book proves, there are very few things spaghetti doesn't go with.

1   Line a sheet pan with parchment paper and generously dust with semolina. Follow the recipe for extruded dough (pages 41).

2   When the machine has warmed and the pasta is properly extruding, gently pull on the pasta to ensure that it comes out evenly in a straight line (you want to avoid the pasta curling as it comes out of the extruder) and lightly dust with semolina.

3   Use a bench scraper to cut the spaghetti into 18-inch lengths, then curl into a horseshoe shape and place in one layer on the prepared sheet pan.

4   Let the pasta dry for 2 to 6 hours, until it has very little give and has semihardened. If not using right away, cover the sheet pan with plastic wrap and refrigerate for up to 36 hours.

Penne

Of the big three tubular pastas (penne, ziti, rigatoni) penne has suffered to find a real footing in the modern hierarchy of store-bought shapes. Perhaps its diagonally cut ends, which recall the shoulders on a Joan Collins suit, have always rooted penne to the 1980s for me. Or maybe it's pasta primavera, that circus show of a '70s dish that ultimately memorialized it as a thing of the past. Either way, part of penne's charm is that it is blissfully outmoded, which is why it's right at home in alla vodka.

Where it's found
Countrywide.

How I serve it
Like ziti, the shape really belongs to one dish for me, and that is, of course, penne alla vodka (page 155).

1   Line a sheet pan with parchment paper and generously dust with semolina. Follow the recipe for extruded dough (page 41).

2   When the machine has warmed and the pasta is properly extruding, use a bench scraper to cut the pasta into 2½-inch pieces and place in a single layer on the prepared sheet pan.

3   Let the pasta dry for 2 to 6 hours, until it has very little give and has semihardened. If not using right away, cover the sheet pan with plastic wrap and refrigerate for up to 36 hours.

Ziti

Traditionally served at weddings in Sicily and Campania (the name is a plural abbreviation of maccheroni di zita, or "bride's macaroni"), the tubular pasta is a narrower version of rigatoni and can be either ridged or smooth.

Where it's found
Countrywide, but most frequently in the south.

How I serve it
I've very rarely used ziti outside the Italian American classics, perhaps mostly because the shape will always be, for me, synonymous with one dish—baked ziti (page 154)—and why compete?

1   Line a sheet pan with parchment paper and generously dust with semolina. Follow the recipe for extruded dough (page 41).

2   When the machine has warmed and the pasta is properly extruding, use a bench scraper to cut the pasta into 2½-inch pieces and place in a single layer on the prepared sheet pan.

3   Let the pasta dry for 2 to 6 hours, until it has very little give and has semihardened. If not using right away, cover the sheet pan with plastic wrap and refrigerate for up to 36 hours.

How to Cook Pasta

Cook Pasta Like a Cook

The day I bounded off the plane in Italy as a soon-to-be apprentice, I assumed that the most difficult work ahead of me was learning how to make pasta, not cook it. After all, how hard could it be to boil, drain, sauce, and serve? What I learned very quickly was that the word "drain" had no use in an Italian kitchen, that boiling is only one part of the cooking process, that "sauce" without pasta water is not sauce at all, and that no matter how well made your actual pasta is, there are about a dozen ways to ruin it.

I, like most Americans, assumed that cooking pasta meant boiling it and that pasta and sauce were separate considerations, combined briefly, stirred together, and served. But cooking pasta is not about boiling it. It's about the marriage of sauce and pasta in the pan over heat, whether it be red sauce, ragù, or a simple combination of butter and pasta water. It's this "marriage ceremony," as my mentor Tony Mantuano calls it (the Italians call it mantecare, which means "to combine or mingle"), that is the most difficult part of the cooking process. It requires that you engage all—or at least four—of your senses. You have to think, and act, like a pasta cook.

By Touch

How do you know when your pasta is ready to go into the pan? If you watch my pasta cooks on the line, you'll see them constantly taking the pasta out of the water to check the texture, whether it's breaking a strand of linguine in half to inspect its interior or pinching the seams on tortelli to test if they've begun to soften. Touch also extends to determining texture by how pasta feels when you taste it. Tasting for texture throughout the cooking process is indispensable, particularly with extruded and dried pastas. The difference between very al dente (which is the point you want to remove your pasta from the water) and al dente is often about 20 seconds, and the difference between al dente and overcooked once the pasta is in the pan can happen equally fast.

Touch continues its important role once your pasta is in the pan. In the recipes, you'll read my advice to add more pasta water to a sauce if it's "tight." You can determine this both by sight and by how the pan or tongs feel in your hand. A "tight" sauce will not glide. When you feel a slight hint of resistance, which will certainly happen a couple of times during the marriage, add a tiny bit of pasta water to loosen up the sauce and keep tossing until you find that friction-free ease.

By Sight

Watching your pan is a given, but knowing what to look for isn't. How do you know, for instance, that your sauce is emulsified? In the case of a pasta water–and–butter sauce, a proper sauce will allow the pasta to move easily in the pan and will coat the pasta with a glossy sheen. If you add too much pasta water, that gloss will begin to dull and your sauce will thin and pool in the pan, losing its essential cling. You can always correct course by dumping a bit of pasta water out of the pan, or by adding a bit more butter and continuously tossing to re-emulsify.

Marrying a red sauce has slightly different visual cues. When it's too tight, it will cling to the sides of the pan and clump up as you toss it with the pasta. You want it to be thin enough to coat the pasta but not so thin that it's pooling at the bottom of the pan. The same is true for a ragù; it should become almost gravy-like when combined with

starchy pasta water, helping it bind to the shape. Too much water, though, and you'll see it immediately: the meat will begin to separate out from the sauce and become coarse, sticking to the bottom of the pan rather than moving with the sauce in a fluid motion. Too little water and your ragù will be cakey and dry and similarly difficult to move in the pan.

By Sound

While sight and touch can get you 90 percent of the way to the altar, so to speak, what tells you a pasta is ready to plate is the sound it makes in the pan as you toss it. Every pasta chef has a way of describing it to young cooks, and in a busy, loud kitchen, it takes a meditative focus not to miss it. To that end, I like to think of it as akin to the sound water makes when gently lapping a shoreline—a calming, uniform sloshing sound. If you're using tongs or a wooden spoon, the sound is similar. If you can't hear it in your mind's ear, but you can recall making a box of Kraft mac and cheese as a kid, it's not all that different from the sound of stirring that macaroni when the combination of powdered cheese, butter, and milk became one in the pot.

By Taste

When a pasta is properly married, it takes on the flavor of the sauce. Remove a piece from the cooking pot and taste it on its own—the savory, bready flavors of the pasta itself should be in relief. But in a properly married dish, the sauce should burrow into the pasta, so much so that if you were to rinse that strand clean, you would still taste the sauce.

The most common question a chef will ask a cook when a dish does not come out of the kitchen properly is, "Did you taste your food?" As you're marrying pasta in the pan, don't forget that you're adding salted, starchy water as you go. Be sure to pause to taste your sauce; if it's starting to edge into "too salty" territory—which can happen with sauces that contain anchovies, cured meats, or aged cheeses—alternate your use of pasta water and regular hot water.

It's been a few years since I've cooked on a line night after night tossing pans. After twenty years of it, I'm about one pan away from shoulder surgery (turns out repetitive motion does get to you eventually). But I still stand at the end of the line, expediting, watching the pasta cooks move in the kitchen. The instinctual choreography of these four senses in a fast-paced kitchen is never not a sight to behold.

Rules to Cook By

I've never been a fan of rules. If I were, I probably wouldn't have ended up in this career. But in pasta cooking, there are several I consider indisputable and essential—rules so easy to follow, so logical, even I don't mind living by them.

Do not put oil in the water.

I wish I could go back in time and reprimand the first person who put this advice to writing. Please do not do this. You want your pasta to absorb the sauce; adding oil pitches a barrier that prevents that from happening.

Do add salt to your pot . . . and then add some more.

The precise ratio of salt to water is 2 tablespoons salt for every quart of water. But if you, like me, are not inclined to measure it out when you're cooking, just remember not to skimp. Add enough salt so the amount makes you just slightly uncomfortable. Taste it, and if you can bear to swallow a spoonful down, add some more.

Mind the temperature of your water.

While most pastas should be dropped into a hard boil (do not turn the temp down once it's in), filled pastas, especially those with delicate fillings that can curdle, such as ones based on ricotta, mascarpone, or other soft cheeses, should go into water that's at a gentle boil. A hard boil also runs the risk of popping filled pastas open in the water since, if made correctly, they will be quite fragile.

Always cook your pasta a little less than you think you should.

The back of your standard-issue pasta box will tell you to boil dried pasta for between 8 and 11 minutes, but my advice is always to take what is on the box and subtract 2 minutes. And for my extruded pasta, I recommend between 5 and 8 minutes. What most home cooks forget is that you will continue to cook your pasta in the pan, so you want to be sure that you're removing it from the pot on the very al dente end of al dente. (For fresh pasta, it's a bit different; cook times vary by shape, but you're generally only boiling it for 1 to 4 minutes, until it just begins to soften.)

Do not drain your pasta.

You want to remove it from the water with a pasta basket, spider, or tongs, so some of the water goes into your sauce-filled pan with the pasta itself. The reserved pasta water is also important, as it plays a multipurpose role in emulsifying, loosening, and/or seasoning your sauce.

Use pasta cooking water and unsalted water.

While pasta cooking water is called for as a component of nearly every sauce in this book, you need to mind your salt levels. If you're working with a sauce that is based on ingredients with a high level of salinity, such as anchovies or cured meats, alternate the use of pasta cooking water and fresh hot water during the marriage.

Do not put too much sauce in the pan.

One of the most common mistakes that home cooks make is adding the pasta to the full volume of sauce they have prepared. Each recipe calls for a specific volume of sauce to be added to the pan that you'll use to marry your pasta. Remember that if the sauce seems scant at first, you'll be adding pasta water to it, increasing its volume, and that your sauce should coat the pasta, not smother it. You can always add a bit more sauce if needed, but it's much harder to subtract. (Note, too, that the recipes will often yield excess sauce because they are best made at a specific volume, and because they are labor intensive. Refrigerate the surplus for later in the week or freeze it for a future dinner. Whoever complained about too much leftover bolognese?)

Do not let the temperature of your sauce-marrying pan drop too low.

The inclination among many cooks is to turn off the heat under the pan when they marry their pasta and sauce. Do not. Keep your sauce on low to begin and turn it up to medium or medium-high when you're ready to add the pasta. Marrying the pasta at a higher temp speeds up the process without overcooking the pasta.

Toss, toss, toss.

You have to be constantly moving the pasta while it's marrying. If you have more than two servings in the pan, use tongs to keep the pasta flowing around the pan in a constant motion, gently picking it up and turning it over to coat.

Don't add cheese until the end.

If you add cheese too early and over heat, it doesn't absorb properly. Instead, it will clump up and distribute unevenly. When the sauce and pasta are almost fully married, take the pan off the heat and add the cheese slowly, toss a few times to integrate, and serve.

Building a Pasta Tool Kit

Chefs have a tool kit, or set of go-to, pan-seasonal ingredients that appear with great frequency across their cooking. In part it is a matter of comfort zone—of returning to ingredients you have a natural attraction to, or a mastery of, as a means of creating a foundation from which you can iterate. Pair those core ingredients with technique and you can define a chef's "style." But this isn't—and shouldn't be—the domain of professionals alone. A "style" is what a home cook should aspire to as well, and that begins with not only building a tool kit of ingredients in general but also drilling down deeper to determine the brand of each one that best suits your taste. My tool kit has certainly changed over the years. Once I left fine dining, the tools in mine were a whole lot less expensive and were pared back, as my mode of cooking became focused on exploring the depth and diversity of fewer staples, not more.

To that end, the following ingredients, plus access to seasonal produce, will get you most of the way through the recipes in this book. And while I have mentioned the brands that I prefer, experiment—play with different finishing olive oils, tomato brands, hell, even make your own ricotta—so your tool kit is, first and foremost, a reflection of your personal taste.

Anchovies: Anchovy fillets packed in olive oil are an essential part of any Italian cook's tool kit, but not just for flavoring seafood pastas or vegetables. In my cooking, anchovies are used as a building block for depth of flavor in braises, sauces, and more. While my preferred brands are Armatore and Euromar, they can be hard to find. The more widely available Agostino Recca brand is a good substitute.

Black pepper: Without black pepper there would be no gricia, no cacio e pepe, and no carbonara, and properly three-quarters of my recipes would be missing that spiciness and levity that only freshly ground black pepper can deliver.

Calabrian chiles: The challenge with Calabrian chiles in oil is to abstain from using them in literally every dish. Their sweet, smoky, hot profile is more than just a key ingredient in my diavola sauce (page 149). In small doses they can take the place of dried red chile flakes in everything from linguine and clams to nearly any vegetable dish. I use Tutto Calabria brand.

Dried red chile flakes: While Calabrian chiles give a dish a potent, deep heat, chile flakes impart a subtler background heat that acts similar to salt in its ability to amplify other flavors in a dish. You will find them called for as flakes and ground.

European-style butter: You will find a number of pasta recipes that call on a simple butter pan sauce, golden and foamy butter, brown butter, or some combination thereof. When I call for butter, it's shorthand for unsalted, high-fat European-style butter.

Extra-virgin olive oil: For all-purpose use in the kitchen (to cure tomatoes or start a ragù, for instance), I look to Monini or Frantoia brand; both are inexpensive and widely available and offer a mild middle way between fruity and green. Viragi Polifemo, made from Tonda Iblea olives from Sicily's Chiaramonte Gulfi, and winemaker Paolo Bea's rich, earthy Umbrian olive oil are my most-used "finishing oils"—that is, what I use to flavor a dish after it has been plated or to make salad dressings. Each has the right balance of sweet, herbal, and spicy. But I am constantly playing around—choosing an oil that is more buttery to finish a steak or more green to finish fish. Olive oil has a seemingly infinite spectrum of profiles, and part of what makes cooking Italian food exciting is being able to constantly experiment with it.

Fennel (bulbs, seeds, fronds, pollen): What *can't* fennel do? Second only to garlic, fennel is the one vegetable I could not live without. I use bulbs raw, roasted, sautéed, and grilled; fennel seed in ragù and other sauces, braises, and marinades; fronds as garnish or in pestos for their aroma and mild flavor; and Antica Drogheria Francioni fennel pollen, which has become such a fixture of my cooking that it's referred to as "magic dust" in the kitchen, on everything from grilled steak to soft-serve gelato.

Flat-leaf parsley, basil, and mint: This is easily my holy trinity of soft herbs. All three show up a lot in my pastas as a means of adding freshness and aroma to a finished dish.

Garlic: Garlic is the foundation of everything that tastes good to me—my one and only, forever ingredient. It is also one of the most difficult to wrangle. How to use it, which means how to cut it, how to cook it, and how to know when too much is too much, has kept me engaged and curious for decades. Every time I think I understand it, it surprises me anew.

Lemons and oranges: Acid is essential to my food—so much so that some might say I take it to the extreme. Citrus peel, perhaps even more than the juice, is a staple. In fact, when I want to add a floral element or perceived acidity to a ragù, it often comes by way of finely diced peel sans the pith (important!).

Marjoram: When we think of Italian food—or at least of Italian American food—we think of oregano. But I am a bigger fan of its sibling of sorts. Marjoram is typically more floral and a bit less pungent and domineering than oregano. Like all of the herbs I use in my pasta dishes, marjoram is often the ingredient I add last to preserve its freshness and aroma.

Nutmeg: A lot of home cooks might be surprised to know how important nutmeg is to northern Italian cooking. It is grated into meat fillings, cheese fillings, and dough for passatelli (page 189) and cooked into ragùs and grated over them. I use it just as frequently, both in sauces and as a finishing ingredient. Make sure you have on hand whole nutmegs, not ground nutmeg, and a Microplane grater.

Parmigiano-reggiano: Parmigiano, like garlic, is not one ingredient but many when you factor in the producer, its age, and how you integrate it in a dish. I use it in myriad ways for both its savory depth of flavor and its texture—specifically, the crystallized crunch it lends when coarsely grated or shaved. I keep a 24-month-aged cheese on hand for all-purpose use and a rich, almost buttery 5-year when I want the cheese to be the star of the dish.

Pecorino romano: Pecorino is just as ubiquitous as parmigiano in my cooking, but its flavor profile is totally different. It's brinier, grassier, and mineral to parm's buttery and earthy. When to use one over the other really comes down to the dish. Subconsciously, I tend to use pecorino in dishes that feel more southern in profile, whereas parmigiano finds its way into those that feel richer, and thus more northern. I like Fulvi pecorino romano, aged between 9 and 12 months.

Red wine vinegar: Although red wine vinegar does not make it into my finished pastas, it is a fixture in my approach to vegetable cookery, which you'll see firsthand in the Contorni chapter. I use only one brand and have been using it for at least ten years: Trucioleto from Emilia-Romagna, which is really high in acid but still preserves the juicy, red-fruit character of a wine you'd actually want to drink.

Ricotta: Ricotta is a fixture of my filled pastas, in doses small and large, as a means of getting a smooth, creamy consistency. But ricotta is about as versatile as any cheese gets. In a nod to my hometown, I've used Calabro hand-dipped ricotta for the better part of two decades. Make sure whatever ricotta you use is hand-dipped, which has a higher fat content and is airier than the regular whole-milk ricotta and tends to be smoother and less dense thanks to the way it's handled. And more importantly, never, ever buy anything but whole-milk ricotta, which has the creaminess (both in texture and flavor) that makes it suitable for binding ingredients in a filling.

Rosemary: Second only to marjoram in the hard-herbs family, rosemary makes it into almost all of my cures, marinades, and braises, and I use it to finish pastas like the chickpea pappardelle on page 338.

Salt: Diamond Crystal kosher salt is my can't-live-without kitchen salt. It's important to pick one brand and stick with it; you will get used to the amount you need of that particular salt when flavoring dishes or salting pasta water. (In other words, not all salts have the same levels of perceptible salinity.) For finishing, I use Ravida sea salt from Trapani or Maldon when I can't get Ravida.

San Marzano tomatoes: When it comes to tomatoes, what brand you use is crucial. Not only is there plenty of false marketing around San Marzano tomatoes, but their flavor varies dramatically by brand and can alter the flavor of not just red sauces but also ragùs and braises. I've been using La Valle DOP San Marzano tomatoes—both their whole peeled tomatoes and their tomato passata, or pureed and strained tomatoes— for as long as I can remember for their balance of sweetness and acidity, the latter of which is on the high side compared with other brands. I also like Gustarosso DOP San Marzano tomatoes, which have a touch more sweetness than La Valle but the same acidic backbone.

Spanish onions: If you're in the business of building flavor, you'd be hard-pressed to do that well without yellow Spanish onions, commonly labeled "yellow onions," in the wings. I use them to build stocks, braises, and of course all on their own, whether roasted, grilled, or raw.

Tomato paste: Tomato paste gets a bad rap. In fact, I didn't use it until I cooked what would become rigatoni diavola (page 289) at home for the first time. When used sparingly, I've come to appreciate high-quality tomato paste (again, quality can really vary; I like Mutti Double Concentrated) for its ability to add depth of flavor.

FAQ

Can I substitute store-bought dried pasta for the extruded shapes?

Absolutely. I do not expect everyone who picks up this book to run out and buy a $2,000 pasta machine. I've included my favorite dried pasta brands on page 39 for this very reason. For cook times, I generally recommend subtracting 2 minutes from what's indicated on the box.

When cooking for two people, can a recipe that yields four to six servings be scaled down?

All of the recipes yield either four to six or six to eight servings (3½ to 5½ ounces per serving, with some exceptions). This is not just because I see pasta as a communal affair but also because making pasta requires a fair amount of labor. I always prefer a recipe that will yield some leftovers versus one that will yield just enough. The easiest way to scale down the recipes while ensuring you aren't compromising their integrity is to cut them cleanly in half. Start with the finished recipe and then work backward—cutting your dough recipe in half and thus the yield of the pasta shape in half.

What does "q.b." mean?

You didn't read the preface, did you? Well, "q.b." stands for quanto basta, or "as needed." In practical terms, I use it to denote an ingredient, most often a seasoning, that does not have an exact measurement and instead should be added to suit the taste of the cook.

What's with the tamis obsession?

You'll see me call for a tamis, or fine-mesh metal sieve, for fillings that rely on either ricotta or vegetable purees—or both. It helps add a textural consistency and refinement to them.

When a recipe calls for olive oil, what kind?

This is always extra-virgin olive oil, and unless otherwise specified, it should be your go-to all-purpose olive oil (see page 135). But be sure to have your finishing oils close by your side.

Why be so careful not to brown garlic?

Garlic can quickly turn bitter in the pan if exposed to too much heat. I am always looking to pull out the sweetness and pungency of garlic and to avoid the acrid flavor of browned garlic, which can easily overpower a dish.

Why chop pith–free citrus peels and not just use a trusty Microplane?

Ask any cook who has ever worked with me and you'll be met with an eye roll. Prep PTSD aside, though, chopping makes a difference. The Microplane yields zest that's hard to manage: it's wetter and clumps, and pith can, and will, find its way into the dish. Chopping simply offers more control. Make sure you remove all of the pith by taking a small, sharp knife to the underside of a peel to carefully shear it—and then chop as finely as you can.

When the recipe calls for "finely chopped," how fine is that?

I've been told that my "fine" is really what the rest of the world calls "minced." Indeed it's true that whenever I call for finely chopped, I mean *very* finely chopped.

Why put vegetables for a ragù through a meat grinder?

As long as I can remember, I have never liked large pieces of cooked vegetables in stews and ragù. But the flavor that a vegetable base, or soffritto, adds is foundational, so I've always compromised by grinding those vegetables into a pulp, squeezing out the water, and then cooking them into the ragù until they effectively dissolve.

Why the love of "whipped" ricotta?

Like the tamis, whipping ricotta is also about textural consistency, though of a different kind. This is my way to get a smooth, silky texture from the ricotta—to will the chalkiness out of it. The technique is all about bringing new intrigue to a familiar ingredient. To whip it, put the ricotta into a food processor and pulse just until it is as smooth as cake frosting and has a sheen, being careful not to process it longer or it will break. I always recommend processing a batch larger than what I need for a recipe. Spoon the excess into a pastry bag and pipe it onto toast or use it on desserts. I assure you it won't go to waste.

What kind of parmigiano and pecorino is best to stock?

If I ever call for an ingredient in a general way—like olive oil, salt, or tomatoes—and you have any doubt as to what you should use or buy, refer to my tool kit on page 135. In the case of the big two, when not otherwise specified, I use parmigiano aged a minimum of 2 years and pecorino romano aged a minimum of 9 months. Be sure to buy both in large chunks and grate right before serving or during your prep to ensure you're getting the maximum flavor.

What kind of mozzarella is best?

Always, always buy cow's milk mozzarella (aka fiore di latte) stored in salted water. Mozzarella that is not packed in water can be so rubbery it squeaks when you bite into it.

When the recipes call for salt, what kind of salt?

Unless I call for "sea salt," "salt" always refers specifically to Diamond Crystal kosher salt, the brand I've used since I first stepped foot in a professional kitchen.

Exactly how much salt should be added to the pot of water for cooking pasta?

I adhere to a ratio of about 2 tablespoons salt for every quart of water.

Why should pasta fillings taste salty? And *how* salty should they taste?

When you cook a filled pasta, the dough acts as a natural buffer to the seasoning of the filling. I've found that in order for the finished dish to be balanced, you have to start out with a filling that tips just slightly into salty territory. Exactly how salty? Just when you feel as though it's properly seasoned—that is, the moment you'd happily eat it right from the mixing bowl—take it just one step further.

Why salt an ice-water bath?

You'll see this throughout the book when greens are called for in a filling, for basil in pesto, and for a number of vegetables in the Contorni chapter. Salted ice water has a dual purpose: it helps the greens retain their color after you've blanched them and it's an extra insurance plan, when it comes to seasoning.

What's with the "cold and cubed" butter?

This is about both consistency in instruction and in the recipe itself. Whenever you're making a sauce that calls for butter, you want to emulsify the sauce gradually, swirling that cube of butter around the edge of the pan to integrate it. All of these recipes are written to accommodate for the time it takes to integrate your butter slowly.

What's the difference between "golden brown and foamy" butter and "brown" butter?

You will find a few different indications of doneness for butter depending on what you're trying to achieve. Most recipes that call for brown butter will instruct you to cook it only until it is golden brown and foamy, meaning before it begins to turn dark brown. A select few will call for brown butter that has gone beyond its active foamy phase and begins to take on a more burnished hue. The differences come down to flavor: As butter continues to brown it becomes sweeter and nuttier, which is great for drizzling over a finished dish in moderation but not in volume. I call for each accordingly.

When checking the closure of filled pastas for doneness, what are you looking for?

Many cooks make the mistake of pulling filled pastas from the water when the thinnest part of the pasta is done rather than the thickest. That can result in the closure being tough and not texturally aligned with the rest of the shape. Make sure it's tender but not limp and floppy.

Why crush tomatoes by hand and not just buy canned crushed tomatoes?

I always buy whole, peeled canned tomatoes, as I want to ensure I am getting the whole tomato to work with so I can control the texture. When you crush by hand, make sure to get the tomatoes as smooth as you can and remove any tough pieces of core. Oh, and if your can has a piece of basil in it, make sure to remove and discard it. Its job is done.

What's with seasoning sauces at the end?

Even a sauce that's cooked on low for just 30 minutes will lose some of its volume. If you season too early, you may end up with a sauce that becomes salty once it concentrates. Seasoning at the end of cooking gives you more control: you can always up the seasoning, but it's hard to take it away.

What to do with leftover sauce or ragù?

Almost every recipe in this book that calls for a sauce or ragù will yield more than needed for the finished recipe. That's intentional. I've always felt that given the considerable effort these sauces require, having just enough is disappointing. All of the sauces can stay for 3 to 5 days in the fridge or can be frozen for a future use. Make pasta again later in the week, cook your eggs in leftover red sauce (i.e., in purgatorio), add to brodo, use as a base for a soup—there are plenty of ways to make the most of all your hard work.

Italian American Classics

What exactly is Italian American food? Is it defined by its calling-card dishes: baked ziti with mozzarella applied with such abandon that no casserole dish is quite capable of corralling its glut; spaghetti topped with meatballs the size of ready-to-pick summer peaches; and cheese ravioli smothered in red sauce, the great cornerstone of red-checkered craving? Is Italian American food simply regional Italian food run through the American comfort mill until it has emerged at twice the size, with twice the sauce, three times the meat, and at least four times the nostalgia? Or is it a cuisine best understood by thinking of it as primarily American food? (For me the answer is some combination of all of the above, but more on that in a second.)

Like the other Italian diaspora cuisines that emerged at the end of the nineteenth century and the beginning of the twentieth, Italian immigrants to America, most of them from the south of Italy, took what they believed to be the best of their traditions—the richer, more complicated dishes often served during holidays and on Sundays—and molded them to reflect their new communities. Gone was the Italian meal structure of antipasto, primo, and secondo, supplanted by the all-at-once American meal. Better access to affordable ingredients—meat, specifically—and the insatiable appetite of an ever-more-prosperous America continued to transform Italian food.

Take spaghetti and meatballs. In Abruzzo, for example, spaghetti alla chitarra are often paired with meatballs (pallottine here, polpettine elsewhere) so modest in size that they do little more than flavor the sauce. Their diminutiveness was not a sign of refinement; it was out of necessity, as meat was a luxury that many people in the country's south and its borderlands could not afford except on special occasions. My point is that "spaghetti and meatballs" can certainly be found in Italy, but none will approach the brashness of the Italian American version. This same super-size-it story applies to many of the genre's standards. Fettuccine Alfredo began as fettuccine al burro, a dish composed of butter, cheese, and pepper. Its induction into the Italian American canon began with an intrepid Roman restaurateur (yes, Alfredo) who, in an effort to appeal to American tourists, added enough cream and tableside flair to catapult the original dish into obscurity. And so it goes: a plate of fettuccine al burro soon becomes fettuccine al burro al panna al (fill in the blank). When the dish settles in America, it acquires all kinds of scandalous adulterations (peas! ham!) that render it ever richer. It's a story whose beginning, middle, and end is more, more—and, even, more.

But this evolution isn't all born of an attempt to pander to an American audience. It was, in its way, Italian immigrants celebrating a new abundance—a sort of joyous molding of Italian traditions to reflect a better position for those who had found their way here. How else would we have ended up with the kind of warm, theatrical atmosphere of the red-sauce joint? How else would the generosity of this experience ultimately change the way we eat in America? And how else, frankly, would I have ever become a chef?

Growing up, I wanted to be Italian. I was born in 1971 in Washington, D.C., and before a year was up, we'd decamped to New Haven, Connecticut, which is home to the state's largest population of Italian Americans. But in my house, it was either Jewish food or 1970s food: chopped liver, chicken Cumberland, and meat loaf that would practically turn to dust when you put a fork to it. My dinner table paled in comparison to just about anything I could find on Wooster Street. This stretch of town was bathed in red, white, and green and packed with pizza and calzone joints, an Italian-ice shop, and a bakery—all of them at once foreign and familiar. I was a notoriously picky eater, but there were very few things on Wooster Street I wouldn't eat, especially if it was stuffed with cheese and plastered in red sauce. It was my introduction to eating as a celebration, and to eating well and abundantly as an *event*.

It's no wonder, then, that the first thing I ever cooked wasn't my mother's brisket or kasha varnishkes, but pasta. Pasta with broccoli. Pasta with red sauce. Fettuccine Alfredo. By college it was penne all'arrabbiata. More than twenty-five years later, when I opened Lilia, the familiarity and the comfort of the ingredients in the Italian American tool kit—garlic, chiles, parsley, oregano, basil, tomatoes, and anchovies—felt exciting again. It was a homecoming of sorts, a trip back to something so simple and foundational that it was new again.

After years spent turning over every stone from north to south to understand regional Italian cuisine, I'd found a new kind of inspiration in the craftsmanship of an excellent red sauce and in the endless possibilities that a bowl of fettuccine with butter, parmigiano, and pepper can present. In a dish such as fettuccine Alfredo, which appears on the menu at Misi (though not by name and in its original fettuccine al burro form), three ingredients present dozens of choices. There are hundreds of parmigiano-reggiano producers, each making cheese that varies, sometimes widely. Which producer to use? Aged three years? Aged five years? And that's before you even get to the butter. A dish as simple as ravioli with red sauce can offer the same bounty of choices if you're willing to look closely. What variety of tomatoes should go into the sauce? Crushed or whole? Tomato paste or none? Wet Calabrian chiles or dried chile flakes?

The Italian American Hall of Fame is sometimes a victim of its own nostalgia. But if we're willing to consider our memories as an ingredient, and to look at each dish more objectively, these classics become a means of understanding both balance and the ingredients that are fundamental to regional Italian cooking. It's why I no longer recoil when my food is sometimes referred to as Italian American. You will not find spaghetti and meatballs or lasagna or penne alla vodka on any of my menus; my food is not Italian American in that sense. But the fact that two of the most beloved dishes at my restaurants—Lilia's mafaldine with pink peppercorns and parmigiano and Misi's fettuccine with buffalo's milk butter, pepper, and aged parmigiano—channel a familiar Italian American kind of comfort is not lost on me.

Think of the ten pasta recipes in this chapter, then, as an opportunity to reconsider dishes that have become so ingrained in our cultural memory that they feel as much American as they do Italian. These are some of the first pastas I learned how to cook, retooled here to be mini master classes in the basics.

On Red Sauce

How many times have you chopped garlic, thrown it into an oiled pan, dumped in a can of tomatoes, salted, simmered, and never had the urge to crack a book, Google a recipe, or even wonder, frankly, if there were a better way? (Be honest.) And how many of us have sated our craving with even the most flawed—chunky, watery, underseasoned, sweet, oregano bombed—red sauce?

Let's face it, how to make a great red sauce isn't exactly a frequent subject of study. But asking what makes a good one is a gateway to better cooking overall. And what makes a red sauce good? A balance of acid, sweetness, and spice, as well as having more than one sauce in your repertoire and knowing when to wield each. A few ground rules:

Choose a go-to tomato brand.

Each brand of peeled tomatoes will vary in sweetness and acidity. Find a go-to (my favorites are mentioned on page 137) and use it as a baseline for all your red sauce recipes, adjusting the seasoning and heat q.b.

Choose a "house" olive oil.

Select a brand that leans neither too grassy nor too peppery. You want an oil without a single dominant note so you have more control over your flavors. I like Monini or Frantoia for all-purpose, everyday cooking oil.

Use tomato paste judiciously.

I spent about ten years paste-abstinent until I started cooking at home; now I use it sparingly in ragùs and red sauces to add a layer of depth.

How you cut and cook your garlic matters.

Add whole cloves to garlic over low heat to soften and caramelize and you get sweetness. Slice or finely chop and sweat and you get pungency and that high-toned, hypnotic aroma that has lured so many of us off sidewalks and into red-sauce restaurants. For my diavola sauce and 30-clove sauce, I cook garlic both ways to get the full spectrum of flavor that ingredient can offer. But for my simple sauce, I stick to sliced for bite and ease. And unlike so many of the Italians I learned from, I do not remove the garlic from the pan—I let it become part of the sauce.

Hell no, dried oregano.

It's personal, but dried oregano has never had a place in my kitchen, and while fresh oregano has a recurring role as an herb I use to finish dishes, I have never used it in sauces. It almost always overpowers, and a great red sauce is ultimately about nuance. I do, however, drop basil into some of my sauces at the end, stirring it in so it can steep for a few minutes before I discard it.

Do not—I repeat, do not—overcook your sauce.

I am not sure where the practice originated, but somewhere along the way people began cooking red sauce like ragù. Do not do that. Once everything is in the pan, you do not need to cook your sauce for more than 30 minutes—45 minutes maximum—over very low heat. Leave the sauce over the heat too long and it not only reduces too much and becomes cloying, but its flavors can caramelize, dulling out the acidity and brightness that is the tomato's gift to us all.

Simple Red Sauce

An everyday, hardworking red sauce should require no more than a small grocery haul and 30 minutes to make. It should also be soul satisfying and should not include too much of any one thing. It should be as good on rigatoni as it is as a bit player in lasagna, and it should leave you with enough left over to ladle into a braise. In other words, this should be the sauce you can make in a pinch, the one that never gets tossed out, and the one you crave when those two words—*red sauce*—are on your mind. It is also the sauce to master first—the one you use to find your go-to tomato brand, your "house" olive oil, and the precise amount of garlic you like. It should be personal, so use mine not as an end point but as a trailhead.

1   Place a large, heavy sauce pot or Dutch oven over low heat. Add the oil and garlic and cook gently until aromatic but without color, 30 seconds to 1 minute. Add the chile flakes q.b.

2   Add the tomatoes and their juice and cook over low heat until the flavors are well blended, 25 to 30 minutes. You are not looking to reduce the mixture, just to bring the flavors together. Season with salt q.b.

3   Set aside off the heat until ready to use, or let cool, transfer to an airtight container, and refrigerate for up to 5 days or freeze for up to 1 month for another use.

Yields 2.25kg / 9 cups

75g / ⅓ cup extra-virgin olive oil
40g / 8 cloves garlic, thinly sliced
Dried red chile flakes, q.b.
3 large (794g / 28 oz) cans
    whole San Marzano tomatoes,
    crushed by hand
Salt, q.b.

30-Clove Sauce

This one is for all the true garlic lovers out there. Thirty cloves, you say? I couldn't tell you how I came up with the number. My best guess is that back in my A Voce days, when this sauce originated, I threw a bunch of whole cloves in a pan, caramelized them, counted thirty, and stuck with that. This sauce began as an audit of everything I'd learned about cooking sauces in Italy—that is, to take the garlic out of the pan after lightly infusing the oil. It was also meant to be an updated take on the red sauces of my youth, which always leaned heavily on garlic and weren't afraid of sweetness. I wanted to channel that without the sauce becoming cloying and found the perfect sweetness via caramelized whole garlic cloves. I also add fennel seed, that essential ingredient in the Italian American pantry. The recipe might read over-the-top on paper, but it yields a versatile sauce that has become my true go-to.

---

1 Place a large, heavy sauce pot or Dutch oven over medium-low heat. Add the olive oil and whole garlic cloves and cook slowly until the garlic is light golden brown, caramelized, and soft enough to mash, 7 to 10 minutes.

2 Gently mash the garlic in the pot with a fork or the back of a spoon.

3 Add the sliced garlic to the pot, decrease the heat to low, and gently cook until aromatic but without color, 30 seconds to 1 minute.

4 Add the tomato paste and cook, stirring, until it starts to turn a deeper red and is well combined with the olive oil and garlic, 3 to 5 minutes.

5 Add the fennel seed and chile flakes, then add the tomatoes and their juice, stir to incorporate all of the ingredients, and cook until the flavors have blended and there is some viscosity to the sauce, 30 to 45 minutes. Season with salt q.b.

6 Stir in the basil and set aside off the heat until ready to use, then remove and discard the basil before using. Or let cool, then remove and discard the basil, transfer to an airtight container, and refrigerate for up to 5 days or freeze for up to 1 month for another use.

Yields 1.7kg / 7 cups

70g / 5 Tbsp olive oil
200g / 35 cloves garlic,
    30 cloves left whole and
    5 cloves thinly sliced
65g / ¼ cup tomato paste
7g / 1 Tbsp plus ¾ tsp
    fennel seed
4g / 2 tsp dried red chile flakes
2 large (794g / 28 oz) cans
    whole San Marzano
    tomatoes, crushed by hand
Salt, q.b.
1 bunch basil, leaves removed
    from stems

Diavola Sauce

As the name suggests, this sauce is all about heat. Not just the kind of dry-spice low buzz you get from your classic dried red chile flakes, but the fruity, smoky pungency of wet Calabrian chiles, which give it a depth that I haven't been able to match with any other red sauce. The base is similar to that of my 30-clove sauce, and while it isn't a utility player in quite the same way, it's the sauce I crave the most. There's a reason it was the first thing I decided to put on the menu at Lilia, and why it will remain there for as long as the restaurant is open.

1   Place a large, heavy sauce pot or Dutch oven over medium-low heat. Add the olive oil and whole garlic cloves and cook slowly until the garlic is light golden brown, caramelized, and soft enough to mash, 7 to 10 minutes.

2   Gently mash the garlic in the pot with a fork or the back of spoon.

3   Add the sliced garlic to the pot, decrease the heat to low, and cook gently until aromatic but without color, 30 seconds to 1 minute.

4   Add the tomato paste and cook, stirring, until the mixture starts to turn a deeper red and is well combined with the oil and garlic, 3 to 5 minutes.

5   Add the Calabrian chiles, chile flakes, and fennel seed, then add the tomatoes and their juice, stir to incorporate all of the ingredients, and cook until the flavors have blended, 30 to 45 minutes. Season with salt q.b.

6   Set aside off the heat until ready to use, or let cool, transfer to an airtight container, and refrigerate for up to 5 days or freeze for up to 1 month for another use.

Yields 1.6kg / 6½ cups

112g / ½ cup olive oil
70g / 14 cloves garlic, 10 cloves left whole and 4 cloves thinly sliced
113g / ¼ cup plus 3 Tbsp tomato paste
15g / 1 Tbsp crushed Calabrian chiles
4g / 2 tsp dried red chile flakes
7g / 1 Tbsp plus ½ tsp fennel seed
2 large (794g / 28 oz) cans whole San Marzano tomatoes, crushed by hand
Salt, q.b.

Fettuccine Alfredo

This was quite literally the only dish I'd eat as a young kid, and the first-ever dish I made—along with a Caesar salad, naturally—for the first-ever "dinner party" I hosted, at fifteen. After I started cooking professionally, I never thought about the dish again—until 2018, when I put a version of the original fettuccine Alfredo (aka fettuccine al burro) on my menu at Misi.

Before we get to how my take is different, let me tell you how it's the same. This is, and always should be, a recipe that celebrates two ingredients, butter and cheese, and boasts the two essential features of a great go-to pasta dish: it's comforting and it's simple. That doesn't mean that how you arrive at simplicity is simple, however. At the risk of getting too heady, this dish became an opportunity to turn over its two main ingredients by sourcing them from different places, animals, ages, and fat levels to figure out how to get the absolute most complexity, flavor, and texture from each. This dish is not so much in how you combine ingredients but rather in how you source them.

To that end, and after more trials than I care to admit, I ended on a combination of buffalo's milk butter, European-style cow's milk butter, a 2-year parmigiano in the sauce, and a 5-year parmigiano to finish. The buffalo's milk butter gives it a tang, while the cow's milk butter ensures the sauce emulsifies properly. It's the 5-year parm that really elevates the dish, giving it a cutting quality that acts as the counterbalance that traditional Alfredo doesn't have. Make sure you coarsely grate the 5-year parm so you get that textured, crystalline crunch. And don't be shy with the pepper.

---

1   Following the instructions for fettuccine on page 49, make 624g / 1 lb 6 oz with the pasta dough.

2   Bring a large pot of water to a boil over high heat. Generously salt the water.

3   Place a large sauté pan over low heat and add 2 to 3 ladles (115 to 170g / ½ to ¾ cup) pasta cooking water to the pan. Add both butters and swirl the contents of the pan to emulsify. Add the black pepper and stir to combine.

4   Add the fettuccine to the water and cook for 1 to 2 minutes, until tender but not soft.

5   Using tongs or a pasta basket, remove the pasta from the pot and transfer to the sauté pan. Turn the heat up to medium. Toss for 1 to 2 minutes to marry the pasta and sauce. Add 2 to 3 additional ladles (115 to 170g / ½ to ¾ cup) pasta cooking water and continue tossing to marry.

6   Remove from the heat. Gradually add the finely grated parmigiano while tossing to integrate. If the sauce begins to tighten, add a splash of pasta cooking water to loosen and continue tossing to integrate.

7   Divide the pasta into bowls. Garnish with the coarsely grated 5-year parmigiano and with pepper q.b.

Yields 4 to 6 servings

1 batch egg dough (page 18)
104g / 7 Tbsp plus 1 tsp
    unsalted buffalo's milk butter,
    cold and cubed
52g / 3½ Tbsp unsalted cow's
    milk butter, cold and cubed
50 grinds black pepper, plus
    more q.b.
231g / 2½ cups plus 1 Tbsp
    finely grated 2-year
    parmigiano-reggiano
120g / 1 cup plus rounded
    3 Tbsp coarsely grated
    5-year parmigiano-reggiano

Nota bene

If you can't find 5-year parmigiano, any parmigiano aged a minimum of two years will still be delicious. And, likewise, if you can't find buffalo's milk butter, using all cow's milk still yields a great dish.

Ravioli Red Sauce

I'll say this straightaway, right from the top: This is probably my favorite recipe in the book. How much of this is colored by nostalgia—the memory of my mom bringing back boxes of fresh ravioli from our go-to New Haven pasta shop, the religious experience (before I had a way of describing it as such) of eating cheese-stuffed pasta for the first time—is hard to say. But let's be honest, for everyone with a pulse, of Italian descent or not, ravioli red sauce is as much about the thing itself as it is about how it makes you feel. It's filled with more than just ricotta and mozzarella; in there, too, is a collective understanding of comfort food. And if you asked me to take my pick from the holy trinity of red sauce—spaghetti and meatballs, baked ziti, and ravioli red sauce—I'd pick ravioli red sauce every time.

The simplicity of this dish appeals to me now more than ever, at least partly because it lays its ingredients bare. To that end, you want to use the best mozzarella, ricotta, and San Marzano tomatoes you can find (my tool kit, page 135, has you covered). Texture is also very important here. While it might seem fussy to pass your ricotta through a tamis, don't skip it; it will make for a more even, creamier filling.

---

1   To make the filling, place a tamis or fine-mesh strainer over a bowl. Pass the ricotta through the tamis.

2   Add the mozzarella, parmigiano, and pecorino to the bowl and fold to mix. Season with pepper and salt q.b. It should taste well seasoned. Refrigerate until ready to use.

3   To finish, following the instructions for ravioli on page 104, make 50 to 60 square pieces with the pasta dough and filling.

4   Bring a large pot of water to a boil over high heat. Generously salt the water.

5   Place a large sauté pan over low heat. Add the red sauce. If needed, add a splash of pasta cooking water to loosen the sauce.

6   Add the ravioli to the water and turn down the heat to bring the water to a gentle simmer instead of a rolling boil. It is important to cook these gently at a simmer instead of a boil. The filling is delicate and can break if cooked over high heat. Cook for 2 to 3 minutes, until tender at the thickest closure point.

7   Using a spider or pasta basket, remove the pasta from the pot and transfer to the sauté pan. Turn up the heat to medium. Swirl the pasta in the sauce for 30 seconds to 1 minute to marry, using a spoon to gently turn the pasta over and coat all sides. If the sauce begins to tighten, add a splash of pasta cooking water to loosen and continue swirling to marry.

8   Transfer to a serving platter or divide onto plates. Garnish with parmigiano and pecorino q.b. Finish with chile flakes q.b.

Yields 6 to 8 servings

Filling

696g / 3 cups ricotta
1 small (85g / 3 oz) ball fresh
      mozzarella, diced into ¼-inch
      pieces
17g / 3 Tbsp finely grated
      parmigiano-reggiano
17g / 3 Tbsp finely grated
      pecorino romano
Black pepper, q.b.
Salt, q.b.

To Finish

1 batch egg dough (page 18)
500g / 2 cups simple red sauce
      (page 147)
Finely grated parmigiano-
      reggiano, q.b.
Finely grated pecorino romano,
      q.b.
Dried red chile flakes, q.b.

Baked Ziti with Aged Provolone and Caciocavallo

Baked ziti is a dish whose appeal hinges not on nuance, but on no-holds-barred comfort—a full resignation to universal satisfaction. While it has origins in southern Italy, baked ziti was as American as apple pie where I grew up. My two favorite versions came from Bimonte's and Leon's in New Haven, Connecticut, which shared nearly identical features: Both were served in family-size portions that no family could reasonably finish, eschewed ricotta, and clocked in at no less than four pounds each—about half of that in mozzarella weight.

   My ziti attempts to channel my nostalgia for the ziti of my youth, while addressing the two key ways a perfectly good baked ziti can go bad. The first concerns the ziti itself. You always have to cook the pasta about half the amount of time you think you do to avoid overcooking it in the oven. The second is the often unbalanced ratio of pasta to cheese. To address this, I rely on a thinner layer of ziti arranged in a large skillet, which ensures that no one is robbed of their golden crust of cheese. And finally, and perhaps scandalously, I swap out mozzarella in favor of funky aged provolone and buttery caciocavallo, which both melt well and add a layer of complexity and refinement to the classic.

---

1   Bring a large pot of water to a boil over high heat. Generously salt the water. Add the ziti to the water and cook for 2 to 3 minutes, until *very* al dente. (It will finish cooking in the oven, so take care not to overcook here.)

2   Using a spider or pasta basket, remove the pasta from the water and transfer to a large mixing bowl. Add 438g to 455g / 1¾ cups of sauce and mix to combine.

3   Preheat the oven to 350°F.

4   Add the remaining tomato sauce to a 10- to 12-inch skillet and spread it evenly.

5   Add half of the ziti and sauce mixture to the pan and spread it evenly. Add the ricotta to the pan in even dollops, followed by half of the caciocavallo and provolone.

6   Add the remaining ziti and sauce mixture, followed by the remaining caciocavallo and provolone, as well as the pecorino.

7   Bake uncovered for 30 to 35 minutes, until golden brown and bubbly.

8   Serve family style from the skillet.

Yields 4 to 6 servings

500 g / 1 lb 2 oz extruded ziti (page 124)
650g / 2½ cups diavola sauce, 642g / 2½ cups 30-clove sauce, or 625g / 2½ cups simple red sauce (pages 147–149)
203g / ¾ cup plus 2 Tbsp ricotta
200g / 1⅔ cups coarsely grated caciocavallo cheese
60g / ½ cup coarsely grated aged provolone
22g / ¼ cup finely grated pecorino romano

Penne alla Vodka

While several people claim this dish has Italian origins, penne alla vodka reeks of American invention to me. How else can you explain the superfluous addition of flavorless liquor to a tomato-based sauce?

Beyond my childhood love of Alfredo, I have always turned the other cheek when it comes to cream sauces. In fact, I had never made alla vodka until a friend begged me to prepare it for her birthday. I did it begrudgingly, but I liked it, perhaps not as an archetype of any sort, but when done right, it is an opportunity for nuance, and I have respect for the combination of sweet, spicy, and rich. It allows you to see tomato in a new light, too, its acidity buffered by cream and, in my version, mascarpone, and its sweetness magnified by both milk fat and onion. But it's red chile that is the real hero here, as it rescues the whole thing from standard-issue indulgence. I use dried red chile flakes, but feel free to work in Calabrian chiles as well. They bring even more heat and an additional bass note to the dish.

1   To make the sauce, place a large sauté pan over low heat and add the olive oil. Add the onion and cook until translucent but without color, 5 to 8 minutes.

2   Add the garlic and cook until aromatic but without color, 10 to 15 seconds. Add the chile flakes and allow them to bloom.

3   Add the tomato paste and cook, stirring constantly, until the color deepens, 2 to 3 minutes. Add the vodka and cook, stirring occasionally, until the alcohol has cooked off, 3 to 5 minutes.

4   Add the tomato passata and stir to combine. Turn the heat down to low and simmer until the flavors have integrated, about 30 minutes.

5   Remove from the heat. Stir in the cream and then gently fold in the mascarpone. Season with salt q.b.

6   Measure out 533g / 2¼ cups sauce and set aside. Transfer the remainder to an airtight container and refrigerate for up to 3 days.

7   To finish, bring a large pot of water to a boil over high heat. Generously salt the water.

8   Add the penne to the water and cook for 5 to 8 minutes, until al dente.

9   While the pasta is cooking, place a large sauté pan over low heat. Add the reserved sauce and 2 to 3 ladles (115 to 170g / ½ to ¾ cup) pasta cooking water and stir to combine.

10   Using a spider or pasta basket, remove the pasta from the pot and transfer to the sauté pan. Turn the heat up to medium. Toss for 30 seconds to 1 minute to marry the pasta and the sauce.

11   Add the butter and continue tossing to marry. If the sauce begins to tighten, add a splash of pasta cooking water to loosen and continue tossing.

12   Divide into bowls and garnish with the parmigiano and with chile flakes and pepper q.b.

Yields 4 to 6 servings

Vodka Sauce

42g / 3 Tbsp olive oil
250g / 1 onion, finely diced
15g / 3 cloves garlic, finely chopped
2g / 1 tsp dried red chile flakes
85g / ⅓ cup tomato paste
73g / ⅓ cup vodka
1 (680g / 24 oz) jar tomato passata (3 cups)
115g / ½ cup heavy cream
56g / ¼ cup mascarpone
Salt, q.b.

To Finish

624g / 1 lb 6 oz extruded penne (page 124)
30g / 2 Tbsp unsalted butter, cold and cubed
22g / ¼ cup finely grated parmigiano-reggiano
Dried red chile flakes, q.b.
Black pepper, q.b.

Spaghetti Meatballs

I never developed a craving for meatballs and spaghetti partly because—and I realize this is controversial—I don't think spaghetti or meatballs gain from being on the same plate with each other. But more on that in a second.

Let's all at least agree that great spaghetti and meatballs starts with great meatballs. And the key to great meatballs is moisture—in this case via milk-soaked bread, olive oil, and gently cooked onions and garlic. The latter is important, as onions and garlic won't soften and integrate if they are not cooked ahead (not to mention the depth of flavor and sweetness you get from cooking them in advance). Another important step is to chill the meatballs after you form them and then to cook them in the oven at high heat so they color on the outside but remain undercooked on the inside. You want them to finish cooking in the sauce.

Which brings us back to the better together (or not) question. To me, the spaghetti-and-meatballs sum is only greater than its parts when you consider what the meatball and the sauce gain from being cooked together: the meatballs lending a savory funk and richness to the sauce, the sauce returning the favor, giving the meatballs greater moisture and a punch of acidity. There is also no shame in allowing them to be masters of their own domain, of marrying a beautiful plate of spaghetti al pomodoro with that meat-infused sauce and serving those meatballs right next door—to integrate (or not) as you wish.

---

1   To make the meatballs, break down the bread into pea-size pieces by rubbing the pieces between your palms. Place the bread in a small bowl and cover with the milk. Let soak until completely softened, 30 to 45 minutes.

2   While the bread is soaking, place a sauté pan over low heat and add 56g / ¼ cup of olive oil. Add the onion and gently cook until very soft but without color, about 10 minutes. Add the garlic and gently cook until aromatic but without color, 10 to 15 seconds. Transfer the mixture to a large bowl to cool.

3   Once the onion mixture is cool, add the beef and pork and fold to combine.

4   Add the eggs, both cheeses, fennel, salt, chile flakes, garlic powder, and pepper and mix well.

5   Drain the milk from the bread. Press and squeeze the bread to force out most of the excess liquid. Make sure the bread is separated into small, crumb-like pieces. Add to the meat mixture and mix well.

6   Gradually add the remaining 56g / ¼ cup olive oil while mixing by hand to integrate. The mixture should be wet, but you should still be able to form balls that hold together. Make a small patty to test your seasoning.

7   Place a small sauté pan over medium heat and add a drizzle of olive oil. Add the test patty and cook, turning once, until cooked through, 2 to 3 minutes on each side. Check your seasoning and add more salt to the meatball mixture q.b.

8   Cover and refrigerate the mixture for 30 minutes to 1 hour.

9   Oil a sheet pan. Form the mixture into 17 to 20 balls, each about 112g. Place them on the prepared sheet pan.

Yields 4 to 6 servings

Meatballs

100g / scant 2 cups torn
    day-old country bread
474g / 2 cups milk
112g / ½ cup olive oil,
    plus more q.b.
250g / 1 onion, very finely
    chopped
15g / 3 cloves garlic, very finely
    chopped
454g / 1 lb ground beef
454g / 1 lb ground pork
150g / 3 eggs
45g / ½ cup finely grated
    pecorino romano
45g / ½ cup finely grated
    parmigiano-reggiano
6g / 1 Tbsp fennel seed
7g / 2 tsp salt, plus more q.b.
6g / 1 Tbsp dried red chile flakes
4g / 1½ tsp garlic powder
50 grinds black pepper, plus
    more q.b.
2.25kg / 9 cups simple red
    sauce (page 147)

10   Chill the balls in the refrigerator for 30 minutes to 1 hour to help them keep their shape.

11   Preheat the oven to 400°F.

12   Place the meatballs in the oven and bake until golden brown on the outside but not cooked all the way through, 10 to 15 minutes.

13   While the meatballs are in the oven, place a large, heavy sauce pot or Dutch oven over low heat. Add the red sauce.

14   Transfer the meatballs to the sauce and continue cooking over low heat until cooked through, about 15 minutes. (Do not boil your sauce or you'll end up with tough meatballs.)

15   To finish, bring a large pot of water to a boil over high heat. Generously salt the water.

16   Place a large sauté pan over low heat. Add 563g / 2¼ cups of the sauce from your pot of meatballs. Add 1 to 2 ladles (55 to 115g / ¼ to ½ cup) pasta cooking water and stir to combine.

17   Add the spaghetti to the water and cook for 5 to 8 minutes, until al dente.

18   Using tongs or a pasta basket, remove the pasta from the pot and transfer to the sauté pan. Turn the heat up to medium. Toss for 1 to 2 minutes to marry the pasta and the sauce. If the sauce begins to tighten, add a splash of pasta cooking water to loosen and continue tossing to marry.

19   Divide the pasta into bowls and garnish with the pecorino, a drizzle of olive oil, and the marjoram and basil. Transfer the meatballs and sauce to a serving bowl and serve alongside the pasta.

To Finish

624g / 1 lb 6 oz extruded spaghetti (page 123)
22g / ¼ cup finely grated pecorino romano
Olive oil, q.b.
3 sprigs marjoram, leaves removed from stems
3 sprigs basil, small leaves removed from stems

Nota bene

When choosing ground beef, opt for a high fat percentage and a coarse grind.

Lobster Fra Diavolo with Linguine

This is another one of those dishes I couldn't eat growing up kosher, which is probably why my memory of those platters of baked ziti at Leon's are so clearly punctuated by shellfish swimming in sauce. Lobster fra diavolo, baked ziti, zuppa di clams, another plate of ziti, mussels marinara—like a Morse code of cans and cannots materializing in front of me. It was always the lobster I yearned for, its hard red shell made cartoonishly vibrant under a cloak of over-reduced marinara sauce.

Many years would pass before I'd satisfy that craving, but rarely with the dish that has become synonymous with the Italian American splurge. I've made grilled lobster tails and bathed them in fra diavolo butter, and I've boiled whole lobsters, cracked them in half, and covered them in a warm fra diavolo vinaigrette. This version, though, takes it all the way back to Leon's. It's inspired by a similarly old-school red-sauce joint in Sheepshead Bay, Brooklyn, whose light, brothy version of the dish is the best I've tasted.

The trick to fra diavolo is not to overcook the lobster, and you do that by *not* cooking it in the sauce. Instead, you partially cook ("parcook" in chef parlance) the lobster in a boil, remove the shells, make a brodo from those, and then use that brodo to flavor your sauce. The lobster gets added back to the sauce right before you marry it with the linguine, warming it through without overcooking it—and, thanks to that lobster brodo, without sacrificing the brininess that makes fra diavolo pop.

1 To cook the lobsters, bring a large pot of water to a boil over high heat. Generously salt the water. Prepare a large ice-water bath.

2 Working with one lobster at a time, remove the body from the tail by twisting them in opposite directions. Reserve the body and the tail separately. Clean and discard any impurities from the body and set aside. Repeat with the remaining lobsters.

3 Remove the claws and set aside.

4 Place the claws in the boiling water and set a timer for 3 minutes. When the timer goes off, add the tails and reset the timer for 3 minutes. After the second 3 minutes, the lobsters will be parcooked, which means they won't overcook when you put them in the sauce later.

5 Using tongs, remove the lobsters from the boiling water and place in the ice bath to stop the cooking and to cool.

6 Once cool to the touch, remove the lobsters from the ice-water bath and place on a sheet pan or in a large bowl.

7 Now, the messy part of cracking the lobsters: For the tails, place one tail on its side on a kitchen towel and wrap the towel around it. Press down firmly until you feel the shell crack. Remove from the towel and, using scissors, cut down the inner spine. Pull the shell off and set aside the meat and shell separately. Repeat with the remaining tails.

8 For the claws, place one claw on the kitchen towel and wrap the towel around it. Using the back of a heavy chef's knife, bang the claw until you hear a crack. Turn the claw over and bang it again. You should be able to remove the shell and keep the claw meat in a single piece. Remove the cartilage from the center of the claw. Repeat with the remaining claws and reserve the meat and shells separately.

Yields 4 to 6 servings

Lobster Brodo

4 (570 to 680g / 1¼ to 1½ lb) live
    lobsters
28g / 2 Tbsp olive oil
20g / 4 cloves garlic
300g / 1 fennel bulb, cut into
    1½-inch pieces
150g / 2 stalks celery, cut into
    1½-inch pieces
150g / 1 large carrot, peeled
    and cut into 1½-inch pieces
65g / ¼ cup tomato paste
220g / 1 cup dry white wine
1 fresh bay leaf
3g / 1 tsp black peppercorns

To Finish

624g / 1 lb 6 oz extruded
    linguine (page 122)
520g / 2 cups diavola sauce
    (page 149)
30g / 2 Tbsp crushed Calabrian
    chiles
Dried red chile flakes, q.b.

continued

9   For the knuckles, use scissors to cut down each side and separate the meat from the shell. Reserve the meat and shells separately.

10   Cut the meat from the lobster tails, claws, and knuckles into ¼- to ½-inch pieces and set aside.

11   To make the brodo, place a large, heavy sauce pot or Dutch oven over medium-low heat. Add the oil, garlic, fennel, celery, and carrot and gently cook until tender, 3 to 5 minutes.

12   Add the tomato paste and cook for another 1 to 2 minutes, stirring frequently.

13   Add the wine and cook, stirring occasionally, until reduced by half, 5 to 7 minutes.

14   Add the reserved lobster shells and lobster bodies, then add cold water to reach just below the top of the shells. Add the bay leaf and peppercorns and bring to a gentle simmer over medium heat. Turn down the heat to low and simmer gently, skimming impurities as it cooks, until you have an aromatic and flavorful brodo, about 30 minutes.

15   Remove from the heat and strain the brodo through a fine-mesh strainer lined with a coffee filter or cheesecloth.

16   Measure out 337g / 1 cup plus 7 Tbsp brodo and set aside. Transfer the remainder to an airtight container and refrigerate for up to 3 days or freeze for up to 1 month for another use.

17   To finish, bring a large pot of water to a boil over high heat. Generously salt the water.

18   Add the linguine to the water and cook for 5 to 8 minutes, until al dente.

19   While the pasta is cooking, place a large sauté pan over medium-high heat. Add the lobster brodo and bring to a gentle boil. Turn down the heat to low and cook for 1 to 2 minutes.

20   Add the diavola sauce and Calabrian chiles and season with chile flakes q.b. Add the lobster meat.

21   Using tongs or a pasta basket, remove the pasta from the pot and transfer to the sauté pan. Turn the heat up to medium. Add 1 to 2 ladles (55g to 115g / ¼ to ½ cup) pasta cooking water. Toss for 1 to 2 minutes to marry the pasta and the sauce. If the sauce begins to tighten, add a splash of pasta cooking water or brodo to loosen and continue tossing to marry.

22   Divide the pasta into bowls and garnish with chile flakes q.b.

Cannelloni

There are a lot of things to love about cannelloni, but there's one that is always my impetus for making them at home: like any good pasta al forno, cannelloni are built for entertaining. If you nail the filling, it allows you to show off the fact that you made fresh pasta without having to excuse yourself to babysit it.

Just be sure to add egg yolks to adapt your filling. Why? The ratio of cheese to pasta in cannelloni can end in tears if you don't have something to bind the filling. That said, this is also a shape that invites self-expression. The most memorable cannelloni I've ever had were at a restaurant in Milan in the 1990s. They were a distant relation of the cannelloni of red-sauce infamy: chestnut dough stuffed with black truffles and ricotta. I mention this to implore you to explore other fillings and doughs in this book.

1   To make the filling, place a tamis or fine-mesh strainer over a large bowl. Pass the ricotta through the tamis. Set aside.

2   Bring a large pot of water to a boil over high heat. Generously salt the water. Prepare a salted ice-water bath and set a colander in it.

3   Drop the spinach into the boiling water and cook until tender but still bright green, about 30 seconds. Transfer the spinach to the salted ice-water bath to stop the cooking. Drain the spinach, transfer to a kitchen towel, and squeeze out the excess water.

4   Once dry, coarsely chop the spinach until there are no large pieces.

5   To the bowl with the ricotta, add the pecorino and spinach. Grate about one-quarter of the nutmeg into the mixture. Add the lemon peel and fold together to combine. Season with salt q.b. It should taste well seasoned.

6   Add the egg yolks and fold together to combine. Set aside until ready to use.

7   To finish, following the instructions for cannelloni on page 86, make 16 pieces with the pasta dough and filling.

8   Preheat the oven to 350°F.

9   Place 500g / 2 cups of the sauce in the bottom and slightly up the sides of a 9 by 13-inch glass or ceramic baking dish.

10   Place the cannelloni on top of the sauce in a single layer, nestling them beside one another. Cover the dish with parchment paper and then seal tightly with aluminum foil.

11   Bake the cannelloni just until warmed through, 15 to 20 minutes. (If you are preparing the dish earlier and refrigerating it, make sure to let it sit at room temperature for 30 to 45 minutes before putting it in the oven, or add 5 minutes to the baking time.)

12   While the cannelloni are baking, place a small sauté pan over low heat. Add the remaining 500g / 2 cups sauce.

13   Remove the cannelloni from the oven and top with a generous grating of nutmeg and with pepper and pecorino q.b.

14   Divide onto plates and spoon the warmed sauce over the top or on the side.

Yields 6 to 8 servings

Filling

928g / 4 cups ricotta
227g / 5 cups loosely packed baby spinach
22g / ¼ cup finely grated pecorino romano
Whole nutmeg
Peel of ½ lemon, pith removed and peel finely chopped
Salt, q.b.
36g / 2 egg yolks

To Finish

1 batch egg dough (page 18)
1kg / 4 cups simple red sauce, at room temp (page 147)
Whole nutmeg, q.b.
Black pepper, q.b.
Pecorino romano, q.b.

Pasta e Fagioli

Every region in Italy has its own version of pasta and beans, and they are all built on the same foundation: dried cannellini or borlotti beans (with a few exceptions, like Campania, where you'll sometimes find fresh shelling beans in the mix), a brodo flavored with cured pork or beef, herbs, often chiles, a measured bit of tomato (whether whole, passata, or paste), and pasta. It's a pretty minimalist peasant dish meant to be filling and practical.

But what we know as pasta fazool (the Italian American name for it, derived from pasta e fasule, its Neapolitan dialectal name) is often embellished. As a kid, I remember seeing it emerge from restaurant kitchens with giant chunks of vegetables in a tomato brodo. You couldn't pay me to order it back then.

In fact, I don't even think I tried it until I went to work in Emilia-Romagna. It was a frequent family meal there, a way to make something out of leftovers, and nothing like the tomato-rich mash-up with minestrone that had gone astray stateside. It was simple: a brodo flavored with pancetta, borlotti beans, and quadrati—fresh pasta squares cut from a sheeted piece of leftover dough. My version is an attempt to right the ship, to find a middle way between the version most of us are likely to have nostalgic feelings for and the true dish, which has managed to withstand regional overhaul and maintain its essential DNA across borders. A good one, contrary to what many of us have been told, is about less, not more.

---

1   To make the beans, place them in a large bowl or pot and cover with room-temperature water. The water level should be about double the volume of the beans. Let soak overnight.

2   When you are ready to cook the beans, drain them. Place the beans in a large pot and add water to cover by 6 to 8 inches. Add the garlic, carrot, onion, celery, and bay leaf.

3   Place the pot over medium-low heat and bring to a very slow simmer. Cook the beans for 1 to 1½ hours. They should be tender but not too soft, as they will continue cooking in the soup. Season with salt q.b. Remove from the heat and let cool.

4   Drain the beans, reserving the cooking liquid.

5   To finish, following the instructions for all-purpose lasagna sheets on page 47, make 283g / 10 oz of quadrati with the pasta dough.

6   Place a large, heavy sauce pot or Dutch oven over medium heat. Add the pancetta and cook until the fat has rendered and the pancetta is cooked but not crispy or brown, 5 to 8 minutes.

7   Add the olive oil and onions and cook until the onions begin to soften, 2 to 3 minutes. Add the garlic and gently cook until aromatic but without color, 10 to 15 seconds.

8   Add the beans and the tomatoes and their juice to the pot. Then add the reserved bean liquid and the water. (The liquid should barely cover the beans.)

9   Add three-quarters of the rosemary, the chile flakes, and the parmigiano rind. Turn the heat down to low and cook until the flavors have melded, 30 to 45 minutes. Season with salt q.b. Remove from the heat and set aside.

continued

Yields 6 to 8 servings

Beans

454g / 1 lb borlotti beans
25g / 5 cloves garlic
150g / 1 large carrot, peeled
    and halved
370g / 1 large onion, halved
75g / 1 stalk celery, split in half
1 fresh bay leaf
Salt, q.b.

To Finish

½ batch egg dough (page 18)
227g / 8 oz pancetta, finely
    chopped
56g / ¼ cup olive oil, plus more
    for drizzling
740g / 2 large onions, finely
    chopped
15g / 3 cloves garlic, thinly sliced
1 large (794g / 28 oz) can whole
    San Marzano tomatoes,
    crushed by hand
948g / 4 cups water
3 sprigs rosemary, leaves
    removed from stems
2g / 1 tsp dried red chile flakes,
    plus more q.b.
1 (4-inch) piece parmigiano-
    reggiano rind
Salt, q.b.
45g / ½ cup finely grated
    parmigiano-reggiano
Black pepper, q.b.

Pasta e Fagioli

continued

10   To finish, bring a large pot of water to a boil over high heat. Generously salt the water.

11   Add the quadrati to the water and cook for 1 to 2 minutes, until tender but not soft.

12   Using a spider or pasta basket, remove the pasta from the pot and transfer to the soup. Stir to combine.

13   Divide into bowls. Garnish with a drizzle of olive oil, the grated parmigiano, the remaining rosemary and the chile flakes and pepper q.b.

Spaghetti Vongole

Spaghetti (or linguine) vongole is such an Italian American staple that you'd be forgiven for assuming it actually originated here. But its origins are Neapolitan, and it dates to at least the nineteenth century, when the first recipe for vermicelli all'aglio con vongole is committed to paper by Ippolito Cavalcanti in his *Cucina teorico-practica*, which also happens to contain the first recipe for pasta sauced with tomatoes. His version is a simple combination of the cooking liquid from the clams, salt, pepper, oil, and parsley.

Today, every Italian region in which clams are sold, from the Veneto to Puglia, Sicily to Sardinia, has its own take. Of course, that's yielded a dish that has taken many forms and collaborated with many shapes. Over here, it has assumed a profile that is like a seaside take on garlic bread: briny, buttery, lemony, garlicky, with a tinge of bitterness from parsley. The Italians, Americans, and Italian Americans will always argue over the addition of tomatoes (or not), or even who can lay claim to the dish, but what we can all agree on is that, whatever the version, the dish has its own gravity. Whole restaurants have been built around its appeal.

My version is fairly straightforward, but it requires attention to cook times. You want to be sure to cook your clams until they are just opened, reserve their briny cooking liquid, and shell them. (You will never find a clam shell in my version; I've never understood it.) I also like to include both chopped and whole bellies so the clams become part of the sauce itself, coating the pasta rather than simply pooling at the bottom of the dish.

---

1   To prepare the clams, place them in a bowl of cold water to soak. Every 10 minutes, drain, rinse away the grit that has accumulated at the bottom of the bowl, and refill with fresh water, continuing until you see no grit after draining, after at least 1 hour of soaking.

2   Place a large sauté pan over medium heat and add the olive oil. Add the sliced garlic and cook until aromatic but without color, 10 to 15 seconds.

3   Working in batches, add the clams to the pan along with the wine, thyme, and chile flakes and cook, stirring occasionally, until the first clam opens. If you want to speed up this process, cover the pan to cook the clams, but begin checking them after 1 minute, removing each one as soon as it opens and transferring it to a bowl.

4   When the clams are cooked, strain the cooking liquid through a fine-mesh strainer. Measure out 228g / 1 cup liquid and set aside.

5   Remove the meat from each clam and discard the shells. Chop half of the clams and add them back to the bowl with the whole clams.

6   To finish, bring a large pot of water to a boil over high heat. Generously salt the water.

7   Add the spaghetti to the water and cook for 5 to 8 minutes, until al dente.

continued

Yields 4 to 6 servings

Clams

3 dozen littleneck clams
224g / 1 cup olive oil
25g / 5 cloves garlic, sliced
660g / 3 cups white wine
10 sprigs thyme
2g / 1 tsp dried red chile flakes

To Finish

624g / 1 lb 6 oz extruded
    spaghetti (page 123)
42g / 3 Tbsp olive oil
5g / 1 clove garlic, finely
    chopped
30g / 2 Tbsp unsalted butter,
    cold and cubed
Peel of 1 lemon, pith removed
    and peel finely chopped, and
    fruit halved and reserved for
    juicing
20g / ¼ cup finely chopped
    parsley
Dried red chile flakes, q.b.

Spaghetti Vongole

continued

8   While the pasta is cooking, place a large sauté pan over low heat. Add the olive oil and chopped garlic and cook until aromatic but without color, 10 to 15 seconds. Add the reserved clam cooking liquid to the pan. Add the butter and swirl to emulsify.

9   Using tongs or a pasta basket, remove the pasta from the pot and transfer to the sauté pan. Turn the heat up to medium. Toss for 1 to 2 minutes to marry the pasta and the sauce.

10   Add the chopped and whole clams and continue to toss for about 30 seconds to distribute the clams evenly and to continue marrying the pasta and the sauce. If the sauce begins to tighten, add a splash of pasta cooking water to loosen and continue tossing. (Check your seasoning, and if it's already quite briny, use a splash of fresh water to loosen instead.) When the pasta is properly married, it will cling to the sauce and have a glossy sheen.

11   Add the lemon peel and parsley, season with chile flakes q.b., and toss to combine.

12   Remove from the heat. Squeeze in the juice from the lemon halves and divide into bowls.

Lasagna

The Internet is so awash in layered pasta that I wondered whether I really needed to toss my hat into the ring. But no book that claims to include the Italian American classics can possibly eliminate lasagna. Like most red-sauce dishes, its origins are Italian—if often twice removed. In Emilia-Romagna, lasagne al forno reaches its apex as lasagne verde, which relies on a delicate layering of paper-thin spinach pasta, béchamel, and Bolognese ragù. Farther north, in the Marche, vincisgrassi, as it is known, sheds the restraint and incorporates rich organ meats into the mix, along with plenty of béchamel. It's a version that makes the red sauce, mozzarella, and ricotta lasagne of my youth seem almost lean by comparison.

My take is pure nostalgia, updated—notably, with parmigiano fonduta in place of béchamel. It gives the dish the same kind of silky richness but with the balancing bite and complexity that only parmigiano can offer.

---

1   To make the fonduta, place a large saucepan over medium heat. Add the cream and bring to a very slow simmer. Decrease the heat to low and cook, stirring occasionally, until the cream has reduced by about one-third, 30 to 45 minutes, being very careful not to scorch the bottom of the pan. Remove from the heat and let cool for 5 minutes.

2   Transfer the warm cream to a high-speed blender. With the blender running on medium-low speed, slowly add the parmigiano, processing until the mixture has emulsified. Taste for seasoning and add salt q.b. (The parmigiano adds plenty of salinity, so you may not need to add much salt.)

3   With the blender running, gradually add the egg yolks, drizzling them in slowly so they temper and the mixture doesn't break. Transfer to a bowl and set aside.

4   To finish, following the directions for lasagna sheets on page 47, make 18 (12-inch) sheets with the pasta dough.

5   Bring a large pot of water to a boil over high heat. Generously salt the water. Line a sheet pan with parchment paper and lightly drizzle with olive oil.

6   Add the pasta sheets to the water in batches, cooking each batch for 20 to 30 seconds (because the pasta will be baked in the oven, there's no need to cook it longer). Using a spider and/or tongs, transfer each batch to the prepared sheet pan in a single layer, separating the layers with lightly oiled pieces of parchment paper.

7   Preheat the oven to 325°F.

8   Add 188g / ¾ cup of the red sauce to a 9 by 13-inch metal or glass baking dish and spread it evenly along the bottom with the back of a spoon.

9   Pat two sheets of pasta dry with a clean kitchen towel and place them lengthwise side by side, in the dish, slightly overlapping their long edges in the middle.

Yields 6 to 8 servings

Parmigiano Fonduta

948g / 4 cups plus 2 Tbsp
    heavy cream
450g / 5 cups finely grated
    parmigiano-reggiano
Salt, q.b.
54g / 2 to 3 egg yolks, stirred

To Finish

1 batch egg dough (page 18)
1.75g / 7 cups simple red sauce
    (page 147)
30g / ⅓ cup finely grated
    parmigiano-reggiano
30g / ⅓ cup finely grated
    pecorino romano
Whole nutmeg, q.b.
Black pepper, q.b.
756g / 1 lb 11 oz fresh mozzarella,
    coarsely grated

10   Spoon or ladle 90g / scant ⅓ cup of the fonduta over the pasta sheets and spread it evenly. (If the fonduta has cooled too much, you may need to warm it slightly by placing the bowl in a warm-water bath.)

11   Sprinkle 3g / ½ Tbsp each of the parmigiano and pecorino over the top of the fonduta, followed by a few gratings of nutmeg and pepper q.b.

12   Add 167g / ⅔ cup of the red sauce and spread it evenly. Sprinkle 85g / packed ½ cup of the mozzarella over the top.

13   Repeat steps 8 through 12 until you have used all of the pasta sheets, leaving the final layer of pasta exposed.

14   Top the final pasta layer with the remaining fonduta, followed by nutmeg, pepper, and remaining red sauce. Finish by sprinkling 8g / 1 heaping Tbsp each of the parmigiano and pecorino evenly on top.

15   Cover the baking dish with a sheet of parchment paper, then top with aluminum foil, rolling the foil over the parchment to seal tightly.

16   Place the baking dish on a sheet pan and bake the lasagna for 40 minutes.

17   Uncover the lasagna. Insert a knife blade into the center. The lasagna should look slightly golden around the edges and the knife blade should be hot.

18   Turn up the oven to 400°F and bake uncovered until the lasagna is golden brown on top and crispy around the edges, 20 to 25 minutes longer, checking after the first 15 minutes of baking. If the lasagna is coloring too rapidly around the edges, cover loosely with a piece of foil for the remaining 5 to 10 minutes to prevent burning.

19   Let the lasagna cool for at least 20 to 30 minutes before serving. Portion onto plates and finish with grated nutmeg q.b.

Nota bene

The pasta sheets will expand when cooked. Depending on the size of your pan, you may need to trim the sheets to fit.

Regional Classics

People love to say that you eat better pasta in America than you do in Italy. But people say all sorts of things. Who among us has not anointed an unworthy cacio e pepe in the shadow of the Pantheon? Who has not declared a subpar tagliatelle alla bolognese enjoyed overlooking the Colli Bolognesi the undisputed archetype? And, more importantly, who has not insisted, while on a successful date at a New York restaurant, let's say, that the versions of the bolognese and the cacio e pepe before them are superior to anything they might find in Italy?

The truth is, you can eat great pasta in Tokyo, London, Mexico City, and New York City. To me, you go to Italy not to find the superior version of each regional dish but to answer questions: Why this dish? Why here? Why this way? Whether it is "better" or "best" is beside the point, although if you're on the right path (or off it, more often), it probably will be.

Answering those questions begins with understanding, as I did the first time I stepped into a kitchen in Udine after two months of cooking in Emilia-Romagna, that Italy is not one country but twenty, and pasta is perhaps best enjoyed as a way—the most delicious way—to partake in that complexity. I've spent years trying to answer these questions in my own cooking in different ways—first as a faithful translator of tradition, and now as a steward of the craft's principles. What follows is my best attempt to explain not only the recipes that have been foundational for me but also where they come from. It's true that you will not find many of these pastas on my menus today, but what they represent still forms the very core of what I do.

So, too, do the places where I've found the most spirited versions of each. I am not talking about Michelin-starred paeans to creativity; I am talking about roadside places so unassuming you'd be forgiven for not even slowing as you pass by. Places like Cianzia, just outside Cortina d'Ampezzo in the Dolomites, a sort of Italian version of Tom's Restaurant that is a welcome foil to the glitz of Italy's Aspen. Or Il Castoro (The Beaver) outside Preci, an Umbrian town at least fifty miles from anywhere you'd want to be, its simple wood-paneled room decorated with photos lifted from a Mac nature screensaver and with an old mounted box TV showing cartoons dubbed over in Italian on a continuous loop. Or Il Borgo dei Fumari in Prata d'Ansidonia, another middle-of-nowhere town (population 500) in the mountains of Abruzzo outside L'Aquila, whose entrance is so unadorned you'd assume it deliberately did not want to be found. This is to say nothing of the homes to which I've been lucky enough to be invited. Each of my trips to Italy has taught me something about the way I cook, or would like to cook, or challenged answers I once held true. These trips are also reminders of the importance of place, and how it can manifest in ways literal and spiritual to form the identity of a dish.

What follows is a collection of the dishes that have, in one way or another, played an important role in my career—and my journey to revisit them. None is an exact replica of a classic pasta I've encountered in Italy; they are adaptations, though they do not stray so far that they could be called by any other name. Each is also, I hope, a reminder that part of understanding pasta is the literal pursuit of a great bowl of it.

Liguria looks exactly how you'd like it to, or at least how I'd like it to: verdant, rolling hills; an endless ripple of ridges topped with pine trees that jut up from the Mediterranean chaparral like straw men standing at attention; seaside towns whose color palette seems to hold the sun in the sky longer than anywhere else on earth. You get the idea. It's only halfway through a drive along the coast from Genoa to La Spezia that I realize that it's all those pine trees that give Liguria its prized pignolo, that rich pill of flavor that meets basil, olive oil, fiore sardo, parmigiano, and garlic in a mortar to make a sauce so spellbinding and variable I could eat it every day. Pesto, it should be known up front, isn't merely a preference in Liguria; it is a birthright, a lifestyle, a religion.

It's almost June, but the weather hasn't gotten the message. All of Italy is essentially under a rain cloud, and the weather report for the next two weeks is nature's version of a shrug. I ask no one in particular whether it always rains this much, as if the hills hadn't already answered the question.

There is no use arguing with the map—we're in the north of Italy. And yet this slice of coastline from the border with France to the northern reaches of Tuscany eats more like an island that broke off from the south of Italy and was bolted onto Lombardy by some enterprising, olive oil–loving Milanese. And herein lies the difficulty of slicing Italy into three pieces. Sure, you can draw a straight line between the indulgence of Emilia-Romagna—with its egg pastas, its balsamic, its prosciutto di Parma, its bolognese—and Piedmont, land of white truffles, Barolo, and some of the country's best cheeses. It's not such a stretch, for instance, to find commonality in tajarin and tagliatelle, or agnolotti dal plin and tortellini in brodo. And if an Alba white truffle landed on a table in Emilia-Romagna, I am pretty sure those present would know what to do with it. In fact, it's this handshake between Piedmont and Emilia-Romagna that, for so many years, was synonymous with "northern Italian" among the American chefs who cooked Italian food and the journalists who ate it. It was also code for serious Italian cooking: If you wanted to cook three-star Italian, it better be the food of these places.

But how do you square the cooking of Piedmont and Emilia-Romagna with Ligurian cuisine, which leans on olive oil and fresh herbs as the axis of almost every dish? Or the food of the Alps, another catchall that obscures the incredible diversity of the cooking found along Italy's northern border and the identity politics that have shaped it? This is without even mentioning Friuli, with its own idiosyncratic slice of the Alps and its prowess with meat by way of the traditional fogolar—a central oven that is the heart of every proper Friulian home—and seafood by way of Trieste, that gateway to the Adriatic. Or Venice, a city that has been co-opted by tourists but still holds tight to many of its culinary traditions, if you know where to look. (Would you believe me if I told you that one of the best pastas I've had in recent memory was at a place nearly in the shadow of the Rialto Bridge? The dish was the city's historic bigoli in salsa—a thick whole-wheat spaghetti served in a sauce of anchovies, garlic, and caramelized onions.)

It's true that the actual craft of pasta making reaches its apex in Emilia-Romagna, which, for my style of pasta making, remains my muse. It's why the dough I use for almost all shapes is made from only egg yolks and 00 flour, including many that might traditionally be made with flour and water. It's also why I find a deep satisfaction in the more stripped-back plates you find in the region, whether tortellini in brodo or balanzoni with butter and sage. These are the dishes that enable you to truly appreciate the actual craft of pasta making—the delicacy and deft touch in forming a filled pasta, for instance, or the richness of the egg yolk dough and how it manages a particular weightlessness and spring when properly cooked. Venture outside of Emilia-Romagna in the north and very quickly the dough you encounter will include the whole egg, which often yields transcendent results but never quite manages the same refinement as the pastas you find in Italy's gastronomic capital.

However, the greatest gift the north has to offer the cook I am now—and, I believe, the home cook—is not that single muse but a diversity that is unparalleled. It is a part of the country that shape-shifts endlessly from west to east and has challenged the very definition of pasta as I understand it along the way. Alto Adige's canederli (aka Knödel), bread dumplings studded with speck (and more, depending on where you are) and drenched in brown butter, are an antidote to both the climate and any diet you may have had in mind. But is it pasta? On paper it is debatable, but spend five days eating it and you understand that it is as true as pasta can be in a place that is as Austrian as it is Italian. Both cultures have their imprint on it.

Consider pizzoccheri, a shape that hails from the Valtellina, which stretches east from the tip of Lake Como and is best known for Valtellina Nebbiolo, the alpine answer to Piedmont's Barolo. Valtellina's hometown dish is like a postcard from eastern Europe: buckwheat pasta boiled together with cabbage and potatoes, strained, and then layered with the local Bitto cheese and topped with hot garlic brown butter that manages to ferry the cheese through every tributary of the dish. It's a triple dare of a pasta that is an island unto itself; it speaks more to my Polish roots than to my Italian allegiances. Or cjalsons, sweet-savory filled shapes from the Carnic Alps that are stuffed with everything from dried fruits to nuts to chocolate to bitter herbs. When writer Meredith Erickson, an expert in all things alpine, said that the only thing anyone knows for sure about cjalsons is that "it's anything you want it to be," she summed them up perfectly. They are different from town to town, house to house, host to host; to eat them in their home region is to partake in an oral history that is continuously unspooling.

It's true, however, that many traditions are dying out. In Liguria, I drove up and down the coast looking for someone—anyone—who was still making trofie, tiny spiraled shapes made by twisting the inside padding of one hand against a flat surface with just the right motion. Only one person could furnish a name, or actually, two: Rosetta and Assuntina, in the town of Sori, about ten miles southeast of Genoa. Modernity has gifted Liguria with its own machine for making trofie, and its efficiency has been almost universally embraced. But in other places, the old traditions are alive and well, and evolving—even at the hands of nonne. Just outside Cortina d'Ampezzo, the home of Veneto's casunziei all'ampezzana, beet-filled mezzelune doused with brown butter, poppy seeds, and smoked ricotta, we found Rita hard at work in the back of the pasta shop she's owned for decades—rolling and cutting and stuffing the classic red casunziei that are doled out to restaurants throughout town. She also makes a golden version stuffed with turnips and potatoes; a green version swollen with beet greens, nettles, and foraged bladder campion; and a number of nontraditional fillings unique to her.

For a country we try so hard to encase in amber, change is everywhere, some of it moving at a generational pace, some of it at a pace that doesn't always feel comfortable for the romantic in me. But all of the tension between old and new is ultimately exciting, challenging, humbling. In fact, I drove twelve hundred miles across northern Italy only to confirm the feelings I had the first time I made cjalsons in the tiny kitchen of Agli Amici, outside Udine, in 1999: I know nothing. There is no swath of the country that confirms this as much as this one. And there's no set of recipes, as evidenced in this chapter, that explains just how woefully insufficient the term "northern Italian food" really is.

Trofie al Pesto Genovese

Pasta with Pine Nut Pesto

My go-to summer pasta is linguine (trenette, if you're in Liguria) with pesto, but along the Italian Riviera, trofie are what pesto al Genovese tangles with most often. And there is a version I now think about each year when New York crests 65 degrees Fahrenheit for the first time. At Manuelina in Recco, the kitchen makes trofie with chestnut flour and tops them with some of the most vibrant, addictive pesto I've ever had. It is the pasta equivalent of an earworm. My version takes inspiration not just from Manuelina but also from myriad others I have encountered along the Ligurian coast, each subtly different from the other: some with green beans, potatoes, and pasta and others with pesto chunky and raw from the mortar or as smooth and rich as peanut butter. All took small liberties but felt tethered to true pesto al Genovese, which calls for just seven ingredients: pine nuts, Genovese basil, garlic, olive oil, salt, parmigiano-reggiano, and pecorino sardo. It took me years to arrive at my go-to recipe and one trip to Genoa to realize that I'd left out the most important ingredient: fiore sardo, a gently smoky version of pecorino from Sardinia.

---

1   Following the instructions for trofie on page 70, make 624g / 1 lb 6 oz with the pasta dough.

2   To make the pesto, preheat the oven to 325°F. Spread the pine nuts in a single layer on a sheet pan and toast until very lightly golden brown, 5 to 7 minutes, checking their progress every few minutes to ensure they don't burn. Set aside to cool, about 15 minutes.

3   Bring a large pot of water to a boil over high heat. Generously salt the water. Prepare an ice water bath and set a colander in it. Add the basil to the pot and cook for 5 seconds. Remove from the water and transfer to the ice water bath to stop the cooking.

4   Remove the basil from the ice water, squeeze out any excess water, and add to the bowl of a high-speed blender. Puree until smooth, adding a splash of water to get it going if needed.

5   Add 150g / 1¼ cups of the pine nuts and puree until they are incorporated.

6   Transfer the pine nut and basil puree to a large mixing bowl. Using a Microplane, grate the clove of garlic into the bowl. Add the olive oil and all three cheeses and fold together until well incorporated.

7   Measure out 320g / 1¼ cups of pesto and set aside. Transfer the remainder to a container, cover with a layer of olive oil, and refrigerate for up to 3 days for another use. Coarsely chop the remaining 30g / ¼ cup pine nuts.

8   Bring another large pot of water to a boil over high heat. Generously salt the water.

9   Add the trofie to the water and cook for 3 to 5 minutes, until tender but still chewy.

10   Using a spider or pasta basket, transfer the pasta directly to the mixing bowl and gently toss to combine. Slowly add 55 to 78g / ¼ to ⅓ cup pasta cooking water to the bowl until the pesto easily coats the pasta.

11   Divide into serving bowls and garnish with the additional fiore sardo q.b., chopped pine nuts, and basil leaves.

Yields 4 to 6 servings

1 batch semolina dough
    (page 19)

Pesto Genovese

180g / 1½ cups pine nuts
210g / 10½ cups basil leaves,
    plus extra for garnish
5g / 1 clove garlic
150g / ⅔ cup olive oil
36g / ⅓ cup plus 1 Tbsp finely
    grated parmigiano-reggiano
36g / ⅓ cup plus 1 Tbsp finely
    grated fiore sardo, plus
    more q.b.
36g / ⅓ cup plus 1 Tbsp finely
    grated pecorino romano

Pansotti con Salsa di Noci

Herb-Filled Pasta with Walnut Sauce

I'd argue that pansotti are really more about the filling than the pasta. Even the shape—essentially a potbellied tortello—announces its priorities. That filling begins with preboggion (or prebuggiun), a collection of wild herbs that changes with the season or with whose house you're eating at. Regardless of the composition, the spirit of preboggion is always the same: it's a reflection of Ligurian seasonality, abundance, and terroir that showcases the three flavor profiles—bitter, herbal, savory—that define Ligurian cooking. No dish expresses this trio quite like pansotti con salsa di noci.

For the filling, the preboggion is traditionally mixed with local prescinsêua cheese (a fresh, slightly acidic cheese) or ricotta mixed with parmigiano. It's finished with salsa di noci, a rich sauce made from ground walnuts, oil, either cream or milk (traditionally milk and old bread), parmigiano, and sometimes marjoram. My preference, ultimately, is for a combination of bread and milk, with yogurt finding its way into the filling. As for marjoram, while it is sometimes added to both the filling and the sauce, my favorite version of the dish (from Trattoria La Brinca, in the hills high above Chiavari) uses it as a garnish for an extra pop of aroma—a move I am quite fond of in my own cooking.

---

1   To make the sauce, place the bread in a small bowl, add the milk (you want the bread to be mostly covered by the milk), and let sit until softened, about 30 minutes.

2   Gently squeeze out the milk from the bread with your hands, reserving the milk in a small bowl, and transfer the bread to a food processor. Add the walnuts, garlic, parmigiano, and half of the reserved milk and puree until smooth.

3   Slowly drizzle in the olive oil, pulsing until the sauce is emulsified. If it seems stiff, add more of the reserved milk as needed to loosen it.

4   Measure out 130g / 9 Tbsp sauce and set aside. Transfer the remainder to an airtight container and refrigerate for up to 3 days for another use (see note).

5   To make the filling, place a large sauté pan over medium heat. Add the oil to the pan, followed by the chard. Toss the chard to coat with the oil and cook until wilted, 1 to 2 minutes. Add the dandelion, arugula, and nettles and continue to cook for 1 to 2 minutes. Transfer to a sheet pan to cool.

6   When the greens are cool, wrap them in a kitchen towel and ring out any excess liquid.

7   Add the greens to a food processor and pulse until smooth. Transfer to a bowl and add the lovage, fennel, parsley, and marjoram.

8   Wash the bowl of the food processor. Put the ricotta into the food processor and pulse just until it is as smooth as cake frosting and has a sheen, being careful not to process it longer or it will break.

9   Fold the ricotta and yogurt into the greens.

10 Add the parmigiano and season with grated nutmeg and salt q.b. It should taste well seasoned. Set aside until ready to use.

Yields 6 to 8 servings

Sauce

54g / 1 cup roughly chopped or torn day-old crustless country bread
237g / 1 cup milk
150g / 1½ cups walnuts
5g / 1 clove garlic
30g / ⅓ cup finely grated parmigiano-reggiano
56g / ¼ cup olive oil

Filling

42g / 3 Tbsp olive oil
168g/ 6 cups Swiss chard leaves, stems removed and reserved (see note) and leaves coarsely chopped
150g / 5 cups dandelion or other bitter green, stems removed
38g / 1¾ cups arugula
42g / 3 cups picked nettles (use gloves!)
8g / ⅓ cup lovage, coarsely chopped

11　To finish, following the instructions for pansotti on page 100, make 40 to 50 pieces with the pasta dough and filling.

12　Bring a large pot of water to a boil over high heat. Generously salt the water.

13　Add the pansotti to the water and turn down the heat to bring the water to a gentle simmer instead of a rolling boil. It is important to cook these gently at a simmer instead of a boil. The filling is delicate and can break if cooked over high heat. Cook for 3 to 5 minutes, until tender at the thickest closure point.

14　While the pasta is cooking, place a large sauté pan over low heat. Add the reserved walnut sauce and 3 ladles (170g / ¾ cup) pasta cooking water and stir to mix well. The mixture should be the consistency of sauce instead of paste.

15　Using a spider or pasta basket, remove the pasta from the pot and transfer to the sauté pan. Swirl the pasta in the sauce for 30 seconds to 1 minute to marry, using a spoon to gently turn the pasta over and coat all sides. If the sauce begins to tighten, add a splash of pasta cooking water to loosen and continue swirling to marry.

16　Divide into bowls or onto plates. Garnish with the walnuts, parmigiano, and marjoram.

12g / 3 Tbsp finely chopped fennel fronds
15g / 3 Tbsp finely chopped parsley
3 sprigs marjoram, leaves removed from stems and coarsely chopped
232g / 1 cup ricotta (see "whipped" ricotta, page 139)
120g / ½ cup plain whole-milk Greek yogurt
45g / ½ cup finely grated parmigiano-reggiano
Whole nutmeg, q.b.
Salt, q.b.

To Finish

1 batch egg dough (page 18)
25g / ¼ cup walnuts, thinly sliced
22g / ¼ cup finely grated parmigiano-reggiano
5g / ¼ cup marjoram leaves

Nota bene

While you may not want Swiss chard stems in your filling, they shouldn't go into the trash. Lightly sauté them, drizzle them with olive oil, a bit of lemon juice, and flaky sea salt, and enjoy as a snack.

The walnut sauce will yield more than you need for the pasta, but it has many other uses. I love to extend it with a bit of olive oil and smear it on crostini, then serve as is or topped with charred vegetables or those sautéed chard stems.

Tajarin al Tartufo

Pasta with White Truffles

I remember the first time I went to Alba. It was the tail end of truffle season, and I'd managed to arrive on the last day of the town's famous truffle festival, which is essentially a trade show for truffle merchants—fifty to one hundred of them, wares displayed. Along the periphery, another set of merchants was arranged to showcase truffle cheese, oil, and paste, and in the corner was a station churning out tajarin, Piedmont's delicate, egg-rich version of tagliolini. Buy yourself a truffle, give it a test drive—that was the idea. I can still remember how my clothes smelled after being in that room that afternoon, and how that smell manages to burrow so deeply that its aroma is able to activate all your senses at once.

I don't need to wax poetic about the white truffle. Too many who have come before have done as much. This recipe is here because it represents an important lesson—albeit an expensive one—in allowing pasta to be a means of showcasing a single ingredient. After all, it's not hard to imagine that whoever shaved the first truffle onto a plate of tajarin with butter and parmigiano would have decided that was all the innovation she, and anyone to come after her, required.

---

1   Following the instructions for tajarin on page 61, make 624g / 1 lb 6 oz with the pasta dough.

2   Bring a large pot of water to a boil over high heat. Generously salt the water.

3   Heat a large sauté pan over low heat. Add the butter and about 2 ladles (115g / ½ cup) pasta cooking water. Swirl the contents of the pan to emulsify. Set aside off the heat.

4   Add the tajarin to the water and cook for 15 to 20 seconds. Tajarin is quite delicate and will cook very quickly.

5   Return the reserved sauté pan to low heat. Using tongs or a pasta basket, remove the pasta from the pot and transfer to the sauté pan. Turn the heat up to medium. Toss for 30 seconds to 1 minute to marry the pasta and the sauce. If the sauce begins to tighten, add a splash of pasta cooking water and continue to marry. When the pasta is properly married, it will cling to the sauce and have a glossy sheen.

6   Remove the pan from the heat and sprinkle in 45g / ½ cup of the parmigiano while tossing to incorporate.

7   Divide the pasta into bowls and garnish with the remaining parmigiano. Shave truffle over each serving q.b.

Yields 4 to 6 servings

1 batch egg dough (page 18)
85g / 6 Tbsp unsalted butter, cold and cubed
68g / ¾ cup finely grated parmigiano-reggiano
White truffle, q.b.

Nota bene

I suggest a minimum of 5g / ⅓ oz truffle per person, but I truly prefer about twice that if you have white truffle to spare. If you do not have a truffle shaver, you can use a mandoline on its narrowest setting; you want the shavings paper thin.

Pizzoccheri alla Valtellinese

Buckwheat Pasta with Potatoes, Cabbage, and Brown Butter

I've spent years reinterpreting this dish, but it wasn't until I drove sixty-five miles north of Milan, hung a right at the northernmost tip of Lake Como, and climbed two dozen switchbacks up above the floor of the Valtellina to the town of Teglio that I realized that it's a dish that doesn't really take to reinterpretation. Pizzoccheri alla Valtellinese dates to at least the eighteenth century. By this point, buckwheat had been planted in the Valtellina for hundreds of years, its hardiness and short growing season the right combo for the forbidding weather. This is alpine food through and through, the sort of pasta you eat when you're heading out into the cold and aren't sure when you'll eat again.

What I learned from visiting Teglio and seeing the dish made according to tradition is that the process is as important as its ingredients: the act of boiling potatoes and cabbage and then boiling the pasta in that same water; the browning of the butter with garlic; the meticulous layering. There is a homespun slowness and comfort in the process, like hygge for Italian mountain folk. The resulting dish, a mass of warm cheese and double starch cloaked in garlicky brown butter, eats like the descent into hibernation must feel. My version keeps this effect intact but cuts back ever so slightly on the cheese and butter, not for the sake of health but to let the pasta itself take more of a starring role.

---

1   Following the instructions for pizzoccheri on page 55, make 454g / 1 lb with the pasta dough.

2   Bring a small pot of water to a boil and salt generously. Add the potatoes and cook until tender, but not without some bite, 3 to 5 minutes. Drain and set aside until ready to use.

3   Place a large sauté pan or Dutch oven over medium-low heat and add the oil and 30g / 2 Tbsp of the butter. Add half of the garlic and gently cook until aromatic but without color, 10 to 15 seconds.

4   Add the cabbage and cook until tender and wilted, 3 to 5 minutes. Remove from the heat and set aside until ready to use.

5   Bring a large pot of water to a boil over high heat. Generously salt the water.

6   Place a small saucepan over medium-low heat. Add the remaining butter and garlic and cook until the butter is golden brown and foamy, 3 to 4 minutes. Set aside and keep warm.

7   Add the pizzoccheri to the water and cook for 3 to 5 minutes, until tender but not too soft.

8   Place the sauté pan with the cabbage over low heat. Using a spider or pasta basket, remove the pasta from the pot and transfer to the sauté pan. Add the potatoes and gently toss to combine.

9   Transfer half of the warm pasta-and-cabbage mixture to a large (9 by 13-inch) casserole dish and arrange in an even layer.

10   Sprinkle half of the fontina and half of the parmigiano over the top. Spoon half of the warm garlic butter over the cheese.

11   Repeat the same layering process with the remaining pasta, cheese, and garlic butter.

12   Serve family style from the casserole dish.

Yields 4 to 6 servings

1 batch buckwheat dough (page 30)
432g / 4 small Yukon gold potatoes, peeled and diced into ½-inch pieces
28g / 2 Tbsp olive oil
165g / 11 Tbsp unsalted butter, cold and cubed
5g / 1 garlic clove, thinly sliced
1 head savoy cabbage, cored and cut into 3- to 4-inch strips (about 1kg)
120g / 1 cup coarsely grated fontina cheese, at room temperature
30g / ⅓ cup finely grated parmigiano-reggiano

Nota bene

Traditionally, this dish calls for Bitto cheese, but availability is limited in the U.S. As a substitute, I use high-quality Fontina Val d'Aosta.

Tortelli di Zucca

Squash-Filled Pasta with Sage Brown Butter

If you've eaten at an Italian restaurant in America in the last twenty years, you have almost certainly encountered squash- or pumpkin-filled pasta. But most of the versions you'll encounter stateside have very little to do with tortelli di zucca, an iconic pasta from Lombardy stuffed with amaretti cookies, Mantua pumpkin, and quince mostarda (candied fruit made pungent with mustard extract) and draped in sage brown butter.

The first time I tried these tortelli was in 1999 at Dal Pescatore, a restaurant near Mantua, the hometown of the dish. Even then, pumpkin-filled pasta was already a staple on New York menus, but it was nothing like the Dal Pescatore version. With turns sweet and savory, the dish makes you question to which category it belongs right up until you've eaten your last bite. My version hews closely to the original with some important modifications based on stateside ingredients. First, the variety of pumpkin (the gray-skinned Capel da Pret) grown near Mantua is firmer and less sweet than the pumpkins we're accustomed to here. Second, most US versions omit mustard extract, which is technically banned in the United States for use as a foodstuff (it is high in erucic acid, which can be toxic).

My approach has always been to re-create the flavor profile of the dish, even if that means altering some of the ingredients to do so. To control the overall sweetness of the filling and elevate the complexity, I don't use pumpkin. Instead, I mix delicata squash with a smaller measure of Honeynut or butternut squash. I swap quince mostarda for pear or apple mostarda, and I take the amaretti cookies out of the filling and use them as a garnish. Finally, I add a small measure of whipped ricotta to the filling, which acts as a final buffer to the sweetness and adds a creaminess to the texture.

---

1   To make the filling, preheat the oven to 350°F.

2   Cut the squashes in half lengthwise and clean out the seeds and fibers.

3   Place the squash halves, hollow side up, on a sheet pan and distribute the butter evenly among the cavities. Season with salt and pepper q.b. Drizzle with the olive oil, then strew with the rosemary, thyme, and garlic.

4   Bake until fork-tender, 45 minutes to 1 hour.

5   Remove from the oven and let cool. Remove the garlic and herbs from the squash halves and discard.

6   Scoop the squash flesh from the skin. You should have about 450g / 2¼ cups total. Discard the skin. Line a chinois or fine-mesh strainer with cheesecloth, set the strainer over a bowl, and spoon the flesh into the strainer. Cover the top with parchment paper or plastic wrap and weight it down with a plate (the parchment keeps the squash from adhering to the plate). Transfer to the refrigerator and let the excess liquid seep out for a minimum of 2 hours or up to overnight. This will prevent the filling from being watery and loose.

7   Place a tamis over a bowl. Pass the squash through the tamis or fine-mesh strainer.

Yields 4 to 6 servings

Filling

900g / 2 lb delicata squash
900g / 2 lb butternut squash
60g / ¼ cup unsalted butter,
    cold and cubed
Salt, q.b.
Black pepper, q.b.
42g / 3 Tbsp olive oil
3 sprigs rosemary
5 sprigs thyme
40g / 8 cloves garlic
232g / 1 cup ricotta (see
    "whipped" ricotta, page 139)
30g / 1½ Tbsp finely chopped
    apple or pear mostarda
90g / 1 cup finely grated
    parmigiano-reggiano
Whole nutmeg, q.b.

8   Put the ricotta into a food processor and pulse just until it is as smooth as cake frosting and has a sheen, being careful not to process it longer or it will break. Transfer to the bowl holding the squash.

9   Add the mostarda and parmigiano to the bowl and mix well. Season with salt and pepper q.b. and with about 15 gratings of nutmeg (don't add more because the spice will bloom when cooked). It should taste well seasoned. Refrigerate until ready to use.

10   To finish, following the instructions for tortelli on page 106, make 60 pieces with the pasta dough and filling.

11   Bring a large pot of water to a boil over high heat. Generously salt the water.

12   Place a small saucepan over medium heat. Add 60g / ¼ cup of the butter and cook until just past golden brown, about 3 to 4 minutes. Add a few of the sage leaves to infuse lightly. Remove from the heat and set aside. You will drizzle this sage brown butter over the plated pasta.

13   Add the tortelli to the water and turn down the heat to bring the water to a gentle simmer instead of a rolling boil. It is important to cook these gently at a simmer instead of a boil. The filling is delicate and can break if cooked over high heat. Cook for 3 to 5 minutes, until tender at the thickest closure point.

14   While the pasta is cooking, place a large sauté pan over low heat. Add 1 to 2 ladles (55 to 115g / ¼ to ½ cup) pasta cooking water. Add the remaining butter and swirl to emulsify.

15   Using a spider or pasta basket, remove the pasta from the pot and transfer to the sauté pan. Turn the heat up to medium. Swirl for 1 to 2 minutes to marry the pasta and the sauce, using a spoon to gently turn the pasta over and coat all sides. If the sauce begins to tighten, add a splash of cooking water to loosen and continue swirling to marry.

16   Divide into bowls and drizzle with the reserved sage brown butter. Garnish with the parmigiano, amaretti, the remaining sage, and with grated nutmeg and pepper q.b.

To Finish

1 batch egg dough (page 18)
114g / ½ cup unsalted butter, cold and cubed
10 small sage leaves
30g / ⅓ cup finely grated parmigiano-reggiano
15g / 1 Tbsp finely crushed amaretti cookies (about 2 large cookies)
Whole nutmeg, q.b.
Black pepper, q.b.

Canederli

Speck and Rye Bread Dumplings

Pull into any restaurant, rifugio, or café between Trento and Merano and I'd wager you've got a 90 percent chance of finding canederli on the menu. Known as Knödel over the northern border in Austria, they become Italianate on this side of the Alps via the introduction of parmigiano-reggiano and speck—that smoky alpine answer to prosciutto. (Often speck is replaced with spinach, but the parmigiano remains.)

Canederli typically present themselves two ways: in brodo or boiled and then finished with brown butter. While I love them both ways, and encourage you to experiment, it's hard to refuse a bowl of smoky, savory bread dumplings doused in butter.

---

1   To make the dough base, break down the bread into 1-inch cubes and transfer to a sheet pan to dry overnight. Alternatively, preheat the oven to 200°F. Place the sheet pan in the oven until the bread is hardened but without color, 1 hour. Set it aside to cool.

2   Place the bread in a large bowl and cover with the milk. Let soak until completely softened, 20 to 30 minutes.

3   While the bread is soaking, place a sauté pan over medium-low heat. Add the olive oil and the onions and gently cook until they just begin to caramelize, 15 to 20 minutes. Transfer the onions to a bowl to cool.

4   Once the onions are cool, add them to the bowl with the bread-and-milk mixture. Add the eggs, speck, flour, and parsley, and fold together to combine. Make sure to break up any large chunks of bread. The mixture should be uniform.

5   Cover and refrigerate the mixture for 30 minutes to 1 hour.

6   Following the instructions for canederli on page 114, make 18 pieces with the dough.

7   To finish, bring a large pot of water to a boil over high heat. Generously salt the water.

8   Line a sheet pan with parchment paper and set aside.

9   Add half of the canederli to the water and turn down the heat to low. Simmer for 20 to 25 minutes, until soft but not mushy. (If you add all of the canederli at once they will not cook evenly.) Using a spider or slotted spoon, remove the canederli from the pot and transfer to the prepared sheet pan. Repeat with the second batch, keeping the first batch separate. Once you have finished cooking the second batch, dip the balls from the first batch back in the water to warm them.

10   Place a saucepan over medium-low heat. Add the butter and cook until golden brown and foamy, 2 to 3 minutes. Keep warm.

11   Divide the canederli between bowls and evenly drizzle the butter over each. There should be a small pool of butter at the bottom of each bowl. Garnish with the parmigiano and the chives.

Yields 4 to 6 servings

Canederli Dough Base

397g / Jewish-style rye bread
474g / 2 cups milk
56g / ¼ cup olive oil
204g / 1½ cups finely diced onions
200g / 4 eggs, mixed
1 small (85g / 3 oz) slab speck, finely diced
40g / 5 Tbsp all-purpose flour
10g / 2 Tbsp finely chopped parsley

To Finish

171g / ¾ cup unsalted butter, cold and cubed
30g / ⅓ cup finely grated parmigiano-reggiano
10g / 2 Tbsp finely sliced chives

Passatelli in Brodo

Bread and Parmigiano Dumplings in Brodo

This was one of the first dishes I learned how to make as a cook in San Marino. Even then, I remember thinking of passatelli as a distant cousin of the matzo ball—more dumpling than pasta, especially when you consider its construction (cheese, egg, bread crumbs, spices). This is a dish that really begins and ends with the shape itself—all of the technique is in getting the texture right. Drop passatelli into hot brodo and you'll know right away if you've done them correctly: they either disintegrate on entry or their shape holds *too* well and they don't swell, like a sponge, when cooked.

The name *passatelli* translates to "to be passed through," referring to the way the shape is made: by passing the dough through either a tool designed specifically for the purpose, known as il ferro or e fér per passatelli (iron for passatelli), or a potato ricer. The little irregular cylinders of dough are then dropped directly into the simmering brodo in which they will be served. While the shape is now sometimes paired with sauces—tomato, meat, or seafood based—passatelli in brodo is far and away its most common guise. That is especially true in its home base of Emilia-Romagna.

The shape, which is described varyingly as "soggy Cheetos" (by a friend, affectionately) and "special fat little noodles" (*The Oxford Companion to Italian Food*), is made by enriching the aforementioned base with bone marrow or minced meat, often salumi or mortadella. To this, both pepper and nutmeg are standard additions, though as far back as Maestro Martino di Como's publication of *Libro de arte coquinaria* in 1465, other spices, like saffron, ginger, and clove, made their way into the mixture. In Umbria and the Marche, passatelli are often further flavored with lemon zest.

Even though the dish always gets second billing to Bologna's other brodo dish (page 198), its humility has always appealed to me. It's a peasant among nobles (tagliatelle alla bolognese, balanzoni, lasagna verde), and a dish that feels about as rooted to my heritage as any Italian dish could.

---

1   To make the dough, preheat the oven to 200°F.

2   Spread the bread on a sheet pan and bake until dried out, 30 to 45 minutes. You do not want any color. To test for doneness, smash a shard of bread with the back of a spoon. The interior should be completely dry. Let cool.

3   Once cooled, place the bread in a food processor and pulse until very finely ground and uniform. Measure out 230g / scant 4 cups bread crumbs and set aside. Transfer the remainder to an airtight container and store in a cool, dry place for up to 2 weeks for another use.

4   Add the reserved bread crumbs and parmigiano to a mixing bowl and stir to combine. Transfer to a wooden work surface and make a well.

5   Add the eggs to a small mixing bowl and quickly whisk to combine. Add 35 to 40 gratings of the nutmeg and the lemon peel, and whisk to combine.

6   Add half of the egg mixture to the well and use a fork to incorporate the inner layer of cheese and bread crumbs, stirring in a continuous motion around the circumference to combine. Continue with the remainder of the egg mixture.

continued

Yields 4 to 6 servings

Passatelli Dough

1 loaf (456g / 16 oz) country
    bread, torn into pieces (about
    8 cups)
214g / 2⅓ cups plus 1 scant Tbsp
    finely grated parmigiano-
    reggiano
300g / 6 eggs
Whole nutmeg, q.b.
Peel of 1 lemon, pith removed
    and peel finely chopped

Brodo

1 (1.6 to 1.8kg / 3½ to 4 lb)
    chicken
2.8 to 4.7kg / 3 to 5 qt water
300g / 2 large carrots, peeled
    and cut into 1-inch pieces
370g / 1 large onion, cut into
    quarters
227g / ½ head celery, cut into
    1-inch pieces
150g / ½ leek, cut into 1-inch
    pieces

7   Once the bread crumbs, cheese, and egg mixture have formed a mass, gently knead the dough just until it comes together. The dough should be firm enough to stay together, yet soft enough that it could easily go through a potato ricer or passatelli press. Form the dough into a ball, cover it with plastic wrap, and let it rest for at least 1 hour. If you're not forming passatelli until the evening or the next day, place the dough in the refrigerator and remove it 20 to 30 minutes before you plan to form the pasta. Use the dough within 24 hours.

8   To make the brodo, place the chicken in a large stockpot and add 2.8kg / 3 qt of the water. If the chicken is not fully covered, add more water to cover by 3 inches. Place over low heat and slowly bring to a simmer, 45 minutes to 1 hour. Once the liquid starts to simmer, scum will begin to rise to the top. Skim continually with a large spoon to keep the brodo very clear.

9   If the water level falls below the chicken after 1 hour, add enough of the remaining water to re-cover it and simmer for 2 hours longer, continuing to skim any impurities and adding more water as needed to keep the chicken covered.

10   After 3 hours, add the carrots, onion, celery, leek, parsley, garlic, peppercorns, and bay leaf and cook at a slow simmer until very flavorful, 1 to 2 hours longer.

11   Line a fine-mesh strainer with a coffee filter or cheesecloth and strain the brodo through it. Measure out 1.4 kg / 6 cups brodo and add to a large sauce pot. Let the remaining brodo cool, then store in an airtight container in the refrigerator for up to 5 days or in the freezer for another use. Refrigerate the chicken meat for another use.

12   To finish, place the large sauce pot with the brodo over medium heat. Bring to a gentle simmer and season with salt q.b.

13   Fit your potato ricer with the medium die.

14   Divide the passatelli dough into four pieces and place one quarter of the dough in the chamber of the potato ricer. Squeeze the handles together directly over the brodo, using a knife to cut 2- to 3-inch strands as they extrude. Repeat with the remaining quarters of dough, adding the passatelli to the pot.

15   Slowly cook the passatelli in the brodo until the pieces begin to float to the top, 2 to 3 minutes.

16   Divide into bowls and garnish with the parmigiano and grated nutmeg q.b.

30g / ½ bunch parsley
100g / 1 head garlic, cut in half
9g / 1 Tbsp black peppercorns
1 fresh bay leaf

To Finish

Salt, q.b.
22g / ¼ cup finely grated parmigiano-reggiano
Whole nutmeg, q.b.

Bigoli in Salsa

Pasta in Anchovy Sauce

Bigoli, a wide spaghetti, has been ubiquitous in Venice since at least the sixteenth century. While its pairing with a sauce made from salted fish and onions originated with the city's Jewish residents, it has since become a dish associated with the Catholic holidays—particularly Lent—and is now served year-round. It's made by sweating down salt-cured fish, typically anchovies (though sardines are sometimes used, especially in the Lombardian town of Mantua), and onions until they dissolve into a creamy consistency. The result is a triumph of savory and sweet, the anchovies lending a subtle funk and depth to the sweetness of the onion and garlic. And while freshly ground pepper might seem like an immaterial inclusion, its bite is a small addition to the traditional recipe that gives the dish levity without compromising its standing as one of the north's strongest arguments for simplicity.

1   Following the directions for bigoli on page 115, make 624g / 1 lb 6 oz with the pasta dough.

2   Place a large sauté pan over low heat. Add the olive oil and butter and swirl to emulsify.

3   Add the onions and continue cooking until they begin to soften, 5 to 8 minutes.

4   Add the garlic, anchovies, and water and continue cooking, stirring often, until the onions are caramelized to a deep golden brown, 45 minutes to 1 hour. Set aside.

5   Bring a large pot of water to a boil over high heat. Generously salt the water.

6   Add the bigoli to the water and cook for 2 to 3 minutes, until tender but not soft.

7   Place the reserved sauté pan over low heat. Using tongs or a pasta basket, remove the pasta from the pot and transfer to the sauté pan. Turn the heat up to medium. Toss for 1 to 2 minutes to marry the pasta and the sauce, gradually adding about 2 ladles (115g / ½ cup) pasta cooking water. If the sauce begins to tighten, add a splash of pasta cooking water to loosen and continue tossing. When the pasta is properly married, it will cling to the sauce and have a glossy sheen.

8   Divide the pasta into bowls and garnish with black pepper q.b.

Yields 4 to 6 servings

1 batch whole-wheat dough (page 26)
56g / ¼ cup olive oil
45g / 3 Tbsp unsalted butter, cold and cubed
454g / 3¼ cups finely diced onions
15g / 3 cloves garlic, finely chopped
114g / 20 to 24 oil-packed anchovy fillets, finely chopped
120g / ½ cup water
Black pepper, q.b.

Casunziei all'Ampezzana

Beet-Filled Pasta with Brown Butter, Poppy Seeds, and Smoked Ricotta

There was a time during the early aughts when this specialty of the ski town of Cortina d'Ampezzo (the Aspen of the Dolomites) hit a bunch of upscale Italian menus in America, though not by its rightful name. What an innovation, we thought, to douse mezzelune ravioli stuffed with bright red beets in brown butter, poppy seeds, and shaved smoked ricotta. But the innovation surely belongs to some enterprising nonna, who likely conceived the dish a century (or several) ago.

The dish, like so many Italian pastas, is built on practicality. In the summer, the ravioli are typically stuffed with beet greens and foraged alpine herbs (chard, nettles, bladder campion), and in the winter, with local root vegetables (beets, turnips, potatoes). How the beet version of casunziei became the town's calling card is not so difficult to guess: it's a sight to behold, and while its combination of sweet, savory, and smoky is something of a holy trinity in the Alps (see cjalsons, page 92), the earthiness imparted by the beets is what gives it an allure all its own.

To master this dish, you must be mindful of both sweetness and texture. While many of the versions I've encountered in Italy cut the beets with potato as a counterpoint, I've always balanced their sweetness and mealy quality with a small measure of whipped ricotta.

---

1   To make the filling, preheat the oven to 350°F. Lay a large sheet of aluminum foil on your work surface and place the beets in the center. Add the coriander seed, fennel seed, chile flakes, rosemary, thyme, olive oil, and a splash of water and season with salt q.b. Seal all the edges and place the foil packet on a sheet pan.

2   Bake the beets until fork-tender, about 2 hours.

3   Open the foil packet and let the beets cool to the touch.

4   To avoid staining your hands semipermanent purple, wear rubber gloves to peel the beets. The skins should slide off easily.

5   Grate half of the beets on the fine side of a box grater.

6   Coarsely chop the other half of the beets and puree in a high-speed blender until smooth (you should not need to add liquid, as the beets should have enough moisture). To ensure the puree is supersmooth, stop and scrape down the sides of the blender jar, then process for 30 seconds longer. Transfer to a bowl and stir in the grated beets.

7   Wash the bowl of the food processor. Put the ricotta into the food processor and pulse just until it is as smooth as cake frosting and has a sheen, being careful not to process it longer or it will break.

8   Add the ricotta to the beets and fold in until fully incorporated.

9   Season with salt and black pepper q.b. It should taste well seasoned. Cover and refrigerate until ready to use. (It will firm up slightly, making it a little easier to work with.)

Yields 6 to 8 servings

Filling

454g / 1 lb beets (about 1 bunch, greens removed)
5g / 1 Tbsp coriander seed
6g / 1 Tbsp fennel seed
2g / 1 tsp dried red chile flakes
3 sprigs rosemary
3 sprigs thyme
42g / 3 Tbsp olive oil
Salt, q.b
116g / ½ cup ricotta (see "whipped" ricotta, page 139)
Black pepper, q.b.

To Finish

1 batch egg dough (page 18)
171g / ¾ cup unsalted butter, cold and cubed
9g / 1 Tbsp poppy seeds
Black pepper, q.b.
1 small (57g / 2 oz) piece smoked ricotta

10   To finish, following the instructions for casunziei on page 89, make 75 to 90 pieces with the pasta dough and filling.

11   Bring a large pot of water to a boil over high heat. Generously salt the water.

12   While the water is heating, place a large sauté pan over medium heat. Add the butter and cook until golden brown and foamy, 2 to 3 minutes. Try and time this step so your butter comes to the foamy stage at the same time as your pasta is ready to hit the pan.

13   Add the casunziei to the water and turn down the heat to bring the water to a gentle simmer instead of a rolling boil. It is important to cook these gently at a simmer instead of a boil. The filling is delicate and can break if cooked over high heat. Cook for 1 to 2 minutes, until tender at the thickest closure point. The center of your pasta will turn a deep magenta during cooking.

14   Using a spider or pasta basket, remove the pasta from the pot and transfer to the sauté pan. Swirl the pasta in the pan to coat with the butter, using a spoon to gently turn the pasta over and coat all sides. This is not a full marriage ceremony; think of it instead as an elopement.

15   Divide onto plates and spoon the remaining butter from the pan over the pasta. Garnish with the poppy seeds and with pepper q.b. Use a Microplane to finely grate the smoked ricotta over the top.

Cjalsons

Sweet and Savory Pasta with Brown Butter and Cinnamon

Are cjalsons sweet? Are they savory? Are they both? No one can even agree on how they are spelled or pronounced (cjalsons, cjarsons, cialzons). There is no precise definition, no codified recipe. Cjalsons are best understood as an expression of the singular slice of the Alps from which they originate. This part of Friuli was once one of the most isolated parts of Italy, so much so that Sauris, the heartbeat of the area, could not be reached by car until the 1930s and was completely inaccessible during the winter months until the midcentury. It's this isolation that has birthed a canon of culinary traditions based on resourcefulness.

There are sweet and savory versions of cjalsons, the former relying on dried fruits, chocolate, ricotta, and biscotti, to name a few components. The savory versions tend to lean on foraged herbs, ricotta, nuts, and spices. But at the center of their Venn diagram is where I've found some of the most interesting examples of the dish. They are typically finished in brown butter with a dusting of cinnamon, sugar, and grated smoked ricotta, but that too can vary. In the home kitchen, I like to think of them as an invitation—a way to study the intersection of savory and sweet, and to delight in their malleability.

1   To make the filling, place a tamis or fine-mesh strainer over a bowl. Pass the ricotta through the tamis. Add the smoked ricotta, apple, pear, raisins, Montasio, citrus peels, cinnamon, and cocoa powder to the bowl and fold together to mix well.

2   Season with salt and pepper q.b. It should taste well seasoned. Cover and refrigerate until ready to use.

3   To finish, following the instructions for cjalsons on page 92, make 48 to 60 pieces with the pasta dough and filling.

4   Bring a large pot of water to a boil over high heat. Generously salt the water.

5   Place a small saucepan over medium heat. Add 114g / ½ cup of the butter and cook until just past golden brown, 3 to 4 minutes. Remove from heat and set aside. You will drizzle this brown butter over the plated pasta.

6   Add the cjalsons to the water and turn down the heat to bring the water to a gentle simmer instead of a rolling boil. The filling is delicate and can break if cooked over high heat. Cook for 2 to 3 minutes, until tender at the thickest closure point.

7   While the pasta is cooking, place a large sauté pan over medium heat. Add 2 ladles (115g / ½ cup) pasta cooking water and the remaining butter and swirl together to emulsify.

8   Using a spider or pasta basket, remove the pasta from the pot and transfer to the sauté pan. Swirl for about 30 seconds to marry the pasta and the sauce, using a spoon to gently turn the pasta over and coat all sides.

9   Divide onto plates and spoon the brown butter over each plate. Garnish with a touch of cinnamon, followed by a tiny dusting of cocoa powder, using a fine-mesh strainer, baker's wand, or sugar shaker (a little goes a long way). Finally, finely grate the ricotta on top, then finish with pepper q.b.

Yields 4 to 6 servings

Filling

348g / 1½ cups ricotta
1 small (57g / 2 oz) piece smoked ricotta, coarsely grated
64g / ½ Granny Smith apple, peeled and finely grated
29g / 1 piece dried pear, finely chopped
15g / 2 Tbsp golden raisins, finely chopped
1 small (28g / 1 oz) piece Montasio cheese, finely grated
Peel of 1 orange, pith removed and peel finely chopped
Peel of 1 lemon, pith removed and peel finely chopped
¼ tsp freshly ground cinnamon
½ tsp natural cocoa powder
Salt, q.b.
Black pepper, q.b.

To Finish

1 batch egg dough (page 18)
150 g / 10 Tbsp plus 1 tsp unsalted butter, cold and cubed
1 stick cinnamon, grated, or ground cinnamon, for garnish
Natural cocoa powder, q.b.
1 small (114g / 4 oz) piece smoked ricotta
Black pepper, q.b.

Tortellini in Brodo

Pork-Filled Pasta in Brodo

Like any proper classic of Emilia-Romagna, tortellini in brodo have spawned no shortage of debate—and that debate centers on what, exactly, the tortellini should be stuffed with. But not enough debate concerns the brodo, which has to pack the same amount of depth and clarity of flavor as the filling. I remember the first time I saw an Italian cook make brodo: a chicken, one piece of beef, a single carrot, a single celery stalk. It was so basic in comparison to the stocks I'd learned to make in French-leaning kitchens, and that minimalism stuck with me. However nontraditional, I only add my vegetables to stock toward the end; what I am looking for from my brodo is the commingling of the pure taste of chicken with the flavor of the filling.

Speaking of that filling, we can at least agree that in the case of classic tortellini in brodo the pasta should be filled with a mixture of meats cured, raw, and/or roasted. I believe it's less important to obsess over the choice of meat than it is to consider what you're trying to get from it. Tortellini are about the size of a quarter, which means the filling is about the volume of a hazelnut, if that. You want enough flavor from that tiny amount of filling to infuse a dish that is backed up solely by brodo.

The second primary consideration is texture. Meat fillings can dry out and become almost grainy. To achieve a smooth, rich texture, I go through the tedium of putting my cured meats through a grinder twice. And to turn things up a few more octaves, I cook pork shoulder in the oven with garlic and aromatics and grind it into the mix along with plenty of parmigiano and freshly grated nutmeg. A tiny taste of that filling should pack some awe. In David and Goliath terms, this is the David of pasta dishes.

1   To make the filling, chill the meat grinder and small die for at least 1 hour before grinding. Salt the pork shoulder on all sides and let sit for 45 minutes to absorb. After it sits, pat it dry with a paper towel to remove any excess moisture.

2   Heat a large sauté pan over medium-high and add 28g / 2 Tbsp of the olive oil. Add the pork shoulder, fat side down, and sear, turning as needed, until golden brown, about 5 minutes on each side.

3   While the pork is browning, preheat the oven to 325°F.

4   Transfer the pork to a heavy sauce pot or Dutch oven, discarding any rendered fat and browned bits in the sauté pan. Add the rosemary, garlic, and lemon peel and cover the pot.

5   Cook the meat until fork-tender and easy to pull apart, about 2½ hours. Set aside for about 20 minutes to cool.

6   When the pork is cool enough to touch, pull it apart into small pieces. Reserve the fat, but remove and discard the sinew. Pour out and discard any rendered fat from the pot.

7   Fit your meat grinder with the small die and put the mortadella, prosciutto, and roast pork through twice.

8   Add the meats and reserved fat to a bowl, and add the parmigiano and the remaining 14g / 1 Tbsp olive oil, season with grated nutmeg and pepper q.b., and mix well. Taste and adjust the seasoning. It should taste well seasoned.

Yields 6 to 8 servings

Filling

Salt, q.b.
1 (567g / 1¼ lb) piece deboned
    pork shoulder with a nice
    fat cap
42g / 3 Tbsp olive oil
3 sprigs rosemary
5 cloves garlic
Peel of ½ lemon, pith removed
1 small (114g / 4 oz) slab
    mortadella
1 small (57g / 2 oz) slab
    prosciutto
90g / 1 cup finely grated
    parmigiano-reggiano
Whole nutmeg, q.b.
Black pepper, q.b.

9   To make the brodo, place the chicken in a large stockpot and add 2.8kg / 3 qt of the water. If the chicken is not fully covered, add more water to cover by 3 inches. Place over low heat and slowly bring to a simmer, 45 minutes to 1 hour. Once the liquid starts to simmer, scum will begin to rise to the top. Skim continually with a large spoon to keep the brodo very clear.

10   If the water level falls below the chicken after 1 hour, add enough of the remaining water to re-cover it and simmer for 2 hours longer, continuing to skim any impurities and adding more water as needed to keep the chicken covered.

11   Add the carrots, onion, celery, leek, parsley, garlic, peppercorns, and bay leaf and cook at a slow simmer until very flavorful, 1 to 2 hours.

12   Line a fine-mesh strainer with a coffee filter or cheesecloth and strain the brodo through it. Measure out 1.6kg / 7 cups brodo and add to a saucepan. Let the remaining brodo cool, then store in an airtight container in the refrigerator for up to 5 days or in the freezer for another use. Refrigerate the chicken meat for another use.

13   To finish, following the instructions for tortellini on page 110, make 150 pieces with the pasta dough and filling.

14   Bring a large pot of water to a boil over high heat. Generously salt the water.

15   Bring the saucepan of brodo to a simmer over low heat and season with salt q.b.

16   Add the tortellini to the water and cook for 1 to 2 minutes, until tender at the thickest closure point.

17   Using a spider or pasta basket, remove the tortellini from the pot and divide into bowls. Ladle the brodo over each serving and garnish with the parmigiano.

Brodo

1 (1.6 to 1.8kg / 3½ to 4 lb) chicken
2.8 to 4.7kg / 3 to 5 qt water
300g / 2 large carrots, peeled and cut into 1-inch pieces
370g / 1 large onion, cut into quarters
227g / ½ head celery, cut into 1-inch pieces
150g / ½ leek, white and light green parts, cut into 1-inch pieces
30g / ½ bunch parsley
100g / 1 head garlic, cut in half
9g / 1 Tbsp black peppercorns
1 fresh bay leaf

To Finish

1 batch egg dough (page 18)
Salt, q.b.
22g / ¼ cup finely grated parmigiano-reggiano

Tagliatelle alla Bolognese

Pasta with Bolognese Ragù

No one is going to argue with bolognese sauce being the true apex of ragù. But that doesn't mean that everyone agrees on what goes into that ragù—or even on what defines a great ragù. All of us, whether or not we've been lucky enough to eat bolognese at its source, understand its universal appeal. This combination of meats slowly simmered together into a gravy doesn't really need a marketing campaign.

The debate about the sauce centers on choosing to include or omit milk or cream and tomato and, of course, the mixture of meat—whether it's all beef, beef and pork, or beef, pork, and veal. Tomato, generally in the form of tomato paste, certainly rankles the most purist nonne. I am in favor of a small dose, which adds a bit of sweetness and tomato flavor without adding liquid.

My version is a tribute to my former neighbor, and now business partner. The first time he ever invited me up for dinner he made bolognese, a bold move. It ultimately became a Sunday standard at our building on Grove Street, a dish I craved and would often beg him to make. It was his version that made me love bolognese. This iteration is inspired by tradition but engineered to compete with his take. If you end up with leftovers, make tagliatelle ripassate in padella, which is essentially refried tagliatelle alla bolognese (the direct translation is "panfried tagliatelle"): simply add oil to a pan over high heat and fry the tagliatelle on both sides until it has a crust on it.

---

1 Place the meat grinder and small die in the refrigerator for at least 1 hour to chill. (You can speed the process by placing it in the freezer for 30 minutes instead.)

2 To make the ragù, fit your meat grinder with the small die. Put the pancetta through the meat grinder twice and set aside.

3 Chop the onion, carrot, and celery into ½- to 1-inch pieces. Put the carrot, celery, and onion through the meat grinder. Once all are ground, gather them in cheesecloth and wring to squeeze out the liquid. This is your soffritto.

4 Place a large, heavy sauce pot or Dutch oven over low heat. Add the pancetta and cook until the fat has rendered and the pancetta is cooked but not crispy or brown, 5 to 8 minutes.

5 Add the beef, pork, and veal and turn the heat up to medium-high. Sauté, breaking up the meat with a wooden spoon, until lightly browned, about 5 minutes.

6 Turn off the heat. Transfer the meat in the pot to a bowl and set aside. Discard any brown bits from the pot.

7 Return the pot to low heat. Add the oil and soffritto and gently cook, stirring frequently, until softened but without color, 5 to 8 minutes. Add the tomato paste and cook for 1 to 2 minutes to integrate. Add the meat back to the pot and stir to combine.

8 Add the wine and cook until reduced by about half and most of the alcohol has cooked off, 2 to 3 minutes.

Yields 4 to 6 servings

Ragù

1 (170g / 6 oz) slab pancetta
370g / 1 large onion
150g / 1 large carrot, peeled
150g / 2 stalks celery
454g / 1 lb ground beef
454g / 1 lb ground pork
454g / 1 lb ground veal
56g / ¼ cup olive oil
130g / ½ cup tomato paste
220g / 1 cup dry white wine
474g / 2 cups water, plus
    more q.b.
237g / 1 cup milk

To Finish

1 batch egg-based dough
    (pages 18, 22, and 26–31)
30g / 2 Tbsp unsalted butter,
    cold and cubed
45g / ½ cup finely grated
    parmigiano-reggiano

9   Add the water and continue to cook over very low heat for 2 to 3 hours. The ragù is ready when the flavors have melded and the meat is fully softened. Check every 30 minutes and add more water q.b. to ensure it doesn't dry out. It should not brown or stick to the bottom of the pot. As it cooks down, it should thickly coat your spoon as you stir.

10   Remove from the heat. Add the milk and stir to incorporate. At this point, your ragù should have a nice sheen.

11   Measure out 512g / 2¼ cups ragù and set aside. Transfer the remainder to an airtight container and refrigerate for up to 5 days or freeze for another use.

12   To finish, following the instructions for tagliatelle on page 57, make 624g / 1 lb 6 oz with the pasta dough.

13   Bring a large pot of water to a boil over high heat. Generously salt the water.

14   Place a large sauté pan over low heat. Add the ragù and 1 to 2 ladles (55 to 115g / ¼ to ½ cup) pasta cooking water and stir to combine.

15   Once the ragù mixture is warm, add the butter and stir to combine. Set aside.

16   Add the tagliatelle to the water and cook for 30 seconds to 1 minute, until tender but not soft.

17   Using tongs or a pasta basket, remove the pasta from the pot and transfer to the sauté pan. Turn the heat up to medium. Add another 1 to 2 ladles (55 to 115g / ¼ to ½ cup) pasta cooking water. Using a large spoon, gently fold together the pasta and sauce for 30 seconds to 1 minute to marry. If the sauce begins to tighten, add a splash of pasta cooking water to loosen and continue folding to marry.

18   Remove from the heat. Add half of the parmigiano and fold to integrate, adding a few more splashes of pasta water if necessary. The meat should cling to the pasta and the sauce should still have a sheen.

19   Divide the pasta into bowls and garnish with the remaining parmigiano.

Balanzoni Burro e Salvia

Mortadella and Ricotta–Filled Pasta with Brown Butter and Sage

Given its visual appeal, I would have thought I'd stumble upon this dish more often. But the first time I had it was in 2019 at Vâgh iń ufézzi, a restaurant in Bologna. Like so many dishes, balanzoni are said to have been born from the ashes of another pasta—in this case tortellini, whose filling would be mixed with ricotta to make balanzoni.

Today, the filling is typically a mixture of mortadella and ricotta seasoned with nutmeg. The balance between the two main ingredients is critical: too much mortadella and the whole affair ends up tasting like a Coney Island hot dog. Mortadella is really only there to add a bit of savory, salty flavor to the ricotta.

While I've had this dish finished with both ricotta salata and smoked ricotta salata, I keep it simple, finishing it in its classic sauce of butter and sage and a not-shy dose of parmigiano. This, like any great filled-pasta dish, is about the pasta itself.

---

1   To make the filling, place the meat grinder and small die in the refrigerator for at least 1 hour to chill. (You can speed the process by placing it in the freezer for 30 minutes instead.)

2   Fit your meat grinder with the small die and put the mortadella through twice.

3   Place a tamis or fine-mesh strainer over a small bowl. Pass the ricotta through the tamis. Add the mortadella and parmigiano to the bowl and stir until well blended.

4   Add 5 or 6 gratings of nutmeg, stir in, and taste. Adjust q.b. (The nutmeg will bloom when the pasta is cooking. It shouldn't be too dominant at this stage.)

5   Season with the salt and then taste. Different mortadellas have varying salt and spice levels, so you may need more. The mixture should taste well seasoned. Cover and refrigerate until ready to use.

6   To finish, following the directions for balanzoni on page 77, make 50 to 60 pieces with the pasta dough and filling.

7   Bring a large pot of water to a boil over high heat. Generously salt the water.

8   While the water is heating, place a small saucepan over medium heat. Add half the butter and cook until just past golden brown, 3 to 4 minutes. Add 5 of the sage leaves and set aside off the heat. You will drizzle this butter over the plated pasta.

9   Place a large sauté pan over low heat. Add 2 ladles (115g / ½ cup) pasta cooking water. Add the remaining butter and swirl to emulsify. Set aside off the heat.

Yields 4 to 6 servings

Filling

1 (120g / 4½ oz) piece
    mortadella
604g / 2⅔ cups ricotta
30g/ ⅓ cup finely grated
    parmigiano-reggiano
Whole nutmeg, q.b.
¾ tsp salt, plus more q.b.

To Finish

1 batch green dough (page 22)
150g / 10 Tbsp plus 1 tsp
    unsalted butter, cold and
    cubed
15 small sage leaves
22g / ¼ cup finely grated
    parmigiano-reggiano
Whole nutmeg, q.b
Black pepper, q.b.

Balanzoni Burro e Salvia

continued

10   Add the balanzoni to the water and turn down the heat to bring the water to a gentle simmer instead of a rolling boil. It is important to cook these gently at a simmer instead of a boil. The filling is very delicate and will break if cooked over high heat. Cook for 1 to 2 minutes, until tender at the thickest closure point.

11   Place the reserved sauté pan over low heat. Using a spider or pasta basket, remove the pasta from the pot and transfer to the sauté pan. Turn the heat up to medium. Swirl the pasta in the sauce for 30 seconds to 1 minute to marry, using a spoon to gently turn the pasta over and coat all sides. If the sauce begins to tighten, add a splash of pasta cooking water to loosen and continue swirling to marry.

12   Divide into bowls and garnish with the parmigiano and with grated nutmeg and pepper q.b. Drizzle the reserved sage butter over the top and finish with the remaining sage leaves.

Agnolotti dal Plin

Brisket and Caramelized Onion–Filled Pasta

My version of agnolotti dal plin traces its origins back to Anne Rosenzweig, the famed New York City chef of Arcadia and Lobster Club, and my former boss in the 1990s. She had a method for cooking brisket that called for covering the whole thing with an obscene amount of sliced onion and then cooking it at a low temp in the oven for at least five hours. The method would essentially cook the meat three ways as the onions caramelized and melted into a flavorful liquid: roast, then steam, then braise. That onion-cloaked brisket is my agnolotti filling—and my sauce.

Is it traditional? Not exactly, but also not-not. In Piedmont, particularly in the hills and plains around Turin, agnolotti are typically stuffed with meat, whether it's beef, pork, or donkey (both horse and donkey are consumed in Italy) that is either braised or roasted or both. Those meats often share at least some of the real estate with a vegetable, like chard or cabbage. And while the filling was once a means of using up leftovers, today it's more often made exclusively for the pasta, and the juices left from the cooking are used for the sugo d'arrosto, or the sauce in which the agnolotti are finished. Like most regional classics, agnolotti dal plin fan out from a central idea rather than a fixed recipe, and my version is still strongly rooted to that idea.

This isn't a dish that you can whip up in the afternoon for dinner the same day. But it's worth carving out some time to make it. What I love about it is the way in which the braise becomes both the filling and the sauce. On paper that might seem like it would lead to monotony, but instead the result is deliciously layered—at once rich, savory, and gently sweet from the inclusion of onion, which is truly the X factor at work here.

1   To make the filling, salt the brisket on all sides and let sit to absorb for at least 1 hour or up to 24 hours in the refrigerator. (If you have refrigerated it, be sure to bring it to room temperature ahead of cooking.) Just before the brisket has sat long enough, preheat the oven to 275°F.

2   Pat the brisket dry with a paper towel to remove any excess moisture. Heat a large sauté pan over medium heat and add 42g / 3 Tbsp of the olive oil. Add the brisket, fat side down, and sear until the fat begins to melt and is golden brown, 4 to 5 minutes. Turn the brisket as needed to sear on all sides until golden brown, 4 to 5 minutes on each side. Transfer the brisket to a sheet pan.

3   Place half of the sliced onions on the bottom of a heavy sauce pot with a lid or a Dutch oven. Place the brisket on top of the onions and place the remaining onions on top of the brisket. Lay the thyme on top of the onions. Add the water, cover the pot with aluminum foil or parchment paper, and place the lid over the foil to seal it in place.

4   Transfer the pot to the oven and cook the brisket and onions until the meat easily pulls apart when tested with a fork, 5 to 6 hours. The onions will have "melted" and caramelized, creating a jus that will form the base of your sauce.

5   Place the meat grinder and small die in the refrigerator for at least 1 hour to chill. (You can speed the process by placing it in the freezer for 30 minutes instead.)

Yields 6 to 8 servings

Brisket Filling

27g / 3 Tbsp salt, plus more q.b.
1 (912g / 2 lb) brisket, center cut with a moderate amount of fat
56g / 4 Tbsp olive oil
1.85kg / 5 or 6 onions, cut into ⅛-inch-thick slices
2 sprigs thyme
474g / 2 cups water
30g / ⅓ cup finely grated parmigiano-reggiano
Whole nutmeg, q.b.

To Finish

1 batch egg dough (page 18)
85g / 6 Tbsp unsalted butter, cold and cubed
22g / ¼ cup finely grated parmigiano-reggiano
Whole nutmeg, q.b.

continued

Agnolotti dal Plin

continued

6   Remove the brisket from the oven, uncover, and, using a spoon, skim any excess fat that has risen to the top. Set aside in the pot until cool to the touch, about 20 minutes.

7   Transfer the brisket from the pot to a sheet pan. Strain the cooking liquid, reserving the solids (150g / ⅔ cup onions) and liquid (474g / 2 cups) separately. (Really squeeze the onions to ensure the liquid is separate.) Set both aside.

8   Pick the meat into small pieces, removing any fat. Fit your meat grinder with the small die and put the meat through the grinder. Then put the braised onions through the grinder.

9   Transfer the meat and onions to a bowl. Add the parmigiano and the remaining 14g / 1 Tbsp olive oil, season with grated nutmeg and salt q.b., and mix well. The mixture should taste well seasoned. Cover and refrigerate until ready to use. The filling is easier to work with at room temperature, so be sure to remove it from the refrigerator about 30 minutes before using.

10   To finish, following the instructions for agnolotti dal plin on page 84, make 160 to 180 pieces with the pasta dough and filling.

11   Bring a large pot of water to a boil over high heat. Generously salt the water.

12   Place a large sauté pan over low heat. Add the reserved braising liquid and butter and swirl to emulsify into a sauce. Keep on low, swirling occasionally.

13   Add the agnolotti to the water and turn down the heat to bring the water to a gentle simmer instead of a rolling boil. It is important to cook these gently at a simmer instead of a boil. Cook for 2 to 4 minutes, until tender at the thickest closure point.

14   Using a spider or pasta basket, remove the pasta from the pot and transfer to the sauté pan. Turn the heat up to medium. Swirl the pasta in the sauce for 1 to 2 minutes to marry, using a spoon to gently turn the pasta over and coat all sides, until the sauce is almost gravy-like and begins to hug the pasta. If the sauce begins to tighten, add a splash of pasta cooking water and continue swirling to marry.

15   Divide into flat-bottomed bowls. Drizzle with the remaining sauce from the pan and garnish with the parmigiano and with grated nutmeg q.b.

Corzetti alle Erbe

Pasta with Herbs and Pine Nuts

It's no secret that I love corzetti, and not just for their delicacy but also for their ease. To me, there is no greater reward than the pasta dish that comes together without much forethought, and in the world of fresh handmade pasta, this recipe is about as easy as it gets.

The sauce is meant to be thrown together quickly—a sort of impressionistic pesto that calls on whatever local herbs are available and in season, good olive oil, and nuts. In Liguria, the pine nut tops the nut food chain and is the most frequent companion of the dish, but it can also be made with walnuts. I find it really becomes its most irresistible when you combine the musky, sweet aroma of marjoram with the richness of pine nuts.

This is a dish that truly allows me to lay bare my obsession with marjoram, which is second only to fennel pollen as a staple for finishing plates in my kitchen. While it's typical to cook the herbs briefly in the sauce, I reserve the marjoram as a garnish, preferring to let its aroma lead the way.

1   Following the instructions for corzetti on page 113, make 80 pieces with the pasta dough.

2   Preheat the oven to 325°F. Spread the pine nuts in a single layer on a sheet pan and toast until very light golden brown, 5 to 7 minutes, checking their progress every few minutes to ensure they don't burn. Set aside to cool, about 15 minutes. Once cooled, coarsely chop and set aside.

3   Bring a large pot of water to a boil over high heat. Generously salt the water.

4   Place a sauté pan over very low heat. Add the olive oil and garlic and gently cook until aromatic but without color, 10 to 15 seconds. Add 2 ladles (115g / ½ cup) pasta cooking water and the butter and swirl to emulsify. Remove from the heat and set aside.

5   Add the corzetti to the water and cook for 1 to 2 minutes, until just tender.

6   Place the reserved sauté pan over low heat. Using a spider or pasta basket, remove the pasta from the pot and transfer to the sauté pan. Turn the heat up to medium. Swirl the pasta and sauce for 30 seconds to 1 minute to marry.

7   Remove from the heat. Add the parsley and half of the pine nuts and stir gently to integrate into the sauce. If the sauce begins to tighten, add a splash of pasta cooking water to loosen and stir gently to integrate.

8   Divide the pasta onto plates in a single layer. Drizzle with the remaining sauce from the pan and garnish with the remaining pine nuts and with the parmigiano and marjoram.

Yields 4 to 6 servings

1 batch egg dough (page 18)
60g / ½ cup pine nuts
42g / 3 Tbsp olive oil
25g / 5 cloves garlic, very finely chopped
45g / 3 Tbsp unsalted butter, cold and cubed
20g / ¼ cup finely chopped parsley
22g / ¼ cup finely grated parmigiano-reggiano
5g / ¼ cup marjoram leaves

Ask me what I think of when I think of central Italy and I'll start by telling you what I do not think of: Tuscany. Nothing against Tuscany, really. I love the region's signature pappardelle al ragù di coniglio, pici al ragù di cinghiale, and gnudi alla fiorentina as much as the next guy. Indeed, one of the most memorable dishes I've had in Italy was at Bar dell'Orso, about twenty minutes outside Siena, where they make beautiful, bright yellow egg-dough pici not by rolling by hand, as is traditional, but via a hand-cranked pasta press called a torchio. It was a bit of innovation that still preserved the rough-hewn quality of that shape—and, arguably, improved how it tasted. It was paired with a ragù di cinghiale flavored with juniper, a masterful addition that gave the richness of the sauce an aromatic, piquant leg up.

But Tuscany can act as a mirage—a region whose marketing prowess has helped it eclipse its neighbors, edging out the competition with its timeless brand of *Under the Tuscan Sun* romanticism. It's a vision so powerful it has even eclipsed the region itself. So, sure, my own vision of central Italy is not completely devoid of those perfectly manicured hilltop tenute with their Apollonian cypress. I am not above its seduction; I've got a whole album full of blurry photos taken from the passenger-side window to prove it. But all other central regions tend to be reduced to comparison with Tuscany instead of appreciated for their distinct merits. And I'd argue that to appreciate the bounty of Italy's borderlands between north and south, you have to venture into its wilder reaches.

Some call Abruzzo "Tuscany without the marketing dollars." They are not wrong. The province of Teramo is home to the same constellation of hilltop towns and olive groves, but it has a wilder, more weathered character. Part of this owes something to the Apennine Mountains, which create a menacing border wall between the province of L'Aquila to the west and the Adriatic to the east, shrugging off a cold wind that gusts all the way to the sea. It's also a study in contrasts—mountain and sea, surely, but also north and south. It's perhaps why a debate exists on whether it should be considered part of southern Italy, and why so many observers (including me) regard it as central. Historical reasons are behind the quibbling, but my argument is based solely on the culinary differences. In Abruzzo, there is a beautiful tension between the brightness, acidity, and heat (the native peperoncino variety, diavolino, shows up *a lot*) that are so central to southern Italian cooking and the richness, both in ingredients and flavors, of regions to the north, primarily Emilia-Romagna. It's borderland food in the truest, most thrilling sense.

Tomatoes, particularly the Pera d'Abruzzo variety endemic to the coast, are abundant here, but they get that touch of the north by their marriage with meat, like the dime-size pallottine (aka polpettine) in the province of Teramo to make the famed spaghetti alla chitarra con le pallottine alla teramana (handmade egg spaghetti with meatballs in red sauce in the style of Teramo). Lasagna shows up as well, though not in its usual guise. Here it comes in the form of a timballo, a baked pasta made by layering paper-thin crespelle, or egg-and-flour crepes, between meat, tomato, cheese, and spinach. It's a dish that achieves the almost impossible task of being both exceptionally rich and almost buoyantly light—a lasagna that gives you wings. The region is also famed for the production of saffron, which finds its way into what seems like about half of the dishes in the province of L'Aquila, often paired with truffles but typically in very humble preparations. One my favorite Abruzzese dishes is spaghetti alla chitarra with saffron, pancetta, and zucchini—a lesson in the sort of simplicity that drives the way I approach pasta today.

Just north, the Marche ("the poor man's Tuscany") also shares a borderland mentality. Here, cappelletti mignon in brodo, each tiny filled pasta getting a mere pinkie nail's worth of meat, act as a far more modest interpretation of Emilia-Romagna's tortellini in brodo. In Fermo, the region's most famous pasta, maccheroncini di Campofilone, essentially a hand-cut egg-dough angel hair, are typically served in a red sauce modestly enriched with meat. No other dish, however, quite showcases the region's position as

Emilia-Romagna's lower half than vincisgrassi, a downright savage interpretation of lasagna that relies on a coarsely chopped ragù often featuring beef or pork, chicken livers, and sweetbreads cooked with cloves and layered with nutmeg-spiked béchamel. It's a buckle-up, middle-finger-to-Emilia pasta if there ever were one.

Umbria ("Tuscany without the crowds") has plenty of those as well, though its middle finger is generally pointed in the direction of its neighbor to the northwest. The tendency to compare Tuscany and Umbria is not unwarranted, especially at their border. Both regions are known for raising cattle, notably the Chianina breed, which is most famous for being the source of bistecca alla fiorentina. Both regions also have a fondness for beans and other legumes and hearty soups, as well as for ragù made from rabbit or hare. Pasta shapes and preparations also cross borders, often traveling under different names.

But the cuisines of both regions diverge as often as they converge, particularly in Umbria's more heavily forested south, where the Sibylline Mountains are home to a fiber optic–like network of tiny, nearly identical roadside towns tucked into the base of the imposing rock faces. Many have been all but abandoned in the wake of two devastating earthquakes in 2016. But they still bear clues to the gastronomical abundance of the area; it's easier to find black truffles along SS685 than it is to find a gas station. That abundance culminates in Norcia, a town worth a pilgrimage through the mountains, provided you care even a bit about cured meat, truffles, or cheese. Norcia is home to some of the finest cured pig in Italy: prosciutto di Norcia, a variant that is dry-cured with salt, pepper, and garlic and then aged with exposure to the mountain wind; ciauscolo, the *other* spreadable sausage, 'nduja, flavored with garlic, spices, and wine (a similar version, called ventricina, hails from Abruzzo); headcheese flavored with orange zest; and so on—and on.

However, the real reason to drive three hours (in a snowstorm, in my case) to this part of Umbria is a single dish: strangozzi alla norcina or simply strangozzi al tartufo, a classic dish of the area that combines black truffle, anchovy, garlic, and olive oil. What makes it great isn't just eating it in the heart of Italy's black truffle zone. It's the revelation in discovering the transcendent, lean-in power of umami that results from combining truffle and anchovy. For me, it defines what Umbria tastes like.

What about Lazio, you say? No one would dare compare the region that houses the former seat of the Holy Roman Empire to anything but itself. That's just as well. When there's a few millennia's worth of history around every Roman street corner and the A-team of pork-spiked pastas, there's little need to wonder how the place stacks up to Tuscany.

Carbonara, cacio e pepe, amatriciana—this hallowed Roman trio looms large in the modern American craving for pasta. Ironically, Rome is not where you go if you want to understand the craft of pasta making, as most of the pasta you'll encounter there is from Gragnano. You go to Rome to better understand the alchemy of combining three or four simple ingredients into a sauce whose sum is greater than its parts—no small feat when those parts consist of pecorino romano and guanciale. These are dishes that loom so large in the American appetite for pasta that they have become synonymous with pasta itself. They are also dishes that offer important lessons in how to properly finish a pasta. I screwed up at least a hundred plates of cacio e pepe before I figured out the right combination of speed, the correct proportion of pasta cooking water to pecorino romano, and precisely when to add the cheese and in what quantity. When done properly, when you get a sauce that perfectly coats each strand of pasta, it's a dish good enough to back up its cult status.

Each of the borderland pastas in this section was chosen for its ability to impart important lessons to the pasta cook and because it reflects the collision of northern and southern Italian food that has become the cornerstone of my approach to pasta today.

Spaghetti alla Carbonara

Pasta with Eggs, Guanciale, and Pecorino

I learned to make carbonara at my first job in Emilia-Romagna. In retrospect, that makes no sense. Even though there is some debate around its origin, there is no debate that today carbonara is a dish of Lazio through and through—Rome to the bone, as one might say. It's also true that there are many different ways to make it: Pancetta or guanciale? Spaghetti or rigatoni? Whole eggs or egg yolks? Parmigiano-reggiano, pecorino romano, or both?

Regardless of how you answer, there is no arguing that carbonara satisfies in its own, almost mystical way. It does not just have fans, it has disciples. It also happens to be a great beginner's pasta in that it's easy to make on the fly with ingredients you're likely to have on hand (though nothing beats guanciale, you can sub in pancetta in a pinch), and even if it does curdle, let's face it, it's still delicious.

But let's not curdle it. That's the most common carbonara mistake. It is easily avoided, however, by what I call the bowl method (not to be confused with the double-boiler method), in which you temper a paste of the cheese and egg yolks—and I use only yolks—with warm guanciale fat in the mixing bowl. Loosening the mixture with pasta cooking water then turns that paste into sauce. After cooking, the pasta goes right into that bowl and gets gently tossed to marry. For extra dimension, I recommend using both pecorino romano (for bite and salinity) and parmigiano-reggiano (for richness and nuttiness). Finally, don't skimp on the black pepper—add a hefty amount, and then add some more.

---

1   Bring a large pot of water to a boil over high heat. Salt the water. Use slightly less than you might for other pastas, as the cheese and pork add quite a bit of salinity to the dish.

2   Place a large sauté pan over low heat. Add the guanciale and cook slowly until the fat has rendered and the meat parts start to get crispy, 5 to 7 minutes. Line a plate with paper towels. Using a slotted spoon, transfer the crisped guanciale to the paper towels to drain. Reserve 55g / ¼ cup of the rendered fat.

3   Add the egg yolks to a large bowl. Use a spoon or spatula to stir them into a smooth liquid. Do not whip them. Add the parmigiano and 68g / ¾ cup of the pecorino and stir to make a paste. Slowly stir in the reserved rendered fat. Add a hefty amount (about 40 grinds) of pepper and half of the reserved guanciale. Stir to combine.

4   Add the spaghetti to the water and cook for 5 to 8 minutes, until al dente.

5   Add 2 ladles (115g / ½ cup) pasta cooking water to the bowl in a slow, steady stream while stirring. This will further temper the eggs so they don't curdle and will also loosen the mixture to form your sauce.

6   Using tongs or a pasta basket, remove the spaghetti from the pot and transfer to the bowl. Quickly but gently toss the pasta and cheese–egg yolk paste. As the sauce tightens, continue to add pasta cooking water a splash at a time until you have a smooth, silky sauce coating the pasta.

7   Divide into bowls and garnish with the remaining 15g / 2½ Tbsp pecorino, the reserved guanciale, and with pepper q.b.

Yields 4 to 6 servings

1 (170g / 6 oz) piece guanciale, finely diced
180g / 10 egg yolks
68g / ¾ cup finely grated parmigiano-reggiano
68g / ¾ cup finely grated pecorino romano, plus 15g / 2½ Tbsp for garnish
Black pepper, q.b.
624g / 1 lb 6 oz extruded spaghetti (page 123)

Nota bene

If using pancetta in place of guanciale, make sure to look for a piece that has plenty of fat.

Timballo alla Teramana

Abruzzese Lasagna with Cheese, Spinach, and Beef

The best way to think about timballo alla teramana is as either a lighter, more obscure cousin to lasagna or as a more polite version of vincisgrassi (there's grasso, or "fat," in the name for a reason), its similarly layered neighbor in the Marche. While there are many versions of the timballo (which refers to the vessel used, not the dish itself) in Italy, the one popular in Teramo often replaces sheets of pasta with crespelle or scripelle (aka paper-thin crepes) to form a dozen or more layers of ground meat, tomato, cheese, greens, you name it. Like lasagna, a timballo is baked, after which it is flipped over, sliced, and served as a showstopping primo.

I made it for the first time with Rosa, the matriarch of the Pepe family (of Montepulciano d'Abruzzo fame), halfway between the Apennines and the Adriatic in Abruzzo's wine country. And when I say "made," I mean that very loosely. This has been Rosa's job for more than a half century, on most Sundays, and certainly for every major occasion. I was there to watch.

My version is an ode to Rosa's, which is divine in its restraint and, as such, in the delicacy of the finished dish. You will be tempted, as I was, to add more to each layer—to pile on an extra scoop or two of beef, a few more dollops of ricotta, a more even layer of sauce. Do not. Trust me when I say that the flavors in this dish are cumulative; never lose sight of the whole in service of a single part.

---

1   To make the crepes, in a large bowl combine the eggs, milk, and olive oil and mix to combine.

2   In a separate bowl, combine the flour, 22 gratings of nutmeg, and salt and mix to combine. Add the egg mixture and whisk until well incorporated. Cover and place in the refrigerator for 30 minutes.

3   Line a sheet pan with parchment paper and set aside.

4   Place an 8-inch nonstick sauté pan over medium-low heat. Dab a paper towel with olive oil and lightly grease the pan.

5   Remove the crepe batter from the refrigerator and stir well. Add 45g / 3 Tbsp of the batter to the sauté pan. Tilt and swirl the pan until the batter coats the bottom and just up the sides in one even layer. Cook for 10 to 15 seconds, until the underside turns faintly golden and little bubbles begin to form on the surface of the crepe. Using a large spatula, flip the crepe over and cook for another 10 to 15 seconds. The crepe should not have more than a little color at the edges. Remove from the pan and transfer to the prepared sheet pan in a single layer. Cover with a sheet of parchment paper.

6   Repeat this process until you have finished cooking all of the batter. You should have 35 to 40 crepes. Set aside.

7   To make the filling, place a large sauté pan over medium-high heat and add 42g / 3 Tbsp of the olive oil. Add the ground beef, breaking it up with a spatula or wooden spoon, and cook until lightly browned, 8 to 10 minutes. Season with about 15 gratings of nutmeg and salt and pepper q.b. Remove from the heat and transfer to a bowl to cool.

Yields 6 to 8 servings

Crepes

750g / 15 eggs
711g / 3 cups milk
42g / 3 Tbsp olive oil, plus
    more q.b.
119g / ¾ cup plus 3 Tbsp
    00 flour
Nutmeg, q.b.
5.5g / ½ tsp salt

Filling

84g / 6 Tbsp olive oil
675g / 1 lb 8 oz ground beef
Whole nutmeg, q.b.
Salt, q.b.
Black pepper, q.b.
10g / 2 cloves garlic, finely
    chopped
342g / 9 cups loosely packed
    baby spinach leaves

Sauce

300g / 6 eggs
178g / ¾ cup milk
397g / 1¾ cups tomato passata
    or 397g / 1½ cups plus
    1½ Tbsp simple red sauce
    (page 147)
Salt, q.b.
Black pepper, q.b.

8　Wipe out the sauté pan with a paper towel and place over low heat. Add the remaining 42g / 3 Tbsp olive oil and the garlic and cook until aromatic but without color, 10 to 15 seconds. Add the spinach and cook until wilted, 1 to 2 minutes. Season with salt q.b. Transfer to a sheet pan or plate and let cool.

9　Once cooled, drain the spinach, transfer to a kitchen towel, and squeeze out the excess water. Finely chop the spinach. Add to the beef and set aside.

10　To make the sauce, place the eggs and milk in a mixing bowl and whisk to combine. Add the tomato passata or simple red sauce and continue whisking to combine. Season with salt and pepper q.b. Set aside.

11　To finish, preheat the oven to 350°F.

12　Line a 9 by 13-inch baking dish with parchment paper and lightly coat with 1 Tbsp of the butter.

13　Add 140g / ½ cup of sauce to the baking dish, doing your best to evenly distribute. Layer the dish with 11 or 12 crepes, allowing them to slightly overlap and extend up and over the sides of the dish.

14　Begin layering the timballo by adding another 140g / ½ cup of sauce, 160g / ⅔ cup of the beef-and-spinach filling, 6g / 1 Tbsp of the parmigiano, 15g / 1 Tbsp butter, and 90g / ½ cup of the mozzarella, doing your best to evenly distribute. Cover with a layer of approximately 4 crepes. Repeat the process of filling and layering 4 crepes four more times, topping with the final layer of crepes. Fold the crepe edges that have draped over the side of the dish over the top.

15　Cover the dish with foil and place in the oven. Cook for 20 to 30 minutes, remove the foil, and continue baking until golden brown, another 20 to 30 minutes. Set aside to cool for 15 to 20 minutes.

16　When the dish is cool enough to handle, place a sheet pan or large flat serving platter over the top of the dish and invert the timballo onto it. Lift away the dish and parchment paper.

17　Cut the timballo into squares and divide among serving plates.

To Finish

60g / ¼ cup butter
28g / 5 Tbsp finely grated
　parmigiano-reggiano
1 large (454g / 1 lb) ball
　mozzarella, cut into
　¼-inch cubes

Nota bene

The crepe recipe yield allows for breakage, but you may still end up with unused crepes. Fill them with parmigiano and/or pecorino and cover with brodo to make another classic Abruzzese dish, crespelle in brodo.

Spaghetti alla Chitarra con Pallottine

Pasta with Abruzzese Meatballs and Lamb Sugo

Spaghetti meatballs (page 156) has become such an American red-sauce standard that you'd be forgiven for assuming it originated here. It's true that in Italy you will not encounter the over-the-top version we so revere in America—spaghetti so heavily cloaked in red sauce you can barely make out the tangle beneath it, meatballs the size of cue balls—but the dish is in fact an Italian regional classic.

In Abruzzo, the native square-sided spaghetti alla chitarra is frequently served in a ragù flavored with lamb, beef, or pork (or all three) along with dime-size meatballs, or pallottine, made of beef or veal. Like timballo (page 220), the dish hails from the province of Teramo, a veritable gold mine of culinary diversity that remains one of the country's true uncut gems. Both this dish and spaghetti meatballs have their time and place, but I'll almost always choose the more measured (yet no less meaty) Abruzzese original.

I choose to flavor my ragù with lamb shoulder, which is removed after being cooked, shredded into tiny pieces and returned to the sauce, which is further flavored with the addition of dozens of tiny beef meatballs.

---

1   To make the pallottine, break down the bread into pea-size or smaller pieces by rubbing the pieces between your palms. Place the bread in a small bowl and cover with the milk. Let soak until completely softened, 20 to 30 minutes.

2   While the bread is soaking, place the beef, pecorino, egg yolk, olive oil, and salt in a bowl and mix until well incorporated.

3   Drain the milk from the bread, reserving the milk. Press and squeeze the bread to force out most of the excess liquid. Make sure the bread is separated into small, crumb-like pieces. Measure 20g / 1 Tbsp plus 1 tsp of the drained milk and discard the rest.

4   Add the bread and measured milk to the beef mixture and mix well. Make a small patty to test your seasoning.

5   Place a small sauté pan over medium heat and add a drizzle of oil. Add the test patty and cook, turning once, until cooked through but still slightly pink in the center, about 3 minutes. Check your seasoning and add more salt to the pallottine mixture q.b.

6   Cover and refrigerate the mixture for 30 minutes to 1 hour. (You can skip this step, but the mixture is quite wet and can be challenging to work with at room temperature.)

7   Oil a sheet pan. Form the mixture into 70 to 80 pallottine, each weighing 3 to 4g, placing them on the prepared pan as you shape them. (You can weigh the first few to get comfortable with the size and then go from there.)

8   Chill the pallottine in the refrigerator for 30 minutes to 1 hour to help them hold their shape.

9   To make the sugo, season the lamb on all sides with salt q.b. Let sit for at least 1 hour or up to 24 hours in the refrigerator. If refrigerated, bring to room temperature.

10   Fit your meat grinder with the small die. Chop the fennel, celery, and onion into ½- to 1-inch pieces. Put the fennel, celery, and onion

Yields 4 to 6 servings

Pallottine

20g / 1 piece day-old country bread, crust removed
118g / ½ cup milk
227g / 8 oz ground beef
22g / ¼ cup finely grated pecorino romano
18g / 1 egg yolk
14g / 1 Tbsp olive oil, plus more q.b.
4g / 1¼ tsp salt

Sugo

454g / 1 lb bone-in lamb shoulder
Salt, q.b.
75g / ¼ fennel bulb, cored
75g / 1 stalk celery
63g / ¼ onion
112g / ½ cup olive oil
55g / 11 cloves garlic, finely chopped
73g / ⅓ cup dry white wine
577g / 2¼ cups whole San Marzano tomatoes, crushed by hand
¾ tsp black peppercorns
1 fresh bay leaf
½ tsp dried red chile flakes
1 sprig rosemary

To Finish

1 batch egg dough (page 18)
Ground red chile, q.b.
30g / ⅓ cup finely grated pecorino romano

through the meat grinder. Once all are ground, gather them in cheesecloth and wring to squeeze out the excess liquid. This is your soffritto.

11   Place a large, heavy sauce pot or Dutch oven over medium heat and add 56g / ¼ cup of the oil. Add the lamb and sear, turning as needed, until golden brown, 3 to 5 minutes on each side. Transfer the lamb to a plate and keep warm.

12   If a lot of brown bits from the lamb are left in the pot, wipe out the pot and return it to the heat. Add the remaining 56g / ¼ cup olive oil and the soffritto, turn down the heat to low, and gently cook, stirring frequently, until softened but without color, 6 to 8 minutes.

13   Toward the very end of cooking, add the garlic and gently cook until aromatic but without color, 10 to 15 seconds. Add the wine and simmer until reduced by half, 3 to 5 minutes.

14   Add the lamb back to the pot. Add the tomatoes and their juice and enough water (237 to 474g / 1 to 2 cups) just to cover the lamb.

15   Make a sachet with cheesecloth for the peppercorns, bay leaf, chile flakes, and rosemary and add to the pot. Cover the pot and gently simmer until the lamb is tender and falling off the bone, 2 to 3 hours.

16   Remove from the heat and let cool.

17   Once cooled, remove the sachet from the pot and discard. Remove the lamb from the liquid and let cool. Using two forks, pull the meat apart into fine strands, run a knife through to cut into smaller pieces, and then add back to the pot.

18   Measure 750g / 3¼ cups sugo and set aside. Transfer the remainder to an airtight container and refrigerate for up to 5 days or freeze for another use.

19   To finish, following the instructions for spaghetti alla chitarra on page 119, make 624g / 1 lb 6 oz with the pasta dough.

20   Bring a large pot of water to a boil over high heat. Generously salt the water.

21   Place a large sauté pan over medium-low heat and add the sugo. Then add the pallottine and cook them gently in the sauce, stirring to keep them poaching evenly, until cooked through, 3 to 4 minutes.

22   Add the spaghetti alla chitarra to the water and cook for 2 to 3 minutes, until tender but not soft.

23   Using tongs or a pasta basket, remove the pasta from the pot and transfer to the sauté pan. Turn the heat up to medium. Fold for 1 to 2 minutes to marry the pasta and the sugo. Add a generous pinch of ground chile and continue folding. If the sugo begins to tighten, add a splash of pasta cooking water to loosen and continue folding to marry. The sugo should nicely coat the pasta without clumping.

24   Divide the pasta into bowls and garnish with the pecorino and with ground chile q.b.

Pappardelle al Ragù di Coniglio

Pasta with Braised Rabbit Ragù

If you asked me to peg a single pasta as capturing the essence of Tuscany, it's a near tie between pici with wild boar ragù (page 333) and pappardelle with rabbit. The latter has the narrow edge primarily because it's the dish I find myself gravitating to most at home—partly because of availability and partly because I just love cooking rabbit. (Note: In Tuscany and other regions of central Italy, especially Umbria, ragù al coniglio is often made with wild hare, a much gamier version of the rabbit we know and love in the States. While it does make for a richer, funkier ragù, I prefer the cleaner flavors of rabbit here.)

In some ways, rabbit is a blank canvas—lean, ever-so-slightly gamy but mostly a mild protein that gets its flavor from the decisions you make while cooking it, particularly what you cook it with when slow roasting or braising it. My rabbit "ragù" (it's really more of a braise) is inspired by rabbit cacciatore, specifically a version I had outside Siena at a roadside trattoria popular with construction workers.

All the usual suspects are here—my fennel soffritto, rosemary, red wine, the juice of San Marzano tomatoes—and one that may appear like an outlier: juniper. While primarily consumed in the United States by way of gin, juniper berries find their way into northern and central Italian cooking, especially in Tuscany and Umbria, where they grow abundantly. They're a frequent companion in braises, like this one, where they act like a more floral, even fruity peppercorn.

---

1   To make the ragù, season the rabbit on all sides with the salt and let sit to absorb for 30 to 40 minutes.

2   Fit your meat grinder with the small die. Peel the carrots. Core the fennel and remove the fronds and stems. Chop the fennel, carrots, and onion into ½- to 1-inch pieces. Put the carrots, fennel, and onion through the grinder. Once all are ground, gather them in cheesecloth and wring to squeeze out the excess liquid. This is your soffritto.

3   Place a large, heavy sauce pot or Dutch oven over medium heat and add the 56g / ¼ cup olive oil. Add the rabbit pieces (you can do this in batches if they don't all fit without crowding) and sear, turning as needed, until golden brown, 3 to 5 minutes on each side. Transfer the rabbit to a plate and keep warm.

4   If a lot of brown bits from the rabbit are left in the pot, wipe out the pot and return it to the heat and add the remaining 28g / 2 Tbsp olive oil. Add the soffritto, turn down the heat to low, and gently cook, stirring frequently, until softened but without color, 6 to 8 minutes.

5   Toward the very end of cooking, add the garlic and gently cook until aromatic but without color, 10 to 15 seconds. Add the wine and simmer until reduced by half, 3 to 5 minutes.

6   Add the rabbit back to the pot. Add the tomatoes and their juice and, if necessary, enough water just to cover the rabbit.

7   Make a sachet with cheesecloth for the parsley, rosemary, and juniper and add to the pot. Cover the pot and gently simmer until the rabbit is tender and falling off the bone, 2 to 3 hours.

Yields 4 to 6 servings

Rabbit Ragù

6 rabbit legs, 228g / 8 oz each, or 1 (1.4kg / 3 lb) whole rabbit, cut into six pieces
36g / ¼ cup salt, plus more q.b.
450g / 3 large carrots
400g / 1 large fennel bulb
370g / 1 large onion
56g / ¼ cup olive oil, plus 28g / 2 Tbsp
25g / 5 cloves garlic, thinly sliced
440g / 2 cups dry red wine
1 large (794g / 28 oz) can whole San Marzano tomatoes, crushed by hand
15g / ¼ bunch parsley
2 sprigs rosemary
6g / 1 Tbsp juniper berries, coarsely crushed

To Finish

1 batch egg dough (page 18)
1g / 1 tsp ground juniper berries
22g / ¼ cup finely grated parmigiano-reggiano

8   Remove from the heat and let cool.

9   Once cooled, remove the sachet from the pot and discard. Remove the rabbit from the liquid and let cool. Pick all of the meat off the bones. Using two forks, pull the meat apart into fine strands, run a knife through to cut into smaller pieces, and then add back to the pot.

10   Measure out 454g / 2 cups ragù and set aside. Transfer the remainder to an airtight container and refrigerate for up to 5 days or freeze for another use.

11   To finish, following the instructions for pappardelle on page 54, make 624g / 1 lb 6 oz with the pasta dough.

12   Bring a large pot of water to a boil over high heat. Generously salt the water.

13   Place a large sauté pan over very low heat and add the ragù.

14   Add the pappardelle to the water and cook for 1 to 2 minutes, until tender but not soft.

15   Using tongs or a pasta basket, remove the pasta from the pot and transfer to the sauté pan. Turn the heat up to medium. Toss or fold for 30 seconds to 1 minute to marry the pasta and the ragù. If the ragù begins to tighten, add a splash of pasta cooking water to loosen and continue tossing or folding to marry. The ragù should nicely coat the pasta without clumping.

16   Divide the pasta into bowls and garnish with the juniper and parmigiano.

Pici al Ragù d'Anatra

Pasta with Duck Ragù

For me, braised meat sauce is synonymous with Tuscany. While ragù often takes the form that we most associate with the word—i.e., based on ground meat, with a touch of tomato, as in Emilia-Romagna—here, it's the rich, rough-hewn ragùs that are based on long braises and large cuts of meat, often incorporating red wine, that speak most to the region. (Neapolitan ragù is similarly based on large cuts of meat, but goes heavy on the tomato, which Tuscan ragù does not.)

    Duck, rabbit, and wild boar are Tuscany's great trifecta, and you will find ragù based on all three in just about every corner of the region and they are often interchangeable in their preparations. While not a classic approach, I confit the duck legs ahead of the braise to give the dish a silky depth and richness without being too weighty.

---

1   To make the duck confit, season the duck on all sides with the salt. Place the duck skin side down and top with the garlic, thyme, juniper, peppercorns, and bay leaf. Let sit at very cool room temperature to cure for 5 hours. (Alternatively, you can cure overnight in the fridge.)

2   Preheat the oven to 225°F.

3   Place a large, heavy sauce pot or Dutch oven over low heat. Transfer the duck legs and the aromatics to the pot and cover with the olive oil. Cook until the oil just begins to bubble, 5 to 7 minutes.

4   Cover the pot, transfer to the oven, and cook the duck until it is tender and falling off the bone but not mushy, 5 to 6 hours.

5   Remove the pot from the oven and let the duck cool in the fat.

6   Once cooled, remove the duck from the pot, being careful to disturb the liquid as little as possible. Pick the meat off of the bones. Using two forks, pull the meat apart into fine strands and then run a knife through to cut into smaller pieces. Set aside.

7   Gently pour or ladle off the fat and strain through a fine-mesh strainer. Measure 98g / 7 Tbsp. Transfer the remaining duck fat to an airtight container and refrigerate for up to 2 weeks or freeze indefinitely for another use. Strain the remaining duck jus through a fine-mesh strainer and set aside (you should have 56g / ¼ cup).

8   To make the ragù, fit your meat grinder with the small die. Chop the celery, carrot, and onion into ½- to 1-inch pieces. Put the celery, carrot, and onion through the meat grinder. Once all are ground, gather them in cheesecloth and wring to squeeze out the excess liquid. This is your soffritto.

9   Place a large, heavy sauce pot or Dutch oven over low heat. Add the reserved duck fat and soffritto and gently cook, stirring frequently, until softened but without color, 6 to 8 minutes. Toward the very end of cooking, add the garlic and gently cook until aromatic but without color, 10 to 15 seconds.

Yields 4 to 6 servings

Duck Confit

4 bone-in duck legs
25g / 2 Tbsp plus 2¼ tsp salt
36g / 7 garlic cloves
10 sprigs thyme
3g / 1½ tsp juniper berries,
   coarsely crushed
½ tsp black peppercorns
1 fresh bay leaf
672g / 3 cups olive oil, plus
   more q.b.

Duck Ragù

150g / 2 stalks celery
150g / 1 large carrot, peeled
250g / 1 onion
25g / 5 cloves garlic, finely
   chopped
220g / 1 cup dry red wine
400g / 1½ cups whole San
   Marzano tomatoes, crushed
   by hand
9g / 1 Tbsp black peppercorns
6g / 1 Tbsp juniper berries,
   coarsely crushed
1 fresh bay leaf
5 sprigs thyme

To Finish

1 batch egg dough (page 18)
22g / ¼ cup finely grated
   parmigiano-reggiano

10   Add the wine and turn up the heat to medium. Cook until the wine is reduced by three-fourths, about 7 minutes. Add the tomatoes and their juice and the duck and stir to combine.

11   Make a sachet with cheesecloth for the peppercorns, juniper, bay leaf, and thyme and add to the pot. Add the reserved duck jus. Turn the heat down to low and cook until the flavors have melded, about 1 hour.

12   Remove from the heat and let cool.

13   Once cooled, remove the sachet from the pot and discard. Measure 592g / 2½ cups duck ragù and set aside. Transfer the remainder to an airtight container and refrigerate for up to 5 days or freeze for another use.

14   To finish, following the instructions for pici on page 71, make 624g / 1 lb 6 oz with the pasta dough.

15   Bring a large pot of water to a boil over high heat. Generously salt the water.

16   Place a large sauté pan over low heat. Add the ragù and 3 to 4 ladles (170g to 230g / ¾ to 1 cup) pasta cooking water and stir to combine.

17   Add the pici to the water and cook for 3 to 5 minutes, until tender but not soft.

18   Using tongs or a pasta basket, remove the pasta from the pot and transfer to the sauté pan. Turn the heat up to medium. Toss or fold for 1 to 2 minutes to marry the pasta and the ragù. If the ragù begins to tighten, add a splash of pasta cooking water to loosen and continue tossing or folding to marry. The ragù should nicely coat the pasta without clumping.

19   Divide the pasta into bowls and garnish with the parmigiano.

Strangozzi alla Norcina

Pasta with Black Truffles and Anchovy

Google "strangozzi alla norcina" and at least two results will be returned. You'll likely find this version tucked into page two of the results behind a dozen or so recipes for the *other* strangozzi alla norcina, a combination of sausage and black truffles spiked with heavy cream. But it's this rendition that first captured my imagination in my early Spiaggia days.

An odd-on-paper combination of black truffles, anchovy, and garlic mashed together into a paste, this is one of those dishes that seems to unlock a sixth taste by combining three ingredients that are singular flavor bombs into a briny, earthy, pungent whole. If pasta had its own seven wonders, this would be one of them.

To really understand this dish, it's helpful to know that while black truffles are white-tablecloth fare in the States, in Umbria they are as everyday and essential as garlic—specifically around the town of Norcia. This is a pasta you'll find in humble trattorias and roadside restaurants all year round. But alas, you're probably not in Umbria, and in the United States, black truffles aren't exactly easy to come by, or cheap. You can find winter and summer blacks in season via specialty online purveyors, or you can substitute preserved black truffles, though they can range in quality quite drastically. I like Savini sliced summer truffles in oil.

---

1   To make the truffle-anchovy paste, place the anchovies, garlic, truffle, and 30g / 2 Tbsp of the water (you want just enough to get it blending) in a high-speed blender and puree until it forms a fine paste.

2   With the blender running at high speed, gradually add the olive oil until the mixture is well emulsified. Set aside until ready to use.

3   To finish, following the instructions for strangozzi on page 56, make 624g / 1 lb 6 oz with the pasta dough.

4   Bring a large pot of water to a boil over high heat. Generously salt the water.

5   Add the strangozzi to the water and cook for 3 to 5 minutes, until tender. (This is a thicker pasta, so it will still have a bit of bite to it, rather than be super tender like fettuccine.)

6   While the pasta is cooking, place a large sauté pan over low heat. Add the truffle-anchovy paste and 2 to 3 ladles (115g to 170g / ½ to ¾ cup) pasta cooking water and stir to combine.

7   Using tongs or a pasta basket, remove the pasta from the pot and transfer to the sauté pan. Turn the heat up to medium. Toss for 1 to 2 minutes to marry the pasta and the sauce.

8   Add the butter and continue tossing to marry. If the sauce begins to tighten, add a splash of pasta cooking water to loosen and continue tossing. When the pasta is properly married, it will cling to the sauce and have a glossy sheen.

9   Divide the pasta into bowls. If you have fresh black truffle to spare, shave some over the top to garnish.

Yields 4 to 6 servings

Truffle-Anchovy Paste

40g / 6 to 8 oil-packed anchovy
fillets, coarsely chopped
5g / 1 clove garlic, roughly
chopped
60g / 2 oz fresh black truffle,
coarsely chopped
30 to 60g / 2 to 4 Tbsp water
42g / 3 Tbsp olive oil

To Finish

1 batch egg dough (page 18)
30g / 2 Tbsp unsalted butter,
cold and cubed
Fresh black truffle, for shaving
q.b. (optional)

Cacio e Pepe

Pasta with Pecorino and Black Pepper

Over the last decade, cacio e pepe has become Cacio e Pepe™, a juggernaut that has inspired everything from doughnuts to street corn. How it became one of Italy's most viral pastas is no secret: it's as easy to make as it is to like. It's much harder, however, to make it well. In fact, I've always considered cacio e pepe to be a pasta cook's litmus test. If you can make great cacio e pepe, chances are the rest of the pastas you cook are great, too.

Just as cannelloni or tortelli are studies in how to make great fillings, making cacio e pepe is a crash course in pasta's great X factor: touch. Success lies in getting the right texture, and that is really about balancing the ratio of pasta water to pecorino, adding the cheese off the heat and tossing consistently, and paying close attention to how the pasta feels in the pan. If it's too hard to control and wants to jump out, your sauce is too loose; add more cheese. If there's friction that slows your motion, it's too tight; add more water. When it's just right, it should feel how the sauce should look: thick and substantial but smooth. It should *glide*.

Every time I eat a perfect plate of cacio e pepe, as I have many times at I Sodi in New York, at Da Cesare in Rome, or at the hands of my former sous chef, Jenny Cianci, who was an absolute master, I say the same thing to myself: How can just three ingredients taste so complex? That is the magic of cacio e pepe.

---

1   Bring a large pot of water to a boil over high heat. Generously salt the water.

2   Place a large sauté pan over low heat. Add the olive oil and pepper, using about 90 turns of the grinder, along with 3 ladles (170g / ¾ cup) pasta cooking water. This will bloom the pepper and extract more of its flavor.

3   Add the spaghetti to the water and cook for 5 to 8 minutes, until al dente.

4   Using tongs or a pasta basket, remove the pasta from the pot and transfer to the sauté pan. Quickly toss to combine.

5   Remove from the heat. Gradually add 160g / 1¾ cups of the pecorino while tossing to combine. As the mixture tightens up from the cheese, alternate sprinkling in some of the remaining cheese and pasta cooking water until you have a smooth, silky sauce that evenly coats the pasta and glides in the pan. It is essential that the pasta water and cheese balance each other out: if you have too much water, the sauce will be soupy; too little and it will have the texture of a dry paste. You want yours to glisten and cling.

6   Divide the pasta into bowls and garnish with the remaining pecorino and with pepper q.b.

Yields 4 to 6 servings

42g / 3 Tbsp olive oil
Black pepper, q.b.
624g / 1 lb 6 oz extruded
    spaghetti (page 123)
180g / 2 cups finely grated
    pecorino romano

Nota bene

I prefer cacio e pepe with spaghetti over fresh tonnarelli, which is what you'll often find in Rome and its environs. I love the bite from extruded pasta against a sauce that doesn't offer much in the way of textural complexity.

Bucatini all'Amatriciana

Pasta with Tomato, Guanciale, and Pecorino

How could a sauce with just three ingredients (or is it four? or five?) inspire so much debate? Despite it being right there in the name, the origin of the dish is also disputed. The Romans often claim the dish as theirs, and not Amatrice's, a town at the crossroads of Lazio, Abruzzo, and Umbria now more famous for its devastating earthquake in 2016 than for its namesake pasta. Some even go so far as to print the rebuke on menus, referring to the dish as la matriciana or alla matriciana instead of all'amatriciana.

The most fervent debate, however, comes down to the use, or not, of onions and garlic. In Amatrice, the dish is unadorned: tomatoes, pecorino cheese, guanciale … *maybe* chile flakes. That's it. But like most dishes that have become part of the Roman canon (carbonara, cacio e pepe) and have thus made their way around the globe, this one invites attempts at improvement. In the past, I was guilty of overcomplicating the dish myself.

Neither onions nor garlic make their way into my interpretation of the dish, despite the fact that the amatriciana I fell in love with leaned so heavily on the former. When I was cooking in Chicago and traveled to New York, my first stop was almost always for a bowl of Mark Ladner's amatriciana. His version is feral and rustic, with pearlescent sheets of red onion the size of walnuts and thick, crispy pieces of guanciale. It's a dish that has a tribe of devotees.

My version is more traditional, and not out of reverence. To me, the genius of amatriciana lies in the combination of tomato, pecorino, and guanciale (plus chile flakes, always). Note that the dish can take additional heat, so feel free to scale up your use of chile if you so desire.

---

1   To make the sauce, place a large sauté pan or Dutch oven over medium-low heat. Line a plate with paper towels.

2   Add the olive oil and guanciale to the sauté pan and cook until the fat has rendered and the pieces are just beginning to turn golden but have not browned (remember that they will crisp up when you remove them from the pan), 5 to 8 minutes.

3   Using a slotted spoon, remove one-quarter of the guanciale and place on the paper towels to drain. Reserve these pieces for garnish.

4   Turn down the heat to low, add the tomato passata and chile flakes, and cook until the rawness of the tomatoes is cooked out and the flavors have melded, 8 to 10 minutes. You are not looking to reduce the sauce.

5   To finish, bring a large pot of water to a boil over high heat. Generously salt the water.

6   Add the bucatini to the water and cook for 5 to 8 minutes, until al dente.

7   Using tongs or a pasta basket, remove the pasta from the pot and transfer to the sauté pan. Add a splash of pasta cooking water and toss for 1 to 2 minutes to marry the pasta and the sauce. Remove from the heat and add 30g / ⅓ cup of the pecorino while tossing or stirring to combine. If the sauce feels tight, add a splash more pasta cooking water to loosen and continue tossing. When the pasta is properly married, it will cling to the sauce and have a glossy sheen.

8   Divide the pasta into bowls and garnish with the remaining pecorino and reserved guanciale.

Yields 4 to 6 servings

Sauce

28g / 2 Tbsp olive oil
160g / 5½ oz guanciale, thinly sliced
456g / 2 cups tomato passata
½ tsp dried red chile flakes

To Finish

624g / 1 lb 6 oz extruded bucatini (page 121)
30g/ ⅓ cup pecorino romano, plus 22g / ¼ cup for garnish

Gnudi alla Fiorentina

Spinach and Ricotta Dumplings with Brown Butter and Sage

There is a reason that the combination of gnudi with butter and sage has become iconic: it offers just the right pairing of herbal levity and richness that amplifies the pasta without overpowering it.

Gnudi are great in concept: ravioli without their casing, or "nude"; pillowy but rich; a pasta without the fuss of having to go through the trouble of actually making pasta. I am certainly not one to deny the appeal. But so often, in practice, gnudi are not as advertised, instead rendered so dense and gummy that you can practically bounce them. In such cases, the blame usually lies with flour, egg, or both.

Cracking your eggs, gently beating them, and folding them into the mixture would make sense. You're making a dumpling after all. And surely you can make great gnudi this way. But for a surefire path to pillowy, I separate the yolks and whites and whip the latter to give them a softness that gets folded into the "dough." On the subject of flour, the dumpling status of gnudi can also lead many astray. Flour is really here to bind, not to build upon. Use it sparingly and integrate it gradually by gently folding it into the mixture. And take it easy: if you fold with too much rigor, you'll activate the gluten and end up with gnudi that have the texture of tapioca pearls.

When you master the "base," you can certain add to or completely abandon spinach in favor of other ingredients, whether that's swapping it for Swiss chard or adding ramp leaves in spring.

---

1   Following the instructions for gnudi on page 65, make 70 to 80 pieces with the dough.

2   To finish, bring a large pot of water to a boil over high heat. Generously salt the water.

3   Place a large sauté pan over medium heat. Add the butter and half of the sage and cook until the butter is golden brown and foamy, 2 to 3 minutes. Set aside. You will drizzle this sage butter over the plated pasta.

4   Using a skimmer or slotted spoon, add the gnudi to the water and turn down the heat to bring the water to a gentle simmer instead of a rolling boil. Cook for about 2 minutes, until they begin to float to the surface. Then cook them for another 30 seconds.

5   Using the spider, remove the gnudi from the pot and divide among shallow bowls or plates.

6   Drizzle the reserved sage butter over the top and garnish with the pecorino, the remaining sage, and with grated nutmeg q.b.

Yields 6 to 8 servings

1 batch gnudi dough (page 25)
114g / ½ cup unsalted butter, cold and cubed
12 to 15 sage leaves
22g / ¼ cup finely grated pecorino romano
Whole nutmeg, q.b.

Maccheroncini di Campofilone al Sugo Tradizionale

Pasta with Short Ribs and Tomato Sugo

South of Emilia-Romagna, ragù shape-shifts. It begins to include less meat, picks up more tomato, and effectively becomes a sauce flavored with meat rather than a sauce starring meat. That approach is born from the Italian tradition of doing more with less, something that defines much of the cuisine of the more impoverished regions of central Italy, such as the Marche, and of the south. Even though the fortunes of the Marche have improved over the last four decades, this restraint is now codified into much of its cuisine.

My take on this lesser-known classic is inspired by a version I had outside Fermo, the maccheroncini so thin and rich that they almost had the texture of custard, the tomato sauce smooth, ever-so-slightly sweet, and funky. The beef bone that had flavored it gave it a wild, rustic edge, and a barely perceptible hint of clove and nutmeg added a warming, sweet-spice depth. The sauce was masterful in its ability to weave all of these flavors together.

Finding my own way to the soul of this dish has been a saga. I've flavored my sauce with beef bones, with and without marrow, with short ribs, with brisket, in the oven and on the stove top. I landed, after a fair amount of subtraction, with a sauce flavored with one marrowbone and short ribs, which I braise in the sauce alongside a single clove and grated nutmeg. I then remove the short ribs, pull the meat into strands and add it back to the sauce, and serve the dish with a dusting of parmigiano.

---

1   To make the sugo, season the short ribs on all sides with salt q.b. and let sit for at least 1 hour at room temperature or up to overnight in the refrigerator.

2   Fit your meat grinder with the small die. Chop the celery, carrot, and onion into ½- to 1-inch pieces. Put the celery, carrot, and onion through the meat grinder. Once all are ground, gather them in cheesecloth and wring to squeeze out the excess liquid. This is your soffritto.

3   Preheat the oven to 275°F.

4   Place a large, heavy sauce pot or Dutch oven over high heat and add 56g / ¼ cup of the olive oil. Add the short ribs and sear, turning as needed, until golden brown on all sides, 3 to 4 minutes per side and 10 to 15 minutes in total.

5   Transfer the short ribs to a plate and set aside. Drain off and discard any remaining oil.

6   Wipe out the pot and place it over medium-low heat. Add the remaining 56g / ¼ cup olive oil and the soffritto and cook, stirring frequently, until softened but without color, 5 to 8 minutes. Add the garlic and cook until aromatic but without color, 10 to 15 seconds.

7   Stud a short rib with the clove and return the short ribs to the pot. Add the wine and simmer until reduced by half, 5 to 7 minutes.

8   Add the marrowbone, followed by the tomato passata, to the pot. Then add water to reach about ½ inch above the top of the meat. Grate the nutmeg into the pot q.b. (The nutmeg will bloom as it cooks, so use a light touch.)

Yields 4 to 6 servings

Sugo

454g / 1 lb beef short ribs, cut into 3-inch pieces
Salt, q.b.
150g / 2 stalks celery
150g / 1 large carrot, peeled
370g / 1 large onion
112g / ½ cup olive oil
25g / 5 cloves garlic, finely chopped
1 whole clove
220g / 1 cup dry white wine
1 (227g / 8 oz) beef marrowbone
1 (680g / 24 oz) jar tomato passata (3 cups)
Whole nutmeg, q.b.

To Finish

1 batch egg dough (page 18)
22g / ¼ cup finely grated parmigiano-reggiano
Whole nutmeg, q.b.

9   Cover the pot and braise the meat in the oven until very tender and falling off the bone, 3 to 4 hours. Remove from the oven and set aside to cool.

10   Once cooled, remove the short ribs from the pot and separate the meat from the bones. Using two forks, pull the meat apart into fine strands, discarding the sinew then run a knife through the strands to cut them into very fine pieces. Using the handle of a spoon, push out the marrow from the marrowbone, reserving the white part and discarding the brown bits and the bone.

11   Skim any excess fat from top of the sauce (leave a little bit in though—that's flavor). Add the meat and marrow back to the pot and stir to combine. The meat should be cut so fine that it almost disappears into the sauce.

12   Measure out 462g / 2 cups sugo and set aside. Transfer the remainder to an airtight container and refrigerate for up to 3 days or freeze for up to 1 month for another use.

13   To finish, following the instructions for maccheroncini di Campofilone on page 50, make 624g / 1 lb 6 oz with the pasta dough.

14   Bring a large pot of water to a boil over high heat. Generously salt the water.

15   Place a large sauté pan over low heat. Add the sugo and 1 to 2 ladles (55 to 115g / ¼ to ½ cup) pasta cooking water to thin it out just slightly.

16   Lightly shake the maccheroncini to separate the strands. Add them to the water and stir immediately to keep them from clumping. Cook for about 30 seconds. (This pasta is very delicate and will cook in a flash.)

17   Using tongs or a pasta basket, remove the pasta from the pot and transfer to the sauté pan. Turn the heat up to medium. Gently toss for 30 seconds to 1 minute to marry the pasta and the sugo. This can be difficult to toss (it's delicate), so feel free to marry by using a spoon rather than tongs to keep the pasta moving in the pan. If the sauce feels tight, add a splash of pasta cooking water to loosen. When the pasta is properly married, it will cling to the sauce and have a glossy sheen.

18   Divide into bowls and garnish with the parmigiano and with grated nutmeg q.b.

"Sunbaked" is the probably the adjective most often used to describe the Italian south. But drive through central Puglia, and "baked" feels a bit too soft, too generous. It has the feeling of driving through a string of old western towns, or at least a postcard from one left abandoned and sun bleached in a store window for the better part of a century. In early fall, the landscape looks as if it's positively exhausted, the tramontana wind kicking up dust, each town with its abandoned storefronts and metal-gated windows a tumbleweed away from a scene out of *Stagecoach*.

The actors, it seems, are always on break. Every now and again, you'll pull into one of the many comatose towns along SP68 in southeastern Sicily or SS172 in Puglia and spot a nonna rounding the corner with a paper bag filled with bread. Or you'll see a couple of kids running down the street in school uniforms, presumably from a school that you'll almost certainly never locate.

The south also has an almost eerie, I've-been-here-before feeling. At times, the rolling hills along Puglia's Salento coast resembling the steep, verdant coastline of Cephalonia, in Greece; the dry, arid interior of Sicily conjuring the trips I took as a kid to Israel; the olive belt in Puglia, which is studded with as many fig trees, recalling all of those brush-filled canyons that splinter off of California's central coast like so many tributaries; or the Supramonte mountains in Sardinia jutting up from the island's center like southern cousins to the Dolomites.

Perhaps this feeling of being someplace and many places at once is fitting. After all, the Mezzogiorno, as it's called, is defined by the blurring of borders, especially when it comes to food. In fact, drawing a strict line to separate what is Spanish or African or Middle Eastern or Greek and what is Italian is more than simply impossible. Its impossibility is the very cornerstone of southern Italian cuisine. As it relates to pasta, this melting pot of influences manifests in the use of saffron in everything from seafood brodo to the tomato-based ragù that smothers Sardinia's native gnocchi, malloreddus (page 258); the prevalence of couscous (cuscusu) on the western side of Sicily (page 264); the combination of nuts, currants, fish, and wild fennel in pasta con le sarde (page 249); the agrodolce, or "sweet-and-sour," profile that Campania's famous puttanesca (page 256) is built on; and so on.

It's fitting, too, that the notion of "tradition" feels more fluid here, or at least more personal than it is collective. It's not difficult to define the rough borders of it, but within those borders there is a lot of space to roam. That sense of personal freedom translates to soulfulness. It's also perhaps why I think of southern Italian cuisine as more of a collection of ingredients than of precise, iconic dishes. And it's why now, as a "midcareer chef," as *New York Times* critic Pete Wells was kind enough to call me, I connect with the food of the south in a way I never did before. I am no longer a chef who's interested in debating the architecture of "true" bolognese or of faithfully reproducing amatriciana. My process now begins with a set of ingredients that have become my tool kit (see page 135)—my own personal sense of regionality, if you will. I build on these ingredients using tradition as a compass, there to steady me when I get too off course, rather than an anchor.

There is no debating that today that tool kit skews southern. But it's also no secret that my style of pasta making is unequivocally northern (egg based, delicate, often filled). Many would argue that these pastas are the most complex to make and master. But spend an afternoon with the Berardi family right outside Bari and tell me that orecchiette isn't at least close to the most difficult shape in the canon to form. Watch Anna, the nonna, flick a piece the size of a thumbnail off the tip of a knife with almost bored nonchalance; believe that nonchalance to be a sign that you, too, can just step in and take over with the same ease, and you will make a fool of yourself. Not even her adult daughters, who take turns diligently trying to outdo each other, can manage to make them with anything even resembling effortlessness.

The south has a complex, varied, and sometimes bewildering relationship to pasta. Sure, it's true that south of Tuscany much of Italy runs on dried pasta. Campania's Gragnano is, after all, the epicenter of the commercial Italian pasta industry and, for my money, is still the place where the highest-quality dried pasta is made. This tradition is as important as the tradition of making filled egg pastas in the north, and most Italians see buying dried pasta not as a rebuke of the craft of making it but rather as a reverence for it—especially in the south. Rigatoni. Fusilli. Anellini. Spaghetti. Paccheri. These are the shapes synonymous with the south of Italy for good reason. But commercially made extruded pastas are only a part of the story.

In Chiaramonte Gulfi, a tiny hilltop town in southeastern Sicily, I ate perfectly plump ravioli filled with ricotta and mint in a red sauce flavored with hunks of pork, a trattoria staple in these parts. In Nuoro, in Sardinia's wild interior, I ate culurgiones, a version of the same, just braided up like an empanada and filled with potato, pecorino, and mint and swimming in a light tomato sauce. On the western side of Sicily, Pino Maggiore, who has worked at the same trattoria for more than fifty years, showed me how to wrap and roll pasta gently around a knitting needle to make busiate. In Guagnano, in Puglia, I made sagne with the Scarciglia family, a similar shape formed sans needle whose difficulty to make varies depending on which wind is blowing: the humid sirocco up from Africa (good!) or the tramontana from the north (bad!). This is to say nothing of Sardinia's hand-stretched noodles, su filindeu, a pasta so rare, labor-intensive, and utterly impossible to make that only three women, all members of the same family, still know how to do it.

The north may be where the craft of pasta making reaches its apex, but the south is where I've come to better understand its spirit, its roots as a piece of familial DNA, an act of devotion, and, above all, a means of attaching meaning to sustenance. The south is also proof that Italian American cuisine and the cuisine of the south may be different on the plate, but they are forever elementally linked. There's no other way to explain why so much of what I've eaten in the south makes me think of my youth in New Haven. You find the same ubiquity of red sauce, sure, and in relation to the rest of Italy, the portion sizes south of Abruzzo are not shy (though not quite to American standards). But the connection is perhaps harder to quantify because it's personal. There is something in this place, about this food—cooking, eating, and, now, after decades of fixing my gaze on the north, taking inspiration from it—that feels like coming home.

Culurgiones alla Nuorese

Cheese and Potato–Filled Pasta in Tomato Sauce

Some call them the chubby Sardinian siblings of ravioli, but I understand culurgiones best as Italy's answer to the pierogi: hefty, starchy, addicting. While they are served all over the island in a variety of guises (in a sauce of brown butter, walnuts, and pistachios; with guanciale and orange zest; deep-fried; pan-seared), it's the version most commonly served in their birthplace, in the province of Nuoro, that has my heart. That version is filled with potato, aged pecorino, sheep's milk ricotta, and mint and is served in a simple tomato sauce often flavored with garlic and onions. It's a dish that requires no explanation, no additional context—a dish for all comers.

My take on culurgiones alla nuorese hews relatively closely to the dish as you'll find it in the wilds of Nuoro, with a couple of notable changes. First, while you'll see it done all over the south of Italy, I do not like to cook mint—it changes the flavor and dulls its impact—so I've taken it out of the filling and used it to garnish the dish instead. Second, as a subtle homage to Panelentu, a tiny husband-and-wife–run restaurant that makes my favorite version of this dish, I include smoky fiore sardo cheese in the filling. At Panelentu, they keep it classic with their filling but serve the dish with a side of very finely grated fiore sardo—a difference-making touch that I've incorporated here.

---

1 To make the filling, place the potatoes in a pot, cover with cold water, and bring to a simmer over medium heat. Cook until fork-tender, 30 to 45 minutes.

2 Using a slotted spoon, transfer the potatoes to a sheet pan and let cool, about 15 minutes. (This will also allow the potatoes to dry out a bit.)

3 When cool enough to handle, peel the potatoes and put them through a potato ricer or a food mill into a bowl.

4 Place a tamis or fine-mesh strainer over the same bowl. Pass the ricotta through the tamis. Add the pecorino and fiore sardo and fold until well integrated. Season with salt q.b. It should taste well seasoned. Cover and refrigerate until ready to use.

5 To finish, following the instructions for culurgiones on page 94, make 32 pieces with the pasta dough and filling.

6 Bring a large pot of water to a boil over high heat. Generously salt the water.

7 Place a small sauce pot over low heat. Add the red sauce.

8 Add the culurgiones to the water and cook until tender at the thickest closure point, 3 to 5 minutes.

9 While the pasta is cooking, ladle 125g / ½ cup sauce into the bottom of each plate or shallow bowl.

10 Using a spider or slotted spoon, remove the pasta from the pot and divide among bowls or plates. Garnish with the fiore sardo and mint leaves.

Yields 4 to 6 servings

Filling

456g / 4 Yukon gold potatoes
232g / 1 cup ricotta
22g / ¼ cup finely grated pecorino romano
30g / ⅓ cup finely grated fiore sardo
Salt, q.b.

To Finish

1 batch semolina dough (page 19)
750g / 3 cups simple red sauce (page 147)
22g / ¼ cup finely grated fiore sardo
Mint leaves, for garnish

Busiate alla Pesto Trapanese

Pasta with Tomato and Almond Pesto

Unlike the north of Italy, where pasta dishes can usually be traced to a single town, in Sicily many pastas—pasta alla Norma and pasta con le sarde—have become synonymous with the island. But busiate alla pesto trapanese proudly declares its origin right in its name. Sandwiched between Palermo and Marsala on Sicily's west coast, Trapani has a few claims to fame aside from its beloved pesto: a particular breed of couscous (page 264) served with fish brodo, a longtime Mafia presence, and excellent salt.

Found all along the west coast, pesto alla trapanese is a variation on pesto al Genovese (page 178) that is said to have originated with Trapani sailors. It grew from a simple agliata sauce (nuts, garlic, oil) to what is effectively Genovese pesto adapted to Sicilian ingredients: almonds replace the pine nuts, basil takes a backseat to ripe tomatoes, mint nudges into the mix. It's traditionally served with busiate, which also hails from Trapani and remains relatively scarce outside of the area. While there are slight variations in consistency and ingredients (the addition of cheese is a matter of debate), it's generally more rough-hewn in texture—the pestle wielded with clemency. My recipe calls for the full force of the pestle. At Corona Trattoria in Palermo, I had a version of the dish that achieved a similar consistency to pesto al Genovese and a greater harmony of ingredients. I use a food processor for ease, but if you're going by hand, you can control the texture to your preference.

1   Bring a small pot of water to a boil over high heat. Prepare an ice-water bath and set a colander in it.

2   Using a sharp paring knife, cut an X into the bottom of each tomato. Drop the tomatoes into the boiling water and leave for 5 to 10 seconds to loosen their skins. Using a slotted spoon, transfer the tomatoes to the ice-water bath. After 30 seconds, transfer the tomatoes to a bowl. Peel the tomatoes and discard the skins. Transfer to a kitchen towel to remove any excess water.

3   Transfer the tomatoes to a high-speed blender. Add the garlic and gently pulse to puree. Add the basil and continue to puree. Add the almonds and continue blending until you have a thick, uniform paste.

4   With the blender running on low speed, drizzle in the 75g / ⅓ cup of oil. Once smooth, transfer the mixture to a mixing bowl. Fold in the cheese until well combined. Check your seasoning and add salt q.b.

5   Measure out 383g / 1½ cups of the pesto. Transfer the remainder to an airtight container, cover with a layer of olive oil, and refrigerate for up to 3 days for another use.

6   To finish, following the instructions for busiate on page 64, make 624 g / 1 lb 6 oz with the pasta dough.

7   Bring a large pot of water to a boil over high heat. Generously salt the water.

8   Add the busiate to the water and cook until al dente, 3 to 5 minutes.

9   Add the pesto to a large mixing bowl. Using a spider or pasta basket, transfer the pasta directly to the mixing bowl. While gently tossing to combine, slowly add pasta cooking water, 15g / 1 Tbsp at a time, until the pesto is creamy and easily coats the pasta.

10   Divide the pasta into bowls.

Yields 4 to 6 servings

545g / 1 lb 3 oz cherry tomatoes
10g / 2 garlic cloves
10 basil leaves
100g / scant ¾ cup Sicilian
    almonds, coarsely chopped
75g / ⅓ cup olive oil plus more
    to cover, as needed
68g / ¾ cup pecorino romano
Salt, q.b.

To Finish

1 batch semolina dough
    (page 19)

Bucatini con le Sarde

Pasta with Sardines, Currants, Pine Nuts, and Fennel

Pasta con le sarde is a perfect expression of Sicily's culinary history in the region—in particular, of the Arab presence for nearly a quarter of a millennium. For that reason, the island still eats like a spiritual borderland between Africa and Europe; pasta con le sarde is a worthy ambassador.

The dish adapts in small ways across the island, but some constants remain: fresh sardines, anchovies, wild fennel, pine nuts, saffron, raisins (more often currants), and bread crumbs. Some variations include Sicilian tomato paste (strattu); others lose the saffron or bread crumbs. Small additions and omissions aside, the dish should always add up to the archetypal Sicilian agrodolce profile.

My version incorporates a prep technique for anchovies that I learned in Trapani, which calls for quickly soaking the fish in vinegar before cooking. This adds a bit of pungency, buffers the fishiness, and firms the fish up, which, in the case of pasta con le sarde, helps ensure that the sardines hold their shape during the marriage process.

1   To prepare the sardines, season the fillets with salt and let sit for 5 minutes.

2   Pour the vinegar into a shallow baking dish or large plate. Place the fillets flesh-side down in the vinegar and let marinate at room temperature until the flesh begins to turn slightly opaque, 5 to 10 minutes.

3   Transfer the fillets to a cutting board and cut each into ¾-inch pieces on a diagonal. Set aside until ready to use, or refrigerate if not using right away.

4   To finish, preheat the oven to 325°F.

5   Add the pine nuts to a sheet pan and toast in the oven until very lightly golden brown, 5 to 7 minutes. Set aside to cool, about 15 minutes.

6   Bring a large pot of water to a boil over high heat. Generously salt the water.

7   Place a large sauté pan over low heat. Add the olive oil. Add the garlic and cook until aromatic but without color, 10 to 15 seconds. Add the fennel bulb and sauté until it begins to soften, 3 to 5 minutes. Set aside.

8   Add the bucatini to the water and cook until al dente, 5 to 8 minutes.

9   Using tongs or a pasta basket, remove the pasta from the pot and transfer to the sauté pan. Turn the heat up to medium. Add 1 ladle (55g / ¼ cup) pasta cooking water and toss to combine. Add the currants, pine nuts, sardines, and chile flakes, and gently toss to combine, being careful not to break up the sardines, 30 seconds to 1 minute. If the sauce begins to tighten, add a splash more pasta cooking water to loosen and continue tossing.

10   Remove from the heat, add the fennel fronds, and toss to incorporate.

11   Divide the pasta into bowls.

Yields 4 to 6 servings

Sardines

8 sardines, scaled, gutted, and filleted
4g / 1¼ tsp salt
220g / 1 cup white wine vinegar

To Finish

70g / 9½ Tbsp pine nuts
75g / ⅓ cup olive oil
40g / 8 cloves garlic, thinly sliced
200g / ½ large fennel bulb, thinly sliced
624g / 1 lb 6 oz extruded bucatini (page 121)
60g / ½ cup dried currants or raisins
Red chile flakes, q.b.
20g / 5 Tbsp chopped fennel fronds

Spaghetti ai Ricci di Mare

Pasta with Sea Urchin

This dish does not have a single regional loyalty—it is pan-southern in the same way that spaghetti aglio, olio e peperoncino, and spaghetti alle vongole are. Where there are sea urchins, there is spaghetti ai ricci di mare.

I've experimented with the dish for years in an effort to find the right balance of richness and salinity without compromising the flavor of sea urchin to the point at which you end up wishing you'd just eaten it raw. It's a dish that takes finesse, not to mention an appetite to splurge. In my A Voce days, I'd make a compound uni butter to create more richness and also a more even distribution of flavor and texture. Of course, butter isn't traditional (this is the south, after all), but I still think finishing the dish with it gives the sauce the cling it needs to marry well with the pasta. It's the one way in which I stray from tradition in this recipe.

1   Place half of the sea urchin in a bowl and mash it into a paste with the back of a spoon. In a separate bowl, use the spoon to gently break the remaining sea urchin into bigger pieces.

2   Bring a large pot of water to a boil over high heat. Generously salt the water.

3   Add the spaghetti to the water and cook for 5 to 8 minutes, until al dente.

4   While the pasta is cooking, place a large sauté pan over low heat. Add the olive oil and garlic and gently cook until aromatic but without color, 10 to 15 seconds. Add 2 to 3 ladles (115 to 170g / ½ to ¾ cup) pasta cooking water and swirl to combine.

5   Right before your pasta is ready, add the sea urchin to the sauté pan and stir to incorporate.

6   Using tongs or a pasta basket, remove the pasta from the pot and transfer to the sauté pan. Turn the heat up to medium. Toss for 30 seconds to 1 minute to marry the pasta and the sea urchin. The urchin will become creamy and begin to cling to the pasta like a sauce.

7   Add the butter and continue tossing to marry. If the sauce begins to tighten, add a splash of pasta cooking water to loosen and continue tossing.

8   Remove the pan from the heat, add the lemon peel and lemon juice, and toss to combine.

9   Divide the pasta into bowls and garnish with a dusting of ground chile q.b.

Yields 4 to 6 servings

240g / 8½ oz sea urchin
624g / 1 lb 6 oz extruded
    spaghetti (page 123)
42g / 3 Tbsp olive oil
15g / 3 cloves garlic, finely
    chopped
60g / ¼ cup unsalted butter,
    cold and cubed
Peel of ⅔ lemon, pith removed
    and peel finely chopped
Juice of ½ lemon
Ground red chile, q.b.

Orecchiette con Cime di Rapa

Pasta with Broccoli Rabe, Anchovies, Garlic, and Chile Flakes

Italians have a particular talent for cooking vegetables to death. When it comes to Puglia's most famous pasta, however, it's a welcome feature, not a bug. What makes this cool-weather dish work is cooking the broccoli rabe until they break down into a kind of ragù alongside the anchovy and garlic. It's bitter, saline, and rich to a point where it functions like a substitute for the original article.

Throughout Puglia you'll find this dish embellished in different ways, whether it's the addition of clams or bread crumbs, or the substitution of smoky grano arso flour (page 11) in combination with, or in place of, semolina. Stateside, it picked up sausage somewhere along the way and ran with it to the point where most Americans assume it is traditional. But what makes this dish great is that it doesn't need the sausage. It's plenty complex in its original form.

---

1   To make the bread crumbs, preheat the oven to 200°F.

2   Spread the bread on a sheet pan and bake until dried out, 30 to 45 minutes. You do not want any color. To test for doneness, crush a shard of bread with the back of a spoon. The interior should be completely dry. Let cool.

3   Once cooled, place the bread in a food processor and pulse until broken down into fine crumbs. You want them to retain some texture, so be careful not to turn them to dust.

4   Place a sauté pan over medium-low heat. Add the oil and garlic cloves and cook until the garlic perfumes the oil, 1 to 2 minutes. Remove the garlic and save for another use.

5   Turn the heat down to low. Line a plate with paper towels. Add the bread crumbs to the pan and cook, stirring occasionally, until golden brown, 5 to 8 minutes. Remove from the pan and transfer to the plate to drain. Let cool.

6   Measure out 40g / ¼ cup bread crumbs and set aside. Transfer the remainder to an airtight container and store in a cool, dry place for up to 1 week for another use.

7   To finish, following the instructions for orecchiette on page 68, make 624g / 1 lb 6 oz with the pasta dough.

8   Separate the broccoli rabe leaves from the stems. Roughly chop the stems and florets into very small pieces. Finely chop the leaves and reserve separately.

9   Bring a large pot of water to a boil over high heat. Generously salt the water.

continued

Yields 4 to 6 servings

Bread Crumbs

½ loaf (228g / 8 oz) country bread, torn into pieces (about 4 cups)
56g / ¼ cup olive oil
10g / 2 cloves garlic

To Finish

1 batch semolina dough (page 19)
346g / 1 large bunch broccoli rabe
42g / 3 Tbsp olive oil
45g / 9 cloves garlic, finely chopped
30g / 4 to 5 large oil-packed anchovy fillets, finely chopped
4g / 2 tsp dried red chile flakes
110g / ½ cup dry white wine
22g / ¼ cup finely grated pecorino romano

Orecchiette con Cime di Rapa

continued

10   Place a large sauté pan over low heat. Add the olive oil and garlic and gently cook until aromatic but without color, 10 to 15 seconds.

11   Add the anchovies, chile flakes, and broccoli rabe stems and florets and stir to combine. Add the wine and about 3 ladles (170g / ¾ cup) pasta cooking water. Braise the broccoli rabe until tender but still bright green, 3 to 5 minutes. Add the leaves and cook for 1 to 2 minutes. Set aside.

12   Add the orecchiette to the water and cook for 4 to 6 minutes, until al dente.

13   Using a spider or pasta basket, remove the pasta from the pot and transfer to the sauté pan. Turn the heat up to medium. Gently toss for 1 to 2 minutes to marry the pasta and the sauce. If the sauce feels tight, add a splash of pasta cooking water to loosen and continue tossing to marry.

14   Divide the pasta into bowls and garnish with the bread crumbs and pecorino.

Spaghetti alla Puttanesca

Pasta with Tomatoes, Olives, Capers, and Anchovies

This dish, the story goes, was popularized in Naples, where the women of the night used its aroma to lure men into the brothel. Puttanesca by that name is fairly new—dating only to the mid-twentieth century, but the dish itself goes back much farther, likely at least to the nineteenth century. In fact, a near-exact version of the dish (missing tomato) appears in Ippolito Cavalcanti's *Cucina teorico-practica* as vermicelli with oil, anchovies, olives, capers, and parsley. Given that the book also contains the first mentions of pasta being sauced with tomato, it's not much of a leap to puttanesca.

The briny, garlic-forward aroma of the sauce is certainly enough to lure anyone, anywhere, even against better judgment. To me, the flavor of Naples is puttanesca, a true assault of pungency and salinity that is as outspoken and frenetic as the city itself. Naples is not a place you go to relax, and puttanesca is not a pasta you serve to folks looking for an innocuous taste of Italy.

In that spirit, my take on the dish is meant to showcase the intensity of each ingredient, rather than cooking them into submission.

---

1   To make the sauce, place a heavy sauce pot or Dutch oven over low heat. Add the olive oil and garlic and gently cook until aromatic but without color, 10 to 15 seconds.

2   Add the anchovies and stir to incorporate. Cook, stirring, until they start to dissolve into the oil, about 30 seconds.

3   Add the chile flakes, followed by the tomato paste. Cook, stirring constantly, until the oil takes on a reddish hue, 30 to 45 seconds.

4   Add the tomatoes and their juice and stir to incorporate. Turn the heat up to medium-low and cook at a slow simmer until the rawness of the tomatoes is cooked out and the flavors have melded, 30 to 45 minutes. You are not looking to reduce the sauce.

5   Remove from the heat and add the olives and capers and stir to incorporate. Season with salt q.b. (Go easy, as olives, anchovies, and capers provide a lot of salinity.)

6   Measure out 540g / 2¼ cups sauce and set aside. Transfer the remainder to an airtight container and refrigerate for up to 3 days or freeze for another use.

7   To finish, bring a large pot of water to a boil over high heat. Generously salt the water.

8   Add the spaghetti to the water and cook for 5 to 8 minutes, until al dente.

9   While the pasta is cooking, place a large sauté pan over low heat. Add the sauce.

10   Using tongs or a pasta basket, remove the pasta from the pot and transfer to the sauté pan. Turn the heat up to medium. Toss for 1 to 2 minutes to marry the pasta and the sauce. If the sauce begins to tighten, add a splash of pasta cooking water to loosen. When the pasta is properly married, it will cling to the sauce and have a glossy sheen.

11   Divide the pasta into bowls.

Yields 4 to 6 servings

Puttanesca Sauce

75g / ⅓ cup olive oil
50g / 10 cloves garlic, thinly sliced
62g / 10 to 12 oil-packed anchovy fillets, very finely chopped
3g / 1½ tsp dried red chile flakes
30g / 2 Tbsp tomato paste
2 large (794g / 28 oz) cans whole San Marzano tomatoes, crushed by hand
140g / 1 cup pitted Taggiasca olives, cut into quarters
32g / 3 Tbsp small salt-packed capers, rinsed
Salt, q.b.

To Finish

624g / 1 lb 6 oz extruded spaghetti (page 123)

Nota bene

Be sure to soak the capers in cold water before using, refreshing the water every 15 minutes or so, until they are briny but not salty, about 2 hours.

Malloreddus alla Campidanese

Sardinian Gnocchi with Sausage, Saffron, and Tomato Ragù

When scientists first went sniffing around Sardinia for an answer as to why the island was home to such a large concentration of centenarians per capita, diet, of course, was a consideration. (Spoiler: it's genetics.) And yes, *that* diet. The thing is, the Sardinians don't adhere to the Mediterranean diet. Compared with their other coastal counterparts, they eat a ton of meat and plenty of dairy, and their wines tend to be quite high in alcohol.

While fregola sarda generously studded with seafood and spaghetti alla bottarga are fixtures all around the island, malloreddus alla campidanese is arguably the island's best-known dish. Originating on the agriculture-rich Campidano plain, which lies just outside the island capital city of Cagliari, the dish combines two of Sardinia's most important staples—saffron and tomatoes—and introduces them to pork sausage. The handshake between the acidity and sweetness of the tomatoes and saffron kicked up with pork fat is a simple revelation. I find it's a dish I crave more than classic bolognese—though, to be fair, choosing one over the other is the very definition of a zero-sum game.

---

1 To make the ragù, combine the pork, the 15g / 3 cloves chopped garlic, fennel seed, salt, and pepper in a bowl. Mix well but gently so as not to break up the fat too much. Make a small patty to test your seasoning.

2 Place a small sauté pan over medium heat and add a drizzle of olive oil. Add the test patty and cook, turning once, until cooked through, 2 to 3 minutes on each side. Check your seasoning and add more salt to the pork mixture q.b. Refrigerate until ready to use.

3 In a small bowl, combine the saffron and wine. Let sit at room temperature for 10 minutes to bloom.

4 Place a large, heavy sauce pot or Dutch oven over medium-low heat. Add 56g / ¼ cup of the olive oil and the onion and cook, stirring occasionally, until very soft and translucent, about 10 minutes. Toward the very end of cooking, add the 25g / 5 cloves garlic and gently cook until aromatic but without color, 10 to 15 seconds. Set aside.

5 Place a large sauté pan over high heat. Add the remaining 56g / ¼ cup oil and begin to cook the pork in batches, one-third of the volume at a time. As the pork starts to brown, break it up with tongs or a wooden spoon into very small, uniform crumbled pieces. Cook until there is no pink in the center, 3 to 5 minutes. Using a slotted spoon, transfer the meat to the pot. Repeat with the remaining batches.

6 Return the sauce pot to low heat. Add the bloomed saffron and wine and cook until reduced by about half, 5 to 6 minutes.

Yields 4 to 6 servings

Ragù

910g / 2 lb high-fat ground pork
40g / 8 cloves garlic, 3 cloves separated from the others, and all finely chopped
23g / scant ¼ cup fennel seed, roughly ground
18g / 2 Tbsp salt, plus more q.b.
55 grinds black pepper
112g / ½ cup olive oil, plus more q.b.
1 tsp saffron threads
220g / 1 cup dry white wine
250g / 2 cups finely chopped onion
1 large (794g / 28 oz) can whole San Marzano tomatoes, crushed by hand

To Finish

1 batch egg-based or semolina dough (pages 18, 22, and 26–31)
1 small (57g / 2 oz) piece fiore sardo

7   Add the tomatoes with their juices to the sauce pot and stir to combine. Cook until the flavors have melded, about 1 hour.

8   Measure out 512g / 2¼ cups ragù and set aside. Transfer the remainder to an airtight container and refrigerate for up to 5 days or freeze for up to 1 month for another use.

9   To finish, following the instructions for malloreddus on page 67, make 624g / 1 lb 6 oz with the pasta dough.

10   Bring a large pot of water to a boil over high heat. Generously salt the water.

11   Place a large sauté pan over low heat. Add the ragù and 2 to 3 ladles (115g to 170g / ½ to ¾ cup) pasta cooking water and stir to combine.

12   Add the malloreddus to the water and cook for 3 to 5 minutes, until tender but not soft.

13   Using a pasta basket or spider, remove the pasta from the pot and transfer to the sauté pan. Turn the heat up to medium. Toss for 1 to 2 minutes to marry the pasta and the ragù. If the sauce begins to tighten, add a splash of pasta cooking water to loosen and continue tossing to marry. The ragù should nicely coat the pasta without clumping in the pan.

14   Divide the pasta into bowls and finely grate the fiore sardo over the top.

Pasta

Casarecce con Pesce Spada, Pistacchi e Capperi

Pasta with Swordfish, Pistachios, and Capers

There's a preponderance of pastas in Sicily that combine nuts—pistachios or almonds, naturally—and tuna, swordfish, or shrimp, primarily. Some versions include wild fennel, others capers, and still others the island-wide pasta staple of bread crumbs. I've had great renditions of all of them, but none that won me over quite like the spaghetti con pesce spada at Da Vittorio, a restaurant perched on the Mediterranean in the sleepy beach town of Menfi. Pungent from the addition of capers and sweet and rich from almonds and cubes of tender, fatty swordfish, it was perfectly balanced. My version hews to Da Vittorio's, but swaps out almonds for pistachios, which add just a touch more richness and depth, and leans on casarecce in place of spaghetti.

1   To make the swordfish, place the cubes in a mixing bowl. Add the salt, toss to coat, and let sit for 10 minutes.

2   Place a sauce pot over low heat. Add the olive oil, citrus peels, garlic, parsley, and marjoram. Make a sachet with cheesecloth for the chile flakes, fennel seed, coriander seed, and black peppercorns and add to the sauce pot.

3   When the oil is just warmed, about 3 to 5 minutes, add the swordfish and stir gently. Slowly poach the fish until opaque, another 3 to 5 minutes. The fish will continue cooking in the sauce so you are only partially cooking it during this step.

4   Remove from the heat and transfer the contents of the pot to a baking dish to cool. Set aside until ready to use. (Alternatively, cover the fish with a layer of olive oil, cover tightly with plastic wrap, and store in the refrigerator for up to 1 day before cooking.)

5   To finish, bring a large pot of water to a boil over high heat. Generously salt the water. Add the casarecce to the water and cook until al dente, 5 to 8 minutes.

6   While the pasta is cooking, place a large sauté pan over low heat. Add the olive oil, garlic, and chile flakes. Gently cook until the garlic is aromatic but without color, 15 to 20 seconds.

7   Add the wine and cook for 30 seconds. Add 3 to 4 ladles (170 to 230g / ¾ to 1 cup) pasta cooking water and swirl the contents of the pan to combine.

8   Just as the pasta is finishing cooking, add the capers to the sauté pan.

9   Using a spider or pasta basket, remove the pasta from the pot and transfer to the sauté pan. Turn up the heat to medium. Using a slotted spoon, remove the swordfish from the oil and add to the pan, tossing the pasta in the sauce to marry, 30 seconds to 1 minute. If the sauce becomes tight, add a splash more pasta cooking water to loosen it.

10   Remove the pan from the heat, add half of the pistachios and all of the parsley, and toss to combine. Add the lemon peel and lemon juice and continue tossing to combine.

11   Transfer the pasta to a large serving platter or divide into bowls, and garnish with the remaining pistachios.

Yields 6 to 8 servings

Swordfish

684g / 24 oz swordfish, cut into ¼- to ½-inch cubes
7g / 2 tsp salt
752g / 3⅓ cups olive oil
Peel of ⅔ lemon, pith removed
Peel of 1 orange, pith removed
25g / 5 cloves garlic, smashed
1 sprig parsley
2 sprigs marjoram
2g / 1 tsp dried red chile flakes
5g / 2 tsp fennel seed
3g / 1½ tsp coriander seed
5g / 2 tsp black peppercorns

To Finish

624g / 1 lb 6 oz extruded casarecce (page 121)
56g / ¼ cup olive oil
25g / 5 cloves garlic, thinly sliced
2g / 1 tsp dried red chile flakes
220g / 1 cup dry white wine
56g / ⅓ cup small salt-packed capers, well rinsed
120g / 1 cup chopped pistachios
10g / 2 Tbsp finely chopped parsley
1 lemon, pith removed from peel and peel finely chopped and lemon halved and juiced

Couscous alla Trapanese

Couscous with Fish Brodo

For most people with a passing acquaintance with couscous, Sicily probably isn't the first place that comes to mind. North Africa? Surely. Israel? Different, but yes. Yet on the island's west coast—particularly in the town that has wedged its way into its most famous preparation, couscous (or cuscusu, as it's called here) is as Sicilian as cannoli.

Couscous was allegedly brought to Sicily by the Arabs a thousand years ago, though some say it came later, during the fifteenth-century arrival of the Sephardic Jews, and still others claim it wasn't truly inducted into Sicilian cuisine until the nineteenth century. Regardless, there is no argument that it is a modern staple of the western Sicilian diet. Like so many of the island's iconic dishes, couscous is the perfect symbol of Sicily's complex, shared foodways.

Sicilian couscous is made by painstakingly hand rolling coarse semolina (or semolato, as it's called) in a terra-cotta vessel called a mafaradda, sometimes for up to an hour, and then serving it with a thick, aromatic fish brodo and chunks of succulent white fish. Many versions will also include shellfish, but at Cantina Siciliana in Trapani, where Pino Maggiore has been working since he was six years old, he balks at the inclusion. "I'm not making paella," he says with a laugh.

What I love about this dish is the zen of making it—the continuous motion, clockwise and then counterclockwise, around the edge of the mafaradda; the consistent adding of water, slowly, and the learned confidence to know when it needs more; and the labor of making the brodo. Making one's regional specialty is always personal, but here this is especially so. Everyone has a different way of working the semolina, a different consistency for which he or she is striving. There's even an embrace of human error that has emerged as its own variation of the dish. Called frescatole, it is a lumpy, overworked couscous that is now made intentionally by clumping the couscous up with the addition of regular soft wheat flour or finely ground semolina.

---

1   To make the brodo, place a large stockpot over medium-low heat. Add the olive oil, fennel, carrot, celery, onion, and garlic. Cook for 8 to 10 minutes, until softened but without color.

2   Add the wine, turn the heat up to medium, and reduce by one-half, 4 to 5 minutes.

3   Add the fish bones, leeks, parsley, peppercorns, fennel seed, chile flakes, and lemon peel. Add the passata and water, and stir to combine.

4   Bring to a slow simmer for 15 minutes, skimming any foam or impurities as they float to the surface, being careful not to let it boil. Turn the heat down to low and cook for another 45 minutes, continuing to skim impurities from the surface of the brodo.

5   Strain the brodo through a fine-mesh strainer. Measure out 1.4kg / 6 cups brodo and set aside. Let the remaining brodo cool, then store in an airtight container in the refrigerator for up to 5 days or in the freezer for another use.

6   To make the couscous, place the semolina in a large mixing bowl, preferably something ceramic and weighty or a stainless-steel bowl with a damp towel placed underneath to hold it in place.

Yields 4 to 6 servings

Brodo

56g / ¼ cup olive oil
600g / 2 fennel bulbs, stems and fronds removed, cut into 1-inch pieces
150g / 1 large carrot, peeled and cut into ½-inch pieces
225g / 3 stalks celery, cut into 1-inch pieces
500g / 2 onions, cut into 1-inch pieces
65g / 13 cloves garlic
330g / 1½ cups dry white wine
452g / 1 lb white fish bones (from a mild fish, such as halibut)
116g / 4 oz leek tops
30g / ½ bunch parsley
9g / 1 Tbsp black peppercorns
½ tsp fennel seed
½ tsp dried red chile flakes
Peel of ½ lemon, pith removed
1 (680g / 24 oz) jar tomato passata (3 cups)
1.4kg / 6 cups cold water

7   Add the water a few drops at a time and begin to swirl the semolina around the interior of the bowl in a circular motion with your dominant hand. Pause every 10 or so rotations to pick up the semolina and gently rub it between your palms. Both these motions alternated between adding small amounts of water will ensure your couscous begins taking on a coarse texture without clumping too much.

8   Continue this process for 45 to 60 minutes (yes, that's right, you may work up a sweat), until the semolina takes on the texture of coarse sea salt. Be sure to continue moving the semolina in the bowl and adding only small amounts of water at a time.

9   Place a large pot of water over medium heat. Set a finely perforated steamer on top of it, and bring to a slow simmer.

10   To the bowl of couscous, add the olive oil, salt, and cinnamon, tossing to combine.

11   Transfer the couscous to the steaming basket; add the onion and parsley, and cook, covered, for 45 minutes to 1 hour, until the couscous is tender but still al dente.

12   Remove the onions and parsley from the couscous and discard. (If you used a whole cinnamon stick, discard that, too.) Cover the couscous and set aside to keep warm or lay out on a sheet pan to cool. Transfer to an airtight container and store in the refrigerator until ready to use.

13   To finish, season the fish, flesh side up, with salt.

14   Place a large sauté pan over medium heat and add the olive oil. Place the fish in the pan skin side down, pressing each fillet down with a fish spatula to ensure they don't curl as they heat. Cook until the skin is golden brown and the flesh is three-quarters of the way cooked through, 3 to 5 minutes. Flip the fillets over, turn the heat down to low, and cook for another 45 seconds to 1 minute.

15   Transfer the fish to a serving platter and drizzle with the lemon juice and olive oil q.b.

16   Divide the couscous into bowls, ladle the brodo over each, and serve alongside the fish.

Couscous

500g / 1 lb coarse semolina
237g / 1 cup room temperature
    water, plus more, q.b.
56g / ¼ cup olive oil
½ tsp salt
¼ tsp ground cinnamon or
    1 whole cinnamon stick
250g / 1 onion, cut into 8 pieces
15g / ¼ bunch parsley

To Finish

4 fillets branzino, cut in half
    (8 pieces)
Salt, q.b.
75g / ⅓ cup olive oil, plus
    more, q.b.
½ lemon, for juicing

Fileja alla 'Nduja

Pasta with 'Nduja and Tomato Sauce

Nobody does heat quite like the Calabrians. While perhaps better known for the production of their eponymous sweet-hot chiles, which always have a prime spot in my pantry (see page 135), they are also known for making 'nduja, the soft sausage made spicy with those very chiles. Over the last decade, both products have received greater US distribution, leading the curious and inclined to discover the regional dishes that celebrate them.

To me, the most triumphant of them is fileja alla 'nduja, a long, handmade tubular pasta (similar to busiate, page 64, without the corkscrew shape) that originated on the western coast of Calabria, served with a simple red sauce turned transcendent by the addition of 'nduja. It's feral and hot, sweet and savory, silky and rich. It's a dish whose treble and bass are turned to ten, and one that should be a more familiar member of the canon.

1   To make the sauce, place a large, heavy sauce pot or Dutch oven over low heat. Add the oil and garlic and gently cook until aromatic but without color, 15 to 30 seconds.

2   Add the fennel seed and tomatoes and their juice and stir to combine. Turn the heat up to medium-low and cook at a slow simmer until the rawness of the tomatoes is cooked out and the flavors have melded, 15 to 20 minutes. You are not looking to reduce the sauce.

3   Gradually add the 'nduja while stirring to break it up as you incorporate it.

4   Remove from the heat. Measure out 342g / 1¼ cups sauce and set aside. Transfer the remainder to an airtight container and refrigerate for up to 5 days or freeze for up to 1 month for another use.

5   To finish, following the instructions for fileja on page 63, make 624g / 1 lb 6 oz from the pasta dough.

6   Bring a large pot of water to a boil over high heat. Generously salt the water.

7   Place a large sauté pan over low heat. Add the sauce.

8   Add the fileja to the water and cook until tender, 3 to 5 minutes.

9   Using a pasta basket or spider, remove the pasta from the pot and transfer to the sauté pan. Toss for 1 to 2 minutes to marry the pasta and the sauce. If the sauce begins to tighten, add a splash of pasta cooking water to loosen and continue tossing to marry. The sauce should evenly coat the pasta.

10 Transfer the pasta to a serving platter or divide into bowls.

Yields 4 to 6 servings

Sauce

42g / 3 Tbsp olive oil
25g / 5 garlic cloves, finely chopped
½ tsp fennel seed, coarsely ground in a spice mill or with a mortar and pestle
1 large (794g / 28 oz) can San Marzano tomatoes, crushed by hand
200g / 7 oz 'nduja, casing removed and discarded and finely chopped

To Finish

1 batch semolina dough (page 19)

Modern Classics

There's a well-worn saying that's been playing in my head for seventeen years: "The most important ingredient is the one you leave out." I'd always attributed it to my early mentor, Tony Mantuano, only to find out later that, according to him, he'd gotten it from Marcella Hazan. But I have found no record of her ever saying it, and it's just as well. It has always felt like an essential truth—a creed passed down from the very inventors of Italian cuisine.

Great cooking is a game of subtraction. How do I get the most out of the fewest ingredients? But as a young chef, I, like most young chefs, played the game of addition, without identifying the difference between innovation and embellishment. To subtract is more difficult; it takes confidence to lay your technique bare, to say less in the hope of saying more. There have certainly been moments when I've doubted my own allegiances, when I worried that "deceptively simple" might be considered just, well, simple. There are certainly critics who have suggested as much. But those ten words—"the most important ingredient is the one you leave out"—have always acted as a steadying reminder to stay the course.

The pastas I cook today draw from the values of both Italian American cooking and classic regional Italian food. From the former, I've developed a dedication to food that places emotional resonance and comfort first. Ten years ago, I am not sure I'd have felt pride if a guest's response to one of my pastas was, "I feel like I've had this before, but I haven't had this before." These days I hear that often, and I could not be paid a higher compliment. I even have those moments with my own dishes, like the rigatoni diavola (page 289) at Lilia, a pasta clearly rooted in red-sauce nostalgia but spiked with ingredients and technique that give it just a slight edge, or my spaghetti alla chitarra with lobster and fresh chiles (page 346), which could easily follow a path back to fra diavolo (page 159). But the connection is often more conceptual than literal—it's about allowing familiarity, in the use of ingredients or the appearance of a dish, to be an ingredient itself. It's a way to relate that, as cliché as it sounds, embraces cooking as an act of love.

How my food is tethered to regional Italian cooking isn't exactly literal, either. I do not have agnolotti dal plin (page 209) or pizzoccheri alla valtellinese (page 183) on my menus. Likewise, you will not find any of my pastas on a menu in Italy. But each dish is based on the techniques I learned by studying and cooking regional Italian pastas for a decade and a half. In other words, they are not called "Modern Classics" as a personal pat on the back, but as an acknowledgment that "modern" is not divorced from tried-and-true Italian traditions. Some pastas are transparent about their inspiration, such as my parmigiano fonduta–filled tortellini in brodo (page 298), an obvious riff on classic tortellini in brodo (page 198), or my eggplant-filled mezzelune with simple sauce and ricotta salata (page 306), essentially Sicily's pasta alla Norma reimagined as a filled pasta. Because I've been at this for so long, I sometimes end up riffing on my own dishes, stepping two to three steps away from Italy (see occhi, page 340, or potato ravioli, page 290), but never so far that I break with its principles.

What unifies all of the following pastas is a sense of regionality achieved through the combination of the ingredients I have available to me in New York and from my personal tool kit (see page 135). Many of these pastas are simple in a casual Tuesday night kind of way. But *simple* doesn't always mean *easy*. There is a graduated scale of complexity in process and technique in these recipes. Yet my aim is always to remain in service to the virtue of subtraction.

Spaghetti with Garlic Four Ways

I really intended this dish to be garlic *one* way—a simple aglio e olio (garlic and oil) based on spring garlic. What I ended up with is a love letter to my favorite ingredient and a celebration of its full spectrum of flavors: a caramelized sweetness, fried sliced garlic for texture and subtle bitterness, and quickly sautéed spring and mature garlic, with each adding a different level of vegetal pungency and a "cold" heat. This is not just a no-holds-barred rebuke of the garlic averse but also an example of how two ingredients can yield all of the complexity you might hope for in a dish if you employ the right techniques.

1 To make the caramelized cloves, place a sauté pan over low heat and add the olive oil. Add the garlic cloves in a single layer and cook, making sure to regularly move them in the pan, until they are light golden brown, caramelized on all sides, and mash easily when pressed, 15 to 20 minutes. This will yield your sweet garlic flavor.

2 Set aside to cool until ready to use or transfer to a lidded glass jar, add olive oil to cover, and store in the refrigerator for up to 1 week.

3 To make the crispy garlic, line a plate with paper towels. Place another sauté pan over low heat and add the olive oil. Add the garlic and cook, stirring occasionally, until the slices begin to turn golden at the edges and harden slightly, 3 to 5 minutes. They will curl up a bit and cluster together as they cook, so be sure to stir occasionally to ensure even coloring.

4 Using a slotted spoon, remove the garlic and place in one layer on the paper towels to drain. They will crisp up as they drain and dry.

5 To finish, bring a large pot of water to a boil over high heat. Generously salt the water.

6 Place a large sauté pan over medium-low heat and add the olive oil. Add the spring garlic and cook until it softens but is without color, 1 to 2 minutes.

7 Add the sliced garlic and continue to cook until it is aromatic and without color, 30 seconds to 1 minute. Add a splash of water to stop the cooking and set aside.

8 Add the spaghetti to the water and cook for 5 to 8 minutes, until al dente.

9 While the pasta is cooking, return the sauté pan to low heat and add 3 ladles (170g / ¾ cup) pasta cooking water and swirl to combine.

10 Using tongs or a pasta basket, remove the pasta from the pot and transfer to the sauté pan. Turn the heat up to medium and add the caramelized garlic cloves and the chile flakes. Toss for 1 to 2 minutes to marry the pasta and the sauce. If the sauce begins to tighten, add a splash of pasta cooking water to loosen and continue tossing.

11 Remove from the heat. Add the parsley and continue to toss until evenly distributed, adding another splash of pasta cooking water if the sauce tightens up.

12 Divide the pasta into bowls and garnish with the crispy garlic.

Yields 4 to 6 servings

Caramelized Cloves

56g / ¼ cup olive oil, plus more q.b. if storing
125g / 25 cloves garlic

Crispy Garlic

224g / 1 cup olive oil
50g / 10 cloves garlic, very thinly sliced (¹⁄₁₆ inch thick) on a mandoline

To Finish

624g / 1 lb 6 oz extruded spaghetti (page 123)
112g / ½ cup olive oil
5 bulbs and stalks spring garlic, sliced into ⅛-inch-thick pieces
36g / 7 cloves garlic, very thinly sliced (¹⁄₁₆ inch thick) on a mandoline
3g / 1½ tsp dried red chile flakes
20g / ¼ cup finely chopped parsley

Spaghetti with Lemon, Pine Nuts, and Parmigiano

This one goes out to Rita Sodi of I Sodi in New York's West Village. When I lived in the neighborhood, I was a longtime devotee of her pappardelle al limone, a soul-satisfying, perfectly simplistic dish. Al limone is a classic Italian dish of ambiguous origins that is generally some combination of olive oil, butter, lemon, and parmigiano—sometimes cream. Mine leans into the first four and adds pine nuts, a superior nut that doesn't see much pasta airtime outside of pesto, for added richness, depth, and texture. Getting this dish right lies in the order of operations—specifically when to add the lemon. Add the lemon juice and lemon zest too early and it ends up dull and bitter, and this is a dish that endorses the opposite.

1   Preheat the oven to 325°F. Spread the pine nuts in a single layer on a sheet pan and toast until very lightly golden brown, 5 to 7 minutes, checking their progress every few minutes to ensure they don't burn. Set aside to cool, about 15 minutes. Once cooled, finely chop and set aside.

2   Bring a large pot of water to a boil over high heat. Generously salt the water.

3   Add the spaghetti to the water and cook for 5 to 8 minutes, until al dente.

4   While the pasta is cooking, place a large sauté pan over low heat and add the olive oil. Add the garlic and gently cook until aromatic but without color, 10 to 15 seconds.

5   Add the butter and 3 to 4 ladles (170g to 230g / ¾ to 1 cup) pasta cooking water. Swirl the contents of the pan to emulsify.

6   Using tongs or a pasta basket, remove the pasta from the pot and transfer to the sauté pan. Toss for about 1 minute to marry the pasta and the sauce.

7   Add the lemon peel and a little less than half of the pine nuts and continue tossing to combine.

8   Remove from the heat and slowly add half of the parmigiano, tossing until it is well incorporated.

9   Squeeze the juice from the lemon halves into the pan and continue tossing to marry. If the sauce begins to tighten, add a splash of pasta cooking water to loosen. When the pasta is properly married, it will cling to the sauce and have a glossy sheen.

10   Divide the pasta into bowls and garnish with the remaining pine nuts and parmigiano.

Yields 4 to 6 servings

80g / ⅔ cup pine nuts
624g / 1 lb 6 oz extruded
    spaghetti (page 123)
28g / 2 Tbsp olive oil
5g / 1 garlic clove, thinly sliced
45g / 3 Tbsp unsalted butter,
    cold and cubed
8g / ⅔ lemon peel, pith removed
    and peel finely chopped
118g / 1⅓ cups finely grated
    parmigiano-reggiano
4 lemons, cut in half and
    seeds removed

Sheep's Milk Cheese–Filled Agnolotti with Saffron, Dried Tomato, and Honey

Like so many of my pastas, this one began with a single ingredient: fiscidu, a Sardinian sheep's milk cheese similar to feta. It's typically served on its own with the island's classic crispy flatbread, pane carasau, but I became obsessed with the idea of working that flavor profile into a filling. It's not imported into United States, so in its place I use Greek feta, which I combine with sheep's milk ricotta to smooth it out and cut the salt. The dish takes inspiration from Sardinia in the use of saffron, tomato (albeit dried tomatoes), and honey, but goes off-piste from there.

Although this dish has become a Lilia standard, it's still very connected to my days at A Voce in its use of technique and ingredients. Fair warning: this is not a beginner's dish, but it is one that rewards heartily in the breadth of flavors it offers, from herbal (thyme) and sweet (honey, tomatoes) to pungent (feta), spicy (chiles), and floral (saffron).

Be judicious with the honey. The balance of sweet, savory, and spicy is a delicate one, so it's always best to start light and slowly adjust up from there.

---

1 To make the filling, put the ricotta into a food processor and pulse just until it is as smooth as cake frosting and has a sheen, being careful not to process it longer or it will break. Transfer to a bowl and set aside.

2 Add the feta to the processor bowl and blend, pulsing to start and then running the machine just until the cheese is smooth. Add the feta to the ricotta along with the honey and season with salt q.b. Fold together until all the ingredients are well integrated. It should taste well seasoned. Cover and refrigerate until ready to use.

3 To make the dried tomatoes, preheat the oven to 200°F. Line a sheet pan with parchment paper.

4 Drain the tomatoes and save the juice for another purpose. Split the tomatoes in half lengthwise and remove the seeds. Lay the tomatoes, cut side up, in a single layer on the prepared sheet pan. Season them with the sugar and salt. Drizzle with the olive oil and evenly top with the garlic and thyme.

5 Bake the tomatoes until they have mostly dried but retain a bit of softness, 2 to 3 hours. You don't want to end up with tomato leather. Set aside.

6 To finish, following the instructions for agnolotti on page 80, make 48 pieces with the pasta dough and filling.

7 Bring a large pot of water to a boil over high heat. Generously salt the water.

8 Place a large sauté pan over low heat and add the olive oil. Add the garlic and gently cook until aromatic but without color, 10 to 15 seconds. Add the dried tomatoes and swirl to warm gently.

Yields 4 to 6 servings

Filling

604g / 2⅔ cups sheep's milk ricotta (see "whipped" ricotta, page 139)
150g / 5¼ oz block high-quality feta in brine
42g / 2 Tbsp honey
Salt, q.b.

Dried Tomatoes

1 large (794g / 28 oz) can whole San Marzano tomatoes
13g / 1 Tbsp sugar
9g / 1 Tbsp salt
14g / 1 Tbsp olive oil
10g / 2 cloves garlic, thinly sliced
15 sprigs thyme

To Finish

1 batch egg-based dough (pages 18, 22, and 26–31)
14g / 1 Tbsp olive oil
10g / 2 cloves garlic, sliced
1½ tsp saffron threads
145g / 10 Tbsp unsalted butter, cold and cubed
14g / 2 tsp honey
2 sprigs thyme, stems removed
Peel of 1 lemon, pith removed and peel finely chopped
½ tsp ground red chile
Black pepper, q.b.

9   Add 2 to 3 ladles (115 to 170g / ½ to ¾ cup) pasta cooking water to the pan. Add the saffron and let it bloom in the water for 30 seconds to 1 minute. It should turn the mixture in the pan a bright yellow.

10   Add the butter and gently swirl the contents of the pan to emulsify. Set aside.

11   Add the agnolotti to the water and turn down the heat to bring the water to a gentle simmer instead of a rolling boil. The filling is very delicate and will break if cooked over high heat. Cook for 1 to 2 minutes, until the pasta is tender to the touch and the filling is warm and oozes when you cut into an agnolotto.

12   Using a spider or pasta basket, remove the pasta from the pot and gently transfer to the sauté pan. Place the pan back over low heat and swirl the contents for 45 seconds to 1 minute to marry the pasta and the sauce.

13   Divide the agnolotti onto plates or into flat-bottomed bowls. Add a splash of pasta cooking water to the sauté pan to loosen the sauce remaining in the pan and then spoon over the pasta. Drizzle each serving with the honey and top with the thyme, lemon peel, ground chile, and with pepper q.b.

Linguine with Anchovies, Corbara Tomatoes, and Lemon

If I gave myself too much leash, I'd probably end up putting anchovies in just about everything. I think of them as a means of enhancing other ingredients—amplifying a vinaigrette or giving a sweetness and salinity to a braise. That profile, when combined with tomato, creates a tension here between sweetness and salinity, with lemon coming in to give the whole arrangement a bit of levity. I think of this dish as an ode, sans clams, to the unloved red version of spaghetti alle vongole.

1   To make the tomatoes, drain them and reserve the juice for another use. Place the tomatoes in a single layer in a colander set over a bowl or sheet pan to catch the juices.

2   Sprinkle the tomatoes with the sugar, salt, fennel seed, and coriander seed and refrigerate overnight.

3   Place a saucepan over very low heat and add the olive oil, basil, thyme, bay leaf, marjoram, citrus peels, and garlic. Heat until just warm, 5 to 8 minutes.

4   While the oil is heating, arrange the tomatoes in a high-sided baking dish or heatproof bowl. Pour the warm oil over the tomatoes and set aside to marinate at room temperature for at least 1 hour. If not using right away, let cool, transfer to an airtight container, and refrigerate for up to 7 days, then bring to room temperature before using.

5   Remove the tomatoes from the oil and process them through a food mill or crush them by hand. Set aside. Reserve the oil for making vinaigrettes or for poaching.

6   To finish, bring a large pot of water to a boil over high heat. Generously salt the water.

7   Add the linguine to the water and cook for 5 to 8 minutes, until al dente.

8   While the pasta is cooking, heat a large sauté pan over very low heat. Add the oil and garlic and gently cook until aromatic but without color, 10 to 15 seconds.

9   Add the anchovies and stir until they start to break up and melt into the oil, about 30 seconds.

10   Add the milled tomatoes and cook just until warm, 1 to 2 minutes. Keep the mixture over very low heat.

11   Using tongs or a pasta basket, remove the pasta from the cooking pot and transfer to the sauté pan. Turn the heat up to medium. Toss for 30 seconds to 1 minute to marry the pasta and the sauce. If the sauce begins to tighten, add a splash of pasta cooking water to loosen and continue tossing to marry. If you need more water, taste as you go and alternate pasta cooking water with fresh water, as the dish will already have a high level of salinity from the anchovies.

12   Remove from the heat. Add the lemon peel, then squeeze the juice from the lemon halves into the pan and continue tossing to combine.

13   Divide the pasta into bowls and garnish with ground chile q.b.

Yields 4 to 6 servings

Cured Corbara Tomatoes

4 (400g / 14 oz) cans Corbara
   tomatoes
13g / 1 Tbsp sugar
9g / 1 Tbsp salt
Rounded ¾ tsp fennel seed,
   coarsely ground in a
   spice mill or with a mortar
   and pestle
2g / 1 tsp coriander seed,
   coarsely ground in a
   spice mill or with a mortar
   and pestle
560g / 2½ cups olive oil
2 sprigs basil
1 sprig thyme
1 fresh bay leaf
1 sprig marjoram
Peel of 1 lemon, pith removed
Peel of 1 orange, pith removed
15g / 3 cloves garlic, smashed
   with the back of a knife

To Finish

624g / 1 lb 6 oz extruded
   linguine (page 122)
56g / ¼ cup olive oil
32g / 6 cloves garlic, finely
   chopped
120g / 16 to 18 large oil-packed
   anchovies, finely chopped
   (about ½ cup)
Peel of ½ lemon, pith removed
   and peel finely chopped
2 lemons, cut in half and seeds
   removed
Ground red chile, q.b.

Potato-Filled Cappelletti with Speck, Horseradish, and Caraway

When I think of Alto Adige, I think of the three ingredients that anchor this dish: speck, horseradish, and caraway. I can trace the dish's inspiration to Merano, a place known not just for its skiing and art nouveau architecture but also for its healing hot springs. There's also a whole lot of speck, Alto Adige's smoky, more rustic mountaineering ham to prosciutto's city-slicker refinement.

This dish is born from an amalgam of two speck dishes: one, a simple piece of fresh bread flecked with caraway and served with a pungent, creamy fresh farmer cheese and a few slices of smoky, salty speck. The second, a plate of speck with fresh horseradish shaved over it in such abundance that it covered the salumi beneath it.

---

1   To make the filling, place the potatoes in a pot, cover with cold water, and bring to a simmer over medium heat. Cook until fork-tender, 30 to 45 minutes.

2   Remove the potatoes from the pot and place on a sheet pan to cool. Peel the potatoes and break them into pieces.

3   Place a tamis or fine-mesh strainer over a large bowl. Pass the potatoes though the tamis.

4   Pass the ricotta through the tamis.

5   Add the crème fraîche to the potatoes and ricotta and fold in.

6   Add the speck and horseradish and continue folding until evenly distributed. Season with salt q.b. It should taste well seasoned. Refrigerate until ready to use.

7   To finish, following the instructions for cappelletti on page 87, make 90 to 100 pieces with the pasta dough and filling.

8   Bring a large pot of water to a boil over high heat. Generously salt the water.

9   Add the cappelletti to the water and turn down the heat to bring the water to a gentle simmer instead of a rolling boil. The filling is delicate and can break if cooked over high heat. Cook for 2 to 4 minutes, until tender at the thickest closure point.

10   While the pasta is cooking, place a large sauté pan over low heat. Add 3 ladles (170g / ¾ cup) pasta cooking water and the butter. Swirl the contents of the pan to emulsify.

11   Using a spider or pasta basket, remove the pasta from the pot and transfer to the sauté pan. Turn the heat up to medium. Swirl the pasta in the sauce for 30 seconds to 1 minute to marry, using a spoon to gently turn the pasta over and coat all sides. If the sauce begins to tighten, add more pasta cooking water to loosen. When the pasta is properly married, it will cling to the sauce and have a glossy sheen.

12   Add the diced speck to the pan and gently stir to combine.

13   Divide the pasta among plates. Spoon the sauce remaining in the pan over each plate. Garnish with the horseradish, caraway, and with pepper q.b.

Yields 6 to 8 servings

Filling

500g / 4 or 5 Yukon gold
    potatoes
232g / 1 cup ricotta
112g / ½ cup crème fraîche
48g / 1¾ oz speck, finely diced
60g / 6 Tbsp finely grated fresh
    horseradish
Salt, q.b.

To Finish

1 batch egg dough (page 18)
150g / 10 Tbsp plus 1 tsp
    unsalted butter, cold
    and cubed
48g / 1¾ oz speck, finely diced
30g / 60 slices fresh
    horseradish, sliced paper-
    thin and put under a damp
    paper towel
12g / 2 Tbsp caraway seed
Black pepper, q.b.

Ricotta Gnocchi with Broccoli Pesto, Basil, and Pistachios

Back in 2015, while I was on Weight Watchers, I was obsessed with developing a pesto that had less oil and more nutritional value and still satisfied my craving for the original. Although the dish has admittedly strayed from its original health-conscious intent, it still ticks the nutritional-value box, and being far from a broccoli lover, it gets me to, well, finish my broccoli.

The texture should mirror the same rich, silky quality you get from Genovese pesto, but it has a sweetness, both from the pistachios and the broccoli; a slight spiciness, thanks to the inclusion of broccoli rabe leaves; and a vegetal quality that, paired with pillowy ricotta gnocchi, I find both unexpected and downright irresistible. In fact, I've tried to take this dish off the menu at Lilia multiple times since we opened, but every time I taste it one last time in an attempt to say goodbye, I can't bear to let it go.

1   To make the pesto, break the broccoli florets into ½-inch pieces.

2   Bring a large pot of water to a boil over high heat. Generously salt the water. Prepare a salted ice-water bath and set a colander in it. Line a sheet pan with paper towels.

3   Drop the broccoli florets into the boiling water and blanch until tender but not soft and still vibrantly green, 2 to 3 minutes. Using a slotted spoon or spider, transfer the florets to the ice-water bath. Transfer the florets to the paper towels to drain.

4   Repeat with the broccoli rabe florets, reserving the leaves. Discard the boiling water and reserve the ice-water bath.

5   Pat the broccoli and broccoli rabe florets dry with the paper towels to remove all the excess water. Set aside.

6   Bring a small saucepan of water to a boil over high heat. Lightly salt the water. Drop the basil and broccoli rabe leaves into the boiling water and blanch until tender but still vibrantly green, about 15 seconds. Using a slotted spoon, transfer the basil and broccoli leaves to the ice-water bath. Remove from the ice-water bath, place in a kitchen towel, and squeeze to remove all the excess water.

7   Place the basil and broccoli rabe leaves in a blender with the water, add the garlic, and blend on high speed to make a very smooth puree. If the mixture is too thick to puree, add a small amount of water to loosen. Set aside.

8   Add the broccoli and broccoli rabe to the bowl of a food processor in batches and pulse to puree until smooth.

9   Place the broccoli mixture in a large bowl. Add the basil puree, olive oil, pistachios, parmigiano, and pecorino. Mix well to combine and season with salt q.b.

10   Measure out 510g / 2 cups pesto and set aside. Transfer the remainder to an airtight container and refrigerate for up to 3 days or freeze for another use.

Yields 4 to 6 servings

Broccoli Pesto

333g / generous 3 cups (about 1 head) broccoli florets
75g / 2½ oz broccoli rabe, leaves and florets separated
20g / 1 cup tightly packed basil leaves
30g / 2 Tbsp water
½ clove garlic
224g / 1 cup olive oil, plus more q.b.
31g / ¼ cup raw pistachios, finely chopped
30g / ⅓ cup finely grated parmigiano-reggiano
30g / ⅓ cup finely grated pecorino romano
Salt, q.b.

To Finish

1 batch ricotta gnocchi dough (page 24)
90g / ⅔ cup chopped raw Sicilian pistachios
60g / ⅔ cup finely grated pecorino romano
20 to 25 small basil leaves
Black pepper, q.b.

Nota bene

Sicilian pistachios are truly in a league of their own, but if you don't have access to them, you can substitute regular pistachios to finish.

11   To finish, following the instructions for ricotta gnocchi on page 74, make 130 to 140 pieces.

12   Bring a large pot of water to a boil over high heat. Generously salt the water.

13   Add the gnocchi to the water and cook for 3 to 5 minutes, until they float to the top of the pot.

14   While the gnocchi are cooking, place a large sauté pan over very low heat. Add the pesto and 1 to 2 ladles (55g to 115g / ¼ to ½ cup) pasta cooking water and stir gently to combine. If it overheats, you will lose the vibrant color quickly, so keep an eye on it.

15   Using a spider or pasta basket, remove the pasta from the pot and transfer to the sauté pan. Keep the pan over low heat and gently toss for 30 seconds to 1 minute to marry the pasta and the sauce. If the sauce begins to tighten, add a splash more pasta cooking water to loosen and continue tossing.

16   Divide into bowls and garnish with the chopped pistachios, pecorino, basil, and with pepper q.b.

Fettuccine with Spicy Lamb Sausage and Tomato Passata

Quite a few recipes in this book began as a way of utilizing ingredients left over from other dishes. In this case, it was the lamb steaks I'd had on the menu at Lilia since we opened. They're cut from a whole leg, and inevitably we'd end up with bones and trim—really flavorful stuff that didn't have an obvious use. In the spirit of many of the sughi or ragùs you see in central Italy, I had the idea to flavor a red sauce with those scraps. I made sausage out of the leftover trim, cooked the sauce with the bones, and then combined the two à la minute.

　　It's everything you might want from a meat-enriched sugo, but what makes this sauce work is the late-breaking addition of chopped lemon peel. I'd tried adding just about every fresh herb in my tool kit to cut through the richness, but it was the lemon (a suggestion from one of my chefs at the time) that gave the dish contour and brightness. It's a reminder that these seemingly optional finishing touches can be the difference between a good and a great dish.

1　To make the sugo, preheat the oven to 350°F.

2　Place the lamb bones in a heavy roasting pan. Roast until golden brown, 45 minutes to 1 hour.

3　Transfer the bones to a heavy sauce pot or Dutch oven. Add the onion, fennel bulb, garlic, coriander seed, chile flakes, peppercorns, fennel seed, and tomato juice to the pot. (You're essentially making a lamb stock with tomato instead of water.)

4　Slowly bring to a simmer over medium-low heat and cook until the flavors have melded, about 1 hour.

5　Remove from the heat and strain through a fine-mesh strainer while still warm. Season with salt q.b. Measure out 700g / 3 cups sugo and set aside. Transfer the remainder to an airtight container and refrigerate for up to 5 days or freeze for up to 1 month for another use.

6　To make the sausage, combine the lamb, fennel seed, peppercorns, coriander, granulated garlic, and salt in a bowl and mix well. Make a small patty to test your seasoning.

7　Place a small sauté pan over medium heat and add a drizzle of olive oil. Add the test patty and cook, turning once, until cooked through, 2 to 3 minutes on each side. Check your seasoning and add more salt to the sausage mixture q.b. Refrigerate until ready to use.

8　To finish, following the instructions for fettuccine on page 49, make 624g / 1 lb 6 oz with the pasta dough.

9　Bring a large pot of water to a boil over high heat. Generously salt the water.

10　Place a large sauté pan over medium heat and add the olive oil. Add the sausage and, as it starts to brown, break it up with tongs or a wooden spoon into very small, uniform crumbled pieces. Cook until caramelized and cooked through, 5 to 8 minutes.

Yields 4 to 6 servings

Lamb Sugo

560g / 1¼ lb lamb bones
125g / 1 small onion
150g / ½ fennel bulb
40g / 8 cloves garlic
4g / 2 tsp coriander seed
4g / 2 tsp dried red chile flakes
4g / 1½ tsp black peppercorns
8g / 1 Tbsp and 1 tsp fennel seed
1.7kg / 7 cups juice from canned San Marzano tomatoes (from about four 794g / 28 oz cans), or 2 (680g / 24 oz) jars tomato passata, thinned with 237g / 1 cup water
Salt, q.b.

Lamb Sausage

454g / 1 lb ground lamb shoulder or leg
8g / 1 Tbsp and 1 tsp fennel seed, ground in a spice mill or with a mortar and pestle
¾ tsp black peppercorns, ground in a spice mill or with a mortar and pestle
3g / 1½ tsp coriander seed, ground in a spice mill or with a mortar and pestle
¾ tsp granulated garlic
¼ tsp salt, plus more q.b.
Olive oil, q.b

11   Add the sugo to the pan with the sausage and cook for 3 to 5 minutes longer.

12   Add the fettuccine to the water and cook for 1 to 2 minutes, until tender but not soft.

13   Using tongs or a pasta basket, remove the pasta from the pot and transfer to the sauté pan. Turn up the heat to medium. Toss for 1 to 2 minutes to marry the pasta and the sauce. If the sauce begins to tighten, add a splash of pasta cooking water to loosen and continue tossing to marry. The sugo should nicely coat the pasta without clumping.

14   Divide the pasta into bowls and garnish with the lemon peel and pecorino.

To Finish

1 batch egg dough (page 18)
42g / 3 Tbsp olive oil
Peel of ⅓ lemon, pith removed and peel finely chopped
60g / ⅔ cup finely grated pecorino romano

Rigatoni Diavola

When people ask me which dish on my menus I crave most—the last-supper, desert-island pasta—it's a toss-up between two dishes: this one and its cousin, the rigatoni with 30-clove sauce (page 148) at Misi. For someone who has spent what feels like a lifetime trying to perfect filled pasta, it comes as a surprise, perhaps, that my craving comes back to dishes so simple that I originally wondered whether or not I'd get away with putting them on a restaurant menu. But when I opened Lilia, I couldn't resist. If I can't put a dish I love this much on a menu, then what's the point of having a restaurant?

This dish will always represent a turning point for me as a chef. It's the moment when I decided to tune it all out and cook the food I wanted to eat. It's a dish I return to not only for comfort but also as a reminder of that moment, and the promise I made to myself, whenever I feel adrift.

1   Bring a large pot of water to a boil over high heat. Generously salt the water.

2   Add the rigatoni to the water and cook for 5 to 8 minutes, until al dente.

3   While the pasta is cooking, place a large sauté pan over low heat. Add the sauce and 1 ladle (55g / ¼ cup) pasta cooking water and stir to combine.

4   Using a spider or pasta basket, remove the pasta from the pot and transfer to the sauté pan. Turn the heat up to medium. Toss for 1 to 2 minutes to marry the pasta and the sauce. If the sauce begins to tighten, add a splash of pasta cooking water to loosen and continue tossing to marry. When properly married, the pasta should absorb the sauce, glide easily when tossed, and there should be little sauce left at the bottom of the pan.

5   Divide into bowls and garnish with the pecorino, marjoram, olive oil, and with pepper q.b.

Yields 4 to 6 servings

624g / 1 lb 6 oz extruded rigatoni (page 123)
585g / 2¼ cups diavola sauce (page 149)
22g / ¼ cup finely grated pecorino romano
3 sprigs marjoram, leaves removed from stems
14g / 1 Tbsp olive oil
Black pepper, q.b.

Potato and Crème Fraîche–Filled Ravioli with Garlic and Rosemary

I feel like I've been doing a version of this dish since the first time I stepped into a kitchen. It dates back at least to my three years at the SoHo Grand, where I made hundreds of pierogi. This filling is essentially a variation on the one in those pierogi. Although you could call the combination of potatoes, cream, garlic, and herbs an accidental hat tip to my Polish roots, it doesn't have a single home, crossing so many borders that it's universal. It spells comfort in every language.

    That's perhaps why it's has been a consistent winter staple for me and a dish I can't seem to keep off the menu for very long, especially come February. After one too many Saturday walks through a nearly deserted New York City greenmarket, it always eats like a bit of encouragement—a dish that shows a way to satisfaction through winter scarcity.

1   To make the filling, place the potatoes in a pot, cover with cold water, and bring to a simmer over medium heat. Cook until fork-tender, about 30 to 45 minutes.

2   Using a slotted spoon, transfer the potatoes to a sheet pan and let cool for about 15 minutes. (This will also allow the potatoes to dry out a bit.)

3   When cool enough to handle, peel the potatoes and put them through a potato ricer or a food mill into a bowl.

4   Reprocess the potatoes gently through a tamis or fine-mesh strainer to ensure they are very smooth.

5   Put the ricotta into a food processor and pulse just until it is as smooth as cake frosting and has a sheen, being careful not to process it longer or it will break. Transfer to a bowl and set aside.

6   Once the potatoes are completely cool, gently fold in the ricotta, crème fraîche, parmigiano, and lemon peel until just combined. Overworking the potatoes will make them gummy. Season with salt q.b. It should taste well seasoned. Refrigerate until ready to use.

7   To make the crispy garlic, line a plate with paper towels. Place a sauté pan over low heat and add the oil. Add the garlic and cook, stirring occasionally, until the slices begin to turn golden and harden slightly, 3 to 5 minutes. They will curl up a bit and cluster together as they cook, so be sure to stir occasionally to ensure even coloring.

8   Using a slotted spoon, remove the garlic and place in one layer on the paper towels to drain. If they aren't fully crispy, do not worry. They will crisp up as they drain and dry.

9   To finish, following the instructions for ravioli on page 104, make 80 to 100 pieces with the pasta dough and filling.

10   Bring a large pot of water to a boil over high heat. Generously salt the water.

Yields 6 to 8 servings

Filling

228g / 2 Yukon gold potatoes
154g / ⅔ cup ricotta (see "whipped" ricotta, page 139)
225g / 1 cup crème fraîche
22g / ¼ cup finely grated parmigiano-reggiano
Peel of ¼ lemon, pith removed and peel finely chopped
Salt, q.b.

Crispy Garlic

224g / 1 cup olive oil
50g / 10 cloves garlic, very thinly sliced (1/16 inch thick) on a mandoline

To Finish

1 batch egg dough (page 18)
28g / 2 Tbsp olive oil
10g / 2 cloves garlic, thinly sliced
60g / ¼ cup unsalted butter, cold and cubed
30g / ⅓ cup finely grated parmigiano-reggiano
2 sprigs rosemary, leaves removed from stems

11   Add the ravioli to the water and turn down the heat to bring the water to a gentle simmer instead of a rolling boil. It is important to cook these gently at a simmer instead of a boil. The filling is delicate and can break if cooked over high heat. Cook for 2 to 3 minutes, until tender at the thickest closure point.

12   While the pasta is cooking, place a large sauté pan over low heat and add the oil. Add the garlic and gently cook until aromatic but without color, 10 to 15 seconds.

13   Add the butter and 3 ladles (170g / ¾ cup) pasta cooking water to the pan. Swirl the contents of the pan to emulsify.

14   Using a spider or pasta basket, remove the pasta from the pot and transfer to the sauté pan. Turn the heat up to medium. Swirl the pasta in the sauce for 30 to 45 seconds to marry, using a spoon to gently turn the pasta over and coat all sides. If the sauce begins to tighten, add a splash of pasta cooking water to loosen. When the pasta is properly married, it will cling to the sauce and have a glossy sheen.

15   Transfer the pasta to a large serving platter or divide onto plates. Spoon the remaining sauce from the pan over the top and garnish with the parmigiano, rosemary, and crispy garlic.

Ricotta and Tuscan Kale–Filled Cappelletti with Fennel Pollen

A lot of my filled pastas build on the classic pairing of spinach and ricotta found in so many of Italy's ravioli—not to mention pies, frittatas, crepes, and pretty much anything capable of containing it. It's a gently sweet, tangy filling that's the perfect base from which to add, subtract, and pivot. The simple swap of kale for spinach gives the filling a heartier, deeper profile, more earthy and rugged than sweet.

I've had versions of this dish on my past menus, and if forced to zoom out on it, I see it as a perfect example of how I approach updating a classic. It's never an overhaul but rather a wardrobe change—in this case, cappelletti in new clothes with my favorite accessory, fennel pollen, an ingredient that regularly finds its way into my vegetable cookery but less often into my pastas. Here it adds a floral quality in collaboration with the bite of parmigiano.

1   To make the filling, strip the kale leaves from their stems. Discard the stems and coarsely chop the leaves into 2-inch pieces. Line a sheet pan with parchment paper.

2   Place a large sauté pan over medium heat and add the oil. Add the garlic and gently cook until aromatic but without color, 10 to 15 seconds.

3   Add the kale in small batches and stir to make sure it is coated with the oil. Cook until wilted and tender, 5 to 8 minutes.

4   Remove the kale and garlic mixture from the pan and spread in a single layer on the prepared sheet pan to cool.

5   Place a tamis or fine-mesh strainer over a bowl. Pass the ricotta through the tamis.

6   Once the kale has cooled, squeeze out any excess liquid and chop it very finely. Add the kale to the bowl with the ricotta. Fold in the mascarpone and parmigiano. Add the fennel pollen q.b., beginning with 1 Tbsp. Season with salt q.b. It should taste well seasoned. Refrigerate until ready to use.

7   To finish, following the instructions for cappelletti on page 87, make 70 to 80 pieces with the pasta dough and filling.

8   Bring a large pot of water to a boil over high heat. Generously salt the water.

9   Add the cappelletti to the water and turn down the heat to bring the water to a gentle simmer instead of a rolling boil. It is important to cook these gently at a simmer instead of a boil. The filling is delicate and can break if cooked over high heat. Cook for 2 to 4 minutes, until tender at the thickest closure point.

Yields 6 to 8 servings

Filling

454g / 1 lb Tuscan kale
28g / 2 Tbsp olive oil
10g / 2 cloves garlic, thinly sliced
116g / ½ cup ricotta
100g / scant ½ cup mascarpone
30g / ⅓ cup plus 22g / ¼ cup
   finely grated parmigiano-
   reggiano
1 Tbsp fennel pollen,
   plus more q.b.
Salt, q.b.

To Finish

1 batch egg dough (page 18)
28g / 2 Tbsp olive oil
5g / 1 clove garlic, thinly sliced
75g / 5 Tbsp unsalted butter,
   cold and cubed
Finely grated parmigiano-
   reggiano, q.b.
Fennel pollen, q.b.

10 While the pasta is cooking, place a large sauté pan over low heat and add the oil. Add the garlic and gently cook until aromatic but without color, 10 to 15 seconds.

11 Add the butter and 2 ladles (115g / ½ cup) pasta cooking water. Swirl the contents of the pan to emulsify.

12 Using a spider or pasta basket, remove the pasta from the pot and transfer to the sauté pan. Turn the heat up to medium. Swirl the pasta in the sauce for 30 to 45 seconds to marry, using a spoon to gently turn the pasta over and coat all sides. If the sauce begins to tighten, add more pasta cooking water to loosen. When the pasta is properly married, it will cling to the sauce and have a glossy sheen.

13 Using a pasta basket, transfer the pasta to a large serving platter or divide onto plates. Spoon the remaining sauce from the pan over the top and garnish with the parmigiano and a generous dusting of fennel pollen q.b.

Parmigiano Fonduta–Filled Tortellini in Brodo

I am not exactly a meat-filling kind of girl. In fact, most of my pastas lean vegetable focused and use meat—often cured meat—as a flavoring agent rather than a base. It was only a matter of time before I took classic tortellini in brodo (page 198) and reworked the filling without the meat. But I still wanted to pay homage to the dish's origin, which I have done by using parmigiano, a revered staple of Emilia-Romagna. Here I make it into a fonduta, which in my case is just parmigiano mixed with cream—no wine, no flour—and a bit of egg to bind it. It's chilled, so it can be piped into the pasta but melts when it cooks, giving the filling the texture of runny egg yolk.

This dish generally finds its way into the restaurants during the late fall, when I offer it with the addition of white truffles. But it's just as good without them.

---

1   To make the filling, place a saucepan over medium heat. Add the cream and bring to a very slow simmer. Turn down the heat to low and very gently simmer until the cream has reduced by about one-third, being very careful not to scorch the bottom of the pan, 1 to 1½ hours. Let cool for 5 minutes.

2   Transfer the cream to a high-speed blender. With the blender running on low-medium speed, slowly add the parmigiano and blend until the mixture is emulsified. Taste to test your seasoning and add salt q.b. (The parmigiano adds plenty of salinity, so you may not need to add much salt.)

3   With the blender still running, gradually add the egg yolk(s), drizzling slowly so the yolk is tempered and the mixture does not break. Cover and refrigerate for at least 1 hour. If you'll be leaving the filling in the refrigerator for several hours or up to overnight, remove it about 30 minutes before using to soften.

4   To make the brodo, place the chicken in a large stockpot and add 2.8kg / 3 qt of the water. If the chicken is not fully covered, add more water just to cover. Place over low heat and slowly bring to a simmer, 45 minutes to 1 hour. Once the liquid starts to simmer, scum will begin to rise to the top. Skim continually with a large spoon to keep the brodo very clear.

5   If the water level falls below the chicken after 1 hour, add enough of the remaining water to re-cover it and simmer for 2 hours longer, continuing to skim off any impurities and adding more water as needed to keep the chicken covered.

6   Add the carrots, onion, celery, leek, parsley, garlic, peppercorns, and bay leaf and continue to cook at a slow simmer until very flavorful, 1 to 2 hours.

Yields 6 to 8 servings

Filling

474g / 2 cups heavy cream
225g / 2½ cups finely grated
    parmigiano-reggiano
27g / 1 to 2 egg yolks, stirred
Salt, q.b.

Brodo

1 (1.6 to 1.8kg / 3½ to 4 lb)
    chicken
2.8 to 4.7kg / 3 to 5 qt water
300g / 2 large carrots, peeled
    and cut into 1-inch pieces
370g / 1 onion, cut into quarters
227g / ½ head celery, cut into
    1-inch pieces
150g / ½ large leek, cut into
    1-inch pieces
30g / ½ bunch parsley
100g / 1 head garlic, cut in half
9g / 1 Tbsp black peppercorns
1 fresh bay leaf

To Finish

1 batch egg dough (page 18)
Salt, q.b.
Olive oil, q.b.
Black pepper, q.b.
45g / ½ cup finely grated
    parmigiano-reggiano

7   Line a fine-mesh strainer with a coffee filter or cheesecloth and strain the brodo. Measure out 1.6kg / 7 cups brodo and set aside. Let the remaining brodo cool, transfer it to an airtight container, and refrigerate for up to 5 days or freeze for up to 1 month for another use. Refrigerate the chicken meat for another use.

8   To finish, following the instructions for tortellini on page 110, make 90 to 120 pieces with the pasta dough and filling.

9   Bring a large pot of water to a boil over high heat. Generously salt the water.

10   While the water is heating, place a saucepan over low heat and add the brodo. Season with salt q.b.

11   Add the tortellini to the water and turn down the heat to bring the water to a gentle simmer instead of a rolling boil. It is important to cook these gently at a simmer instead of a boil. The filling is very delicate and will break if cooked over high heat. Cook for 1 to 2 minutes, until tender at the thickest closure point. The filling should be melted and creamy.

12   Using a spider or pasta basket, remove the tortellini from the water and divide into bowls. Ladle the brodo over the tortellini and garnish with a drizzle of oil, with pepper q.b., and with the parmigiano.

Spaghetti alla Chitarra with Ramps, Lemon, and Ricotta Salata

If you've spent any time on the East Coast, you're likely aware of the hype surrounding ramp season. After all, ramps have all the necessary features of a fad: a short window of availability, a totally singular flavor profile, high demand.

Every spring, my first ramps of the season make their way up from West Virginia by way of Russ the Ramp Guy (not his real name), freshly foraged and caked full of dirt. As the season progresses, they begin moving north. By the time they're being harvested closer to the city, we're going through eighty to one hundred pounds of ramps per week at the restaurants, much of it integrated into my focaccia and vegetable dishes. This dish began as a play on aglio e olio, swapping garlic for ramps. I also wanted to use the whole ramp but find different uses for its parts, integrating the leaves (tops) into the dough and chopping the bulbs (bottoms) and cooking them into a sauce. It's one of the only ramp pastas I've made that I feel pays proper tribute to the ramp's spicy, musky, sweet profile.

---

1 Following the instructions for spaghetti alla chitarra on page 119, make 624g / 1 lb 6 oz with the pasta dough, substituting ramp tops for half of the spinach.

2 Heat a large sauté pan over medium-low heat and add the olive oil. Add the ramp bottoms and gently cook them, stirring occasionally, until soft but without color, 5 to 8 minutes. Set aside.

3 Bring a large pot of water to a boil over high heat. Generously salt the water.

4 Add the spaghetti alla chitarra to the water and cook for 2 to 3 minutes, until tender but not soft.

5 While the pasta is cooking, place the sauté pan with the ramp bottoms over low heat. Add the butter and 3 ladles (170g / ¾ cup) pasta cooking water. Swirl the contents of the pan to emulsify.

6 Using tongs or a pasta basket, remove the pasta from the pot and transfer to the sauté pan. Turn the heat up to medium. Toss for 1 to 2 minutes to marry the pasta and the sauce. If the sauce begins to tighten, add a splash of pasta cooking water to loosen and continue tossing to marry.

7 Turn off the heat. Add the ramp tops, lemon peel and juice, and chile flakes to the sauté pan and continue tossing to combine.

8 Divide the pasta into bowls and shave the ricotta salata on top.

Yields 4 to 6 servings

1 batch green dough (page 22)
42g / 3 Tbsp olive oil
220g / 2 cups thinly sliced ramp bottoms (from about 454g / 1 lb ramps)
30g / 2 Tbsp unsalted butter, cold and cubed
16g / ¼ cup finely sliced ramp tops
Peel of 1 lemon, pith removed and peel finely chopped
Juice of 1 lemon
2g / 1 tsp dried red chile flakes
1 small (114g / 4 oz) piece ricotta salata

Nota bene

If you do not have enough ramp tops for making the dough, you can make your spaghetti alla chitarra with the basic green dough using only spinach or with classic egg dough (page 18).

Ravioli with Taleggio Fonduta, Peas, and Speck

Fonduta is alpine Italy's answer to fondue. It's a staple in Piedmont and in the Aosta Valley, where it's generally comprised of Fontina cheese and local wine. I've stretched the concept, calling on a variety of cheeses, ditching the wine, and adding cream to "lengthen" the cheese and give it a creamy texture. I use it in fillings, on vegetables, and with grilled bread as sort of the upper register of richness in my cooking.

This is the dish that made fonduta part of my repertoire. I was cooking at the James Beard House for the first time on my own, and I wanted to impress. Runny, funky fondue-filled ravioli felt like a statement. I've always considered this dish to be important from a technique perspective, as it set me on a path to working and then reworking every one of my cheese-based fillings for greater richness and textural consistency.

1   To make the filling, place a saucepan over medium heat. Add the cream and bring to a very slow simmer. Turn down the heat to low and very gently simmer until the cream has reduced by about one-third, being very careful not to scorch the bottom of the pan, 1 to 1½ hours. Let cool for 5 minutes.

2   While the cream is reducing, remove the rind from the cheese, reserving just the creamy interior. Chop the cheese into 1-inch pieces.

3   Transfer the cream to a high-speed blender. With the blender running on low-medium speed, slowly add the cheese and blend until the mixture is emulsified. Taste to test your seasoning and add salt q.b. (The Taleggio adds plenty of salinity, so you may not need to add much salt.)

4   With the blender still running, add the egg yolk. Cover and refrigerate for at least 1 hour. If you'll be leaving the filling in the refrigerator for several hours or up to overnight, remove it about 30 minutes before using to soften.

5   To finish, following the instructions for ravioli on page 104, make 35 to 40 pieces with the pasta dough and filling.

6   Bring a small pot of water to a boil over high heat. Generously salt the water. Prepare a salted ice-water bath and set a colander in it.

7   Add the peas to the boiling water and blanch until barely tender and still bright green, 20 to 30 seconds. Using a slotted spoon, transfer the peas to the ice-water bath to stop the cooking. Lift the colander out of the ice-water bath and set aside.

8   Bring a large pot of water to a boil over high heat. Generously salt the water.

9   Place a large sauté pan over low heat and add the oil. Add the garlic and gently cook until aromatic but without color, 10 to 15 seconds. Add the peas to the pan, stir to combine, and set aside.

Yields 4 to 6 servings

Filling

474g / 2 cups heavy cream
340g / 12 oz Taleggio with rind
Salt, q.b.
10g / ½ egg yolk

To Finish

1 batch egg dough (page 18)
150g / 1 cup shelled English peas
42g / 3 Tbsp olive oil
5g / 1 clove garlic, thinly sliced
60g / ¼ cup unsalted butter, cold and cubed
85g / 3 oz speck, finely diced
20g / 1 cup tender pea tendrils
22g / ¼ cup finely grated parmigiano-reggiano
Black pepper, q.b.

10   Add the ravioli to the water and turn down the heat to bring the water to a gentle simmer instead of a rolling boil. It is important to cook these gently at a simmer instead of a boil. The filling is very delicate and will break if cooked over high heat. Cook for 2 to 3 minutes, until tender at the thickest closure point and the filling is warm and oozes when you cut into one.

11   While the pasta is cooking, place the pan of peas back over medium-low heat. Add the butter and 2 to 3 ladles (115g to 170g / ½ to ¾ cup) pasta cooking water. Swirl the contents of the pan to emulsify. Add half of the speck.

12   Using a spider or pasta basket, remove the pasta from the pot and transfer to the sauté pan. Turn the heat up to medium. Swirl the pasta in the sauce for 30 seconds to 1 minute to marry, using a spoon to gently turn the pasta over and coat all sides. If the sauce begins to tighten, add a splash of pasta cooking water to loosen and continue swirling to marry.

13   Add half of the pea tendrils and let them gently wilt in the pan, 10 to 15 seconds.

14   Divide onto plates and garnish with the remaining speck and pea tendrils, the parmigiano, and with pepper q.b.

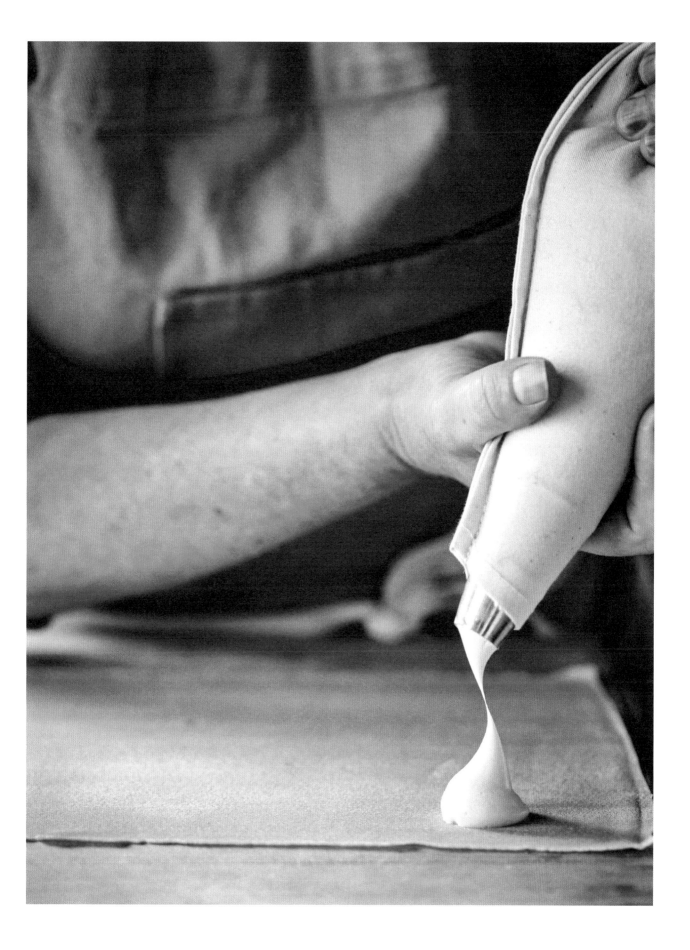

Eggplant-Filled Mezzelune with Simple Sauce and Ricotta Salata

I can trace this dish back to an eggplant-filled pasta I had at a mediocre restaurant in Rome. The dish itself was forgettable, but the concept of a smoky eggplant–filled pasta was not. I came home determined to find the right combination of flavors to support it and ultimately landed on pasta alla Norma, a classic Sicilian combination of tomato sauce, eggplant, and ricotta salata typically served with rigatoni.

While pasta alla Norma is undoubtedly comforting, I've never found that those three ingredients add up to a dish that is sufficiently complex. Part of it is that the eggplant rarely gets the space to shine. Too often it's in a deadlock with a rich tomato sauce and a very generous layer of ricotta salata, its creamy texture and earthiness unable to take the lead. This dish was my way to give eggplant its rightful Norma moment.

1   To make the filling, heat a grill to medium or preheat your broiler and position an oven rack closest to the heat source.

2   Place the eggplants on the grill or under the broiler. If using the broiler, be sure to arrange the eggplants on a broiler pan or wire rack set in a sheet pan so that air is circulating around them. Grill or broil the eggplants, rotating and flipping them every 5 to 10 minutes, until charred on all sides and very soft in the center, 30 to 45 minutes.

3   Let the eggplants cool at room temperature until cool to the touch.

4   Cut the eggplants open and, using a spoon, scrape out the interior from each one. It should come away from the skins easily. Discard the skins.

5   Line a chinois with cheesecloth or place a fine-mesh strainer over a bowl. Place the eggplant flesh in the chinois or strainer and weight it down with a plate. Transfer to the refrigerator for a minimum of 2 hours or up to 24 hours to allow the excess liquid to seep out. This will prevent the filling from being watery and loose.

6   After the eggplant flesh has drained, transfer it to the bowl of a food processor and puree until smooth, stopping once or twice to scrape down the sides of the bowl to ensure it's well processed.

7   Place a tamis or fine-mesh strainer over a bowl. Pass the ricotta through the tamis. Add the eggplant to the ricotta and fold until well integrated. Mix in the salt, then taste and add more q.b. It should taste well seasoned. Cover and refrigerate until ready to use.

8   To finish, following the instructions for mezzelune on page 95, make 80 to 100 pieces with the pasta dough and filling.

9   Bring a large pot of water to a boil over high heat. Generously salt the water.

Yields 6 to 8 servings

Filling
10 (1.6 to 1.8kg / 3½ to 4 lb)
    Japanese eggplants
174g / ¾ cup ricotta
5.5g / 1½ tsp salt, plus more q.b.

To Finish
1 batch egg dough (page 18)
500g / 2 cups simple red sauce
    (page 147)
Ground red chile, q.b.
120g / 4¼ oz ricotta salata
20 to 25 small basil leaves

10   Place a large sauté pan over low heat. Add the red sauce. Add 1 to 2 ladles (55g to 115g / ¼ to ½ cup) pasta cooking water to the sauté pan and stir to combine.

11   Add the mezzelune to the water and turn down the heat to bring the water to a gentle simmer instead of a rolling boil. It is important to cook these gently at a simmer instead of a boil. The filling is delicate and can break if cooked over high heat. Cook for 1 to 2 minutes, until tender at the thickest closure point.

12   Using a spider or pasta basket, remove the pasta from the pot and transfer to the sauté pan. Turn the heat up to medium. Swirl the pasta in the sauce for 30 seconds to 1 minute to marry, using a spoon to gently turn the pasta over and coat all sides. If the sauce begins to tighten, add a splash of pasta cooking water to loosen and continue swirling to marry.

13   Transfer the pasta to a serving platter or divide onto plates and garnish with the ground chile q.b. Coarsely grate the ricotta salata over the top and garnish with the basil leaves.

Pappardelle with Porcini and Veal Bolognese

Heading into the opening of Lilia, I was fresh off of a significant weight loss, which meant meat—particularly beef and pork—were not a huge part of my diet. I'd finished writing the menu and realized that there was not a single meat pasta on it.

This was born as a lighter attempt at bolognese, using veal, which is softer and milder than beef or pork, backed up by the earthiness of dried porcini—both the water left over from soaking them and the mushrooms themselves, which get chopped and integrated into the sauce. There is also no milk here, and instead of tomato paste, I use just a splash of tomato juice to ensure that the bouillon-like notes of the porcini and the subtlety of the veal are not masked by too much fat or sweetness. This is a ragù in pursuit of a cleaner profile.

1 To make the ragù, in a bowl, cover the porcini with cool water and soak for about 5 minutes, sloshing the mushrooms around with your hand a few times to remove dirt and other impurities. Drain the porcini, return them to the bowl, add the room-temperature water, and set aside to soften, 30 minutes to 1 hour.

2 Once the mushrooms are fully hydrated and softened, drain them, reserving the water (you should have about 948g / 4 cups water), and finely chop. Set the mushrooms and soaking water aside separately.

3 While the porcini hydrate, fit your meat grinder with the small die. Core the fennel and remove the fronds and stems. Chop the onion and fennel into ½- to 1-inch pieces. Put the onion, fennel, and garlic through the meat grinder. Once ground, gather them in cheesecloth and wring to squeeze out the liquid. This is your soffritto.

4 Place a heavy sauce pot or Dutch oven over medium-high heat and add 28g / 2 Tbsp of the olive oil. Add the veal and sauté, breaking it up with a wooden spoon into small, uniform crumbled pieces, until just cooked through, 5 to 7 minutes. Using a slotted spoon, transfer the meat to a bowl and set aside.

5 Turn the heat down to low and add the remaining 112g / ½ cup olive oil, the soffritto, and the porcini to the pot. Continue to cook, stirring frequently, until softened but without color, 3 to 5 minutes.

6 Add the wine and cook until almost fully evaporated, about 5 minutes.

7 Return the veal to the pot and add the reserved porcini liquid and the San Marzano juice.

continued

Yields 4 to 6 servings

Ragù

56g / 2 oz dried porcini
    mushrooms
1.4kg / 6 cups room-temperature
    water
200g / ½ large fennel bulb
236g / 1 onion
10g / 2 cloves garlic
28g / 2 Tbsp plus 112g / ½ cup
    olive oil
896g / 2 lb ground veal
220g / 1 cup dry white wine
122g / ½ cup juice from canned
    San Marzano tomatoes
1 fresh bay leaf
2 sprigs thyme
2 sprigs rosemary
1 sprig sage
2g / 1 tsp coriander seed
9g / 1 Tbsp black peppercorns
Salt, q.b.

To Finish

1 batch egg dough (page 18)
30g / 2 Tbsp unsalted butter,
    cold and cubed
20g / ¼ cup finely chopped
    parsley
22g / ¼ cup finely grated
    parmigiano-reggiano
Whole nutmeg, q.b.
Black pepper, q.b.

Pappardelle with Porcini and Veal Bolognese

continued

8 Make a sachet with cheesecloth for the bay leaf, thyme, rosemary, sage, coriander seed, and peppercorns. Add to the veal and porcini mixture.

9 Cook the sauce over low heat for 2 to 3 hours. The flavors should be melded and the meat fully softened.

10 Remove from the heat and season with salt q.b. Measure out 606g / 2¼ cups ragù and set aside. Transfer the remainder to an airtight container and refrigerate for up to 5 days or freeze for up to 1 month for another use.

11 To finish, following the instructions for pappardelle on page 54, make 624g / 1 lb 6 oz with the pasta dough.

12 Bring a large pot of water to a boil over high heat. Generously salt the water.

13 Place a large sauté pan over medium-low heat. Add the ragù.

14 Add the pappardelle to the water and cook for 1 to 2 minutes, until tender but not soft.

15 Using tongs or a pasta basket, remove the pasta from the pot and transfer to the sauté pan. Turn the heat up to medium. Add the butter and 1 ladle (55g / ¼ cup) pasta cooking water and alternate tossing and folding the pasta and sauce together with a wooden spoon for about 1 minute to marry. If the sauce begins to tighten, add a splash of pasta cooking water to loosen and continue tossing and folding to marry. Add the parsley and fold or toss to integrate. The ragù should nicely coat the pasta without clumping.

16 Divide the pasta into bowls and garnish with the parmigiano and with grated nutmeg and pepper q.b.

Prosciutto and Goat Cheese–Filled Cappelletti with Pistachios

I've been riffing on this dish since my Spiaggia days, when it originated as a way to use up prosciutto butts—the scraps left behind after you've sliced it to the nub. While goat cheese adds the grassy tang that really makes this dish, ricotta is the unsung hero, per usual, making up for the textural shortcomings of goat cheese (its chalkiness, namely) and tempering the flavor profile. The filling also gets spinach, again bolting this to that foundational combo of spinach and ricotta on which so many of my filled pastas are built.

Pistachios swoop in for added texture and flavor, a common move in the south of Italy, where nuts and bread crumbs seem to top nearly every pasta dish but are a rarer sight in the north. Here they give the dish just the right amount of subtle sweetness.

1   To make the filling, chill the meat grinder and all the dies for at least 1 hour before grinding. Cut the prosciutto into ½- to 1-inch cubes and chill in the freezer until cold, about 15 minutes. You do not want them frozen, but you do want them colder than they will get in the refrigerator. Fit the grinder with the larger of the two dies (or the medium die if you have three). Grind the prosciutto twice. Set aside.

2   Put the ricotta into a food processor and pulse just until it is as smooth as cake frosting and has a sheen, being careful not to process it longer or it will break. Transfer to a bowl and set aside.

3   Bring a large pot of water to a boil over high heat. Generously salt the water. Prepare a salted ice-water bath and set a colander in it.

4   Drop the spinach into the boiling water and cook until tender but still bright green, about 1 minute. Transfer the spinach to the salted ice-water bath to stop the cooking. Drain the spinach, transfer to a kitchen towel, and squeeze out the excess water.

5   Once dry, finely chop the spinach.

6   In a bowl, combine the whipped ricotta, goat cheese, prosciutto, spinach, and parmigiano and mix until all of the ingredients are well integrated. Taste and adjust the seasoning with salt q.b. It should taste well seasoned. Add the egg yolk, mix well, and refrigerate until ready to use.

7   To finish, following the instructions for cappelletti on page 87, make 70 to 80 pieces with the pasta dough and filling.

8   Bring a large pot of water to a boil over high heat. Generously salt the water.

9   Place a large sauté pan over low heat. Add the butter and 2 to 3 ladles (115g to 170g / ½ to ¾ cup) pasta cooking water. Swirl the contents of the pan to emulsify.

Yields 4 to 6 servings

Filling

128g / 4½ oz prosciutto, in a
    single piece
116g / ½ cup ricotta (see
    "whipped" ricotta, page 139)
114g / 3 cups lightly packed
    spinach leaves
168g / ¾ cup fresh goat cheese
22g / ¼ cup finely grated
    parmigiano-reggiano
Salt, q.b.
18g / 1 egg yolk

To Finish

1 batch egg dough (page 18)
45g / 3 Tbsp unsalted butter,
    cold and cubed
31g / ¼ cup raw Sicilian
    pistachios, very finely
    chopped
22g / ¼ cup finely grated
    parmigiano-reggiano

10 Add the cappelletti to the water and turn down the heat to bring the water to a gentle simmer instead of a rolling boil. It is important to cook these gently at a simmer instead of a boil. The filling is delicate and can break if cooked over high heat. Cook for 2 to 4 minutes, until tender at the thickest closure point.

11 Using a spider or pasta basket, remove the pasta from the pot and transfer to the sauté pan. Turn the heat up to medium. Swirl the pasta in the sauce for 30 seconds to 1 minute to marry, using a spoon to gently turn the pasta over and coat all sides. If the sauce begins to tighten, add a splash of pasta cooking water to loosen and continue swirling to marry. When the pasta is properly married, it will cling to the sauce and have a glossy sheen.

12 Divide the pasta onto plates. Drizzle the remaining sauce from the pan over the top. Garnish with the pistachios and parmigiano.

Caramelle with Caramelized Onion, Brown Butter, and Balsamic

This is situated squarely at the intersection of sweet, savory, and sour—an agrodolce in pasta form. I first made a variation on this at Spiaggia, but I've updated the filling along the way, adding both bread crumbs and parmigiano to give it just a bit more binding and creaminess. For the balsamic, you want to make sure you're using an aged version that has some sweetness and viscosity. It doesn't have to be twenty-five years old, but it shouldn't be the kind you'd regularly use in vinaigrette. For quality, price, and versatility, I like Massimo Bottura's Villa Manodori.

1   To make the bread crumbs, preheat the oven to 200°F.

2   Spread the bread on a sheet pan and bake until dried out, 30 to 45 minutes. You do not want any color. To test for doneness, smash a shard of bread with the back of a spoon. The interior should be completely dry. Let cool.

3   Once cooled, place the bread in a food processor and pulse until broken down into fine crumbs. You want them to retain some texture, so be careful not to turn them to dust.

4   Place a sauté pan over medium-low heat. Add the olive oil and garlic and cook until the garlic perfumes the oil, 1 to 2 minutes. Remove the garlic and save for another use.

5   Turn the heat down to low. Line a plate with paper towels. Add the bread crumbs to the pan and cook, stirring occasionally, until they are golden brown, 5 to 8 minutes. Remove from the pan and transfer to the plate to drain. Let cool.

6   Measure out 104g / ⅔ cup crumbs and set aside. Transfer the remainder to an airtight container and store in a cool, dry place for up to 1 week for another use.

7   To make the filling, place a large Dutch oven over low heat. Add the oil and butter and swirl to emulsify.

8   Add the onions and stir to make sure they are fully coated in the butter and olive oil. Cook until soft and translucent, 10 to 15 minutes. Stir occasionally so they cook evenly and do not burn.

9   Add the water and stir to combine. Tie the rosemary and thyme together with kitchen twine and add to the pot.

10   Cover the onions with a piece of parchment paper placed directly on top of them and cook, lifting the parchment to stir occasionally, until completely softened and a deep brown, 2 to 3 hours. At this point, all of the water should have evaporated. Remove from the heat and let cool.

Yields 6 to 8 servings

Bread Crumbs

½ loaf (228g / 8 oz) country
    bread, torn into pieces
    (about 4 cups)
56g / ¼ cup olive oil
10g / 2 cloves garlic

Filling

125g / ⅔ cup olive oil
60g / ¼ cup unsalted butter,
    cold and cubed
1.8kg / 5 large yellow onions,
    thinly sliced
237g / 1 cup water
2 sprigs rosemary
2 sprigs thyme
60g / ⅔ cup finely grated
    parmigiano-reggiano
Salt, q.b.
Black pepper, q.b.

To Finish

1 batch egg dough (page 18)
150g / 10 Tbsp plus 1 tsp
    unsalted butter, cold
    and cubed
Aged balsamic vinegar, q.b.
1 sprig rosemary, leaves removed
    from stem
2 sprigs thyme, leaves removed
    from stems
22g / ¼ cup finely grated
    parmigiano-reggiano
Black pepper, q.b.

11   Once cooled, transfer the onions to a high-speed blender and puree until smooth.

12   Transfer the onion puree to a bowl. Add the bread crumbs and parmigiano and season with salt and pepper q.b. Cover and refrigerate until ready to use.

13   To finish, following the instructions for caramelle on page 88, make 80 to 100 pieces with the pasta dough and filling.

14   Bring a large pot of water to a boil over high heat. Generously salt the water.

15   Place a small saucepan over medium heat. Add 85g / 6 Tbsp of the butter and cook until just past golden brown, 3 to 4 minutes. Set aside. You will drizzle this over the plated pasta.

16   Add the caramelle to the water and turn down the heat to bring the water to a gentle simmer instead of a rolling boil. It is important to cook these gently at a simmer instead of a boil. The filling is delicate and can break if cooked over high heat. Cook for 2 to 3 minutes, until tender at the thickest closure point.

17   Place a large sauté pan over low heat. Add the remaining 65g / ¼ cup plus 1 tsp butter and 2 to 3 ladles (115g to 170g / ½ to ¾ cup) pasta cooking water. Swirl the contents of the pan to emulsify.

18   Using a spider or pasta basket, remove the pasta from the pot and transfer to the sauté pan. Turn the heat up to medium. Swirl the pasta in the sauce for 30 seconds to 1 minute to marry, using a spoon to gently turn the pasta over and coat all sides. If the sauce begins to tighten, add a splash more pasta cooking water to loosen and continue swirling to marry.

19   Transfer the pasta to a serving platter or divide onto plates. Spoon the remaining sauce from the pan over the pasta, first loosening it with a splash of pasta cooking water if necessary. Drizzle the balsamic and reserved brown butter over the pasta. Garnish with the rosemary, thyme, parmigiano, and with pepper q.b.

Mafaldine with Pink Peppercorns and Parmigiano-Reggiano

Lilia's beloved mafaldine with pink peppercorns was a bit of an accident. I was home testing out custom pasta bowls for Lilia and, well, I needed to see what they looked like with pasta in them. All I had in the house was spaghetti, butter, and parmigiano; I threw them together and gave the dish a last-minute dusting of ground pink peppercorns for color. I loved it. Before we opened, we tested the combination with a number of different shapes before settling on mafaldine, a long, ribbon-shaped pasta that's ruffled at the edges, offering perfect little coves for parmigiano and butter to hide in.

With just four ingredients, it's stripped down—so stripped down, in fact, that I initially wondered if anyone would order it. (It's now one of Lilia's most-ordered pastas.) It turned out to be a powerful argument for quanto basta, and a true teaching pasta: It's all about balance, attention to detail, and the all-important marriage ceremony.

---

1   Bring a large pot of water to a boil over high heat. Generously salt the water.

2   Add the mafaldine to the water and cook for 5 to 8 minutes, until al dente.

3   While the pasta is cooking, place a large sauté pan over low heat. Add 4 ladles (230g / 1 cup) pasta cooking water to the pan. Gradually add half of the butter to the pan and stir to emulsify.

4   Using tongs or a pasta basket, remove the pasta from the pot and transfer to the sauté pan. Turn up the heat to medium. Toss for 1 to 2 minutes to marry the pasta and the sauce. Add the remaining butter and keep tossing the pasta until the butter is absorbed. If the sauce begins to tighten, add a splash of pasta water and continue tossing. The sauce should cling to the pasta but still glide easily in the pan.

5   Remove from the heat and add 90g / 1 cup of the parmigiano and 5g / 2 Tbsp of the pink peppercorns. Continue tossing until evenly distributed.

6   Divide the pasta into bowls. Garnish with the remaining 22g / ¼ cup parmigiano and 3g / 1 Tbsp pink peppercorns.

Yields 4 to 6 servings

567g / 1 lb 4 oz extruded
  mafaldine (page 122)
114g / ½ cup unsalted butter,
  cold and cubed
90g / 1 cup plus 22g / ¼ cup
  finely grated parmigiano-
  reggiano
8g / 3 Tbsp coarsely ground
  pink peppercorns

Tagliatelle with Ossobuco and Soffritto

I've been making the same ossobuco recipe for the better part of two decades. It was inevitable that it would find its way into a pasta at some point. This dish originated as a way to use up night-before ossobuco by making a ragù with the meat and the base of the braise, or soffritto, which in this case is a combination of onion, fennel, carrot, and garlic.

What I love about this recipe is that it's actually applicable to any braise that you want to make another meal out of. Some may need to be finished with a bit of butter to emulsify, but the combination of marrow and the gelatin from the bones in ossobuco gives it enough richness to stand on its own.

---

1   To make the ragù, season the shanks with the salt. Set aside for 1 to 2 hours before cooking or, if you have time, refrigerate overnight. When ready to cook, season with pepper q.b. and set aside.

2   Fit your meat grinder with the small die. Core the fennel and remove the fronds and stems. Peel the carrot. Chop the fennel, carrot, and onion into ½- to 1-inch pieces. Put the fennel, onion, and carrot through the meat grinder. Once all are ground, gather them in cheesecloth and wring to squeeze out the liquid. This is your soffritto.

3   Place a large, heavy sauce pot or Dutch oven over medium heat and add the olive oil. Add the veal shanks and sear, turning as needed, until golden brown on all sides, 7 to 9 minutes. Transfer to a plate. Clean out any burned bits from the pot.

4   Add the soffritto to the pot, turn down the heat to low, and gently cook, stirring frequently, until softened but without color, 5 to 8 minutes. Toward the very end of cooking, add the garlic and gently cook until aromatic but without color, 10 to 15 seconds.

5   Return the shanks to the pot and add the wine. Simmer until the wine has almost fully evaporated, 5 to 8 minutes.

6   Add the tomatoes and their juice and enough water to cover the shanks by 1 inch. Make a sachet with cheesecloth for the fennel seed, chile flakes, rosemary, and thyme. Add to the pot and bring to a simmer over low heat, cover, and cook on the stove top for 2 to 3 hours. Alternatively, transfer to a 275°F oven for the same amount of time. The meat is ready when it is tender and easily falling off the bone but not mushy. Let the meat cool in the braising liquid.

7   When the meat has cooled, remove the sachet from the pot and discard. Remove the meat from the sauce. Separate the meat from the bones, discarding any sinew or tough membranes. Remove the marrow from the bones and reserve for spreading on bread as a snack.

Yields 4 to 6 servings

Ossobuco Ragù

910g / 2 lb center-cut veal shanks, in 2-inch-thick pieces
14g / 1½ Tbsp salt, plus more q.b.
Black pepper, q.b.
400g / 1 large fennel bulb
150g / 1 large carrot
370g / 1 large onion
75g / ⅓ cup plus 28g / 2 Tbsp olive oil
20g / 4 cloves garlic, thinly sliced
360g / 1⅔ cups dry white wine
1 large (794g / 28 oz) can whole San Marzano tomatoes, crushed by hand
6g / 1 Tbsp fennel seed
4g / 2 tsp dried red chile flakes
5 sprigs rosemary
2 sprigs thyme

To Finish

1 batch egg dough (page 18)
Fennel pollen, q.b.
Black pepper, q.b.
22g / ¼ cup finely grated parmigiano-reggiano

8   When all of the meat has been stripped from the bones, pull it apart with two forks into strands. Run a knife through the strands, cutting them into ¼- to ½-inch pieces.

9   Skim any fat from the braising liquid and return the meat to the liquid. Stir to combine and season with salt q.b. Measure out 450g / 2 cups ragù and set aside. Transfer the remainder to an airtight container and refrigerate for up to 5 days or freeze for up to 1 month for another use.

10   To finish, following the instructions for tagliatelle on page 57, make 624g / 1 lb 6 oz with the pasta dough.

11   Bring a large pot of water to a boil over high heat. Generously salt the water.

12   Place a large sauté pan over medium-low heat. Add the ragù.

13   Add the tagliatelle to the water and cook for 30 seconds to 1 minute, until tender but not soft.

14   Using tongs or a pasta basket, remove the pasta from the pot and transfer to the sauté pan. Toss for about 1 minute to marry the pasta and the sauce. If the sauce begins to tighten, add a splash of pasta cooking water to loosen and continue tossing to marry. The ragù should nicely coat the pasta without clumping.

15   Divide the pasta into bowls and garnish with fennel pollen and pepper q.b. and with the parmigiano.

Spinach and Ricotta-Filled Tortelli with Brown Butter and Ricotta Salata

When I was workshopping this dish for Misi, the premise was simple: turn the classic spinach and ricotta filling on its head, making the greens, not the cheese, the star. Cheese being cheese, it's hard to replace its texture and flavor and not miss it. But I thought back a few decades to my time with Wayne Nish at March. He used to do a brown butter and spinach puree that tasted like complex creamed spinach. I combine that puree with a fifty-fifty split of ricotta and mascarpone, the latter of which is denser and slightly sweeter.

The dish has become, far and away, the most popular pasta at Misi, finding an addictive intersection of sweet, savory, and salty that always catches people by surprise. In fact, I don't think anyone *means* to eat a whole portion themselves, but it happens more often than not. I've even seen guests on such a pasta high that they've "encored" this dish for dessert.

---

1   To make the filling, remove and discard the stems and ribs from the Swiss chard and set the leaves aside.

2   Bring a pot of water to a boil over high heat. Generously salt the water. Prepare a salted ice-water bath and set a colander in it.

3   Drop the spinach into the boiling water and cook until tender but still bright green, 10 to 15 seconds. Transfer the spinach to the ice-water bath to stop the cooking. Drain the spinach, transfer to a kitchen towel, and squeeze out the excess water.

4   Repeat the same process with the chard but cook for 30 seconds to 1 minute, as it will take a bit longer to become tender.

5   Transfer the greens to a high-speed blender and puree until smooth. (You may need to add a splash of water to get the blade moving.) Set aside.

6   Place a small saucepan over medium heat. Add the butter and cook until just past golden brown, 3 to 4 minutes. Measure out 52g / ¼ cup, and set aside in a small saucepan. You will use this to finish your pasta.

7   Turn the blender on low and drizzle in the remaining 60g / ⅓ cup brown butter to gently emulsify. Transfer the greens and butter mixture to a bowl.

8   Put the ricotta into a food processor and pulse just until it is as smooth as cake frosting and has a sheen, being careful not to process it longer or it will break.

9   Fold the ricotta, mascarpone, and parmigiano into the spinach and chard mixture until they are fully incorporated and the mixture is a uniform green. Season with salt q.b. It should taste well seasoned. Cover and refrigerate until ready to use.

continued

Yields 6 to 8 servings

Filling

114g / 4 cups Swiss chard leaves
114g / 3 cups loosely packed
 baby spinach
171g / ¾ cup unsalted butter,
 cold and cubed
116g / ½ cup ricotta (see
 "whipped" ricotta, page 139)
112g / ½ cup mascarpone
45g / ½ cup finely grated
 parmigiano-reggiano
Salt, q.b.

To Finish

1 batch egg dough (page 18)
28g / 2 Tbsp olive oil
5g / 1 clove garlic, thinly sliced
75g / 5 Tbsp unsalted butter,
 cold and cubed
1 small (57g / 2 oz) piece ricotta
 salata

Spinach and Ricotta-Filled Tortelli with Brown Butter and Ricotta Salata

continued

10   To finish, following the instructions for tortelli on page 106, make 75 to 100 pieces with the pasta dough and filling.

11   Bring a large pot of water to a boil over high heat. Generously salt the water.

12   Add the tortelli to the water and turn down the heat to bring the water to a gentle simmer instead of a rolling boil. The filling is very delicate and will break if cooked over high heat. Cook for 3 to 5 minutes, until tender at the thickest closure point.

13   While the pasta is cooking, place a large sauté pan over low heat and add the olive oil. Add the garlic and gently cook until aromatic but without color, 10 to 15 seconds. Add 2 to 3 ladles (115 to 170g / ½ to ¾ cup) pasta cooking water and the butter. Swirl the contents of the pan to emulsify.

14   Using a spider or pasta basket, remove the pasta from the pot and transfer to the sauté pan. Turn the heat up to medium. Swirl the pasta in the sauce for 30 to 45 seconds to marry, using a spoon to gently turn the pasta over and coat all sides. If the sauce begins to tighten, add a splash of pasta cooking water to loosen and continue swirling in the pan.

15   Place the saucepan with the reserved brown butter over low heat and gently warm the butter.

16   Transfer the pasta to a large serving platter or divide into flat-bottomed bowls. Spoon the remaining sauce from the pan over the top, then drizzle on the brown butter. Use a Microplane to finely grate the ricotta salata over the top.

Sunchoke-Filled Agnolotti with Walnuts, Lemon, and Thyme

This dish has no Italian ancestry. It instead sprung forth from the sunchoke craze in the early aughts, when just about every Manhattan restaurant south of Fourteenth Street had a sunchoke puree under a piece of salmon.

I got on board in my way. This dish begins with a single, and very singular, flavor profile and builds around it. The creamy, earthy flavor of sunchoke is amplified by the walnuts and countered by citrus and thyme, which add a bit of brightness without being overpowering. While a bit of a one-off in my repertoire, this has always been one of my favorite wild-card pastas.

---

1   To make the filling, place the sunchokes in a pot and pour in the milk and cream. Add the parmigiano rind and garlic.

2   Make a sachet with cheesecloth for the peppercorns, thyme, and bay leaf.

3   Add the sachet to the pot. Cover the sunchokes with a piece of parchment paper placed directly on top of them.

4   Turn on the heat to very low and cook the sunchokes until cooked through and soft, 30 to 45 minutes.

5   Using a slotted spoon, transfer the garlic and sunchokes to a high-speed blender. Discard the sachet and parmigiano rinds. Reserve the liquid.

6   Add 30g / 2 Tbsp of the sunchoke liquid to the blender and puree until smooth. If needed, add a bit more liquid, about 15g / 1 Tbsp at a time, until loosened enough to blend. You need just enough liquid to get the mixture going. Do not add too much or your filling will be too loose.

7   Prepare an ice-water bath and set a bowl in it. Transfer the sunchoke puree to the bowl to chill. (The puree must be fully cooled before blending it with the ricotta or it will curdle the ricotta.)

8   Put the ricotta into a food processor and pulse just until it is as smooth as cake frosting and has a sheen, being careful not to process it longer or it will break.

9   Fold the ricotta into the sunchoke mixture. Season with salt q.b. It should taste well seasoned. Refrigerate until ready to use.

10   To finish, following the instructions for agnolotti dal plin on page 84, make 100 to 150 pieces with the pasta dough and filling.

Yields 6 to 8 servings

Filling

684g / 1½ lb sunchokes, trimmed
    and peeled
474g / 2 cups milk
474g / 2 cups heavy cream
1 (114g / 4 oz) parmigiano-
    reggiano rind (from 2 large or
    4 smaller pieces parmigiano)
25g / 5 cloves garlic
3g / 1 tsp black peppercorns
5 sprigs thyme
1 fresh bay leaf
464g / 2 cups ricotta (see
    "whipped" ricotta, page 139)
Salt, q.b.

To Finish

1 batch egg dough (page 18)
85g / 6 Tbsp unsalted butter,
    cold and cubed
30g / ⅓ cup finely grated
    parmigiano-reggiano
35g / ⅓ cup walnuts, finely
    chopped
Peel of 1 lemon, pith removed
    and peel finely chopped
3 sprigs thyme, leaves removed
    from stems

11   Bring a large pot of water to a boil over high heat. Generously salt the water.

12   Add the agnolotti dal plin to the water and turn down the heat to bring the water to a gentle simmer instead of a rolling boil. The filling is very delicate and will break if cooked over high heat. Cook for 2 to 4 minutes, until tender at the thickest closure point.

13   While the pasta is cooking, place a large sauté pan over medium-low heat. Add the butter and 2 to 3 ladles (115 to 170g / ½ to ¾ cup) pasta cooking water. Swirl the contents of the pan to emulsify.

14   Using a spider or pasta basket, remove the agnolotti dal plin from the pot and transfer to the sauté pan. Turn the heat up to medium. Swirl the pasta in the sauce for 30 seconds to 1 minute to marry, using a spoon to gently turn the pasta over and coat all sides. If the sauce begins to tighten, add a splash of pasta cooking water to loosen and continue swirling to marry. When the pasta is properly married, it will cling to the sauce and have a glossy sheen.

15   Divide the pasta onto plates and garnish with the parmigiano, walnuts, lemon peel, and thyme.

Spaghetti with Pancetta, Black Pepper, and Spring Onions

If you do not crave, love, or even like cured pork, keep moving. This is a simple tribute: a sauce made from two ingredients—pasta water and pork fat—emulsified into a velvety, unctuous pairing with spaghetti. The spring onion tops made their way into the mix to cut through the fat and as a way of utilizing the whole vegetable and minimizing waste (we were, at the time, using the bulbs for a number of dishes). Spring onions have a short season and can be hard to find, but you can substitute scallions, which will be slightly less sweet but no less delicious.

1   Chill the meat grinder and the larger of the two dies (or the medium die if you have three) for at least 1 hour before grinding. Cut the pancetta into ½- to 1-inch cubes and chill in the freezer until cold, about 15 minutes. You do not want them frozen, but you do want them colder than they will get in the refrigerator.

2   Fit the grinder with the large (or medium) die. Grind the pancetta twice.

3   Place a large sauté pan over very low heat and add the pancetta. Slowly cook, stirring occasionally, until the fat is rendered and the meat is cooked but not crispy, 10 to 15 minutes. Separate the meat from the fat, reserving both.

4   Bring a large pot of water to a boil over high heat. Lightly salt the water. (Pancetta has a high salt content. Go too heavy with your pasta water and your finished dish will end up very salty.)

5   Add the spaghetti to the water and cook for 5 to 8 minutes, until al dente.

6   While the pasta is cooking, place a large sauté pan over low heat and add 55g / ¼ cup of the rendered pork fat. Add the garlic and gently cook until aromatic but without color, 10 to 15 seconds.

7   Add the cooked pancetta and 3 ladles (170g / ¾ cup) pasta cooking water to the pan and stir to combine.

8   Using tongs or a pasta basket, remove the pasta from the pot and transfer to the sauté pan. Turn the heat up to medium. Toss for 1 to 2 minutes to marry the pasta and the sauce. Because of the high level of fat, the sauce will tighten quickly, so you will need to add more pasta cooking water to emulsify.

9   Add the butter to the pan and continue tossing to emulsify.

10   Remove the pan from the heat and add a very generous amount—20 to 30 grinds—black pepper and toss to incorporate. Add half of the spring onion tops and toss. Add half of the parmigiano and continue tossing. If your sauce tightens again, add a bit more pasta cooking water to loosen until the pasta glides easily in the pan. When properly married, it should have a glossy sheen.

11   Divide the pasta into bowls and garnish with the remaining spring onion tops and parmigiano.

Yields 4 to 6 servings

1 (227g / 8 oz) piece pancetta
624g / 1 lb 6 oz extruded
   spaghetti (page 123)
15g / 3 cloves garlic, finely
   chopped
30g / 2 Tbsp unsalted butter,
   cold and cubed
Black pepper, q.b.
25g / ½ cup thinly sliced spring
   onion tops
45g / ½ cup finely grated
   parmigiano-reggiano

Strangozzi with Pork Sugo, Nutmeg, and Parmigiano

This is scrap sauce. Or at least it was originally, when I featured it as a special at Lilia after discovering a bunch of salumi butts in the walk-in refrigerator. I ran them all through the meat grinder until the mixture was fine enough to cook down, and then I combined it with San Marzano juice for a very savory, very porky ragù. I returned to it at Misi, where I knew I wanted—and needed—a hearty, meat-forward dish to be a staple on a menu focused squarely on vegetables. In the spirit of the genesis of the dish, if you're missing one or two of the salumi called for, or if you want to swap in a different type, by all means do so. The result will still be delicious.

Like any ragù, you want to cook this low and slow. Note that the cured meats release a lot of fat, which is great for flavor but will need to be skimmed periodically to keep the sauce from getting too rich. Nutmeg also plays an important role. As a garnish, it brings a sense of levity and brightness to the dish.

---

1   To make the sugo, chill the meat grinder and the dies for at least 1 hour before grinding. Cut the pork shoulder, soppressata, guanciale, pancetta, and prosciutto into ½- to 1-inch cubes and chill in the freezer until cold, about 15 minutes. You do not want them frozen, but you do want them colder than they will get in the refrigerator.

2   Fit the grinder with the large die. Grind the shoulder twice. Set aside.

3   Grind the soppressata and guanciale separately, putting each through the grinder once. Grind the pancetta and prosciutto separately, putting each through the grinder twice.

4   Clean the meat grinder, then fit it with the small die. Core the fennel and remove the fronds and stems. Chop the fennel, onion, and celery into ½- to 1-inch pieces. Put the fennel, onion, celery, and garlic through the meat grinder. Once all are ground, gather them in cheesecloth and wring to squeeze out the liquid. This is your soffritto.

5   Cut the lardo into ½-inch pieces. Place a large sauté pan over low heat and add the lardo. Slowly render the pieces until liquefied, 10 to 15 minutes. Remove from the heat.

6   Place a large, heavy sauce pot or Dutch oven over medium-high heat and add the melted lardo and oil. Add the pork shoulder and break it up with a wooden spoon into small pieces in an even layer. Cook until light brown but not deeply caramelized, 3 to 4 minutes. Using a slotted spoon, transfer the meat to a bowl.

7   Add the soffritto to the pot and cook, stirring frequently, until softened but without color, 3 to 4 minutes. Add the soppressata, guanciale, pancetta, and prosciutto and stir to distribute them in an even layer. Add the guanciale skin. (It adds a bit more flavor to the sauce and will ultimately be removed.)

continued

Yields 4 to 6 servings

Sugo

1 (250g / 8¾ oz) boneless pork shoulder
1 (200g / 7 oz) piece spicy soppressata
1 (100g / 3½ oz) piece guanciale
1 (100g / 3½ oz) piece pancetta
1 (200g / 7 oz) piece prosciutto
150g / ½ fennel bulb
125g / 1 small onion
75g / 1 stalk celery
75g / 15 cloves garlic
125g / 4¼ oz lardo
56g / ¼ cup olive oil
1 (50g / 1¾ oz) piece guanciale skin
1 large (794g / 28 oz) can whole San Marzano tomatoes, crushed by hand
4 sprigs sage
25g / ¼ bunch parsley
36g / ¼ cup black peppercorns
Salt, q.b.

To Finish

1 batch egg dough (page 18)
85g / ⅓ cup 30-clove sauce (page 148)
45g / 3 Tbsp unsalted butter, cold and cubed
22g / ¼ cup finely grated parmigiano-reggiano
Whole nutmeg, q.b.
Black pepper, q.b.

Strangozzi with Pork Sugo, Nutmeg, and Parmigiano

continued

8　Add the tomatoes and their juice and stir well to incorporate. Turn the heat down to low and cook very slowly, stirring occasionally, for about 1 hour. The sauce will give off a large amount of fat that will need to be carefully skimmed off the surface as it cooks.

9　Make a sachet with cheesecloth for the sage, parsley, and peppercorns. Add the sachet to the sauce. Cook for 1 more hour, continuing to stir and skim.

10　Remove from the heat and let cool, continuing to skim any additional fat that rises to the surface. Remove the sachet and the guanciale skin. Season with salt q.b. Measure out 660g / 2¾ cups sugo and set aside. Transfer the remainder to an airtight container and refrigerate for up to 5 days or freeze for up to 1 month for another use.

11　To finish, following the instructions for strangozzi on page 56, make 624g / 1 lb 6 oz with the pasta dough.

12　Bring a large pot of water to a boil over high heat. Generously salt the water.

13　Place a large sauté pan over low heat. Add the sugo, 30-clove sauce, and butter and stir to integrate.

14　Add the strangozzi to the water and cook for 3 to 5 minutes, until tender. (This pasta is on the thick side, so it will take a bit longer to cook than thinner varieties, such as pappardelle or fettuccine.)

15　Using tongs or a pasta basket, remove the pasta from the pot and transfer to the sauté pan. Turn the heat up to medium. Toss for 1 to 2 minutes to marry the pasta and the sauce, using your tongs to help you move the pasta in the pan. (This one can be tough to toss.) If the sauce begins to tighten and feel coarse as you move it in the pan, add a splash of pasta cooking water to loosen it and continue tossing to marry. The sugo should nicely coat the pasta without clumping.

16　Transfer the pasta to a large serving platter or divide into bowls. Garnish with the parmigiano and with grated nutmeg and pepper q.b.

Nota bene

If you do not have 30-clove sauce on hand and do not want to make a batch, you can substitute 76g / ⅓ cup jarred tomato passata for ease.

Cocoa Pici with Braised Cinghiale

Of all of the dishes in this chapter, this remains closest to the hip of tradition. Chocolate has been a staple of savory Italian cooking for at least three centuries, finding its way into torte, pastas, and sauces and as a finishing ingredient deployed in the way herbs or parmigiano might be. Meat and chocolate, strange bedfellows though they may seem, are a common pairing, whether in the meat-and-chocolate cookies called 'mpanatigghi that I couldn't get enough of in the Sicilian town of Modica or the classic southern Tuscan combination of dark chocolate and wild boar. Today, dough infused with cocoa powder is not an uncommon sight in Tuscany, mostly coupled exactly this way.

   This recipe is an homage to boar, a beloved staple of the central Italian diet. The profile is noticeably different than pork: It's deeper, richer, and gamier rather than subtly sweet. It's also leaner and darker in color, its richness the product of depth of flavor rather than fat content. It's feral to pork's domestic, and it's precisely that wild quality that commingles so well with the bitter flavor of cacao. While boar is not quite as abundant here as it is in Tuscany, you can still find it in the States, mostly by way of Texas.

1   To make the ragù, salt the boar on all sides. Cover with plastic wrap and let sit at room temperature for 1 to 2 hours.

2   Fit your meat grinder with the small die. Peel the carrot. Chop the carrot, celery, and onion into ½- to 1-inch pieces. Put the carrot, celery, and onion through the meat grinder. Once all are ground, gather them in cheesecloth and wring to squeeze out the liquid. This is your soffritto.

3   Place a large, heavy sauce pot or Dutch oven over medium heat and add the 42g / 3 Tbsp olive oil. Pat the meat dry with paper towels. Add it to the pot and sear, turning as needed, until golden brown, 3 to 5 minutes on each side. Transfer to a plate. Clean out any burned bits from the pot.

4   Add the soffritto to the pot. Add the remaining 28g / 2 Tbsp olive oil. Turn the heat to low and gently cook, stirring frequently, until softened but without color, 4 to 6 minutes. At the very end of cooking, add the garlic and gently cook until aromatic but without color, 10 to 15 seconds.

5   Turn the heat up to medium. Add the wine and simmer until reduced by half, 3 to 5 minutes.

6   Return the boar to the pot. Add the tomatoes and their juice and enough water to reach to within 1 inch from the top of the meat.

7   Make a sachet with cheesecloth for the peppercorns, cinnamon, chile flakes, juniper, rosemary, and bay leaf and add to the pot.

8   Turn the heat to low, cover the pot, and simmer until the boar is tender and falling off the bone but not mushy, 3 to 4 hours.

continued

Yields 4 to 6 servings

Cinghiale Ragù

912g / 2 lb bone-in wild boar
   shoulder
Salt, q.b.
150g / 1 large carrot
150g / 2 stalks celery
370g / 1 large onion
42g / 3 Tbsp olive oil,
   plus 28g / 2 Tbsp
25g / 5 cloves garlic, finely
   chopped
440g / 2 cups dry red wine
1 large (794g / 28 oz) can whole
   San Marzano tomatoes,
   crushed by hand
9g / 1 Tbsp black peppercorns
1 cinnamon stick
2g / 1 tsp dried chile flakes
2g / 1 tsp juniper berries
1 sprig rosemary
1 fresh bay leaf

To Finish

1 batch cocoa dough (page 31)
1 (30g / 1 oz) piece bittersweet
   chocolate
Ground red chile, q.b.
Black pepper, q.b.

Cocoa Pici with Braised Cinghiale

continued

9   Remove from the heat and let cool.

10   Once cooled, remove the sachet and discard. Remove the boar from the liquid and pick all of the meat off the bones. Using two forks, pull the meat apart until you have fine strands, run a knife through the strands, and add back to the pot. Season with salt q.b.

11   Measure out 560g / 2¼ cups ragù and set aside. Transfer the remainder to an airtight container and refrigerate for up to 5 days or freeze for another use.

12   To finish, following the instructions for pici on page 71, make 624g / 1 lb 6 oz with the pasta dough.

13   Bring a large pot of water to a boil over high heat. Generously salt the water.

14   Place a large sauté pan over very low heat. Add the ragù.

15   Add the pici to the water and cook for 3 to 5 minutes, until tender but not soft.

16   Using tongs or a pasta basket, remove the pasta from the pot and transfer to the sauté pan. Turn the heat up to medium. Toss or fold for 1 to 2 minutes to marry the pasta and the sauce. If the sauce begins to tighten, add a splash of pasta cooking water to loosen and continue tossing or folding to marry. The sauce should nicely coat the pasta without clumping.

17   Divide the pasta into bowls. Finely grate the chocolate over the top and garnish with ground chile and pepper q.b.

Nota bene

Feel free to match other doughs with the wild boar ragù. It's at home with anything that complements its hearty, savory bass tones, such as chestnut or espresso.

Corn-Filled Cappelletti with Black Pepper and Pecorino

Despite the expanses of cornfields in the Po Valley, corn typically makes its way into the Italian diet in one form: polenta. But come August, corn is an American imperative. So, I decided to build a pasta around it. This is really about the purity of corn flavor at the very height of its season, when it's so sweet and creamy that it has all of the flavor this pasta needs to stand on its own. It has become a summer staple at Lilia, where it shows up for about a month at the tail end of the season.

1   To make the filling, place the corn and milk in a heavy saucepan over low heat. Gently heat the milk mixture and cook, stirring occasionally so the milk does not scorch, until the corn is tender enough to be pureed, 20 to 30 minutes.

2   Using a slotted spoon, transfer the corn to a high-speed blender. Reserve the milk.

3   Blend the corn into a smooth, thick paste, adding 1 Tbsp of the reserved milk at a time if necessary to achieve a good consistency.

4   Prepare an ice-water bath and set a bowl in it. Transfer the corn mixture to the bowl to cool, 5 to 10 minutes.

5   Put the ricotta into a food processor and pulse just until it is as smooth as cake frosting and has a sheen, being careful not to process it longer or it will break.

6   When the corn mixture is cool, remove the bowl from the ice-water bath and fold the ricotta into the mixture. Season with salt q.b. It should taste well seasoned. Refrigerate until firm, 1 to 2 hours.

7   To finish, following the instructions for cappelletti on page 87, make 90 to 100 pieces with the pasta dough and filling.

8   Bring a large pot of water to a boil over high heat. Generously salt the water.

9   Add the cappelletti to the water and turn down the heat to bring the water to a gentle simmer instead of a rolling boil. The filling is very delicate and will break if cooked over high heat. Cook for 2 to 4 minutes, until tender at the thickest closure point.

10   While the pasta is cooking, place a large sauté pan over low heat and add the olive oil. Add the garlic and cook until aromatic but without color, 10 to 15 seconds. Add the butter and 3 ladles (170g / ¾ cup) pasta cooking water. Swirl the contents of the pan to emulsify.

11   Using a spider or pasta basket, remove the pasta from the pot and transfer to the sauté pan. Turn the heat up to medium. Swirl the pasta in the sauce for 30 to 45 seconds to marry, using a spoon to gently turn the pasta over and coat all sides. If the sauce begins to tighten, add more pasta cooking water to loosen, and continue swirling the pasta in the pan.

12   Transfer the pasta to a large serving platter or divide onto plates. Spoon the remaining sauce from the pan over the top and garnish with the pecorino and with pepper q.b.

Yields 6 to 8 servings

Filling

3 or 4 ears corn, kernels cut off cobs to make 500g / 3¾ cups
474g / 2 cups milk
44g / 3 Tbsp ricotta (see "whipped" ricotta, page 139)
Salt, q.b.

To Finish

1 batch egg dough (page 18)
28g / 2 Tbsp olive oil
5g / 1 clove garlic, thinly sliced
75g / 5 Tbsp unsalted butter, cold and cubed
30g / ⅓ cup finely grated pecorino romano
Black pepper, q.b.

Chickpea Pappardelle with Chickpeas, Rosemary, and Garlic

I ate a version of this dish almost every night when I was living in the small Tuscan town of Sansepolcro. It was the dead of winter, and the house I was living in didn't have heat. I found myself at the enoteca that served this dish, staying until it closed to avoid having to go home and put on every sweater and half of my socks to make it through the night. I ate pappardelle with chickpeas, rosemary, and parmigiano alongside a glass of Sangiovese most nights. It was simple and rustic but so satisfying—enough that I have been thinking about it for twenty years.

I finally put this dish on a menu when I opened Misi. Like any dish that is this spartan, I like to focus on a single ingredient to try and get the most from it. This is really about the chickpeas, which I incorporate into the dough as chickpea flour and into the finished dish whole.

1   To make the chickpeas, place them in a large bowl or pot and cover with room-temperature water. The water level should be about double the volume of the chickpeas. Let soak at room temperature overnight.

2   When you are ready to cook, drain the chickpeas. Place them in a large pot and add water to cover by 4 to 6 inches. Add the garlic, carrot, onion, celery, and bay leaf.

3   Place the pot over medium-low heat and bring to a very slow simmer. Cook the beans until tender and creamy, 1 to 2 hours. When the beans are three-quarters cooked, season with salt q.b. Remove from the heat and cool.

4   Drain the chickpeas, reserving the cooking liquid. Measure out 115g / ½ cup chickpea cooking liquid and 270g / 1½ cups cooked chickpeas and set aside. Combine the remaining chickpeas and their cooking liquid, transfer to an airtight container, and store in the refrigerator for up to 5 days for another use.

5   Remove the chickpea skins that may have loosened (this is tedious, I know, but worth it for a texturally improved final dish).

6   To finish, following the instructions for pappardelle on page 54, make 624g / 1 lb 6 oz with the pasta dough.

7   Bring a large pot of water to a boil over high heat. Generously salt the water.

8   Separate the pappardelle piece by piece from their neat stacks to ensure the pieces do not stick together. Add them to the water and cook for 1 to 2 minutes, until tender but not soft.

9   While the pasta is cooking, place a large sauté pan over low heat and add the oil. Add the garlic and gently cook until aromatic but without color, 10 to 15 seconds.

Yields 4 to 6 servings

Chickpeas

454g / 1 lb dried chickpeas
25g / 5 cloves garlic
150g / 1 large carrot, peeled and halved
250g / 1 onion, peeled and halved
75g / 1 stalk celery, halved
1 fresh bay leaf
Salt, q.b.

To Finish

1 batch chickpea dough (page 29)
28g / 2 Tbsp olive oil
15g / 3 cloves garlic, finely chopped
Peel of 1 lemon, pith removed and peel finely chopped
30g / 2 Tbsp unsalted butter, cold and cubed
1 sprig rosemary, leaves removed from stems, half coarsely chopped and remainder left whole
Juice of ½ lemon
34g / 6 Tbsp finely grated parmigiano-reggiano

10   Add the chickpea cooking liquid and cooked chickpeas to the pan and stir to combine.

11   Using tongs or a pasta basket, remove the pasta from the pot and transfer to the sauté pan. Turn the heat up to medium. Alternate gently tossing and folding the pasta and sauce together with a wooden spoon for 30 to 45 seconds to marry. Be careful not to move the pasta in the pan too aggressively as it can break.

12   Add half of the lemon peel and gently toss to combine.

13   Add the butter and continue to toss. If the sauce tightens and you feel a bit of friction in the pan, add a splash of pasta cooking water to loosen it. It should glide when properly married.

14   Remove from the heat. Add the chopped rosemary, the lemon juice, and 11g / 2 Tbsp of the parmigiano and continue tossing until well integrated.

15   Divide the pasta into bowls or place on a serving platter. Spoon any chickpeas and sauce left in the pan over each bowl or the platter, adding a splash of pasta cooking water to the pan to loosen the sauce if needed. Garnish with the remaining lemon peel, whole rosemary leaves, and remaining parmigiano.

Nota bene

Cooking 454g / 1 lb dried chickpeas will yield quite a bit more than you need for this recipe. Cover and refrigerate the excess to use for salads or a stew.

Sheep's Milk Ricotta–Filled Occhi with Lemon and Bottarga

Ever since I very possibly made this shape up (see page 98), I've been wanting to use it in a dish I'd long imagined as spaghetti al limone in stuffed pasta form. I'd been workshopping it for weeks at Misi but couldn't get it quite right. From here, the story is a familiar one to anyone who's worked in a kitchen: We had bottarga in for a salad I'd been creating, and I figured what the hell, I'll shave it over the top of this dish as if it were parmigiano and see if it works.

To anyone acquainted with bottarga, and I hope you are, the combination of cured fish roe and ricotta, both staples of the Italian south, might sound like an error in judgment. But pairing fish and cheese is not a sin in the south, and here, I thought, is one good reason why. The tang and richness of ricotta combined with the minerally, briny bitterness of the bottarga kicked up with lemon has become one of my favorite combinations.

---

1   To make the filling, put the sheep's milk ricotta and cow's milk ricotta in a food processor and pulse just until they are as smooth as cake frosting and have a sheen, being careful not to process the mixture longer or it will break. Transfer to a bowl.

2   Season the ricotta mixture with salt q.b. It should taste well seasoned. Refrigerate until ready to use.

3   To finish, following the instructions for occhi on page 98, make 90 pieces with the pasta dough and filling.

4   Bring a large pot of water to a boil over high heat. Generously salt the water.

5   Add the occhi to the water and turn down the heat to bring the water to a gentle simmer instead of a rolling boil. The shape and filling are very delicate and will break if cooked over high heat. Cook for 1 to 2 minutes, until tender at the thickest closure point and the filling is warm and oozes when you cut into it.

6   While the pasta is cooking, place a large sauté pan over very low heat. Add the butter and 2 to 3 ladles (115 to 170g / ½ to ¾ cup) pasta cooking water. Swirl the contents of the pan to emulsify.

7   Using a spider or pasta basket, remove the pasta from the pot and transfer to the sauté pan. Swirl the pasta in the sauce for 30 to 45 seconds to marry, using a spoon to gently turn the pasta over and coat all sides. If the sauce begins to tighten, add a splash of pasta cooking water to loosen and continue swirling to marry. When the pasta is properly married, it will cling to the sauce and have a glossy sheen.

8   Transfer the pasta to a large serving platter or divide onto plates in a single layer. Add a few drops of pasta water to the sauté pan to loosen the sauce and drizzle over the platter or plates. Garnish with the lemon peel and, using your Microplane, a generous grating of bottarga.

Yields 6 to 8 servings

Filling

348g / 1½ cups sheep's
  milk ricotta (see "whipped"
  ricotta, page 139)
348g / 1½ cups cow's
  milk ricotta
Salt, q.b.

To Finish

1 batch egg dough (page 18)
75g / 5 Tbsp unsalted butter,
  cold and cubed
Peel of 1 lemon, pith removed
  and peel finely chopped
About ¼ lobe bottarga, or q.b.

Nota bene

Look for grey mullet bottarga, which tends to be slightly milder in flavor and less fishy than other types.

Espresso Tagliolini with Smoked Ricotta and Chiles

One Google search is all you need to know that, perhaps unsurprisingly, most espresso pasta is being peddled by coffee companies or espresso machine manufacturers. La Marzocco has a recipe for it. So does De'Longhi. And you best believe Lavazza isn't missing out. Mine can be traced back to a coffee shop in Venice, where I impulse-bought a bag of their espresso tagliatelle and then promptly forgot about it in my cupboard for a year and a half.

Leading up to the opening of Lilia, I came home with a chunk of Andrew Marcelli's addictive smoked ricotta peperoncino that his family makes in Abruzzo. I went digging in the cupboard and grabbed that espresso tagliatelle. I loved the juxtaposition of hot, bitter, smoky, and creamy and began working on it with different shapes. I landed on tagliolini, which have a way of giving the heady intensity of the dough a touch of elegance. It was meant to be on the opening menu at Lilia, but it was a dish too delicate to execute at volume. It's become a personal favorite of mine at home instead.

---

1   Following the instructions on page 60, make 624g / 1 lb 6 oz tagliolini with the pasta dough.

2   Bring a large pot of water to a boil over high heat. Generously salt the water.

3   Place a large sauté pan over low heat and add the olive oil. Add the garlic and gently cook until aromatic but without color, 10 to 15 seconds. Add 3 ladles (170g / ¾ cup) pasta cooking water and the butter. Swirl the contents of the pan to emulsify.

4   Add the tagliolini to the water and cook for 30 seconds to 1 minute, until tender but not soft.

5   Using tongs or a pasta basket, remove the pasta from the pot and transfer to the sauté pan. Toss for 30 seconds to 1 minute to marry the pasta and the sauce. If the sauce begins to tighten, add a splash of pasta cooking water and continue tossing to emulsify.

6   Remove from the heat. Season with pepper and chile flakes q.b. and continue tossing to combine.

7   Divide into bowls and coarsely grate the smoked ricotta over the top.

Yields 4 to 6 servings

1 batch espresso dough
   (page 28)
42g / 3 Tbsp olive oil
15g / 3 cloves garlic, thinly sliced
30g / 2 Tbsp unsalted butter,
   cold and cubed
Black pepper, q.b.
Dried red chile flakes, q.b.
114g / 4 oz Marcelli smoked
   ricotta peperoncino

Nota bene

You can find Marcelli's cheeses online (Marcelli Formaggi), but this particular cheese tends to be limited. If you don't have access to it, you can substitute smoked ricotta or ricotta salata and use more chile flakes to make up for the lost heat.

Corzetti with Sungold Tomatoes, Pecorino, and Herbs

Certain dishes end up defining a season for me, and most of them naturally hinge on ingredients that have a limited window of availability: ramps, spring garlic, chanterelles, white asparagus. In summer, it's this pasta in a sauce of barely cooked Sungold tomatoes, a little pecorino, butter, and fresh herbs. Austerity is easy at the height of summer.

This dish relies on one of the few techniques left over from my fine-dining days. I peel the tomatoes not just because I despise tomato skins—and certainly not to make my cooks' lives a living hell—but because when you remove that outer cloak, the tomatoes end up absorbing not only their marinade but also the sauce, becoming pillowy bombs of sweetness, acidity, and buttery richness.

---

1   To make the tomatoes, bring a large pot of water to a boil over high heat. Prepare an ice-water bath and set a colander in it.

2   Using a sharp paring knife, cut a small X in the bottom of each tomato. Drop the tomatoes into the boiling water and leave for 5 to 10 seconds to loosen their skins. Using a slotted spoon, transfer the tomatoes to the ice-water bath. After 30 seconds, transfer the tomatoes to a bowl. Working over another bowl to capture any juices, peel the tomatoes and discard the skins.

3   Add the olive oil and garlic to the bowl with the tomato juices. Then add the peeled tomatoes and salt and stir to mix. Set aside.

4   To finish, following the instructions for corzetti on page 113, make 80 pieces with the pasta dough.

5   Bring a large pot of water to a boil over high heat. Generously salt the water.

6   Add the corzetti to the water and cook for 1 to 2 minutes, until tender but not soft.

7   While the pasta is cooking, place a large sauté pan over low heat. Add the contents of the bowl holding the tomatoes and cook for 1 to 2 minutes, lightly mashing the tomatoes with the back of a spoon to release their juices.

8   Add the butter and 1 ladle (55g / ¼ cup) pasta cooking water. Swirl the contents of the pan to emulsify.

9   Using a spider or pasta basket, remove the pasta from the pot and transfer to the sauté pan. Turn the heat up to medium. Swirl the pasta in the sauce for 1 to 2 minutes to marry, using a spoon to gently turn the pasta over and coat all sides. If the sauce begins to tighten, add more pasta cooking water to loosen and continue swirling to marry. When the pasta is properly married, it will cling to the sauce and have a glossy sheen.

10   Divide the pasta among plates in a single layer. Spoon the sauce remaining in the pan over each plate. Garnish with the pecorino, chervil, basil, and marjoram.

Yields 4 to 6 servings

Tomatoes

500g / 1 lb 1½ oz Sungold
    tomatoes (from about
    2 pint-size baskets)
56g / ¼ cup olive oil
40g / 8 cloves garlic, finely
    chopped
Salt, q.b.

To Finish

1 batch egg dough (page 18)
30g / 2 Tbsp unsalted butter,
    cold and cubed
22g / ¼ cup finely grated
    pecorino romano
5g / ¼ cup tender chervil leaves
5g / ¼ cup small to medium
    basil leaves
5g / ¼ cup marjoram leaves

Spaghetti alla Chitarra with Lobster and Fresh Chiles

I like to think of this as fra diavolo (page 159) funneled through coastal California, by way of Sheepshead Bay, Brooklyn. In other words, it's a cleaner, greener, brighter version of the red-sauce standard that hinges on the interplay of the salinity of the lobster and the gentle heat and aromatics of the Fresno chiles and fresh herbs, which give the whole dish a cheerful lift.

I've made several variations on this but ended back here, with a stark template and uninvolved prep. It's all about brightness and ease, which is everything I look for in a summer seafood pasta.

1   To cook the lobsters, bring a large pot of water to a boil over high heat. Generously salt the water. Prepare a large ice-water bath.

2   Working with one lobster at a time, remove the body from the tail by twisting them in opposite directions. Reserve the body and tail separately. Clean and discard any impurities from the body and reserve for stock or discard. Repeat with the remaining lobsters.

3   Remove the claws and set aside.

4   Place the claws in the boiling water and set a timer for 3 minutes. When the timer goes off, add the tails and reset the timer for 3 minutes. After the second 3 minutes, the lobsters will be parcooked, which means they won't overcook when you put them in the sauce later.

5   Using tongs, remove the lobsters from the boiling water and place in the ice-water bath to stop the cooking and to cool.

6   Once cooled to the touch, remove the lobsters from the ice-water bath and place on a sheet pan or in a large bowl.

7   Now, the messy part of cracking the lobsters. For the tails, place one tail on its side on a kitchen towel and wrap the towel around it. Press down firmly until you feel the shell crack. Remove from the towel and, using scissors, cut down the inner spine. Pull the shell off and set the meat aside. Repeat with the remaining tails.

8   For the claws, place one on the kitchen towel and wrap the towel around it. Using the back of a heavy chef's knife, bang the claw until you hear a crack. Turn the claw over and bang it again. You should be able to remove the shell and keep the claw meat in a single piece. Remove the cartilage from the center of the claw. Repeat with the remaining claws and set the meat aside.

9   For the knuckles, use scissors to cut down each side and separate the meat from the shell. Set the meat aside.

Yields 4 to 6 servings

3 (570 to 680g / 1¼ to 1½ lb) live lobsters
1 batch egg dough (page 18)
42g / 3 Tbsp olive oil
15g / 3 cloves garlic, finely chopped
2 or 3 fresh chiles (preferably Fresno), thinly sliced crosswise
55g / ¼ cup dry white wine
30g / 2 Tbsp unsalted butter, cold and cubed
Peel of 1 lemon, pith removed and peel finely chopped
20g / ¼ cup finely chopped parsley
1 lemon, cut in half and seeds removed
20 small to medium basil leaves

10   Discard all of the shells or save them for stock. Cut the meat from the tails, claws, and knuckles into ¼-inch pieces and set aside.

11   Following the instructions for spaghetti alla chitarra on page 119, make 624g / 1 lb 6 oz with the pasta dough.

12   Bring a large pot of water to a boil over high heat. Generously salt the water.

13   Place a large sauté pan over low heat and add the olive oil. Add the garlic and gently cook until aromatic but without color, 10 to 15 seconds.

14   Add the chiles and cook for another 5 to 10 seconds. Add the wine and 1 ladle (55g / ¼ cup) pasta cooking water and cook for 20 to 30 seconds. Set aside.

15   Add the spaghetti alla chitarra to the water and cook for 2 to 3 minutes, until tender but not soft.

16   While the pasta is cooking, place the sauté pan back on the heat and add an additional 3 to 4 ladles (170g to 230g / ¾ to 1 cup) pasta cooking water. Add the lobster meat and stir to combine.

17   Using tongs or a pasta basket, remove the pasta from the pot and transfer to the sauté pan. Turn the heat up to medium. Add the butter and toss for 1 to 2 minutes to marry the pasta and the sauce. If the sauce begins to tighten, add a touch more pasta cooking water to loosen.

18   Remove from the heat. Add the lemon peel and parsley and toss to combine. Squeeze in the juice from the lemon halves, toss, and continue tasting to combine.

19   Divide into bowls and garnish with the basil.

Spaghetti with Colatura, Garlic, and Bread Crumbs

I've had variations on this dish all along the Amalfi Coast, and especially in the town of Cetara, a small fishing village between Positano and Salerno that is known for its production of funky, salty colatura. Colatura is essentially aged Italian fish sauce made from anchovies that are salt-cured and left to ferment, under pressure, in chestnut barrels. After three years in the barrel, their amber-colored liquid is drained and bottled. All along the coast of Campania you'll find spaghetti con la colatura di alici, which is essentially aglio e olio with a strong dose of colatura. It's like spaghetti alle vongole without the clams and with twice the brine.

This is a near replica, but I diverge in the addition of toasted bread crumbs, which give the dish texture and, to me, recall the flavor of garlic bread dipped in a briny bowl of clams.

1   To make the bread crumbs, spread the bread out on a sheet pan. Let sit at room temperature until crunchy on the outside with a bit of give in the interior, 2 to 3 hours.

2   Line a plate with a paper towel. Place a small saucepan over medium heat and add the olive oil. Add the bread crumbs and cook, stirring occasionally, until golden brown, 5 to 7 minutes.

3   Transfer the bread crumbs to the plate and let cool.

4   To finish, bring a large pot of water to a boil over high heat. Generously salt the water.

5   Add the spaghetti to the water and cook for 5 to 8 minutes, until al dente.

6   While the pasta is cooking, place a large sauté pan over low heat and add the olive oil. Add the garlic and gently cook until aromatic but without color, 10 to 15 seconds.

7   Add the anchovies and stir to break them up. Add 2 to 3 ladles (115g to 170g / ½ to ¾ cup) pasta cooking water and stir to combine.

8   Using tongs or a pasta basket, remove the pasta from the pot and transfer to the sauté pan. Turn the heat up to medium. Toss for 1 to 2 minutes to marry the pasta and the sauce. If the sauce begins to tighten, add a splash of room-temperature water to loosen and continue tossing to marry. (Colatura and anchovies have a high level of salinity, so adding too much pasta cooking water during the marriage can tip the dish into too-salty territory. Feel free to alternate between pasta water and fresh water or use only fresh water.)

9   Remove from the heat. Add the colatura and toss to incorporate. Add the parsley and chile flakes and continue tossing. Squeeze in the juice from the lemon halves and toss again to combine.

10   Divide the pasta into bowls and garnish with the bread crumbs.

Yields 4 to 6 servings

Bread Crumbs

30g / 1 piece fresh country bread, crust removed and bread torn into pea-size pieces
28g / 2 Tbsp olive oil

To Finish

624g / 1 lb 6 oz extruded spaghetti (page 123)
42g / 3 Tbsp olive oil
15g / 3 cloves garlic, finely chopped
40g / 6 to 8 oil-packed anchovy fillets, finely chopped
15g / 1 Tbsp colatura
20g / ¼ cup finely chopped parsley
2g / 1 tsp dried red chile flakes
1 lemon, cut in half and seeds removed

Corzetti with Chanterelles and Aged Goat Cheese

When chanterelles come into season, generally early summer through late fall, I have to restrain myself from turning my restaurants over to them entirely. I've got a chanterelle dish for every day of the year by now, but this is one of my favorites.

While Sardinia is known for its abundance of sheep and thus pecorino, there are two aged goat cheeses from the island that I love—pantaleo and capra sarda—used here in combination with the earthy sweetness of chanterelles, which I cook in garlic and white wine. While capra sarda tends to be a bit richer and deeper in profile, and pantaleo more herbal, they both have a buttery, lemony quality that I find irresistible.

1 Following the instructions for corzetti on page 113, make 80 pieces with the pasta dough.

2 Place a large sauté pan over medium heat. Add the olive oil, followed by the chanterelles. Stir to make sure the mushrooms are well coated in the oil. Cook until they begin to soften, 2 to 3 minutes.

3 Add the garlic, stir to combine, and cook for 20 to 30 seconds.

4 Add the wine and cook until the liquid has almost evaporated and the mushrooms are tender but not mushy, 5 to 8 minutes. (There should be a little pan juice released from the mushrooms; that will become part of your sauce.) Set aside.

5 Bring a large pot of water to a boil over high heat. Generously salt the water.

6 Add the corzetti to the water and cook for 1 to 2 minutes, until tender but not soft.

7 While the pasta is cooking, place the sauté pan back over low heat. Add 2 ladles (115g / ½ cup) pasta cooking water and stir to combine.

8 Using a spider or pasta basket, remove the pasta from the pot and transfer to the sauté pan. Turn the heat up to medium. Add the butter and swirl the pasta in the sauce for about 1 minute to marry, using a spoon to gently turn the pasta over and coat all sides. If the sauce begins to tighten, add a splash of pasta cooking water to loosen and continue swirling. When properly married, the sauce should coat the pasta and have a glossy sheen.

9 Divide onto plates in a single layer and garnish with the thyme and cheese.

Yields 4 to 6 servings

1 batch egg dough (page 18)
75g / ⅓ cup olive oil
454g / 1 lb chanterelles, cleaned, small and medium ones left whole and larger ones cut in half or into quarters
10g / 2 cloves garlic, finely chopped
220g / 1 cup dry white wine
45g / 3 Tbsp unsalted butter, cold and cubed
5 sprigs thyme, leaves removed from stems
57g / ½ cup coarsely grated aged Italian goat cheese (such as pantaleo or capra sarda)

Mandilli di Seta with Dried Cherry Tomatoes and Herbed Bread Crumbs

Like the corzetti with Sungold tomatoes on page 343, this is one of those perfect summer dishes for me—light, acidic, herbal, sweet, nice to look at. In their home region of Liguria, mandilli di seta (or saea, in dialect) are a common companion to pesto al Genovese. But I love how the shape, which translates to "silk handkerchiefs," plays against a minimalist palette and a bit of texture.

1   To make the tomatoes, preheat the oven to 225°F. Line two sheet pans with parchment paper.

2   Cut the tomatoes in half and place on one of the prepared sheet pans. Season them with the salt and drizzle with the oil.

3   Bake the tomatoes until slightly dried, 2 to 3 hours. They should lose about half their volume but still feel plump and juicy to the touch. Remove from the oven and set aside to cool. (They can be made ahead and stored in an airtight container in the refrigerator for up to 5 days.)

4   To make the bread crumbs, place the bread, parsley, chives, and tarragon in a food processor and pulse until the bread is reduced to fine crumbs and the bread and herbs are well mixed, 30 to 45 seconds. The mixture should be green.

5   Spread the bread crumb mixture on the second prepared sheet pan. Set aside to dry at room temperature for 2 to 3 hours. (They will not be quite as crispy as your typical bread crumbs.) The bread crumbs are best when freshly made but can be stored in an airtight container at room temperature for up to 24 hours before using.

6   To finish, following the instructions for mandilli di seta on page 51, make 624g / 1 lb 6 oz with the pasta dough.

7   Bring a large pot of water to a boil over high heat. Generously salt the water.

8   Place a large sauté pan over low heat and add 42g / 3 Tbsp of the oil. Add the garlic and gently cook until aromatic but without color, 10 to 15 seconds.

9   Add 2 to 3 ladles (115g to 170g / ½ to ¾ cup) pasta cooking water and the butter. Swirl the contents of the pan to emulsify.

10 Add the mandilli di seta to the water and cook for 20 to 30 seconds, until tender but not soft.

11 Using a spider, carefully remove the pasta from the pot and transfer to the sauté pan. Add the tomatoes. Turn the heat up to medium. Fold the pasta and the sauce together for 30 seconds to 1 minute to marry, gently turning the sheets of pasta over in the pan to coat all sides. If the sauce begins to tighten, add a splash of pasta cooking water to loosen and continue folding the pasta and sauce.

12 Using a large spoon, divide onto plates. Drizzle with the remaining olive oil and garnish with the pecorino and bread crumbs.

Yields 4 to 6 servings

Tomatoes

560 to 620g / 2 pints cherry tomatoes
18g / 2 Tbsp salt
42g / 3 Tbsp olive oil

Bread Crumbs

114g / 2 cups roughly torn country bread
20g / 1 cup packed parsley leaves
20g / ⅓ cup finely sliced chives
11g / ⅓ cup packed tarragon leaves

To Finish

1 batch egg dough (page 18)
70g / 5 Tbsp olive oil
15g / 3 cloves garlic, thinly sliced
60g / ¼ cup unsalted butter, cold and cubed
30g / ⅓ cup finely grated pecorino romano

Nota bene

A note of caution on the pasta itself: it's a very delicate shape, so go easy and avoid using tongs.

Stricchetti with Smashed Peas and Prosciutto

Peas and prosciutto are a classic springtime combination in Emilia-Romagna, where they are often similarly combined with stricchetti (aka farfalle) or tagliatelle and a generous dusting of parmigiano-reggiano. In Italian American cuisine, they are also canon, perhaps most famously as an Alfredo invader. This is my take on the former.

This dish relies on both fresh peas in season and a technique that gets them soft enough to mash without sacrificing their color or flavor. I blanch and shock the peas three times, then mash them while drizzling in olive oil to make a paste that breaks down into a sauce when the dish is married. This is far more pea-forward than the original and is yet another dish that makes the vegetable, rather than its porky counterpart, the star.

1   To make the peas, bring a small saucepan of water to a boil over high heat. Generously salt the water.

2   Prepare a salted ice-water bath and place a colander in it. (The salt will help preserve the vibrant green color of your peas.)

3   Add the peas to the boiling water and blanch until they begin to soften, 1 to 2 minutes. Using a spider, transfer the peas to the ice-water bath. Keep the pot of water boiling; you will use it two more times.

4   Once the peas have cooled, repeat the process of dumping them into the boiling water and then shocking them in the ice water two more times, until they are soft enough to smash easily with a fork or between your fingertips.

5   Remove the peas from the ice-water bath for the final time and turn them out onto a kitchen towel to drain.

6   Transfer the peas to a bowl and begin to smash them with a fork. Continue smashing while drizzling in the olive oil to create a rough mash with the consistency of a rustic pesto. Set aside.

7   To finish, following the instructions for stricchetti on page 75, make 624g / 1 lb 6 oz with the pasta dough.

8   Bring a large pot of water to a boil over high heat. Generously salt the water.

9   While the water is heating, place a sauté pan over low heat and add the olive oil. Add the onion and gently cook until soft but without color, 5 to 8 minutes. Add the garlic and gently cook until aromatic but without color, 10 to 15 seconds.

10 Add the crushed peas and stir to combine. Set aside.

continued

Yields 4 to 6 servings

Smashed Peas
300g / 2 cups shelled English peas
56g / ¼ cup olive oil

To Finish
1 batch egg dough (page 18)
42g / 3 Tbsp olive oil
370g / 1 large onion, finely diced
10g / 2 cloves garlic, finely chopped
75g / 5 Tbsp unsalted butter, cold and cubed
45g / ½ cup finely grated parmigiano-reggiano
1 (80g / scant 3 oz) piece prosciutto, 40g / ¼ cup finely diced and 40g / ¼ cup julienned
Black pepper, q.b.

Stricchetti with Smashed Peas and Prosciutto

continued

11   Add the stricchetti to the water and cook for 2 to 3 minutes, until tender at the center of the shape.

12   While the pasta is cooking, put the sauté pan over low heat. Add 3 ladles (170g / ¾ cup) pasta cooking water and the butter. Swirl the contents of the pan to emulsify.

13   Using a spider or pasta basket, remove the pasta from the pot and transfer to the sauté pan. Turn the heat up to medium. Toss for 1 to 2 minutes to marry the pasta and the sauce.

14   Remove from the heat. Add half of the parmigiano while tossing or stirring to combine. Add the diced prosciutto and continue tossing or stirring to integrate. If the sauce begins to tighten, add a splash of pasta cooking water to loosen. When the pasta is properly married, it will cling to the sauce and have a glossy sheen.

15   Divide onto plates and garnish with the julienned prosciutto, the remaining parmigiano, and with pepper q.b.

Tagliatelle with Matsutake Mushrooms, Lemon, and Mint

Matsutake mushrooms—stubby and firm with a piney herbal quality—are one of those cheffy ingredients that I'd never really been able to find a true use for. When faced with the mushroom kingdom's two firm, upscale species, I'd always choose porcini. But matsutakes are another ingredient entirely, and this dish was the first time I figured out how not only to wrangle their chewiness and flavor profile but also to celebrate both. The addition of mint was a means to amplify the inherent green quality of the mushrooms and an ode to a dish I had in Rome with porcini and nepitella, a perennial herb with an aromatic profile that falls between the mint we know and marjoram.

1   Following the instructions for tagliatelle on page 57, make 624g / 1 lb 6 oz with the pasta dough.

2   Clean the dirt from the mushrooms by peeling off the first layer of flesh on the stems with a paring knife. Be careful to avoid taking off too much. With a slightly damp towel, gently but thoroughly clean away any remaining dirt.

3   Slice the mushrooms very thinly, cutting through both the caps and the stems so you end up with slices about ⅛ inch thick by about 2 inches long.

4   Place a large sauté pan over high heat and add 56g / ¼ cup of the olive oil. Add about one-third of the mushrooms in an even layer and sear, turning to ensure even coloring, until golden brown around the edges and cooked through, 5 to 7 minutes. (Matsutakes are very meaty mushrooms, so they will still feel firm but have a glossy sheen.) Transfer the mushrooms to a plate or bowl and set aside.

5   Repeat this process, adding 56g / ¼ cup of the olive oil with each batch of mushrooms until you have cooked all of the mushrooms. Reserve the sauté pan.

6   Bring a large pot of water to a boil over high heat. Generously salt the water.

7   While the water is heating, return the sauté pan to low heat and add the remaining 14g / 1 Tbsp olive oil. Add the garlic and gently cook until aromatic but without color, 10 to 15 seconds. Return the mushrooms to the pan and stir to combine.

8   Add the tagliatelle to the water and cook for 30 seconds to 1 minute, until tender but not soft.

9   While the pasta is cooking, add 2 to 3 ladles (115g to 170g / ½ to ¾ cup) pasta cooking water to the pan. Add the butter and swirl the contents of the pan to emulsify.

continued

Yields 4 to 6 servings

1 batch egg dough (page 18)
454g / 1 lb matsutake
  mushrooms
168g / ¾ cup plus 14g / 1 Tbsp
  olive oil
25g / 5 cloves garlic, finely
  chopped
60g / ¼ cup unsalted butter,
  cold and cubed
45g / ½ cup finely grated
  parmigiano-reggiano
Peel of 1 lemon, pith removed
  and peel finely chopped
20g / ¼ cup finely chopped
  parsley
30 mint leaves
Black pepper, q.b.

Tagliatelle with Matsutake Mushrooms, Lemon, and Mint

continued

10   Using tongs or a pasta basket, remove the pasta from the pot and transfer to the sauté pan. Turn the heat up to medium. Toss for 1 to 2 minutes to marry the pasta and the sauce.

11   Remove the pan from the heat and add half of the parmigiano. Add the lemon peel and parsley and continue tossing to combine. If the sauce begins to tighten, add a splash of pasta cooking water to loosen. When the pasta is properly married, it will cling to the sauce and have a glossy sheen.

12   Divide into bowls and garnish with the remaining parmigiano, the mint, and with pepper q.b.

Nota bene

Matsutake mushrooms have a short fall season, from September through November, and can be tough to find in that window. If you can't get your hands on them, you can substitute porcini or king oyster (aka trumpet royale) mushrooms. Although their profiles differ from that of the matsutake, both are meaty enough to keep the texture of the dish intact.

Contorni

I tend to think good old-fashioned Jewish guilt is at play in making vegetables so central to my cooking. Perhaps it's my way of apologizing to my mother for refusing to even lock eyes with anything green when I was growing up. A bit of repentance. She's appreciative, for what it's worth, but suspects her green beans probably deserved my disdain.

My approach to vegetable contorni, or side dishes, is simple: treat them like the main event. Offer them the same reverence you might a great piece of fish or meat and apply the same techniques and principles. Braise them, sear them, baste them, poach them, marinate them. When I opened Misi, with a menu of just ten pastas and ten vegetables, I wasn't trying to be contrarian or push an agenda. I was just putting together a menu that would allow guests to enjoy what I believe to be an ideal meal: a bowl of fresh pasta and a well-cooked vegetable.

With that belief in mind, I couldn't possibly put eighty pasta recipes to paper and not include a way to complete the meal. The following fifteen recipes are dishes I crave alongside pasta, chosen not just because I eat them with frequency but also because most of them include preparations that can apply to vegetables across seasonal availability. Hot honey is as at home on kabocha squash as it is on roasted tomatoes; the mint pesto is a worthy companion to pasta or crostini; and it's no exaggeration when I say that the garlic vinaigrette that cloaks grilled summer beans is truly good on everything, provided you're like me and you crave garlic and vinegar with the same passion as gelato.

Take these recipes, in part, as lessons in vegetable cookery techniques. Feel free to mix and match with whatever seasonal produce you have available to you when you decide to make yourself some pasta for dinner. Be as bold as your vegetables should be.

Charred Treviso with Walnuts and Saba

When I was opening Lilia, I made a concerted effort to use less cheese, not because I was on a diet (even though I was), but because I recognized that cheese had become a bit of a crutch in my cooking—or perhaps more accurately, a reflex. I started asking myself what truly needed it and what was actually improved without it. A lot of dishes, like this one, fell in that latter camp. What I love about this dish is the depth of flavor and richness you get from the saba, aka mosto cotto, or reduced grape must (think of it as a less acidic, slightly fruitier aged balsamic). It counters both the bitterness of the Treviso, a type of radicchio, and the acidity of both orange juice and red wine vinegar.

---

1   Heat a grill to medium or place a grill pan over medium-high heat on the stove top.

2   Cut the Treviso heads in half lengthwise, leaving the core on to keep the halves intact.

3   Place the heads in a bowl and drizzle 56g / ¼ cup of the olive oil over them. Turn them in the bowl to make sure they are well coated on all sides.

4   Season well on all sides with salt q.b., being sure to peel back the leaves a bit to season the interior.

5   Place the Treviso halves, cut side down, on the grill or grill pan and cook until they begin to wilt and lightly char, 3 to 5 minutes.

6   Turn the Treviso over and cook until there is an even char on all sides, 3 to 5 minutes longer.

7   Remove the Treviso from the grill or grill pan. Cut the core off of each half and separate the leaves. Transfer the leaves to a bowl.

8   Squeeze the juice from the orange halves into the bowl. Add the vinegar and orange peel and stir to combine.

9   Transfer one-third of the leaves to a serving bowl. Add a generous drizzle of saba, one-third of the walnuts, and pepper q.b. Repeat with the remaining leaves and walnuts, one-third at a time, to make two more layers, adding a drizzle of saba and some pepper to each layer. The saba plays an integral role in the dish, so after the first layer, taste the dish and adjust so you are adding enough saba as you build.

10   Drizzle the remaining 28g / 2 Tbsp olive oil over the top.

Yields 4 to 6 servings

4 heads Treviso radicchio
84g / 6 Tbsp olive oil
Salt, q.b.
1 orange, halved and seeds removed
55g / ¼ cup red wine vinegar
Peel of 1 orange, pith removed and peel julienned
Saba, q.b.
50g / ½ cup walnuts, coarsely chopped
Black pepper, q.b.

Bitter Lettuces and Herbs with House Vinaigrette

It's just a salad, you say. You would be right. But everyone needs a house salad and a good house vinaigrette to match. This is mine: a combination of bitter greens, herbs, and a Dijon vinaigrette kicked up with garlic that is integrated via Microplane for even distribution. The inclusion of Dijon might seem like a diversion from the Italian pantry, but together with the lettuces, herbs, red onions, and shaved parmigiano, the salad still tastes firmly Italian. Make sure to prepare the dressing ahead so the garlic has time to bloom, and be generous with the parmigiano. I use a combination of Treviso, escarole, and Little Gem, but feel free to mix and match.

1   To make the vinaigrette, add the mustard to a bowl.

2   Using a Microplane, grate the garlic into the mustard and stir to incorporate.

3   Add the red wine vinegar to the bowl. While stirring, drizzle in the olive oil.

4   Season with the salt and pepper q.b. Measure 84g / 6 Tbsp vinaigrette and set aside. Transfer the remainder to an airtight container and refrigerate for up to 3 days for another use.

5   To finish, remove the outer leaves and the cores of the lettuce, Treviso, and escarole. Separate the leaves from the Little Gem and the Treviso. Tear the escarole leaves into pieces about the size of the Little Gem leaves.

6   Transfer the lettuces to a large mixing bowl. Add the parsley, basil, onion, and reserved vinaigrette and mix well. Season with salt and pepper q.b.

7   Transfer the salad to a serving bowl. Shave the parmigiano over the top.

Yields 4 servings

Vinaigrette

12g / 1 Tbsp Dijon mustard
5g / 1 clove garlic
55g / ¼ cup red wine vinegar
112g / ½ cup olive oil
Salt, q.b.
Black pepper, q.b.

To Finish

1 head Little Gem lettuce
1 head Treviso
1 small head escarole
10g / ½ cup packed parsley
    leaves
6g / ½ cup lightly packed small
    basil leaves
62g / ¼ red onion, thinly sliced
Salt, q.b.
Black pepper, q.b.
1 (112g / 4 oz) piece parmigiano-
    reggiano

Escarole with Anchovy Vinaigrette, Ricotta Salata, and Crispy Garlic

This dish is the ultimate expression of my flavor preferences. There's a slight bitterness from the escarole, savory depth and salinity from the anchovies, richness from the ricotta, texture from the garlic, and lots and lots of acidity. This dish would not have been a Lilia standard if it weren't for Patty Gentry of Early Girl Farms on Long Island, whom I've worked with since we opened. Her escarole is sweeter and less bitter when cooked and works perfectly as a "quick pick-up." It's a dish that can be made without a ton of prep.

1 To make the vinaigrette, combine the anchovies, chile flakes, vinegar, and olive oil in a bowl and mix well. Set aside until ready to use.

2 To make the crispy garlic, line a plate with paper towels. Place a sauté pan over low heat and add the olive oil. Add the garlic and cook, stirring occasionally, until the slices begin to turn golden and harden slightly, 3 to 5 minutes. They will curl up a bit and cluster together as they cook, so be sure to stir occasionally to ensure even coloring.

3 Using a slotted spoon, remove the garlic and place in one layer on the paper towels to drain. If they aren't fully crispy, do not worry. They will crisp up as they drain and dry.

4 To finish, discard any bruised outer leaves from the escarole, then cut the escarole in half lengthwise and rinse well to remove any dirt from the inner leaves. Pat dry with a kitchen towel.

5 Place a large sauté pan over high heat. Add the olive oil.

6 Season the cut side of the escarole with salt q.b., making sure to open the leaves to get inside. (The anchovy and ricotta salata are both salty, so don't go too heavy.)

7 Add the escarole, cut side down, to the pan. Place another heavy pan on top of the escarole to weight it down and get the most possible surface contact.

8 Cook the escarole until it is golden on the cut surface and wilted but still has a bit of bite, 3 to 5 minutes.

9 Turn off the heat and flip the escarole over in the pan. Add the vinegar to the pan. It will create a bit of steam and evaporate rather quickly.

10 Using tongs, transfer the escarole, seared side up, to a serving platter. Spoon the vinaigrette over the escarole, shave the ricotta salata over the top, and garnish with the crispy garlic.

Yields 4 to 6 servings

Vinaigrette

85g / 15 to 18 oil-packed
    anchovy fillets, finely
    chopped
3g / 1½ tsp dried red chile flakes
14g / 1 Tbsp red wine vinegar
20g / 1 Tbsp plus 1½ tsp olive oil

Crispy Garlic

224g / 1 cup olive oil
50g / 10 cloves garlic, very thinly
    sliced on a mandoline

To Finish

1 large head escarole
56g / ¼ cup olive oil
Salt, q.b.
20g / 1 Tbsp plus 1 tsp red wine
    vinegar
1 small (20g / ¾ oz) piece ricotta
    salata

Snap Peas with Black Pepper, Lemon, and Lardo

Perhaps I should be embarrassed to admit that I am more proud of this dish, barely cooked and only four ingredients, than most of what I've made over the last two decades. The intent was to turn the idea of the traditional springtime combination of peas and prosciutto on its head. You still get the greenness, the sweetness, and the funk, but the format is different. I use raw snap peas at the height of the season and trade out the prosciutto for melted lardo, which is poured over the top of the dish. It provides a diffuse richness that still eats clean and lets the peas own the plate. The dish is then topped with plenty of lemon and a liberal amount of black pepper, itself a nod to that classic combination of pork and pepper that forms the foundation of more than one Roman classic. I have only one rule with this dish, which is to please, please eat it with your hands.

1   Remove the peas and lemons from the refrigerator and let them come to room temperature.

2   Cut the lardo into 2-inch cubes. Place a small saucepan over low heat. Add the lardo and slowly render until the pieces have liquefied, 6 to 8 minutes. Strain through a fine-mesh strainer (lardo is cured with a lot of spices and herbs, and you want the fat to be very clean) into a separate small saucepan. You should have about 40g / 3 Tbsp.

3   Remove the stem from each snap pea by snapping it from the top and pulling the stringy part with it (this part can be a bit tough to bite through, so it's best to remove).

4   Lay each pea on its side and, using a sharp paring knife, split it in half along the seam; you are cutting right through the center so that when you open up the pod, like a book, each side should have sliced peas still attached. Try to keep the halved peas on each side intact as much as possible.

5   As you cut the peas, carefully lay the halves, cut side up, in a single layer on a serving platter. A little overlapping is okay.

6   Place the saucepan with the lardo over low heat. Heat until the lardo is just warmed, about 30 seconds.

7   Drizzle the lardo over the snap peas. If the lardo or peas are too cool, the lardo will tighten up and coagulate. Be sure the peas are at room temp and that you warm the lardo sufficiently.

8   Squeeze the juice from the lemon halves evenly over the snap peas. Drizzle with the olive oil and season with the pepper and salt.

Yields 4 to 6 servings

300g / 10 oz snap peas
   (about 60)
1½ lemons, cut in half and
   seeds removed
1 (3 by 1-inch) piece lardo
28g / 2 Tbsp olive oil
18 grinds black pepper
3g / 1 tsp flaky sea salt

Broccoli Rabe with Parmigiano and Calabrian Chile Oil

I've always been equal parts alarmed and intrigued by the Italian propensity to cook vegetables to their last gasp. I tend to cook most of my green vegetables to al dente, preferring to salvage bite and vibrancy. This dish is an exception. It's not quite to Italian standards, but I do take it just past crunch to blunt some of the bitterness of the rabe and give it a comforting textural creaminess. Note that good vintage-dated olive oil is paramount here. Be sure to use the most recent release, which will always be the year prior to the one we're in, as you'll get more brightness and flavor from it.

1   Bring a large pot of water to a boil over high heat. Generously salt the water.

2   Cut the tough bottoms off the broccoli rabe, trimming off about ¼ inch.

3   Add the broccoli rabe to the water and cook until quite tender but still bright green, 2 to 3 minutes.

4   Drain the broccoli rabe and wrap in a kitchen towel to absorb any excess water.

5   Spread 30g / ⅓ cup of the parmigiano on a serving platter.

6   Layer half of the broccoli rabe over the cheese. Squeeze the juice from two lemon halves over the top.

7   Drizzle 28g / 2 Tbsp of the olive oil over the top.

8   Sprinkle half of the remaining parmigiano evenly over the broccoli, covering it fully.

9   Place the remaining broccoli on top of the first layer. Squeeze the juice from the remaining lemon halves over the top. Drizzle with the remaining 28g / 2 Tbsp olive oil and then with the chile oil. Top with the remaining parmigiano and serve warm.

Yields 4 to 6 servings

570g / 1¼ lb broccoli rabe (about 2 bunches)
135g / 1½ cups finely grated parmigiano-reggiano
2 lemons, cut in half and seeds removed
56g / ¼ cup olive oil
28g / 2 Tbsp Calabrian chile oil (drained from jarred Calabrian chiles)

Nota bene

If you want to prepare this dish ahead of time, set up an ice-water bath and shock the broccoli rabe in the ice water, then drain. When ready to serve, dunk the broccoli rabe in boiling water to reheat.

Olive Oil–Poached Zucchini with Grilled Bread and Oregano

Who among us does not love panzanella? Who cannot salute a salad made of bread that still dares to call itself a salad? This dish really began with the technique of olive oil poaching, which I like to use for squashes and mushrooms, in particular. Zucchini on its own doesn't have a ton of bold flavor, and while the tendency to grill or sauté it is just fine, too often the subject ends up tasting like the method. Poaching in olive oil is meant to bolster its mild, sweet profile, which gets a subtle leg up by way of the aromatics in the oil. This dish is all about preserving cleanliness of flavor and countering the softness of the zucchini with torn grilled bread. It has since become my favorite go-to summer "salad."

1   To make the roasted garlic, preheat the oven to 300°F.

2   Lay a double layer of aluminum foil large enough to wrap the garlic on your work surface. Place the garlic heads in the center of the foil. Drizzle with the olive oil, then enclose the garlic completely in the foil, sealing all of the edges well.

3   Place the foil packet in the oven and roast the garlic until lightly golden and soft enough to mash easily, 1 to 1½ hours. Set the packet aside to cool.

4   Unwrap the garlic and cut each head in half horizontally to remove the top quarter.

5   Squeeze the garlic from its papery sheaths into a bowl and mash with a fork until creamy. Measure out 90g / 6 Tbsp roasted garlic and set aside until ready to use. Transfer the remainder to an airtight container and refrigerate for up to 1 week for another use.

6   To make the garlic butter, place a sauté pan over low heat and add the olive oil. Add the chopped garlic and gently cook until aromatic but without color, 10 to 15 seconds. Remove from the heat.

7   Place the butter, sautéed garlic, roasted garlic, and lemon peel in a bowl and fold the ingredients together until well integrated. Set aside until ready to use, or transfer to an airtight container and refrigerate for up to 1 week.

8   To make the zucchini, cut them lengthwise into quarters. Cut the quarters into 1-inch cubes.

9   Spread the zucchini cubes on a sheet pan and sprinkle evenly with the salt. Let sit at room temperature for about 30 minutes. This will help season the zucchini internally and draw out some of the moisture.

continued

Yields 6 to 8 servings

Roasted Garlic

400g / 4 large heads garlic
14g / 1 Tbsp olive oil

Garlic Butter

14g / 1 Tbsp olive oil
5g / 1 clove garlic, finely
    chopped
228g / 1 cup unsalted butter,
    at room temperature
Peel of ¼ lemon, pith removed
    and peel finely chopped

Poached Zucchini

1kg / 6 to 8 large zucchini
18g / 2 Tbsp salt
1.5kg / 7 cups olive oil
150g / 30 cloves garlic
Peels of 5 lemons, pith removed
6 to 8 sprigs oregano

To Finish

4 (1-inch-thick) slices country
    bread
112g / ½ cup olive oil
30g / 6 cloves garlic, thinly
    sliced
Peels of 2 lemons, pith removed
    and peels finely chopped
3g / 1½ tsp dried red chile flakes
42g / ¼ cup small salt-packed
    capers, rinsed
55g / ¼ cup red wine vinegar
Salt, q.b.
10 sprigs oregano, leaves
    removed from stems

Olive Oil–Poached Zucchini with Grilled Bread and Oregano

continued

10   Place a large saucepan over low heat. Add the olive oil, garlic, lemon peels, and oregano and gently heat until slightly warm and the flavors have come together, 5 to 10 minutes.

11   Add the zucchini and gently poach in the olive oil, stirring and testing periodically to check for doneness, 20 to 25 minutes. The zucchini should retain its bright green color and be tender but not mushy.

12   Remove the pan from the heat and transfer the zucchini to a sheet pan to cool more rapidly. Reserve the olive oil. Once both the zucchini and olive oil are cool, recombine them and set aside until ready to use. Or combine them, transfer to a container, and refrigerate for up to 5 days, then, when ready to use, remove from the refrigerator and bring to room temperature. (You can speed this up by gently heating the zucchini in the olive oil.)

13   To finish, heat a grill to medium or preheat your broiler and position an oven rack closest to the heat source.

14   Slather the garlic butter on both sides of each bread slice. Place the bread on the grill or arrange the slices on a sheet pan and place under the broiler. Toast, turning once, until golden brown and slightly crunchy, 1 to 2 minutes on each side.

15   Remove the bread from the grill or broiler and place on a wire rack to cool slightly.

16   Place a large sauté pan over low heat and add 28g / 2 Tbsp of the olive oil. Add the garlic and gently cook until aromatic but without color, 10 to 15 seconds. Set aside to cool.

17   Tear the bread into 1- to 2-inch pieces.

18   Remove the zucchini from the olive oil and place it in a large bowl along with the gently cooked garlic, the lemon peels, chile flakes, capers, vinegar, and the remaining 84g / 6 Tbsp olive oil. Toss to combine. Add the torn bread.

19   Season with salt q.b. and add most of the oregano leaves, reserving a few for garnish. Toss to combine.

20   Divide into bowls and garnish with the remaining oregano.

Nota bene

Be sure to soak the capers in cold water, refreshing the water every 15 minutes or so, until they are briny but not salty, about 2 hours. The zucchini poaching oil can be strained and reserved to poach other vegetables.

Roasted Eggplant with Olives and Sun-Dried Tomato Vinaigrette

Puttanesca—the briny, sweet-and-sour sauce native to Napoli—need not be reserved for pasta alone. Here I slightly alter the iconic combination of olives, capers, anchovy, and tomato to create a warm vinaigrette for eggplant that has been slow roasted until creamy. I call for sweet, savory sun-dried tomatoes.

1   To make the eggplant, place the quarters skin side down on a sheet pan. Salt and let sit for 10 to 15 minutes. Use a paper towel to wipe off any moisture that leaches out.

2   Place a large sauté pan over medium heat. Add half of the olive oil. Add half of the eggplant quarters to the pan flesh side down and cook, turning to ensure even cooking, until golden brown and tender, 6 to 8 minutes. Eggplant absorbs a lot of oil so you may need to add more as you go if the pan starts to look dry.

3   Flip the eggplant over so the skin side is down and cook for another 1 to 2 minutes until the flesh is soft and cooked all the way through.

4   Add half of the red wine vinegar to the pan and cook until evaporated, 1 to 2 minutes. Remove the eggplant from the pan and set aside. Repeat with the second batch of eggplant and remaining olive oil and vinegar.

5   To make the vinaigrette base, place a small saucepan over low heat. Add the olive oil and the garlic and cook until aromatic but without color, 10 to 15 seconds. Add the tomato paste and cook, stirring, until it starts to turn a deeper red and is well combined with the olive oil and garlic, 3 to 5 minutes. Remove from the heat and set aside to cool.

6   Place the sun-dried tomatoes in a small bowl and add warm water to cover. Set aside until just softened, 3 to 5 minutes.

7   Add the olives to a food processor and pulse until very fine, but not pureed. Transfer to a mixing bowl.

8   Drain the tomatoes and place in the food processor. Add the tomato paste mixture and pulse until a uniform paste forms.

9   Add the paste to the bowl with the olives and add the anchovies, capers, orange peel, and the chile oil and fold to combine. Set aside 120g / ½ cup. Transfer the remainder to an airtight container, cover with a layer of olive oil and refrigerate for up to 2 weeks for another use.

10   To finish, juice the orange. Add the red wine vinegar, orange juice, olive oil, and chile oil to the reserved base in a bowl and stir to combine.

11   Place the eggplant in a large mixing bowl. Add the vinaigrette and gently stir to coat. You want the eggplant to maintain its shape.

12   Transfer the eggplant to a serving platter and garnish with the basil leaves.

Yields 4 to 6 servings

Eggplant

907g / 4 Japanese eggplants, quartered lengthwise and widthwise
9g / 1 Tbsp salt
112g / ½ cup olive oil, plus more q.b.
55g / ¼ cup red wine vinegar

Vinaigrette Base

38g / 2 Tbsp plus 2 tsp olive oil, plus more q.b.
15g / 3 cloves garlic, finely chopped
48g / 3 Tbsp tomato paste
100g / 1⅔ dry-packed cups sun-dried tomatoes
149g / 1 cup plus 1 Tbsp pitted Taggiasca olives
25g / 4 to 5 anchovies, finely chopped
74g / ¼ cup plus 3 Tbsp salt-packed capers, rinsed and finely chopped
1 orange, ¼ peel, pith removed and finely chopped and fruit reserved
½ tsp Calabrian chile oil

To Finish

55g / ¼ cup red wine vinegar
84g / 6 Tbsp olive oil
7g / 1½ tsp Calabrian chile oil
2 sprigs basil, stems removed

Nota bene

The recipe will yield quite a bit more vinaigrette base than you'll need. Spread it on crostini or use as a sauce for pasta.

Fennel with Celery, Walnuts, and Parmigiano

When it comes to salads, fennel is not given the chance to be the main event often enough. This dish is a variation on a salad I had in Sardinia that combined celery, fennel, celery leaves, and no less than a half lobe of bottarga shaved in sheets over the top. This removes the bottarga, which is often dubbed the "parmigiano of the sea," and replaces it with actual parmigiano, similarly shaved in generous sheets to finish. It's a hearty salad that can double as a meal on its own.

1   Stand a fennel bulb upright and cut in half lengthwise. Make a deep triangular cut to remove the toughest part of the core. Repeat with the remaining bulbs. One at a time, thinly slice each half, cut side down, on a mandoline.

2   Break apart the celery head into stalks and trim off the tops and bottoms. Remove the leaves, coarsely chop, and reserve.

3   Using a vegetable peeler, lightly peel the celery stalks, removing their stringy exterior layer. Then, using the mandoline or a knife, slice crosswise on the diagonal about ⅛ inch thick.

4   Combine the fennel and celery in a large bowl. Add 45g / ½ cup of the parmigiano and 45g / ½ cup of the walnuts. Squeeze the juice from the lemon halves over the bowl and add the olive oil. Add the celery leaves, reserving a tablespoon or so for garnish.

5   Mix everything together and season with salt q.b.

6   Divide into bowls and garnish with the remaining nuts, parmigiano, and celery leaves and with chile flakes q.b.

Yields 4 to 6 servings

1.5kg / 5 fennel bulbs, stems and fronds removed
500g / 1 head celery
85g / ¾ cup shaved parmigiano-reggiano
90g / ¾ cup chopped walnuts
3 lemons, cut in half and seeds removed
56g / ¼ cup olive oil
Salt, q.b.
Dried red chile flakes, q.b.

Porcini with Rosemary and Garlic

I can trace this dish back to a lunch I had in Rome about thirteen years ago with my friend Craig. It was early in my career cooking Italian, and I was still trying to grasp both the template and the spirit of it and to train myself away from the New American food I'd been making. The combination of mushrooms, garlic, and rosemary was then, as it remains now, so obvious, but it was about the product: the subtle, mellow earthiness of porcini, the sweetness and bitter edge of caramelized garlic, the heady pop of rosemary. Italian cooking is only simple because it's imbued with a confidence in ingredients that goes back centuries. That clicked for me in that moment. I've kept this dish close since.

1   To make the caramelized garlic, place a large sauté pan over low heat and add the olive oil. Add the garlic, arranging the cloves in a single layer. Cook slowly, stirring to ensure even cooking, until they are light golden brown and soft enough to mash, 7 to 10 minutes.

2   Remove from the heat and let cool. Set aside until ready to use, or transfer the garlic and oil to an airtight container and refrigerate for up to 3 days.

3   To finish, clean the dirt from the mushrooms by peeling off the first layer of flesh on the stems with a paring knife. Be careful to avoid taking off too much. With a slightly damp towel, gently but thoroughly clean away any remaining dirt.

4   Cut the mushrooms in half lengthwise.

5   Place a sauté pan over low heat and add 42g / 3 Tbsp of the olive oil. Add the chopped garlic and gently cook until aromatic but without color, 10 to 15 seconds. Set aside.

6   Place a large sauté pan over medium heat and add the remaining 56g / ¼ cup olive oil. Add the porcini, cut side down, in a single layer. Place another pan on top to weight them down for a more even sear (they tend to curl a bit when they hit the pan) and cook for 1 to 2 minutes. Remove the top pan and continue to cook until golden brown and glossy, 2 to 3 minutes.

7   Turn the mushrooms over and continue cooking until golden brown and cooked through but not mushy, another 2 to 3 minutes. You may need to add a bit more olive oil, as mushrooms absorb quite a bit as they cook. During the last minute of cooking, season the mushrooms on both sides with salt q.b. and toss. Set aside.

8   Remove the caramelized cloves from their oil and transfer to a large bowl. Lightly mash them with the back of a fork.

9   Add the mushrooms and gently cooked chopped garlic, then squeeze in the juice from the lemon halves and stir to combine.

10   Transfer the mushrooms, cut side up, to a serving platter or divide onto plates. Garnish with the lemon peel, rosemary, a drizzle of olive oil, and sea salt q.b.

Yields 4 to 6 servings

Caramelized Garlic
56g / ¼ cup olive oil
75g / 15 whole cloves garlic

To Finish
1.2kg / 2½ lb porcini mushrooms (about 8)
42g / 3 Tbsp plus 56g / ¼ cup olive oil, plus more q.b.
30g / 6 cloves garlic, finely chopped
Salt, q.b.
1 lemon, cut in half and seeds removed
Peel of ½ lemon, pith removed and peel finely chopped
3 sprigs rosemary, leaves removed from stems
Flaky sea salt, q.b.

Nota bene

It's impossible to replicate the flavor and texture of porcini, but they can be hard to find. If you must make a swap, king oyster (aka trumpet royale) mushrooms are the best substitute.

Asparagus with Mint Pesto and Almonds

Many of my pasta dishes center on just a few ingredients, which are then repeated in a single dish in different ways. A piece of garlic, for instance, cooked four different ways (see page 273), each meant to give a different profile and texture. My approach to vegetables often plays out in a similar way. This dish is essentially blanched spring asparagus with a pesto made from mint, parsley, and almonds. I then take those ingredients—essentially the prep, pre-pesto—and incorporate them into a garnish. What might seem like a redundancy ends up giving the dish another layer of texture and brightness.

1   To make the pesto, bring a large pot of water to a boil over high heat. Generously salt the water. Set up a salted ice-water bath.

2   Add the mint and parsley leaves to the boiling water and blanch for 10 to 15 seconds. This will help them retain their brightness.

3   Using a spider, transfer the leaves to the ice-water bath to stop the cooking. Let them sit in the ice-water bath until thoroughly chilled, about 5 minutes. Otherwise they may continue to oxidize when you process them, as blending introduces a little heat.

4   Gather the leaves in your hands and squeeze out the water. Place them in a high-speed blender and puree until smooth, stopping and scraping down the blender jar to ensure they are well blended. (You may need to add a splash of water to get the blade moving.)

5   Transfer the herb puree to a bowl. Add the oil, almonds, pecorino, and parmigiano. Using a Microplane, grate the garlic into the mixture. Add the salt and stir to combine. Check the seasoning and add more salt q.b. It should be loose enough to easily smother the asparagus. If needed, add olive oil to thin q.b.

6   Measure out 64g / ¼ cup pesto. Cover with a thin layer of oil and set aside. Transfer the remaining pesto to an airtight container, cover with a thin layer of oil, and refrigerate for up to 3 days for another use.

7   To finish, bring a large pot of water to a boil over high heat. Generously salt the water. Set up a salted ice-water bath.

8   Cut off and discard the bottom 2 inches of each asparagus spear. Then, using a vegetable peeler, peel the bottom 4 inches of each spear.

9   Add the asparagus to the boiling water and blanch for 45 seconds to 1 minute. The asparagus should still be firm and bright green.

10 Using a spider, remove the asparagus from the water and immediately transfer to the ice-water bath to stop the cooking. Remove from the ice-water bath when completely cool and pat dry with a kitchen towel.

11 Transfer the asparagus to a platter. Squeeze the juice from the lemon halves over the top. Drizzle with oil and sprinkle with sea salt q.b. Spoon the pesto in a wide strip across the middle of the asparagus. Garnish with the almonds, then shave the pecorino over the top and finish with the mint leaves.

Yields 4 to 6 servings

Pesto

50g / 2½ cups tightly packed mint leaves

15g / ¾ cup tightly packed parsley leaves

70g / 5 Tbsp olive oil, plus more q.b.

22g / 3 Tbsp finely chopped raw almonds

11g / 2 Tbsp finely grated pecorino romano

11g / 2 Tbsp finely grated parmigiano-reggiano

½ clove garlic

½ tsp salt, plus more q.b.

To Finish

900g / 2 lb asparagus (about 2 bunches)

1 lemon, cut in half and seeds removed

Olive oil, q.b.

Flaky sea salt, q.b.

30g / ¼ cup finely chopped raw almonds

28g / 1 oz pecorino romano

5g / ¼ cup mint leaves

Nota bene

This recipe yields more pesto than you will need. Use the remainder on eggs, in a frittata, or on crostini. It's versatile and the excess will reward you.

Pinzimonio

Pinzimonio is essentially crudités with a better name. Like the French version, this is a minimalist affair: seasonal vegetables arranged with whatever level of fanfare you can muster, salted, hit with a squeeze of lemon juice, and served with the best olive oil you can get your hands on. What differentiates this from crudités is often the choice of which vegetables end up on the plate. For me, it's a mix of fennel, Treviso, broccoli rabe, puntarelle (if you can get it), radish, and romanesco. In other words, I always treat pinzimonio like bagna cauda, with olive oil subbed in for that hot bath of anchovy and garlic.

1 Arrange all of the vegetables—lettuce, Treviso, fennel, radishes, carrots, broccoli rabe, romanesco, and others if using—on a serving platter.

2 Squeeze the juice from the lemon halves over the top and sprinkle with salt q.b.

3 Place the olive oil in a small serving bowl and add salt and pepper q.b.

4 Serve the olive oil alongside the vegetables for dipping.

Yields 4 to 6 servings

1 head Little Gem lettuce, outer leaves removed and head cut into 8 wedges, with core trimmed but left on

1 head Treviso, cut lengthwise into 6 pieces

1 fennel bulb, stems and fronds removed, cut in half lengthwise and each half cut into ¼-inch-thick slices

1 bunch breakfast radishes (or other type of radish), left whole with tops attached

1 bunch baby carrots, peeled

½ bunch broccoli rabe, leaves removed

½ head romanesco, cut into small wedges

Any other seasonal vegetables you want to add

1 lemon, cut in half and seeds removed

Flaky sea salt, q.b.

336g / 1½ cups olive oil

Black pepper, q.b.

Grilled and Marinated Baby Artichokes with Bay Leaf and Orange

This dish leans on my go-to technique for cooking artichokes, which begins with poaching them in a "stock" of equal parts water, white wine, and olive oil, plus aromatics, in this case bay leaf, orange zest, parsley, and garlic. Once poached, you can grill, sear, or cover them in olive oil and store them. Here I throw them on the grill (a grill pan works, too) to add a touch of heat and flavor before they hit the plate. I then finish them with a spin on salmoriglio, a classic southern Italian sauce of lemon, garlic, olive oil, and oregano that makes its way into a lot of my cooking.

1   To make the artichokes, fill a large bowl half full with cold water. Squeeze the juice from the lemon halves into the bowl. Reserve the lemon halves.

2   Remove the tough outer leaves from an artichoke. Using a small knife, cut off about ½ inch from the top and pare the stem to remove the tough outer fibers. Once trimmed, rub the artichoke with a reserved lemon half and transfer to the bowl of lemon water. This will prevent the artichoke from discoloring. Repeat with the remaining artichokes.

3   Drain the artichokes and add them to a large Dutch oven. Add the wine, olive oil, water, and orange juice. The liquid should nearly cover the artichokes. Add more water if needed. Add the garlic, orange peel, bay leaves, parsley, and salt. Stir to combine.

4   Place the Dutch oven over medium heat and bring to a simmer. Turn the heat down to low and cook, stirring occasionally, until the artichoke stems are just fork-tender and you can easily pull an outer leaf from the body, 20 to 30 minutes.

5   Turn off the heat. Using a slotted spoon, transfer the artichokes to a sheet pan and spread in a single layer in order to cool more rapidly. Set them aside until ready to use.

6   To make the salmoriglio, place a small saucepan over low heat. Add 112g / ½ cup of the oil and the garlic and gently cook until aromatic but without color, 10 to 15 seconds. Transfer to a small bowl and set aside to cool.

7   Once cooled, add the remaining 168g / ¾ cup oil, the orange peels, parsley, and chile flakes. Set aside.

8   To finish, heat a grill to medium or place a grill pan over medium-high heat on the stove top.

9   Gently open the artichokes so they resemble an open flower. Drizzle with olive oil q.b. and place, face down, on the grill or grill pan. Cook for 1 minute or so, then rotate the artichokes onto their sides and cook for a total of 1 to 2 minutes, turning as needed to allow them to heat through and become slightly charred on all sides.

10   Transfer the artichokes to a serving platter and squeeze the juice from the lemon halves over the top. Add the orange juice to your salmoriglio, stir to combine, and spoon over the artichokes. Garnish with sea salt q.b. and with the parsley and mint.

Yields 6 to 8 servings

Artichokes

3 lemons, cut in half
1.1kg / 2½ lb baby artichokes (about 32)
367g / 1½ cups plus 3 Tbsp dry white wine
380g / 1½ cups olive oil
357g / 1½ cups water
45g / 3 Tbsp fresh orange juice
25g / 5 garlic cloves
Peel of 1 orange, pith removed
4 fresh bay leaves
15g / ¼ bunch parsley
38g / ¼ cup plus ½ tsp salt

Salmoriglio

280g / 1¼ cups olive oil
75g / 15 cloves garlic, finely chopped
Peels of 2 oranges, pith removed and peels finely chopped
20g / ¼ cup finely chopped parsley
2g / 1 tsp dried red chile flakes
60g / ¼ cup fresh orange juice

To Finish

Olive oil, q.b.
2 lemons, cut in half and seeds removed
Flaky sea salt, q.b.
6g / ½ cup loosely packed parsley leaves
3g / ¼ cup loosely packed mint leaves

Grilled Summer Beans and Garlic Vinaigrette

This dish has been a standard at Misi since we opened. I use runner beans there, but the vinaigrette is as good a partner to pretty much any summer beans—haricot vert to wax—or really any vegetable you have coming off the grill. If you don't have access to a grill, you can do this on the stove top in a grill pan or even in a sauté pan over high heat. What you're looking for is a healthy char and a bit of blistering on the exterior.

1 To make the vinaigrette, put the shallot and the olive oil in a small saucepan over very low heat and cook until the shallot starts to soften and becomes completely translucent, 5 to 8 minutes. Add the garlic and continue to cook, stirring frequently, until the shallots are totally softened and the garlic is softened but without color, 2 to 3 minutes.

2 Transfer the contents of the pan to a heatproof bowl and let cool.

3 Once cooled, add the marjoram, parsley, and chile flakes. This is your vinaigrette base. Measure out 80g / ⅓ cup and set aside. Transfer the remainder to an airtight container and refrigerate for up to 5 days for another use.

4 To finish, preheat your grill to high or place a grill pan over high heat on the stove top.

5 Place the beans in a large bowl. Add the olive oil and salt and mix well. (You will finish with flaky sea salt, so you don't need to go too heavy now.)

6 Use a grill topper or grill basket on the grill to prevent the beans from falling through the bars of the grate. Arrange the beans in an even layer on the topper or basket. If using a grill pan, cook in batches to avoid crowding the pan. Cook, turning once, until they begin to char and soften but still have some crunch, 2 to 4 minutes on each side.

7 While the beans are cooking, pour your vinaigrette base into a small measuring cup or bowl. Add the vinegar and stir to combine.

8 When the beans are ready, transfer them to a large bowl. Add the vinaigrette and chile flakes and stir to combine.

9 Transfer to a serving platter and garnish with sea salt q.b.

Yields 6 to 8 servings

Garlic Vinaigrette

25g / 1 small shallot, finely diced
150g / ⅔ cup olive oil
125g / 25 cloves garlic, finely chopped
6g / 2 Tbsp finely chopped marjoram
15g / 3 Tbsp finely chopped parsley
¼ tsp dried red chile flakes
55g / ¼ cup red wine vinegar

To Finish

794g / 1¾ lb summer beans, trimmed
42g / 3 Tbsp olive oil
½ tsp salt
¼ tsp dried red chile flakes
Flaky sea salt, q.b.

Nota bene

You can add vinegar to the leftover vinaigrette base and use it as a salad dressing, marinade, or a warm vinaigrette for fish.

Braised Savoy Cabbage with Onions and Nutmeg

In the winter, vegetable cookery is about resourcefulness. How many different ways can I cook a squash? How do I turn cabbage into something craveable? This was my attempt to elevate Savoy cabbage by putting enough trust in it to carry the dish with almost nothing else to support it. There is one differentiation: parmigiano rind, which imparts a creamy, buttery richness without any cheese actually making its way into the final dish. It's meant to be a simple, hearty, satisfying reminder that there's more to cabbage than meets the eye.

1   Cut the Savoy cabbage in half through the stem end, then cut each half lengthwise into quarters. Core each quarter and separate the leaves, keeping them intact.

2   Place a large Dutch oven over low heat and add 56g / ¼ cup of the olive oil. Add the onion and gently cook until soft but without color, 5 to 8 minutes. Add the garlic and gently cook until aromatic but without color, 10 to 15 seconds.

3   Add the cabbage in small batches, allowing each batch to gently wilt before adding the next to the pan, 1 to 2 minutes per batch.

4   Add the wine, increase the heat to medium, and cook until the wine has reduced by half, 5 to 8 minutes.

5   Turn the heat down to low. Add the butter and water and then the parmigiano rinds.

6   Grate the nutmeg over the pan. Add the chile flakes and stir to combine.

7   Place a piece of parchment paper directly on top of the cabbage and braise over low heat until softened but not mushy, 20 to 30 minutes. You still want a little bite.

8   Add the salt and stir to combine. Check your seasoning and add more salt q.b.

9   Using a slotted spoon, transfer the cabbage to a large serving bowl. Add just enough of the braising liquid from the pan to cover the bottom of the bowl. The dish shouldn't be soupy.

10   Sprinkle the ground chile over the top. Grate nutmeg and grind pepper q.b. over the top. Then drizzle over the remaining 42g / 3 Tbsp olive oil.

Yields 4 to 6 servings

1 large head Savoy cabbage (about 1kg)
56g / ¼ cup olive oil, plus 42g / 3 Tbsp to finish
180g / 1 onion, cut in half and sliced
40g / 8 cloves garlic, sliced
367g / 1½ cups plus 3 Tbsp dry white wine
120g / ½ cup plus 1 tsp unsalted butter, cold and cubed
357g / 1½ cups water
120g / 1 or 2 pieces parmigiano-reggiano rind
¼ whole nutmeg, plus more q.b.
2g / 1 tsp dried red chile flakes
6g / 2 tsp salt, plus more q.b.
½ tsp ground red chile
Black pepper, q.b.

Roasted Kabocha Squash with Hot Honey and Bread Crumbs

There is no denying the lure of mild honey and hot Calabrian chiles. I've used it on roasted tomatoes, at home on chicken, on ricotta, and on anything in need of a bit of confident flair. Here I roast squash with butter, herbs, and garlic, then toss the caramelized pieces with honey vinegar and drizzle it with the hot honey and a final dusting of bread crumbs for texture. It's a dish that finds its home somewhere in the overlap of sweet, spicy, and bright.

1   To make the bread crumbs, preheat the oven to 200°F.

2   Spread the bread on a sheet pan and bake until dried out, 30 to 45 minutes. You do not want any color. To test for doneness, smash a shard of bread with the back of a spoon. The interior should be completely dry. Let cool.

3   Once cooled, place the bread in a food processor and pulse until broken down into fine crumbs. You want them to retain some texture, so be careful not to turn them to dust.

4   Place a sauté pan over medium-low heat. Add the olive oil and garlic and cook until the garlic perfumes the oil, 1 to 2 minutes. Remove the garlic and save for another use.

5   Turn the heat down to low. Line a plate with paper towels. Add the bread crumbs to the pan and cook, stirring occasionally, until they are golden brown, 5 to 8 minutes. Remove from the pan and transfer to the plate to drain. Let cool.

6   Measure out 20g / ⅓ cup bread crumbs and set aside. Transfer the remainder to an airtight container and store in a cool, dry place for up to 1 week for another use.

7   To make the hot honey, mix together the honey, chiles, and chile oil in a small bowl. Measure out 80g / ¼ cup and set aside. Transfer the remainder to an airtight container store at room temperature for up to 2 weeks for another use.

8   To make the squash, preheat the oven to 400°F.

9   Place a small saucepan over low heat. Add the butter and gently melt. Remove from the heat and stir in the olive oil.

10   Place the squash wedges in a large bowl. Add the butter mixture and toss or stir to coat on all sides.

continued

Yields 4 to 6 servings

Bread Crumbs

½ loaf (228g / 8 oz) country bread, torn into pieces (about 4 cups)
56g / ¼ cup olive oil
10g / 2 cloves garlic

Hot Honey

340g / 1 cup honey
45g / 3 Tbsp crushed Calabrian chiles
7g / 1½ tsp Calabrian chile oil (drained from jarred Calabrian chiles)

Squash

30g / 2 Tbsp unsalted butter, cold and cubed
42g / 3 Tbsp olive oil
1.4 to 1.8kg / 3 to 4 lb kabocha squash, cut into 2-inch-thick wedges
50g / 10 cloves garlic
7 sprigs rosemary
7 sprigs thyme
Salt, q.b.

To Finish

55g / ¼ cup honey vinegar or apple cider vinegar
3 sprigs thyme, leaves removed from stems
2 sprigs rosemary, leaves removed from stems
2g / 1 tsp dried red chile flakes
Flaky sea salt, q.b.

Roasted Kabocha Squash with Hot Honey and Bread Crumbs

continued

11   Place the squash wedges, skin side down, on a sheet pan. Arrange the garlic cloves around and on the squash and lay the rosemary and thyme sprigs on top. Sprinkle with salt q.b.

12   Roast the squash until fork-tender and slightly caramelized, about 45 minutes.

13   To finish, transfer the squash to a large bowl, add the vinegar, and gently stir to coat.

14   Transfer the squash to a large serving platter and drizzle with the hot honey. Garnish with the thyme and rosemary leaves, chile flakes, and bread crumbs, then sprinkle with sea salt q.b. to finish.

Nota bene

Honey vinegar is vinegar made from honey. I use Lindera Farms' honey vinegar, which you can purchase online. In a pinch, you can substitute apple cider vinegar.

Acknowledgments

First and foremost, thank you to the team who made this book possible. *Pasta* is as much yours as it is ours. To Kelly Puleio: your talent is undeniable, but it's your spirit that made its way onto the pages of this book and brought it to life. Thank you for sharing *you* with us. To Stephan Alessi and Kelly Britton: you are magic. To travel Italy from north to south, while the country was in lockdown, and capture what you did? Thank you for your sense of adventure, kindness, and friendship, and thank you for sharing Italy through your eyes, with us. To Laurie Ellen Pellicano: you are a fearless recipe tester, endless source of humor, and fierce talent. Thank you for your dedication and willingness to jump in head-first. To Nick Hensley: what can't you do? Thank you for patiently translating pasta making into illustrated form, and for your unwavering optimism. To our editor, Lorena Jones: thank you for patiently, steadfastly leading us every step of the way. Your attention to detail is the stuff of legend and your belief, support, and parallel vision made this book what it is. To our designer, Lizzie Allen: thank you for your ability to translate soulfulness through minimalism. Thank you for all the image swaps, the type studies, and for your dedication to getting it right. To our publisher, Aaron Wehner: thank you for your support and friendship, A+ cheerleading, and expert eye. To our research assistant, Alexandra Coraluzzi: thank you for the many hours on JStor and your willingness to read Renaissance cookbooks. To Lish Steiling: many thanks for being an absolute boss in the kitchen and running the most organized shoot in history. To Payson Stultz and Casey Bayer: thank you for bringing your cooking talent and good humor to our shoots. To Tamara Costa: thank you for being the quiet force that you are, and for bringing your talent for organization and sense of humor to the entire project. To Suzie Myers: thanks for your kick-butt expertise in propping, your passion for this project, and for never hesitating to try to sneak a fork into the shot. To Adrienne Anderson at Columbia Products: we appreciate your support, creative energy, and knack for the best damn cortado in Brooklyn. Thank you to Made In and Le Creuset for outfitting us in style. To the entire team at Ten Speed Press: from art direction (Emma Campion) to production design (Mari Gill), production management (Jane Chinn), marketing (Windy Dorresteyn, Samantha Simon, Stephanie Davis), and publicity (Kate Tyler, David Hawk, Leilani Zee), you are simply best in class. To Kari Stuart, for the guidance and support, always.

Thank you to all of the friends, advisors, families, hosts, pasta makers, and guides who helped lead us on a journey to better understand the thirty-five regional classics in this book. Thanks to Kim Sayid, for being our unofficial guide to Puglia and Sicily. Thank you to Katie Parla for your generosity in sharing your knowledge and passion for Italy, and for always being game for an adventure. Thanks to Roberto Panizza, for sharing the gospel of pesto and for being our guide to the Riviera. To Beatrice Ughi, Faith Willinger, and David Kinch for sharing contacts, hotspots, and advice. To the friends and winemakers who unscored the inseparable connection between pasta and wine, north to south, and hosted us along the way: Arianna Occhipinti, Elisabetta Foradori, Giampiero Bea, Emanuele Pelizzatti Perego, the entire Pepe family (Emidio, Rosa, Chiara, Elisa, Sofia, and Daniela), and the Nonino ladies (Elisabetta, Cristina, Francesca). To Rocco and Viola of Borgo Eibn for sharing Sauris with us. To all of the families, cooks, and pasta makers who invited us into their homes and shops to reveal the alchemy of devotion—to craft, to family, to tradition—that has made pasta what it is: Salvatore Rocco, Maria Berardi and family, Lisetta Scarciglia and family, Pino Maggiore, Antonio Cimenti, Rita and family, the Cosano family, Luca and Meica of Panelentu and so many more. Your generosity led the way.

Talia: There are truly more people to thank than these pages can contain. Thank you to everyone who lent an ear, a hand, a glass of wine during the three years we spent on this book. You know who you are. Thank you to Leslie Pariseau, for the early read and for being a constant source of encouragement. Thank you to my parents, who made loving food a family imperative. And thank you to all the Baiocchis, from Lucca to Los Angeles, past and present, for the Italian DNA and pride in possessing it. More specifically, to Elio and Italia Baiocchi, who were along for this ride with me the whole way. To Jacquelyn Morris, Dana Chivvis, Rachel Hammerman, and many more: thank you for always being game to eat the test batch and for supporting the both of us along the way. To Missy Robbins: you are a force. The only thing that matches your determination is your heart. Thank you for never doing anything halfway, and that includes loving me. Telling your story has been one of the great privileges of my life. This is, and will always be, for you.

Missy: To Talia Baiocchi: thank you for so selflessly immersing yourself in this book. We set out on a journey to create something truly special and your drive, passion, and pursuit of perfection led the way. I will always be grateful for your writing, your vision, and for you pushing me every day to be better at what I do. But mostly, I will be grateful that we got to share this experience together and deepen our love for Italy and each other. To Mom and Dad: without you and your love of food, dining, and entertaining, I would have never become a chef. Thank you for always believing in me and instilling in me the idea that I could do, and be, anything I wanted to. To Tony Mantuano: you are simply the greatest mentor, friend, and ambassador of all things Italian. The principles of Italian cooking that you drilled into me from day one as a novice chef have been my guide for the last eighteen years and inspired me daily to honor Italian tradition. To Sean Feeney: thank you for believing in the power of pasta and building a restaurant and company with me that celebrates it. Our evening over a bowl of your perfect bolognese and a negroni will forever be a moment that changed both of our lives.

No chef is complete without a great team. Thank you to ALL the chefs, sous chefs, and cooks from Spiaggia, A Voce, Lilia, and Misi that have been a part of developing recipes alongside me, testing and retesting until we got it right, and bringing them to life on a daily basis. A special thanks to Will Unseld, Aaron Diener, Kyle MacKinnon, and David Kaplan for putting up with my daily asks throughout this project to make sure every detail was correct.

Index

A

Abruzzo, 39, 68, 86, 119, 144, 172, 216, 217, 220, 245
Accademia Italiana della Cucina, 57
AEX5 "Vita," 38
Agli Amici, 4, 177
agnolotti, 80–81
    Agnolotti dal Plin, 84–85, 209–10
    Sheep's Milk Cheese–Filled Agnolotti with Saffron, Dried Tomato, and Honey, 276–77
    Sunchoke-Filled Agnolotti with Walnuts, Lemon, and Thyme, 326–27
Alba, 182
Alfonso I d'Este, 57
almonds
    Asparagus with Mint Pesto and Almonds, 378
    Busiate alla Pesto Trapanese, 248
Alto Adige, 95, 114, 177, 281. *See also* Trentino–Alto Adige
Amalfi Coast, 348
Amatrice, 234
anchovies, 135
    Anchovy Vinaigrette, 367
    Bigoli in Salsa, 191
    Linguine with Anchovies, Corbara Tomatoes, and Lemon, 280
    Orecchiette con Cime di Rapa, 253–55
    Puttanesca Sauce, 256
    Spaghetti alla Puttanesca, 256
    Spaghetti with Colatura, Garlic, and Bread Crumbs, 348
    Strangozzi alla Norcina, 232
    Truffle-Anchovy Paste, 232
Aosta Valley, 302
L'Aquila, 172, 216
Arcadia, 2, 209

Arcobaleno, 38
Arezzo, 65, 71
Artichokes, Grilled and Marinated Baby, with Bay Leaf and Orange, 380
Artusi, Pellegrino, 54
Ascoli Piceno, 50
Asparagus with Mint Pesto and Almonds, 378
A Voce, 5, 37, 148, 252, 276

B

balanzoni, 77–78
    Balanzoni Burro e Salvia, 205–6
Bar dell'Orso, 216
Bari, 68, 244
basil, 136
    Pesto Genovese, 178
Basilica di San Luca, 57
Basilicata, 68
Bea, Paolo, 135
beans
    Grilled Summer Beans and Garlic Vinaigrette, 383
    Pasta e Fagioli, 162–64
    See also chickpeas
beef
    Agnolotti dal Plin, 209–10
    Bolognese Ragù, 202–3
    Maccheroncini di Campofilone al Sugo Tradizionale, 240–41
    Spaghetti alla Chitarra con Pallottine, 224–25
    Spaghetti Meatballs, 156–57
    Tagliatelle alla Bolognese, 202–3
    Timballo alla Teramana, 220–21
beets
    Casunziei all'Ampezzana, 194–95
Berardi family, 244
bigoli, 115
    Bigoli in Salsa, 191
Bimonte's, 1, 154

boar, wild
    Cinghiale Ragù, 333–34
    Cocoa Pici with Braised Cinghiale, 333–34
Bologna, 57, 77, 110, 189, 202, 205
Bolognese Ragù, 202–3
Borgia, Lucrezia, 57, 110
Il Borgo dei Fumari, 172
Bottarga, Sheep's Milk Ricotta–Filled Occhi with Lemon and, 340
Bottura, Massimo, 316
branzino
    Couscous alla Trapanese, 264–65
bread
    Canederli, 188
    Olive Oil–Poached Zucchini with Grilled Bread and Oregano, 371–72
    Passatelli in Brodo, 189–90
Brescia, 65
bringoli, 71
broccoli
    Broccoli Pesto, 282
    Ricotta Gnocchi with Broccoli Pesto, Basil, and Pistachios, 282–83
broccoli rabe
    Broccoli Rabe with Parmigiano and Calabrian Chile Oil, 370
    Orecchiette con Cime di Rapa, 253–55
    Pinzimonio, 379
bucatini, 121
    Bucatini all'amatriciana, 234
    Bucatini con le Sarde, 249
buckwheat dough, 30
    Pizzoccheri alla Valtellinese, 183
buckwheat flour, 11
busa, 64
busiate, 64
    Busiate alla Pesto Trapanese, 248

butter, 135
brown, 141
cold and cubed, 140
Garlic Butter, 371

C

cabbage
Braised Savoy Cabbage with
Onions and Nutmeg, 384
Pizzoccheri alla
Valtellinese, 183
Caciocavallo, Baked Ziti with
Aged Provolone and, 154
Cacio e Pepe, 233
Cagliari, 67, 258
Calabria, 11, 64, 68, 267
Camogli, 70
Campania, 36, 39, 86, 121, 124,
162, 244, 245
Campidano, 258
Campofilone, 50
Canederli, 114, 188
canestri. See stricchetti
Cannelloni, 86, 161
Cantina Siciliana, 264
cappelletti, 87
Corn-Filled Cappelletti
with Black Pepper and
Pecorino, 335
Potato-Filled Cappelletti
with Speck, Horseradish,
and Caraway, 281
Prosciutto and Goat
Cheese–Filled Cappelletti
with Pistachios, 312–13
Ricotta and Tuscan Kale–
Filled Cappelletti with
Fennel Pollen, 294–95
caramelle, 88
Caramelle with Caramelized
Onion, Brown Butter, and
Balsamic, 316–17
Carnic Alps, 11, 92, 177
casarecce, 121
Casarecce con Pesce Spada,
Pistacchi e Capperi, 263
casoncelli, 89

Casoni, Franco, 12
Il Castoro, 172
casunziei, 89
Casunziei all'Ampezzana,
194–95
Catania, 121
Cavalcanti, Ippolito, 165, 256
Cetara, 348
cheese. See individual cheeses
chestnut dough, 27
cannelloni, 161
corzetti, 113
trofie, 70
chestnut flour, 11
Chiaramonte Gulfi, 245
Chiavari, 180
chickpeas
Chickpea Pappardelle with
Chickpeas, Rosemary, and
Garlic, 338–39
dough, 29
flour, 11
chiles
Broccoli Rabe with
Parmigiano and
Calabrian Chile Oil, 370
Calabrian, 135
Diavola Sauce, 149
Espresso Tagliolini with
Smoked Ricotta and
Chiles, 342
flakes, dried red, 135
Spaghetti alla Chitarra with
Lobster and Fresh Chiles,
346–47
chitarra, 12, 119
chocolate
cocoa dough, 31
Cocoa Pici with Braised
Cinghiale, 333–34
See also cocoa dough
Cianci, Jenny, 233
Cianzia, 172
Cjalsons, 92–93, 197
clams
Spaghetti Vongole, 165–67

cocoa dough, 31
Cocoa Pici with Braised
Cinghiale, 333–34
Colina, 4
Conant, Scott, 5
Connie's Macaroni, 1
Il Convivio, 4
Corn-Filled Cappelletti
with Black Pepper and
Pecorino, 335
Corona Trattoria, 248
Cortina d'Ampezzo, 89, 172,
177, 194
corzetti, 113
Corzetti alle Erbe, 213
Corzetti with Chanterelles
and Aged Goat
Cheese, 350
Corzetti with Sungold
Tomatoes, Pecorino, and
Herbs, 343
stamps, 12
Cosetti, Gianni, 92
Couscous alla Trapanese,
264–65
croxetti, 113
culurgiones, 94
Culurgiones alla
Nuorese, 246

D

Da Cesare, 233
Dal Pescatore, 5, 186
Da Vittorio, 263
De Cecco, 39
De'Longhi, 342
Del Posto, 5
DeLucie, John, 4
Diavola Sauce, 149
Di Martino, 39
dough
buckwheat, 30
chestnut, 27
chickpea, 29
cocoa, 31
egg, 18
espresso, 28

dough, *continued*
    extruded, 41
    flour for, 10–11
    gnudi, 25
    green, 22
    importance of, 17
    ramp, 22
    ricotta gnocchi, 24
    rolling and sheeting, 32–35
    semolina, 19
    whole-wheat, 26
duck
    Duck Confit, 228
    Duck Ragù, 228–29
    Pici al Ragù d'Anatra,
        228–29

E

Early Girl Farms, 367
egg dough, 18
    Agnolotti dal Plin, 209–10
    Cannelloni, 161
    Caramelle with Caramelized
        Onion, Brown Butter, and
        Balsamic, 316–17
    Casunziei all'Ampezzana,
        194–95
    Cjalsons, 197
    Corn-Filled Cappelletti
        with Black Pepper and
        Pecorino, 335
    Corzetti alle Erbe, 213
    Corzetti with
        Chanterelles and Aged
        Goat Cheese, 350
    Corzetti with Sungold
        Tomatoes, Pecorino, and
        Herbs, 343
    Eggplant-Filled Mezzelune
        with Simple Sauce and
        Ricotta Salata, 306–7
    Fettuccine Alfredo, 150
    Fettuccine with Spicy Lamb
        Sausage and Tomato
        Passata, 286–87

Lasagna, 168–69
Maccheroncini di
    Campofilone al Sugo
    Tradizionale, 240–41
Mandilli di Seta with
    Dried Cherry Tomatoes
    and Herbed Bread
    Crumbs, 351
Pansotti con Salsa di Noci,
    180–81
Pappardelle al Ragù di
    Coniglio, 226–27
Pappardelle with Porcini
    and Veal Bolognese,
    309–10
Parmigiano Fonduta–Filled
    Tortellini in Brodo,
    298–99
Pasta e Fagioli, 162–64
Pici al Ragù d'Anatra,
    228–29
Potato-Filled Cappelletti
    with Speck, Horseradish,
    and Caraway, 281
Potato and Crème Fraîche–
    Filled Ravioli with Garlic
    and Rosemary, 290–91
Prosciutto and Goat
    Cheese–Filled Cappelletti
    with Pistachios, 312–13
Ravioli Red Sauce, 153
Ravioli with Taleggio
    Fonduta, Peas, and Speck,
    302–3
Ricotta and Tuscan Kale–
    Filled Cappelletti with
    Fennel Pollen, 294–95
Sheep's Milk Ricotta–Filled
    Occhi with Lemon and
    Bottarga, 340
Spaghetti alla Chitarra con
    Pallottine, 224–25
Spaghetti alla Chitarra with
    Lobster and Fresh Chiles,
    346–47

Spinach and Ricotta-Filled
    Tortelli with Brown
    Butter and Ricotta Salata,
    322–25
Strangozzi alla Norcina, 232
Strangozzi with Pork Sugo,
    Nutmeg, and Parmigiano,
    330–32
Stricchetti with Smashed
    Peas and Prosciutto,
    354–56
Sunchoke-Filled Agnolotti
    with Walnuts, Lemon,
    and Thyme, 326–27
Tagliatelle with Matsutake
    Mushrooms, Lemon, and
    Mint, 357–58
Tagliatelle with Ossobuco
    and Soffritto, 320–21
Tajarin al Tartufo, 182
Tortellini in Brodo, 198–99
Tortellli di Zucca, 186–87
eggplant
    Eggplant-Filled Mezzelune
        with Simple Sauce and
        Ricotta Salata, 306–7
    Roasted Eggplant with
        Olives and Sun-Dried
        Tomato Vinaigrette, 374
eggs
    Spaghetti alla Carbonara, 218
    See also egg dough
Emilia-Romagna, 2, 17, 33, 57,
    75, 77, 86, 87, 88, 98, 106,
    110, 162, 168, 172, 176, 189,
    198, 216, 217, 218, 228, 240,
    298, 354
Emiliomiti Lillo Due, 38
equipment, 12, 14–15
Erickson, Meredith, 177
escarole
    Bitter Lettuces and
        Herbs with House
        Vinaigrette, 366

Escarole with Anchovy
Vinaigrette, Ricotta
Salata, and Crispy
Garlic, 367
espresso dough, 28
Espresso Tagliolini with
Smoked Ricotta and
Chiles, 342
extruded pasta
brands of, 39
commercial production of,
36–37
cook times for, 138
dough for, 41
drying, 37, 42
importance of, 36
making at home, 37–38,
41–42
shapes of, 121–24
See also individual shapes
extruders, 14, 15, 37–38

F

Faella, 36, 39
Fara San Martino, 39
farfalle. *See* stricchetti
farina di grano tenero
integrale, 10
farina di grano tenero
tipo 00, 10
Felidia, 4
fennel, 136
Bucatini con le Sarde, 249
Fennel with Celery, Walnuts,
and Parmigiano, 375
Pinzimonio, 379
Fermo, 50, 216, 240
Ferrara, 106
feta
Sheep's Milk Cheese–Filled
Agnolotti with Saffron,
Dried Tomato, and Honey,
276–77

fettuccine, 49
Fettuccine Alfredo, 144,
145, 150
Fettuccine with Spicy Lamb
Sausage and Tomato
Passata, 286–87
fileja, 63
Fileja alla 'Nduja, 267
fiocchetti. *See* stricchetti
Florence, 12
flour, 10–11
Frederick II (Holy Roman
emperor), 92
Friuli, 4, 11, 92, 176, 197
fusarioi, 115

G

garlic, 136, 146
browned, 139
Caramelized Garlic, 377
Chickpea Pappardelle with
Chickpeas, Rosemary, and
Garlic, 338–39
Escarole with Anchovy
Vinaigrette, Ricotta
Salata, and Crispy
Garlic, 367
Garlic Butter, 371
Garlic Vinaigrette, 383
Orecchiette con Cime di
Rapa, 253–55
Porcini with Rosemary and
Garlic, 377
Potato and Crème Fraîche–
Filled Ravioli with Garlic
and Rosemary, 290–91
Roasted Garlic, 371
Salmoriglio, 380
Spaghetti with Colatura,
Garlic, and Bread Crumbs,
348
Spaghetti with Garlic Four
Ways, 273
30-Clove Sauce, 148

Genoa, 51, 178
Gentile, 39
Gentry, Patty, 367
gnocchi, 74
board, 14
dough, ricotta, 24
Ricotta Gnocchi with
Broccoli Pesto, Basil,
and Pistachios, 282–83
gnudi, 65
dough, 25
Gnudi alla Fiorentina, 238
goat cheese
Corzetti with
Chanterelles and Aged
Goat Cheese, 350
Prosciutto and Goat
Cheese–Filled Cappelletti
with Pistachios, 312–13
Gragnano, 36, 39, 217, 245
grano arso, 11
grano duro, 10
grano tenero, 10
green dough, 22
Balanzoni Burro e Salvia,
205–6
Spaghetti alla Chitarra
with Ramps, Lemon, and
Ricotta Salata, 300
Grosseto, 71
Guagnano, 245
guanciale
Bucatini all'amatriciana, 234
Pork Sugo, 330–32
Spaghetti alla Carbonara, 218

H

Hazan, Marcella, 5, 270
House Vinaigrette, 366

I

Istria, 115
Italian American food,
definition of, 144

J

James Beard House, 302

K

kale
  Ricotta and Tuscan Kale–
    Filled Cappelletti with
    Fennel Pollen, 294–95
KitchenAid stand mixers, 14,
    24, 34–35

L

Ladner, Mark, 234
lamb
  Fettuccine with Spicy Lamb
    Sausage and Tomato
    Passata, 286–87
  Lamb Sausage, 286
  Lamb Sugo, 224–25, 286
  Spaghetti alla Chitarra con
    Pallottine, 224–25
Langhe, 61, 84
Lasagna, 47, 168–69
Lavazza, 342
Lazio, 49, 57, 71, 74, 119, 121,
    123, 217, 218
lemons, 136
  Linguine with Anchovies,
    Corbara Tomatoes, and
    Lemon, 280
  peel, chopped, 139
  Sheep's Milk Ricotta–Filled
    Occhi with Lemon and
    Bottarga, 340
  Snap Peas with Black
    Pepper, Lemon, and
    Lardo, 369
  Spaghetti alla Chitarra
    with Ramps, Lemon, and
    Ricotta Salata, 300
  Spaghetti with Lemon,
    Pine Nuts, and
    Parmigiano, 274
  Sunchoke-Filled Agnolotti
    with Walnuts, Lemon,
    and Thyme, 326–27

Tagliatelle with Matsutake
    Mushrooms, Lemon, and
    Mint, 357–58
Leon's, 1, 154, 159
lettuce
  Bitter Lettuces and
    Herbs with House
    Vinaigrette, 366
  Pinzimonio, 379
Liguria, 11, 12, 51, 64, 70, 100,
    113, 122, 176, 177, 180,
    213, 351
Lilia, 37, 145, 149, 270, 276, 282,
    286, 289, 309, 319, 335,
    342, 364, 367
Lillo Due, 38
linguine, 122
  Linguine with Anchovies,
    Corbara Tomatoes, and
    Lemon, 280
  Lobster Fra Diavolo with
    Linguine, 159–60
lobster
  Lobster Fra Diavolo with
    Linguine, 159–60
  Spaghetti alla Chitarra with
    Lobster and Fresh Chiles,
    346–47
Lobster Club, 2, 209
Lombardy, 5, 11, 55, 65, 80, 89,
    106, 115, 186, 191
lombrichetti, 71

M

macarrones de busa, 63
maccheroncini di
    Campofilone, 50
  Maccheroncini di
    Campofilone al Sugo
    Tradizionale, 240–41
maccheroni al ferretto, 63
maccheroni alla chitarra, 119
Mafalda of Savoy, Princess, 122
mafaldine, 122
  Mafaldine with Pink
    Peppercorns and
    Parmigiano-Reggiano, 319

Maggiore, Pino, 245, 264
malfatti, 65
malloreddus, 67
  board, 14
  Malloreddus alla
    Campidanese, 258–59
maltagliati, 47
mandilli di seta, 51
  Mandilli di Seta with
    Dried Cherry Tomatoes
    and Herbed Bread
    Crumbs, 351
manicotti, 86
Mantua, 115, 186, 191
Mantuano, Tony, 4, 5, 128, 270
Manuelina, 178
Marcelli, Andrew, 342
March, 2
Marche, 50, 60, 168, 189,
    216–17, 220, 240
marjoram, 136
Martino di Como, 104, 189
La Marzocco, 342
meatballs
  Spaghetti alla Chitarra con
    Pallottine, 224–25
  Spaghetti Meatballs, 156–57
Menfi, 263
Merano, 114, 188, 281
mezzelune, 95
  Eggplant-Filled Mezzelune
    with Simple Sauce and
    Ricotta Salata, 306–7
Milan, 106, 161
mint, 136
  Mint Pesto, 378
Misi, 98, 145, 150, 289, 322, 330,
    338, 340, 362, 383
Modena, 110
Modica, 333
Molise, 60, 68
Monferrato, 84
Monograno Felicetti, 39
mortadella
  Balanzoni Burro e Salvia,
    205–6
  Tortellini in Brodo, 198–99

mozzarella, 140
    Lasagna, 168–69
    Ravioli Red Sauce, 153
    Timballo alla Teramana,
       220–21
mushrooms
    Corzetti with
       Chanterelles and Aged
       Goat Cheese, 350
    Pappardelle with Porcini
       and Veal Bolognese,
       309–10
    Porcini with Rosemary and
       Garlic, 377
    Tagliatelle with Matsutake
       Mushrooms, Lemon, and
       Mint, 357–58

N

Naples, 39, 165, 228, 256, 374
Nish, Wayne, 2, 322
nocchette. *See* stricchetti
Norcia, 217, 232
Norma, 306
Nuoro, 94, 245, 246
nutmeg, 136

O

occhi, 98–99
    Sheep's Milk Ricotta–Filled
       Occhi with Lemon and
       Bottarga, 340
olive oil, 135–36, 138, 146
olives
    Puttanesca Sauce, 256
    Roasted Eggplant with
       Olives and Sun-Dried
       Tomato Vinaigrette, 374
    Spaghetti alla
       Puttanesca, 256
onions, 137
    Agnolotti dal Plin, 209–10
    Braised Savoy Cabbage with
       Onions and Nutmeg, 384
    Caramelle with Caramelized
       Onion, Brown Butter, and
       Balsamic, 316–17

    Spaghetti with Pancetta,
       Black Pepper, and Spring
       Onions, 329
oranges, 136
    Grilled and Marinated Baby
       Artichokes with Bay Leaf
       and Orange, 380
    peel, chopped, 139
orecchiette, 68–69
    Orecchiette con Cime di
       Rapa, 253–55
oregano, 146
L'Oriecchietta, 17

P

Palermo, 248
Pallottine, 220
pancetta
    Bolognese Ragù, 202–3
    Pasta e Fagioli, 162–64
    Pork Sugo, 330–32
    Spaghetti alla
       Carbonara, 218
    Spaghetti with Pancetta,
       Black Pepper, and Spring
       Onions, 329
    Tagliatelle alla Bolognese,
       202–3
Panelentu, 246
pansotti, 100–101
    Pansotti con Salsa di Noci,
       180–81
pappardelle, 54
    Chickpea Pappardelle with
       Chickpeas, Rosemary, and
       Garlic, 338–39
    Pappardelle al Ragù di
       Coniglio, 226–27
    Pappardelle with Porcini
       and Veal Bolognese,
       309–10
parmigiano-reggiano, 136, 139
    Broccoli Rabe with
       Parmigiano and
       Calabrian Chile Oil, 370
    Fennel with Celery, Walnuts,
       and Parmigiano, 375

    Fettuccine Alfredo, 150
    Lasagna, 168–69
    Mafaldine with Pink
       Peppercorns and
       Parmigiano-Reggiano, 319
    Parmigiano Fonduta–Filled
       Tortellini in Brodo, 298–99
    Passatelli in Brodo, 189–90
    Spaghetti with Lemon,
       Pine Nuts, and
       Parmigiano, 274
    Strangozzi with Pork Sugo,
       Nutmeg, and Parmigiano,
       330–32
parsley, 136
Passatelli in Brodo, 189–90
pasta
    cooking, 128, 131–33
    fresh, 17
    ingredient tool kit for,
       135–37
    making, 9–12, 14–15, 17
    shapes of, 46–47
    See also dough; extruded
       pasta; *individual shapes*
Pasta e Fagioli, 162–64
Pastificio Gaetano
    Sergiacomo, 39
peas
    Ravioli with Taleggio
       Fonduta, Peas, and Speck,
       302–3
    Snap Peas with Black
       Pepper, Lemon, and
       Lardo, 369
    Stricchetti with Smashed
       Peas and Prosciutto,
       354–56
pecorino romano, 136, 139
    Bucatini all'amatriciana, 234
    Cacio e Pepe, 233
    Corn-Filled Cappelletti
       with Black Pepper and
       Pecorino, 335
    Corzetti with Sungold
       Tomatoes, Pecorino, and
       Herbs, 343

pecorino romano, *continued*
Spaghetti alla
Carbonara, 218
Pellicano, Laurie Ellen, 15
penne, 124
Penne alla Vodka, 155
Penne (town), 39
pepper, black, 135
pesto
Broccoli Pesto, 282
Mint Pesto, 378
Pesto Genovese, 178
Pesto Trapanese, 248
Piacenza, 88
Picetti, Pietro, 12
pici, 71
Cocoa Pici with Braised
Cinghiale, 333–34
Pici al Ragù d'Anatra,
228–29
Piedmont, 60, 61, 80, 84, 176,
177, 209, 302
pine nuts
Bucatini con le Sarde, 249
Corzetti alle Erbe, 213
Pesto Genovese, 178
Spaghetti with Lemon,
Pine Nuts, and
Parmigiano, 274
Pinzimonio, 379
pistachios
Casarecce con Pesce Spada,
Pistacchi e Capperi, 263
Prosciutto and Goat
Cheese–Filled Cappelletti
with Pistachios, 312–13
Ricotta Gnocchi with
Broccoli Pesto, Basil, and
Pistachios, 282–83
pizzoccheri, 55
Pizzoccheri alla
Valtellinese, 183
pork
Bolognese Ragù, 202–3
Malloreddus alla
Campidanese, 258–59
Pork Sugo, 330–32

Sausage, Saffron, and
Tomato Ragù, 258–59
Spaghetti Meatballs, 156–57
Strangozzi with Pork Sugo,
Nutmeg, and Parmigiano,
330–32
Tagliatelle alla Bolognese,
202–3
Tortellini in Brodo, 198–99
See also guanciale;
mortadella; pancetta;
prosciutto; speck
potatoes
Culurgiones alla
Nuorese, 246
Pizzoccheri alla
Valtellinese, 183
Potato-Filled Cappelletti
with Speck, Horseradish,
and Caraway, 281
Potato and Crème Fraîche–
Filled Ravioli with Garlic
and Rosemary, 290–91
Po Valley, 335
Prata d'Ansidonia, 172
Preci, 172
Predazzo, 39
prosciutto
Pork Sugo, 330–32
Prosciutto and Goat
Cheese–Filled Cappelletti
with Pistachios, 312–13
Stricchetti with Smashed
Peas and Prosciutto,
354–56
Tortellini in Brodo, 198–99
Provolone, Aged, Baked Ziti
with Caciocavallo
and, 154
Puglia, 17, 68, 80, 244, 245, 253
Puttanesca Sauce, 256

Q
q.b. (quanto basta), meaning
of, xi, 138
quadrati, 47

R
rabbit
Pappardelle al Ragù di
Coniglio, 226–27
Rabbit Ragù, 226–27
ragùs. *See* sauces and ragùs
ramps
dough, 22
Spaghetti alla Chitarra
with Ramps, Lemon, and
Ricotta Salata, 300
ravioli, 104–5
Potato and Crème Fraîche–
Filled Ravioli with Garlic
and Rosemary, 290–91
Ravioli Red Sauce, 153
Ravioli with Taleggio
Fonduta, Peas, and Speck,
302–3
Recco, 70, 178
Reggio Emilia, 87
ricotta, 137
Balanzoni Burro e Salvia,
205–6
Cannelloni, 161
Casunziei all'Ampezzana,
194–95
Cjalsons, 197
Culurgiones alla
Nuorese, 246
Espresso Tagliolini with
Smoked Ricotta and
Chiles, 342
gnocchi, 74
gnocchi dough, 24
Gnudi alla Fiorentina, 238
gnudi dough, 25
Pansotti con Salsa di Noci,
180–81
Potato-Filled Cappelletti
with Speck, Horseradish,
and Caraway, 281
Potato and Crème Fraîche–
Filled Ravioli with Garlic
and Rosemary, 290–91

Prosciutto and Goat Cheese–Filled Cappelletti with Pistachios, 312–13
Ravioli Red Sauce, 153
Ricotta and Tuscan Kale–Filled Cappelletti with Fennel Pollen, 294–95
Ricotta Gnocchi with Broccoli Pesto, Basil, and Pistachios, 282–83
Sheep's Milk Cheese–Filled Agnolotti with Saffron, Dried Tomato, and Honey, 276–77
Sheep's Milk Ricotta–Filled Occhi with Lemon and Bottarga, 340
Spinach and Ricotta-Filled Tortelli with Brown Butter and Ricotta Salata, 322–25
whipping, 139
ricotta salata
Eggplant-Filled Mezzelune with Simple Sauce and Ricotta Salata, 306–7
Escarole with Anchovy Vinaigrette, Ricotta Salata, and Crispy Garlic, 367
Spaghetti alla Chitarra with Ramps, Lemon, and Ricotta Salata, 300
Spinach and Ricotta-Filled Tortelli with Brown Butter and Ricotta Salata, 322–25
rigatoni, 123
Rigatoni Diavola, 289
Ristorante Righi, 2, 4
Rome, 217, 218, 233, 234, 306, 357, 377
Romoli, Domenico, 54
Rosato, Mino, 17
rosemary, 137
Rosenzweig, Anne, 2, 209
Rustichella d'Abruzzo, 39
rye flour, 11

S
Salimbene di Adam, 65
Salmoriglio, 380
salt, 132, 137, 140
San Marino, 2, 189
Sansepolcro, 4, 33, 54, 338
sardines
Bucatini con le Sarde, 249
Sardinia, 63, 64, 67, 94, 178, 244, 245, 246, 258, 350, 375
sauces and ragùs
Bolognese Ragù, 202–3
Cinghiale Ragù, 333–34
Diavola Sauce, 149
Duck Ragù, 228–29
Lamb Sugo, 224–25, 286
leftover, 141
Ossobuco Ragù, 320–21
Pork Sugo, 330–32
Puttanesca Sauce, 256
Rabbit Ragù, 226–27
red, 146–47
Salmoriglio, 380
Sausage, Saffron, and Tomato Ragù, 258–59
seasoning, 141
Simple Red Sauce, 147
30-Clove Sauce, 148
Veal Bolognese, 309–10
Vodka Sauce, 155
Walnut Sauce, 180, 181
See also pesto
Sauris, 197
sausage
Fettuccine with Spicy Lamb Sausage and Tomato Passata, 286–87
Fileja alla 'Nduja, 267
Lamb Sausage, 286
Malloreddus alla Campidanese, 258–59
Sausage, Saffron, and Tomato Ragù, 258–59
See also mortadella
Scarciglia family, 245
Scarpetta, 5

schlutzkrapfen, 95
sciancon. See stricchetti
sea urchin
Spaghetti ai Ricci di Mare, 252
semola rimacinata di grano duro, 10
semolina dough, 19
Busiate alla Pesto Trapanese, 248
Culurgiones alla Nuorese, 246
Fileja alla 'Nduja, 267
Malloreddus alla Campidanese, 258–59
Orecchiette con Cime di Rapa, 253–55
Trofie al Pesto Genovese, 178
Senatore Cappelli, 11
1789, 2
sfoglino method, 33
Sicily, 11, 39, 63, 104, 121, 123, 124, 135, 244, 245, 248, 249, 263, 264, 333
Siena, 71, 216
Sodi, Rita, 274
I Sodi, 233, 274
Soho Grand, 4, 290
Sori, 177
spaghetti, 123
Cacio e Pepe, 233
Spaghetti ai Ricci di Mare, 252
Spaghetti alla Carbonara, 218
Spaghetti alla Puttanesca, 256
Spaghetti Meatballs, 156–57
Spaghetti Vongole, 165–67
Spaghetti with Colatura, Garlic, and Bread Crumbs, 348
Spaghetti with Garlic Four Ways, 273
Spaghetti with Lemon, Pine Nuts, and Parmigiano, 274
Spaghetti with Pancetta,

spaghetti, *continued*
Black Pepper, and Spring
Onions, 329
spaghetti alla chitarra, 119
Spaghetti alla Chitarra con
Pallottine, 224–25
Spaghetti alla Chitarra with
Lobster and Fresh Chiles,
346–47
Spaghetti alla Chitarra
with Ramps, Lemon, and
Ricotta Salata, 300
speck
Canederli, 188
Potato-Filled Cappelletti
with Speck, Horseradish,
and Caraway, 281
Ravioli with Taleggio
Fonduta, Peas, and Speck,
302–3
Spiaggia, 4, 5, 17, 312, 316
spinach
Cannelloni, 161
Gnudi alla Fiorentina, 238
gnudi dough, 25
Prosciutto and Goat
Cheese–Filled Cappelletti
with Pistachios, 312–13
Spinach and Ricotta-Filled
Tortelli with Brown
Butter and Ricotta Salata,
322–25
Timballo alla Teramana,
220–21
See also green dough
Spinosi, 50
Spoleto, 56
squash
Olive Oil–Poached Zucchini
with Grilled Bread and
Oregano, 371–72
Roasted Kabocha Squash
with Hot Honey and
Bread Crumbs, 385–86
Tortellli di Zucca, 186–87

strangozzi, 56
Strangozzi alla
Norcina, 232
Strangozzi with Pork Sugo,
Nutmeg, and Parmigiano,
330–32
strascinati, 68
stricchetti, 75
Stricchetti with Smashed
Peas and Prosciutto,
354–56
stringozzi, 56
Sunchoke-Filled Agnolotti
with Walnuts, Lemon,
and Thyme, 326–27
Swiss chard
Pansotti con Salsa di Noci,
180–81
Spinach and Ricotta-Filled
Tortelli with Brown
Butter and Ricotta Salata,
322–25
swordfish
Casarecce con Pesce Spada,
Pistacchi e Capperi, 263

T

tagliatelle, 57
Tagliatelle alla Bolognese,
202–3
Tagliatelle with Matsutake
Mushrooms, Lemon, and
Mint, 357–58
Tagliatelle with Ossobuco
and Soffritto, 320–21
tagliolini, 60
Espresso Tagliolini with
Smoked Ricotta and
Chiles, 342
tajarin, 61
Tajarin al Tartufo, 182
Taleggio Fonduta, Ravioli with
Peas, Speck, and, 302–3
tamis, 16, 138
Teglio, 183
Teramo, 216, 220

30-Clove Sauce, 148
Timballo alla Teramana,
220–21
tomatoes, 137, 146
Bucatini all'amatriciana, 234
Busiate alla Pesto
Trapanese, 248
Corzetti with Sungold
Tomatoes, Pecorino, and
Herbs, 343
crushing by hand, 141
Culurgiones alla
Nuorese, 246
Cured Corbara
Tomatoes, 280
Diavola Sauce, 149
Dried Tomatoes, 276
Eggplant-Filled Mezzelune
with Simple Sauce and
Ricotta Salata, 306–7
Fettuccine with Spicy Lamb
Sausage and Tomato
Passata, 286–87
Fileja alla 'Nduja, 267
Linguine with Anchovies,
Corbara Tomatoes, and
Lemon, 280
Maccheroncini di
Campofilone al Sugo
Tradizionale, 240–41
Malloreddus alla
Campidanese, 258–59
Mandilli di Seta with
Dried Cherry Tomatoes
and Herbed Bread
Crumbs, 351
paste, 137, 146
Puttanesca Sauce, 256
Ravioli Red Sauce, 153
Roasted Eggplant with
Olives and Sun-Dried
Tomato Vinaigrette, 374
Sausage, Saffron, and
Tomato Ragù, 258–59

Sheep's Milk Cheese–Filled
    Agnolotti with Saffron,
    Dried Tomato, and Honey,
    276–77
Simple Red Sauce, 147
Spaghetti alla
    Puttanesca, 256
30-Clove Sauce, 148
Vodka Sauce, 155
tonnarelli, 119
torchio bigolaro, 15
Torre Annunziata, 39
tortelli, 106–7
    Spinach and Ricotta-Filled
    Tortelli with Brown
    Butter and Ricotta Salata,
    322–25
    Tortellli di Zucca, 186–87
tortellini, 110–11
    Parmigiano Fonduta–Filled
    Tortellini in Brodo,
    298–99
    Tortellini in Brodo, 198–99
Trapani, 63, 248, 264
Trattoria I Rizzari, 121
Trattoria La Brinca, 180
Trattoria La Buca, 98
trenette, 122
Trentino–Alto Adige, 11, 39,
    60, 114
Trento, 188
Treviso
    Bitter Lettuces and
    Herbs with House
    Vinaigrette, 366
    Charred Treviso with
    Walnuts and Saba, 364
    Pinzimonio, 379
Trieste, 176
trofie, 70
    Trofie al Pesto Genovese, 178
Tropea, 64
truffles
    Strangozzi alla Norcina, 232
    Tajarin al Tartufo, 182
    Truffle-Anchovy Paste, 232

Turin, 61, 209
Tuscany, 4, 33, 54, 65, 71, 80,
    86, 216, 217, 226, 228, 333

U
Udine, 4, 92, 172, 177
Umbria, 56, 71, 74, 172, 189, 217,
    226, 232
umbricelli, 71
umbrichelli, 71
umbrici, 71

V
Vâgh iń ufézzi, 77, 205
Valtellina, 55, 177, 183
Va Tutto, 4
veal
    Bolognese Ragù, 202–3
    Ossobuco Ragù, 320–21
    Pappardelle with Porcini
    and Veal Bolognese,
    309–10
    Tagliatelle alla Bolognese,
    202–3
    Tagliatelle with Ossobuco
    and Soffritto, 320–21
Veneto, 89, 115, 177
Venice, 115, 176, 191, 342
Victor Emmanuel II, 61
vinaigrettes
    Anchovy Vinaigrette, 367
    Garlic Vinaigrette, 383
    House Vinaigrette, 366
vinegar, red wine, 137
Vivano, Antonio, 123
vodka
    Penne alla Vodka, 155
    Vodka Sauce, 155

W
Walbichl, 114
walnuts
    Charred Treviso with
    Walnuts and Saba, 364
    Fennel with Celery, Walnuts,
    and Parmigiano, 375
    Pansotti con Salsa di Noci,
    180–81

Sunchoke-Filled Agnolotti
    with Walnuts, Lemon,
    and Thyme, 326–27
    Walnut Sauce, 180, 181
Waxman, Jonathan, 4
Wells, Pete, 244
White, Michael, 5
whole-wheat dough, 26
    Bigoli in Salsa, 191

Z
Zafirano, 57
Zibello, 98
ziti, 124
    Baked Ziti with Aged
    Provolone and
    Caciocavallo, 154
Zucchini, Olive Oil–Poached,
    with Grilled Bread and
    Oregano, 371–72

Published in the United States by Ten Speed Press, an imprint of Random House,
a division of Penguin Random House LLC, New York.
www.tenspeed.com

Ten Speed Press and the Ten Speed Press colophon are registered trademarks
of Penguin Random House LLC.

Library of Congress Cataloging-in-Publication Data is on file with the publisher.
LCCN 2021933187

Hardcover ISBN: 978-1-9848-5700-2
eBook ISBN: 978-1-9848-5701-9

Printed in China

Editor: Lorena Jones
Designer: Elizabeth Allen | Art director: Emma Campion
Production designers: Mari Gill and Mara Gendell
Production manager: Jane Chinn
Prepress color manager: Nick Patton
Culinary shoot producer: Lish Steiling
Culinary shoot assistants: Payson Stultz and Casey Bayer
Prop stylist: Suzie Myers
Recipe tester: Laurie Ellen Pellicano
Copyeditor(s): Sharon Silva | Proofreader(s): Nancy Bailey and Rachel Markowitz
Indexer: Ken DellaPenta
Marketers: Samantha Simon and Stephanie Davis | Publicist: David Hawk

10 9 8 7 6 5 4 3 2 1